Pacific Mythology

Pacific Mythology

An Encyclopedia of Myth and Legend

Jan Knappert

Illustrated by Elizabeth Knappert

Aquarian/Thorsons

An Imprint of HarperCollins*Publishers*

The Aquarian Press
An Imprint of HarperCollins*Publishers*
77–85 Fulham Palace Road,
Hammersmith, London W6 8JB

Published by The Aquarian Press 1992
1 3 5 7 9 10 8 6 4 2

A catalogue record for this book
is available from the British Library

ISBN 1 85538 133 8

Typeset by Harper Phototypesetters Limited
Northampton, England
Printed in Great Britain by
Mackays of Chatham, Kent

Contents

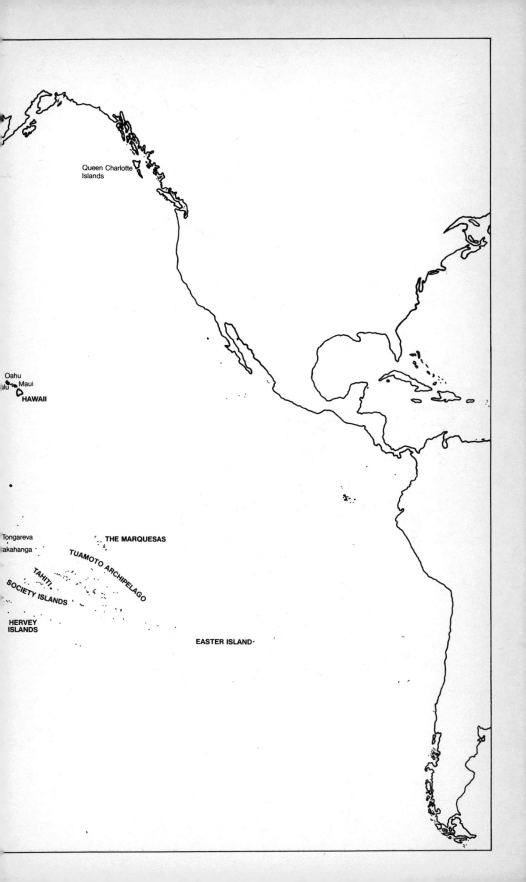

Preface

This first Encyclopedia of Pacific Mythology covers countries and islands from Thailand to Tahiti, from Japan to Java and from New Zealand to New Britain. As no single person can be an expert in the mythologies of all these nations, nor, supposing such a scholar could be found, would it be possible for him to include all the mythologies of the Pacific in one volume, it is offered with apologies for any shortcomings. A severe selection had to be made, and another problem faced: the available literature on Pacific mythology is very unequal. The myths of countries like Hawaii, Indonesia, Japan, Korea and New Zealand have been well described, but many other mythologies are still waiting for competent scholars to catalogue them. The reader should not underestimate the creative verbal arts, the oral and written traditions, religions and rituals even in the smallest islands. As soon as a scholar begins his research, it is like excavating a palace full of treasures. The language, the folktales, proverbs, songs, myths and legends of every single people in the Pacific is well worth studying, collecting and publishing.

In recent times more detailed research has begun into the 'ethnobotany', the arts and knowledge of the medicine-men and midwives, the wise herbalists and other healers. This has already brought to light not only new knowledge of the native plants of the Pacific islands but also of their medicinal application.

Besides legends and natural history, the local scholars are also mines of information on their 'ethnohistory', another subject that requires at least one volume all to itself. 'Learning is like an ocean without beaches,' one scholar told me, as he was gazing out over the sunny ocean.

Jan Knappert

Introduction

The Pacific is the largest ocean; it covers almost a third of the earth's surface: from Singapore to Panama is almost 20,000km, halfway around the globe. Innumerable islands rise from the blue waters, mostly pushed upwards by volcanic forces. Seven of the world's nine greatest countries border on the Pacific (Australia, Canada, China, Indonesia, Japan, Russia and the USA). Of the nine, only Brazil and India have no Pacific ports.

The Pacific has a long history *as an ocean*. The Atlantic may have been crossed by the peoples of antiquity (Egyptians, Greeks, Celts, Vikings), but it did not become a seaway for regular traffic, unlike the Indian Ocean, where the Sumerians frequently sailed. The Pacific was perhaps crossed by the Chinese and the Incas in antiquity, but it became a regularly navigated sea only with the arrival of the Austronesians, more precisely the Malayo-Polynesians, in the first millennium before Christ.

It is obviously impossible to present in one book the mythology of the entire Pacific area, containing over 50 political units, including the vast USA Pacific Islands Trust Territory, which comprises the Carolines, the Mariana and Marshall Islands. Excluded from this guide are Australia, China, Vietnam, Siberia and the Americas. Hong Kong and Taiwan have entries, but their mythologies are not dealt with in this survey, because their cultures are now essentially Chinese.

Three continental Asian countries of the Pacific littoral *are* included in this survey, viz. Malaya, i.e. the Malay Peninsula, which participates in the Malaysian-Indonesian culture whose vehicle is the Malay-Indonesian language; Thailand, which has preserved its medieval Buddhist culture and mythology, unlike its more secularized neighbours; and Korea, that beautiful peninsula between the Yellow Sea and the Sea of Japan (this author knows only South Korea), where another, very distinct Buddhist culture flourishes side by side with an ancient pattern of local religions.

The following countries in the Indian Ocean are included in our survey:

Polynesia, which covers the entire eastern half of the Pacific. It is defined by the so-called 'Polynesian Triangle' whose corners are Easter Island in the east, Hawaii in the north and New Zealand in the south. An almost straight line from Midway Island west of Hawaii to Three Kings Island north-west of New Zealand separates Polynesia on the east from Melanesia south of the Equator, and Micronesia north of it. Fiji belongs linguistically to Polynesia, though most anthropologists classify it within Melanesia; the same applies to Kiribati, previously the Gilbert Islands, and Tuvalu, once called the Ellice Islands, though the latter are sometimes included in Micronesia. The problem is that geographers, anthropologists and linguists have different criteria for their classification, but that need not concern us here. Micronesia has been receiving scant attention from mythologists, partly because, as the name implies, all the islands are only specks on the map. The largest, Guam, is only just under 30 miles long. In contrast, the largest island of Melanesia, New Guinea, is a little bigger than France and Italy combined. Politically, New Guinea is divided into Irian Jaya, or west New Guinea, part of Indonesia, and Papua, or east New Guinea, part of the Republic of Papua New Guinea.

In the western regions of the Pacific we include Indonesia, Japan and the Philippines in our guide, apart from the countries already mentioned. The Philippines have not received the attention they deserve in the scholarly literature on languages and mythology – although a fascinating blend of Spanish and native Filipino folktales has been discovered – while Indonesian mythology is so incredibly rich that a library-full has been published about it.

As for Japan, it has an ancient, unique culture with two historical religions, Shinto and Japanese Buddhism, the latter being quite distinct from any other branch of the great Buddhist cultural system. As the field is so wide, a complete list of Japanese mythological names could not be included, nor was there sufficient time to study the beautiful Japanese language to the level required for an adequate study of the sources, but fortunately, excellent works have already been published about Japan's myths in European languages.

Regarding Indonesian and Polynesian languages (including Tagalog, and Malay in Arabic script), this writer is sufficiently qualified to go to the sources, but the island of New Guinea speaks an estimated 500 languages; in some areas every village has its own language. Fortunately, numerous works have been published on its many mythologies in European languages, including Dutch and German.

In such a wide and varied area it has been necessary to treat many mythological phenomena under general headings such as 'Gods', 'Demons' and 'Witches'. Some animals feature almost universally in mythology, such as cats and bats, others only in the larger tropical land areas such as crocodiles, tigers, buffaloes and elephants.

The Pacific supplies half the fish caught on earth, so naturally the majority of the Pacific peoples are engaged in fishing or collecting shellfish, and seafood provides most of their protein intake. No wonder that there are many odysseys in Pacific mythology, numerous heroes who set sail to discover unknown islands where they meet and marry lovely princesses. In other mythologies, the gods are fishes and the first people were mermaids and mermen, while the seagulls and skuas are messengers of the gods. The preponderance of agriculture can also be gauged by the widespread veneration of the Rice-Goddess or the many myths of a god's head growing into a coconut palm.

Many questions remain unanswered, such as the problem of the origin of the Pacific peoples. Where did the Japanese and the Koreans come from, with their totally unrelated languages? How, on the other hand, do we explain that all the Malayo-Polynesian languages, from Hawaii and Easter Island via Indonesia all the way to Madagascar, more than half way round the globe, are quite clearly related? It was assumed for a long time that the Malayo-Polynesians had entered the Pacific area from Malaya, having migrated south from what is now Burma and Thailand. However, the Malay legends of origin seem to indicate, on the contrary, that the Malays settled the Peninsula from Sumatra. The Pacific peoples themselves relate that they just rose out of the ocean like morning mist, or grew in shaded pools like eels or frogs.

In the arts too, questions remain. What, for instance, explains the obvious resemblance of the famous statues on Easter Island with the tall stone statues which the Koreans used to place outside their villages?

As for religion, ancestor worship seems to be the oldest and the most widespread form of ritual. Hinduism and Buddhism are the two great religions whose country of origin is ancient India. The reader is referred to the author's *Indian Mythology* for descriptions of the gods of Hinduism and the mythological concepts of Buddhism, but details of the great oriental religions are not discussed in this work. The immense influence of Islam on many of the peoples of Malaysia, Indonesia and the Philippines is likewise only mentioned sporadically, for details are available elsewhere.

There can be little hope of completeness in a work of this modest size. Still as much data as possible has been packed into this book. The Pacific Ocean has almost as many cultures as there are islands, so that its spiritual world is as multicoloured as its coral reefs or the flora of its coasts, where over a thousand different languages are spoken. There are myths in every single one of them.

The whispering palm trees, the tall volcanoes, the morning mists on the slopes, it all invites the people with a natural gift for oral art to compose poetic tales. A few of these are represented in this book. May their beauty be a source of enjoyment.

Note: The spelling of Oriental names has been kept simple and as close to English as possible. Note the *ch* in Japanese and other languages is pronounced in the same way as *c* in modern Malay-Indonesian spelling (as in ket*ch*up).

Table of some common words demonstrating the close relationship of the Malayo-Polynesian languages:

English	Malay	Javanese	Tagalog	Fijian	Samoan	Maori	Hawaiian
boat	bangka	–	bangka	waka	va'a	waka	wa'a
breast	susu	susu	suso	suu	susu	uu	uu
death	mati	mati	ka-matay-an	mate	mate	mate	make
drink	minum	umbe	uminom	unuma	inu	inu	inu
ear	telinga	telingan	tainga	dalinga	talinga	taringa	–
eight	(delapan)	wolu	walu	walu	valu	waru	walu
eye	mata	mata	mata	mata	mata	mata	maka
fire	api	api	apoy	avi	afi	ahi	ahi
five	lima	lima	lima	lima	lima	rima	lima
fruit	buah	woh	bua	vua	fua	hua	hua
four	empat	pat	apat	va	fa	wha	ha
hair (fur)	bulu	wulu	buhok	vulua	lau-ulu	huruhuru	hulu
house	balai	bale	bahay	vale	fale	whare	hale
leaf	daun	ron	dahon	drau	lau	rau	lau
plank	papan	papan	papan	papa	papa	papa	papa
rain	hujan	udan	ulan	ua	ua	ua	ua
road	jalan	dalan	daan	sala	ala	ara	ala
six	enam	enem	anim	ono	ono	ono	ono
sky	langit	langit	langit	langi	langi	rangi	lani
two	dua	loro	dalawa	drua	lua	rua	lua
water	air	we	–	wai	vai	wai	wai

A

Ama Terasu returning light to the earth (Japan)

Abang Salamat The faithful helper of *Sijobang*.

Abdu Rahman A Malay sultan. See *Puntianak*.

Abdu'l Ra'uf of Singkel (or as-Sinkili) Abdu'l-Ra'uf bin 'Ali al-Jawi as-Sinkili was born in Singkel on the west coast of Sumatra in what was then the Sultanate of Acheh, *c.*1620. He studied for 19 years in Arabia and in 1660 he returned to his native land where he began preaching Islam. His fame as a mystic and ascetic spread along the coasts and across the *islands*, and he became especially popular in *Java*.

His best known work is the *Support for those who are in need of Travelling Forth on the Path of those who are Absorbed in the Unity of Being*. This title refers to the Sufi doctrine of the seven steps or stages, which the ardent student has to climb towards becoming the image of *God*.

Abdu'l-Ra'uf was buried after 1693 near the mouth of the river Acheh, and after his death he was venerated as a saint and his tomb became a centre of pilgrimage, so that he became known as *Teungku di Kuala*, Achinese for 'My Lord of the Estuary'.

Abiasa In Javanese mythology, Raden Abiasa or Kresna Dwipayana was the son of Palasara and Princess Durgandini ('Woman of Unpleasant Odour'). He was an unkempt ascetic who became the ancestor of the *Korawas* and the *Pandawas* by embracing the sisters *Ambiki* and

Ambahini, in spite of their aversion to him.

Abreu, Gomes d'   A Portuguese sailor. See *Indonesia*.

Adab ('Civilization') One of the Indonesian Five Virtues. See *Pancha-Sila*.

Adi-Buddha ('The principal original, essential Buddha') The Supreme *Buddha*, who incorporates all the other (i.e. later) Buddhas and Bodhisattvas within his being.

Adi Mailagu   See *Goddess of the Sky*.

Adi Putra   A Malay saint. His name is probably a corruption of *Adi-Buddha*, the Eternal Teacher. See *Hang Tuah*.

Adil ('Justice') One of the Indonesian Five Virtues. See *Pancha-Sila*.

Aditinggi   God of the volcano Gunung Awu on Siau in Indonesia. See *Volcano God*.

Adam and Eve

1. In Hawaiian tales they are called *Kumu-Honua* 'First on Earth' and Lalo-Honua 'Below Earth', his wife; her name may be an echo of the belief in the Earth-Goddess. This first couple were not allowed to eat a certain fruit, but this part of the tale seems Christianized.
2. The first man in Polynesian mythology was *Kane* (Hawaiian) or *Tane* (*Maori*). When he felt lonely he asked *Papa*, the earth, his mother and the first woman, to give him a companion. Her response was to bring forth trees – the pine trees of different colours, and many others, then plants, then flax, then birds of diverse plumage, then forest pools filled with clear water. If only Man had read the meaning of these signs: let nature be your company; but Man was dissatisfied and persistent. Finally, the earth told him to shape a body like his own from earth but without his genitals. He did and lay down on it, embracing it. It came to life in his arms and became his wife.
3. In other Polynesian myths, *Tiki*, the first man and ancestor, is the husband of Hine or Hina (meaning 'woman', 'goddess'). He was created by the god Tu Matauenga, or according to another version, by Tane. Tiki himself was a demi-god who could lift up the sky, thereby becoming co-creator. One day Tiki found a woman in a pond. She became his wife by seducing him. Maori women used to wear a phallus-shaped charm round their necks, called *tiki*, to protect them against barrenness. See also *Woman*(1).
4. In Samoan mythology, Ele'ele was the first woman, wife of Fetu ('Star'), a god of the night sky.
5. Wakea was the Hawaiian equivalent of Vatea, the *Creator* and the first man, son of Varima. His wife Papa gave birth to a calabash, out of which Wakea fashioned the vault of the sky.

   A variant of this myth relates that Papa was a giant bird who laid an egg which opened and became the island of *Hawaii*, which soon grew green trees. Later, Wakea and Papa lived on the island themselves, as the first human beings. It is quite 'normal' for *gods* to 'descend' to earth and live human lives for a time.

6. In the religion of the people of *New Britain*, the Creator, the 'One who was first there', drew blood from his own body and sprinkled it on the earth. From this earth he formed the first man, To-Kabinana, who lived thanks to the Creator's blood. This first man always did the right things. He climbed a coconut palm, cut down a coconut and, when he opened it, discovered a beautiful woman. To-Kabinana carved a fish from wood and placed it in the sea. This grateful fish drove the other fish into the lagoon so the first couple always had plenty of food.

See also *Creator; Creation; Na Atibu; Nareau; Opossum.*

Adarna In Philippine mythology, Adarna was a magical bird which could make a certain sick king better, so his three sons were sent in search of it. The first two were careless and were turned into stone by the *magic* which protected the bird. But the youngest son showed kindness to a leper who told him how to avoid the evil spell, and so he finally captured the magical bird. The king was cured.

Adaro In the myths of the *Solomon Islands*, an *adaro* is a malevolent sea-spirit in the shape of a fish-man, a man with tail fins on his feet and gills behind his ears. He has a horn like a shark's back fin and a pike on his head like a sword fish or sawfish. An *adaro* can travel along rainbows and kill men by shooting poisonous flying fish at them.

Adat (also *ada*; literally: custom, recurrent behaviour, morals) *Adat* is the ancient tradition of the local peoples of *Indonesia*, the morality and correct behaviour, the sacred *law* of the ancestors. The authority of the *adat* is often invoked when modern Muslim scholars insist on applying Islamic law, especially regarding inheritance.
   See also *Pancha-Sila.*

Adi Mailagu   See *Goddess of the Sky.*

Aditya-Raja   See *White Raven.*

Afa   The Samoan Storm-God. See also 'Gods of the Pacific' under *Gods.*

Aftabul Ardi   A Malayan king. See *Malay Annals.*

Agung Abdur Rahman   A sultan of *Java.* See *Indonesia.*

Ahi   See *Fire.*

Ahoeitu   A legendary King of Tonga, grandson of Kohai who may have been a primeval earth *serpent.* The Sky-God Eitumatupua descended from *heaven* one day and married Ilaheva, an earth-goddess. Until their son Ahoeitu was full grown, he had never seen his father, who lived in heaven. Eitumatupua had begotten other sons in heaven who were jealous when Eitumatupua mentioned his earth-son, so they ambushed

Ahoeitu and devoured him. As soon as Eitumatupua discovered this conspiracy, he summoned all his heavenly sons to him and ordered them to vomit. As soon as he had all the pieces of Ahoeitu gathered together, he rejoined them using *magic* herbs, and Ahoeitu came to life again. He was given the kingdom of *Tonga* as recompense for his pain.

Ahu   An *ahu* is a burial platform on Easter Island (see *Rapanui*). There were 160 on the island, where the ancestors lay entombed.

Ai Kanaka   See *Lona; Mahina.*

Ai-Tupuai   The daughter of *Oro*. See *Oro*(1).

Air   (*Fuku-Nyorai*) One of the *elements* in Japanese cosmology.

Airlanga   A medieval King of Java. See *Arjuna; Java.*

Aizen-Myoo   (or Aizen Myo-o) The personification of the Spirit of Love for Illumination in Japanese *Buddhism*, guardian of the pilgrims on the True Path. See also 'Gods of Japan' under *Gods.*

Ajapal   (or Ajalpala) In Thai mythology, the second king of the city of *Ayodhya* and the son of King *Anomatan* and Queen Manikesara. He slew the demon Asura. His son was Dasaratha (= *Dasarata*).

Ajari Joan   A Japanese priest. See *Skeleton.*

Aji Saka   In Javanese legend a prince, or, according to some, a scholar, who came from the west bringing science and civilization to the island, including the Javanese script.

Aji-Shiki   See 'Gods of Japan' under *Gods.*

Akasa-Garbha   (or Akasha; 'The Womb of the Sky' or 'The Nucleus of the Universe'; in Japanese, Kokuzo Bosatsu) The name of the twelfth Bodhisattva, whose mantra is considered specially effective.

Ake Antak   See *Creation*(16).

Akechi   See *Fireball.*

Ako   A young Japanese lord. See *Peony*(1).

Alberto   A Philippine hero. See *Monsters*(3).

Albino   A white-skinned person believed to be the child of a fairy and a woman.

Alexander the Great   See *Iskandar; Malay Annals.*

Aluelap   See *Ligoupup.*

Alutanga Nuku   See *Atonga.*

Ama Terasu   The 'illustrious ancestress of the Emperor' (according to Japanese school history textbooks prior to 1945), the Japanese Sun-Goddess, eldest daughter of the first couple, *Izanagi* and *Izanami*. Ama Terasu was so bright and radiant that her parents sent her up the

Celestial Ladder to *heaven*, where she has ruled ever since. She was a proud Queen of Heaven, for she quarrelled with both her brothers – Tsuki-Yumi the Moon-God, whom she banished to the night sky when she no longer wanted to see his face, and *Susanowo* the Storm-God. When he caused storms she locked herself up in a rock-cave, moping, because he was so noisy. The gods were in despair as darkness descended upon the world. They decided to create a great feast of entertainment, decorating the space in front of the cave, which Ama Terasu had closed with a boulder, with colourful jewels and songbirds. The Goddess of the Dance, *Uzume* ('Whirling'), performed an elaborate dance, decked out in a large head-dress and armed with a spear. Of course, as expected, curiosity got the better of Ama Terasu. She opened her cave door just enough to see what was going on, so that a streak of light escaped and lit up the dark sky. Today, people call that streak *dawn*, for it is as if someone has lifted the dark lid of the night sky so that the light behind it breaks through.

Later, Ama Terasu created *rice* fields, *inada*, where she cultivated the rice without which the people of the Far East could not live. Ama Terasu also invented the art of weaving with the loom and taught the people how to cultivate wheat and silkworms.

See also 'Gods of Japan' under *Gods; Ise-Jingu*.

Amai-Te-Rangi A Polynesian deity of the sky who 'angles' for mortal men on earth, pulling them up in baskets to devour them.

Amatsu-Kami See *Kami*.

Ambiki In Javanese mythology, a queen who shuts her eyes while she is being embraced by the terrifying and unkempt ascetic *Abiasa*, causing her son, *Drestarata*, to be born blind.

Ambu Dewi (or Sunan Ambu, 'Divine Mother') Ambu Dewi is another name for Ambika, *Kali, Bairawi, Durga,* and *Lara Jonggrang,* the spouse of *Siwa*. In numerous Indonesian tales of the Hindu repertoire, the god and goddess who are married in heaven are born on earth as human beings, each with the same sex as in heaven. They then have offspring who are again *incarnations* of the same *gods*. Gods may marry their siblings, in heaven and on earth.

In the Sundanese mythology of West *Java*, Ambu Dewi is the mother of *Guru Minda* and other gods, and the wife of the Supreme God, *Guriang Tunggal*. Her son Guru Minda, alias *Lutung Kasarung*, dreams that he has a wife like his mother. His mother, as the goddess *Dewi Sri*, has already incarnated in a lovely princess, Purba Sari, who is tyrannized by her elder sister, Purba Rarang. For the full story, see *Lutung Kasarung*.

Amei Awi See *Dayaks*.

Amida (Amitabha or Amida Butsu; Japanese, Taho) In *Japan*, the *Buddha* of Pure Light, one of the most revered of the five great Bodhisattvas. The pure light is the Ultimate Yearning for Enlightenment upon which some Buddhists concentrate in their dying moment. Amida lives in Gokuraku *Jodo*, the 'Pure Land', in *heaven* where he resides near a pond of pure ambrosia surrounded by blossoming trees in which colourful birds sing harmoniously with the temple bells. This is based on the early translations of the *Amitayur-Dhyana-Sutra*, the 'Textbook for the Contemplation of Infinite Life', and other fundamental Buddhist textbooks.

Amida was in a previous life the devout monk Dharmakara who vowed that his devotees would be reborn in the Pure Land (Prasadana Kshetra) and there attain Enlightenment. This Pure Land bathes in the rays of light that emanate from the Buddha's own essence. For his reward, Dharmakara was reborn as Amida, ruler of Sukhavati, the Land of Happiness. The worshippers concentrate on his essence by repeating *Namu Amida Butsu*, 'Hail, Amitabha Bodhisattva'. By this exercise, seated in front of Amida's statue, they hope to attain the Pure Land.

See also *Amida-Nyorai*(1); 'Gods of Japan' under *Gods*.

Amida Butsu See *Amida*.

Amida-Nyorai

1. The *Buddha* of Immeasurable Light – the wisdom distinguishing truth from error. Another name for *Amida*.
2. In Japanese cosmology, the element of water, signifying law. See *Elements*.

Amir Hamza An uncle of the Prophet Muhammad who has become the eponymous hero of a long romance in Malay. Amir Hamza and his followers (later accompanied by his son Badiu Zaman) experience the most fantastic adventures in numerous imaginary countries, performing exploits of incredible valour, amongst which they defeat, single-handedly, armies of horrifying *demons*. Hamza makes love to many beautiful, amorous princesses, while their fathers send fierce armies against him. He defeats them all and always escapes. He is known as Menak in the Javanese puppet theatre *wayang golek*. The real Hamza died in 625.

Amitabha See *Amida*.

Amoghasiddhi See *Shaka*.

Amori See *Kangaroo*.

Amulet (*Heitiki*) An amulet is an object which, either by its nature or as a result of special magical rites, contains supernatural powers which protect the wearer against danger. (The word amulet derives from the Latin *amolitio*, 'averting, keeping away'.)

1. In *Thailand*, thousands of amulets are sold by vendors. The commonest type are the well-known *Buddha* images made from every conceivable material including clay, wood, gold, ivory and compressed plant matter. Mixed in are the ashes of priceless old manuscripts. The most effective amulets – we are told – are those

made by old monks who have led lives of virtue and abstemiousness. Amulets protect the wearer against evil *spirits*, the beings of *Saksit*. Amulets also promise success and prosperity so that the wearer feels confident.

2. The Torajas of *Sulawesi* used pieces of ramified coral worn on a string round their necks to make them invulnerable in battle. After the fighting was over, the amulet had to be 'fed' pieces of scalps.

3. On Timor, the *kakaluk* is a bag filled with *stones* which have been chosen by the owner following his *dreams*. He keeps it in his attic. Offers have to be brought twice daily to the *kakaluk* spirits. In time of war this amulet will protect its owner against missiles.

4. On Halmahera, a phial of sacred oil was worn on the neck by warriors for the same purpose, and *tiger* teeth are considered useful for courage in battle.

5. In many parts of *Indonesia*, a *matakau* ('red-eyes') is an object hung in a fruit tree which will cause a thief wounds if he touches the fruit. Often these objects are animal figures with red eyes intended to deter the thief, who will not dare to touch such a tree. See also *Fetish*.

Anan See 'Gods of Japan' under *Gods*.

Ananta Nakhon In Thai mythology, the city of King *Sison*.

Ananta Thewi In Thai mythology, the Goddess of Good Fortune, whose consort is the great God of Fortune, Saturn (see *Phra Sao*). Her Sanskrit name is *Ananda Devi*.

Anantaboga In the Javanese *wayang* myths, the King of the Dragons in the *Underworld*, father and husband of *Dewi Nagagini*. See also *Dragon*.

Ancor Vat See *Angkor-Wat*.

Andelas Former name of *Sumatra*. See *Malay Annals*.

Aneka-Warna ('More than one colour') The palace garden of the *gods* in *heaven*, described in Malay and Indonesian myths, especially those of the *wayang* cycles.

Angels In Japanese Buddhist mythology, *tenshi*, angels, are not only the messengers of the *gods* but also work for the benefit of people. They prevented *Kobo* Daishi from sacrificing his life by throwing himself from a high rock, telling him that a lifetime of teaching the lore of *Buddha* is better than propitiation. See also *Heaven*(1); *Tennin*.

Anjing Ajak See *Werewolf*.

Anggun Nan Tungga See *Sijobang*.

Angkor-Wat (or Ancor Vat) A Khmer sanctuary in Cambodia. The vast rectangular temple complex was sacked by Thai troops in 1431. It was meant as a habitation for the *gods*, including the spirit of King Suryavarman, who built it before 1150.

Annam The old name of North Vietnam, An-nan is the Chinese for 'The Pacified South'. For centuries the Annamites resisted Chinese invasions. This made them a militant nation.

See also *Green Demon; Magic Flute; Tortoise.*

Anomatan In Thai mythology, the first king of the city of *Ayodhya*, son of the god *Narayana*, in the *epic* of *Ramakirti* (see *Ramakien*). The name means 'He who has no mother', since Anomatan was born from a lotus flower in the middle of the Ocean of Milk. The *gods* presented him with gifts: *Indera* gave him a queen named Manikesara, *Shiva* gave him his trident, Vishnu gave him his mace.

Anshitsu A Japanese hermitage for a solitary Buddhist monk. The lonely traveller should be wary of asking for shelter there at night, for it may happen that the gloomy figure who opens the door is only the ghost of the monk who once lived there.

Anta Kusuma (Kusomo) In old Javanese and Balinese mythology, a *magic* jewel in the shape of a beautiful flower, which belongs to *Dewi Sri*. Its possession secures enduring love, long life, good health and happiness. It is an elusive object.

Antang The falcon of *Mahatara*, the Supreme God of the *Dayaks*.

Antoku Tenno A Japanese emperor. See *Epic Poetry.*

Anuman See *Hanuman.*

Anut The Supreme God. See *Race*(1).

Ao ('Light', the opposite of Po, 'Night'; also called Ao Toto, 'Blood-Red Dawn') The Polynesian God of the Clouds, the first ancestor of the *Maoris*. In the Pacific clouds are not associated with darkness, for they often look like columns of light. See also *Creation*(5); 'Gods of the Pacific' under *Gods.*

Ao Toto See *Ao.*

Ape In the *Philippines* they relate that a certain ape who was born from human parents and baptized by a Christian priest could take off his furry skin and become a handsome young man. See also *Monkeys.*

Api See *Fire.*

Apu-Hau ('Fierce Squall') The Storm-God of *Hawaii*. See 'Gods of the Pacific' under *Gods; Storm.*

Apu Lagang The World of the Spirits in the mythology of the *Dayaks*. See also *Spirits.*

Apu Matangi ('Howling Rainfall') The *Maori* God of Storms. See *Fire*(4); 'Gods of the Pacific' under *Gods; Storm.*

Ara Tiotio (or Awhiowhio) The Polynesian God of the Tornado. See 'Gods of the Pacific' under *Gods;* see also *Storm.*

Arahuta The daughter of *Tawhaki* and *Tangotango*.

Aremata-Rorua and Aremata-Popoa ('Long-Wave' and 'Short-Wave') Two ocean *demons* greatly feared by Polynesian mariners because they were totally at the mercy of their immense power. See also *Navigators*.

Areoi In the mythology of the Tuamotu (Society) Islands, a religious order first organized by the *gods* Oro-Tetefa and Uru-Tetefa, two brothers living in *heaven* but later settling on earth. Like the Knights of St John, they were celibate warriors, who recruited their members from among the nobility.

Arhat (or Arahant) From Sanskrit *arhanta*, 'worthy, deserving'. A Buddhist who has abolished all desire, an ascetic, a monk.

Ariki Rahi See *King*.

Arimbi A giantess. See *Gatutkaca*.

Arisatun Shah Son of Alexander the Great. See *Malay Annals*.

Arjuna In the Javanese *Mahabharata*, the son and *incarnation* of the god *Indera*, a great warrior and hero, whose charioteer was the god Krishna (see *Kresna*). The medieval King Airlanga (Erlangga) was idealized by his chroniclers as the Prince Arjuna himself. See also *Janaka*(1).

Arjuna-Wiwaha ('The Marriage of Arjuna') A famous old Javanese *epic* poem, in which Arjuna, the great hero of the *Mahabharata*, married the nymph Suprabha. Later, this son of *Indera* married six other nymphs as well.

Arohirohi The *Maori* Goddess of Mirages. See *Mirage; Woman*(1).

Aroture The daughter of *Ina* and *Tini Rau*.

Aru Aru An Orokolo man. See *Yam*(2).

Arugo The *soul*. See also *Hiyoyoa*.

Asagao See *Morning-Glory*.

Ashuku-Nyorai ('The Immovable Buddha') In Japanese cosmology, the element of *earth* (see *Elements*); in Sanskrit, *Akshobhya Adarsanajnana*, the knowledge of the unseen. It signifies the power of making images manifest.

Asai See *Sangiang*.

Asama ('Dawn of Good Luck') See *Sengen*.

Asmara ('Passionate Love') A cycle of legends played by Javanese actors.

Asmara Dewa A Malay hero. See *Yatim Nustapa*.

Assembly of the Gods Every year, according to Japanese mythology, the *gods* assemble in the holy temple at *Izumo*. They hold council in order to predestine the love affairs of people: who will love whom, and whose love will be requited.

Astrology See *Fortune-Tellers*(2).

Asura See *Ajapal*.

Ata An island in the Tongan archipelago. The story runs that Ata was thrown down from *heaven*. Such stony *islands* were called *Maka-Fonua* 'Thrown-Land'.

Atanua See *Dawn; Tangaroa*.

Atarapa ('Daybreak') See 'Gods of the Pacific' under *Gods; Haronga*.

Atea ('Space') Atea was the Sky-God in the cosmology of the people of Tuamotu. He married Fa'ahotu. Their first son was Tahu, 'Knowledge', who became a great magician. Their second son was *Tane*, according to some versions of the myth, and another son was *Ro'o*. Tane and Atea were later locked in a deadly struggle, like Zeus and Kronos. Finally Tane, using the thunderbolt Fatu-Titi, slew Atea. Many kings of the Tuamotu *islands* trace their descent to Atea. See also *Tangaroa*.

Athityarat The Thai Sun-King. See *White Raven*.

Ati The Maori chief who managed to catch a lovely fairy in a net, and married her.

Atlantis There is a theory, first expounded by Dr J. Macmillan Brown, that there was once a continent right in the centre of the Pacific, where the genesis of the Polynesian *race* took place. When the land began to sink back into the ocean, the people scattered and settled on the other Polynesian *islands*. The central Polynesian Sporades is all that remains of that great land.

Atonga In Samoan myth, a hero who is half-human, half-spirit. He built a miraculous *canoe* which he completed in one night. Then he summoned the birds from heaven to carry the light craft to the beach of Upolu where chief Alutanga Nuku was awaiting it impatiently. Atonga even taught the birds the song he wanted them to sing. Thus Atonga is a culture hero who invented canoe-building as well as the songs for the rowers.

Atu Name of the first man on *Fiji* and the first man on *Tonga*, according to Samoan myth. See *Islands*.

Atua An *atua* is the spirit of an ancestor in *Polynesia*, who is revered like a god. The family *gods*, Lares and Penates, are also *atua*. Shrines may be erected for the *spirits*. Some demand to drink the blood of slain enemies. Even though the *atua* are not worshipped like gods, they do receive veneration. *Karakia* (*magic* formulae in poetic form) may be recited to them, and they may have to be exorcised. They are sometimes referred to as Nuku-mai-Tore, the 'People of the Other World'. They can fly, and they live in trees, like birds.

1. One day a man called Tura wandered inland from the coast of a certain island called Otea, where, he knew, spirits wandered. A girl called Turakihau, the daughter of an old woman, befriended him and agreed to marry him. She took him to her people who lived in the trees. So Tura had married a spirit! However, unafraid, he built a hut and they lived together as human beings. Turakihau became pregnant and when her time approached two women arrived to cut the child out of her side. Tura however, forbade them to touch her, and instead, helped his wife to give birth in the human way. The child, a son, was called Tauira-Ahua.

   When the boy was grown up, Tura got grey hairs. His wife asked him what that was and he replied, 'Old age. I am going to die.' So they wept. Among the *atua* there is no death. Then one night Tura dreamt that his father called him and he died soon after.

2. In Rarotonga, some spirits rose from the water of a clear pond on the first night of the full moon, to steal human food. Once one of them was caught in a net. She was brought to Chief Ati, who liked her so much that he married her. He had the pond filled in, lest she dive back into it. They had a son who was born in the natural human way, because Chief Ati refused to cut open his wife's belly and remove the child, as she had asked him to do. For that was the custom, she had said, in the world of the spirits. One day later she asked Ati to accompany her to the spirit world and teach the spirits to have children in the human way, but he could not follow her, though he tried. So, she went alone and never came back to earth.

(Killing the mother by carving the child out of her side is vestigially mentioned in oriental myths. In ancient times princely babies were sometimes delivered by Caesarean, for safety.)

See also *God*(1); *Io*; *Ngarara*.

Atutuahi (or Autahi) The south star, Canopus, Alpha Carinae, God of the Heavens, which guided Polynesian *navigators* on their voyages lasting many months. Atutuahi is addressed in hymns as the 'Mother of the Moon and the Stars'. See also 'Gods of the Pacific' under *Gods; Matariki; Milky Way; Morning Star; Ru*(2); *Star; Star Spirit*.

Auahi-Turoa and the Fire Children According to Polynesian myth, Auahi-Turoa was the son of the Sun-God Tama Nui-Te-Ra, who sent him down to earth as a comet, carrying the Seed of Fire. On earth, Auahi-Turoa married Mahuika, the Fire-Goddess, or Mother of Fire. They had five sons, the Fire Children, who bear the names of the fingers: Koiti (little finger), Konui (thumb), Koroa (index finger), Manawa (ring finger) and Mapere (middle finger). See also *Fire*.

Aula See *Eleio*.

Auparu ('Gentle Dew') A stream in Rarotonga where nymphs are known to bathe.

Auraka ('The All-Devouring') A deity of *death* in Polynesian mythology.

Auriaria A king in *Kiribati* mythology. See *Neititua Abine*.

Australids The first people to populate Australia. See also *Indonesia*.

Austronesia The Austronesian peoples are characterized by their preference for living on *islands*. Only the Malay peninsula is not an island, though very nearly so. Secondly they are characterized by their appearance. They have more orthognathic faces than the Indians (they are more 'moon-faced'), and they are not always easily distinguished from the Siamese peoples.

The original Formosans (as opposed to the Chinese immigrants in *Taiwan*) have quite obvious Indonesian and Filipino features. There is also an older Indonesian race, a people who were already settled in *Indonesia* when the Javanese and the Malays arrived in the early first millennium BC. In *New Guinea* and Melanesia live a race of African-type peoples. One theory of historical ethnology endeavours to explain this fact by the hypothesis of 'overlayering'. Originally, according to this theory, in the first period of human *expansion* there was only the black race which spread out across all of Africa as well as South Asia and Melanesia. Then several waves of lighter coloured races arrived from the north and 'washed out' the blackness. In this way the Indians became 'shades of brown', from almost white in the north to quite dark in the south.

The Indonesians may have come from what is now South Vietnam (where pockets of Indonesian *languages* are still spoken), when South-East Asia was invaded by peoples speaking Sinic (Chinese-related) languages. That does not explain, however, the presence of the quite distinct, noble race of the *Polynesians* east of a straight line that runs from Midway, the westernmost island of the Hawaiian chain, to Auckland Island off New Zealand. These Polynesians speak closely related dialects, which clearly belong to the same family as Malay–Indonesian and Filipino–Tagalog, as the comparative word list on p.12 shows. The Melanesian languages, like their speakers, are clearly mixed. Many words in these languages can be identified as Malayo–Polynesian; many others are of unknown origin.

Autahi See *Atutuahi*.

Avaiki According to some Polynesian myths, this is their land of origin. It may be near *Indonesia*, *New Zealand* or *Samoa*. Others maintain that Avaiki is the *Nether World*, where the *spirits* live, who may ascend to this world through a hole in the ground. According to this view, Avaiki is the 'root of the world' from which the rest of the earth was created, the home of *Rongo*, the twin-brother of the god *Tangaroa* (the one with black hair), and his family. From there he built up the island of Mangaia in the *Cook Islands*.

Avaiki was constructed by the *gods* in a series of strata, with spaces separated by ceilings like caves, and tunnels giving access to its halls. In the lowest hall lives *Varima-Te-Takere*, the Goddess of Beginning. See also *Hades*(1); *Hina-Ika*; *Miru*; *Reinga*; *Tangi'ia*.

Avaiki Tautau Ancient name of *New Zealand* in *Maori* myth.

Avo and Ohare Akore See *Creation*(2); *Sex*.

Awa

1. The Hawaiian form of *kava* plant. See also *Eleio*.
2. A province of *Japan*.

Awabi A god of the sea who lives near Nanao in *Japan*. These sea-demons eat the fishermen when they drown. They are the guardians of large seashells containing shining jewels. See also *Demons*.

Awatara An *avatar* or *incarnation* of a god or goddess. Most commonly in Javanese myths it is *Narayana* (*Wisnu*), who is born as a baby, i.e. he is said to 'enter the womb', of a woman who has just conceived so that she gives birth to a son who is also her husband's son, but his spirit is a divine spirit, the *semangat* of the god. 'Naturally', the deity can divide his (or her) powerful spirit so that several babies are born at the same time as incarnations of the same divinity. *Dewi Sri*, Wisnu's consort, incarnates as Sita, Rukmini and other princesses. Each of her incarnations marries an incarnation of Wisnu (Rama, *Kresna*), though often only after numerous adventures. Just as a god may appear in more than one body, so his earthly life may expand in more than one time, thus Kresna marries several times, but in 'mythical time', i.e. in more than one human lifespan. Though brother and sister in *heaven*, *gods* may marry on earth.

Awha The *Maori* Storm-God. See also 'Gods of the Pacific' under *Gods*; *Storm*.

Awhiowhio See *Ara Tiotio*.

Aya A Japanese princess. See *Peony*(1).

Ayame A Japanese lady, related to the emperor. See *Yorimasa*.

Ayodhya (or Ayuthya) A city in Thai mythology. See *Ajapal*; *Anomatan*; *Dasarata*; *Dwarawati*.

B

Buddha on Naga Muchilinda (Cambodia)

Badang ('Forest ghost') A Malay fisherman from Johore, whose fish were destroyed by a *badang*, found the monster's vomit and ate it up. As a result he became immensely strong. Then he slew the ghost and all his other enemies so that the ruler of his country made him *hulubalang*, field marshal. See also *Ghosts*.

Badger

1. There is a Japanese tale about a bad badger who killed a woman because she would not let him eat her pet hare. He took on her appearance and cooked a soup from her body. When the husband returned home he was served this soup by the disguised badger. The hare later took revenge for his mistress by killing the badger with an oar, while his boat sank. The badger is not always so ruthless in Japanese tales. It often plays the part of a jester.
2. A wise young man called Kadzutoyo once found a lovely girl by the roadside, weeping in the rain. She implored him to help her but he cut off her head instead. When later questioned about his reasons he answered, 'I saw that her clothes stayed dry in spite of the rain, and her beauty was not like that of a human being.'

   Later, they found a dead badger instead of a girl's body on that spot.

3. A tinker who had bought an old tea-kettle from an old priest observed how, in the middle of the night, it became a badger, which started dancing and bouncing. For some years he made money with it, showing it at markets and fairs to the public who were much amused by the badger's agility in walking the tightrope.

See also *Raiju*.

Badi An evil spirit. See *Cat*(2); also *Soul*.

Badiu Zaman See *Amir Hamza*.

Badui A Javanese mountain people. See *Hanuman*.

Bagaspati A fierce Balinese forest god. The name is from the Sanskrit *Brihaspati*, the planet Jupiter.

Bagawan In Javanese mythology, a nobleman who retires and becomes an ascetic.

Bahasa Indonesia The national language of *Indonesia*. See *Indonesia, Modern History*.

Bahau Dayaks See *Dayaks*.

Bairawi In old Javanese and Balinese mythology, the terrifying aspect of *Dewi*, wife of *Siwa*. She is the Goddess of Death, wearing a garland of skulls; she is identified with Maha *Kali* and *Durga*, who killed the *buffalo* demon *Mahisa*. See also *Ambu Dewi; Death*.

Bajang In *Malaysia*, this is an evil spirit which usually takes the shape of a *musang*, polecat. When it mews at night, a child will die. It is said that a *bajang* is obtained from the newly buried body of a still-born child, the dwelling-place of a spirit, and can be lured from it by the powerful incantations of a wicked *sorcerer*. Such a criminal is punished by drowning, but the *bajang* will escape through his mouth. See also *Lizard*(2).

Bakoa A demi-god. See *Taburimai*.

Baku See *Dreams*(2).

Baladewa In the *Ramayana*, brother of Krishna, son of *Vasudeva*.

Bale-Fe'e The palace of the Samoan War-God. See *Fe'e*.

Bale Kenchur ('House of the Dead') In *Java*, the mortuary near the cemetery, where the *dead* await burial. A living man may go and lie down there for a night if he expects to receive messages from the dead.

Balepa See *Spirits*(5).

Bali Bali is a volcanic island of 5,591 sq km (2,159 sq m) just east of *Java, Indonesia*. The capital is Denpasar and the population 2.5 million. Balinese is a distinct Indonesian *language* with a script of its own and a very rich literature. On Bali the ancient traditions of Hinduism and *Buddhism* have survived for 2,000 years.

See also *Bagaspati*; *Bairawi*; *Colours and Compass*; *Goddess*; *Gods*; *Manjushri*; *Prawati*; *Rati*; *Sakti*; *Saraswati*; *Sesa*; *Siwa*; *Waruna*; *Wayang*; *Wisnu*; *Witch*; *Yama-Raja*.

Balinese Gods See 'Gods of Bali' under *Gods*.

Baloma In Melanesia the spirit of a dead relative, often seen in a dream. See *Dreams*(1).

Bambam Early name of the island on which *Singapore* now stands. See *Malay Annals*.

Bangar See *Goddess*(1).

The Banks Islands See *Marawa*; *Vanuatu*.

Banoi In the cosmology of the people of the New Hebrides (see *Vanuatu*), Banoi is the Land of the Dead. For several days after *death* the *soul* lingers above the earth until it starts off on its voyage to Banoi, which lies somewhere in the ocean. The souls live there in peace for they do not have to work, because there are no fields to tend. See also *Death*; *Hades*.

Bantam (or Banten) The chronicle of the Sultanate of Bantam, the *Sejarah Banten*, opens with the myth of the *Wali* (Islamic saint) who was insulted by the Hindu Raja of Pajajaran, the last Hindu kingdom of West *Java*. The saint cursed the Raja, predicting that his religion would be superseded by a new religion brought by the 'Man from the Mountain', Sunan Gunung Jati. In due course the Sunan appeared and preached Islam, which spread across Java. The chronicle goes on to describe the exploits of the Islamic rulers of Bantam.

Banten See *Bantam*.

Bao Round ancestral *stones*. See *New Caledonia*.

Barat See *Bharata*. 'Phrot' is the Tai pronunciation.

Baratra See *Batara Guru*.

Basir The priest-shaman of the Ngaju *Dayaks* in *Kalimantan*, southern *Borneo*, dressed like a woman.

Basudewa See *Vasudeva*.

Basuki See *Sesa*.

Batak The name of a people living in *Sumatra* around Lake Toba. They speak a distinct Indonesian *language* with its own script in which many works on *magic* have been written. See also *Creation*(9); *Demons*(3); *Devata*; *Eggs*; *Gnomes*; *Predestination*(4); *Rice Soul*; *Shaman*(3).

Batala The *Tagalog* form of Batara or *God*. See *Monkeys*(1).

Batara Guru (or Baratra Guru; 'Venerable Teacher' or 'Worshipful Master') In pre-Islamic Indonesian and Malaysian myths, Batara Guru was the Supreme God, sometimes identified with *Indera*, but usually with *Siwa*. See also *Creation*(7)(9); *Lutung Kasarung; Mahayogi; Ratna Dumilah*.

Batari See *Bairawi; Durga; Kali; Sakti*.

Bathala See *Batala; Siwa*.

Bato The Japanese horse-headed goddess, identified with *Kannon*.

Bats In the *Philippines* they relate the following myth about the origin of bats. In the beginning there was only one man on earth. His body was composed of numerous tiny beings who were constantly at war with one another. In the end one night the man was so exhausted that he lay down to die. With him died all the beings he was made up of, except the bats, who like flying at night, so they flew away.

Bayang See *Soul*.

Bayu ('Action and learning') See *Saraswati*.

Bear See *Haida*.

Bees Almost a millennium ago in *Japan*, General Yogodayu was defeated, and retreated to the valley of Kizugawa. There, one evening, he saw a bee caught in a spider's web. He liberated the poor bee and let it fly free. That night he saw, in a dream, a man dressed in black and yellow who gave him some instructions: 'Go and collect 1,000 jars like the ones used by beekeepers, place them in a big barn in yonder plain; let it be known to your enemies that you are there with all your men and leave the rest to me. You shall be rewarded for your kindness.'

The man disappeared and the next morning Yogodayu sent his men out to collect 1,000 jars and place them in the barn. As soon as the enemy knew where Yogodayu and his men were, they marched in force to attack him. By that time all the jars were full of bees. As soon as the enemy approached, the bees flew out, millions of them, and stung the enemy troops. Those who did not turn and run at once were stung until they died or went mad and were cut down by Yogodayu's men. He later built a shrine for the bees who had died in the battle, whose bodies he had collected and buried there.

See also *Honey Tree Song*.

Begu A ghost. See *Demons*(3); *Soul*.

Bela See *Tree-Spirit*(3)(8).

Bells Great *bronze* temple bells can be seen outside many Buddhist temples in *Japan* and *Korea*.

One day a strong man called Benkei (not the swordsman, see below) unhooked the famous bell from the monastery at Miidera in Japan and carried it to his own town. But when struck the bell would only complain, 'I want to go back to Miidera.' Finally, Benkei carried it out of his town and it was brought back to Miidera.

See also *Kane*(1); *Kiyo*.

Benkei A famous fighter and swordsman in Japanese mythology.

Benten The Japanese name for the goddess *Saraswati*, patroness of learning, especially language and eloquence, and music. She is also Goddess of the Sea, one of the *Shichi Fukujin*, seven Gods of Good Luck. She rides a *dragon* (sometimes painted as a *serpent* in Japanese art). She has eight arms; six of her hands hold a symbol – bow, arrow, wheel, sword, key and jewel – while the two remaining hands are joined in prayer. It is related that when a wicked dragon devoured many children, she descended to earth to put a stop to his evil work. The island of Enoshima rose up specially to receive her footsteps.

One day a young poet, Hanagaki Baishu, while worshipping Benten in her temple at Amadera, found a poem written in an exquisite feminine hand. He fell in love with the poetess-calligrapher and prayed to Benten that she should be given to him in marriage. The goddess appeared to the girl's father and told him that she had found an excellent husband for his daughter, a poet for the poetess. She described Baishu in such detail that the next day the father recognized him in the street and made him his son-in-law.

See also *Enoshima*; 'Gods of Japan' under *Gods*.

Beras Thrashed rice in *Indonesia*.

Betel (in *Indonesia*, *sireh* or *sirih*; in Melanesia, *kwega*) The leaves of the plant *Piper betel* which, when wrapped around the crushed nut of the areca palm, *pinang*, are chewed by millions, their red-stained lips bearing witness to their inclination. In Indonesia, *pinang* is identical with the word for marriage proposal. During negotiations, *betel* is chewed. On Boyowa Island in Melanesia there is *magic* connected with it which is believed to make women pregnant. *Betel* is universally associated with ceremonies introducing the proceedings for matchmaking and marriage.

See also *Owl*(2).

Beyawa The name of a beautiful woman in Melanesia. When she died, her husband Tomwaya could not forget her, so, by putting himself into a trance, he visited her in the spirit town, Vabusi.

Bezoar Stone (Malay, *guliga* or *mustika*) An antidote against poison, found, according to Malay mythology, in some *coconuts*. It seems to be limestone. It is used for medical purposes as a styptic. See also *Fetish*.

Bhaishajya See 'Gods of Japan' under *Gods*; *Yakushi-Nyorai*.

Bharada A Balinese ascetic. See *Witch*(2).

Bharata In Hindu–Javanese myths, the son of King Dusianta and ancestor of the *Korawas* and *Pandawas*. See *Mahabharata*.

Bharatayuda   The Javanese *Mahabharata*.

Bherava (or Maha Bherava; Sanskrit, Bhairava) The terrifying manifestation of *Siwa* (Shiva), in the Hindu–Javanese and Balinese mythology. In Buddhist philosophy likewise, Siwa Maha Bherava is the numinous manifestation of the *Buddha*.

Bidadari   In Javanese myths a kind of nymph of heavenly beauty who may rescue the hero with her *magic* knowledge and even marry him. See also *Widyadari*.

Bidan   ('Midwife') See *Fortune-Tellers*(2).

Bidasari   A Malay *epic* poem of *love* and romance, with a happy ending. King Mengindera of Indrapura, while hunting in the darkest part of the forest, discovers a sleeping beauty in a cabin. It appears she wakes up only at night. She confesses that she is persecuted by his own queen who took her *semangat* (*soul*) and locked her up in the cabin for fear that the king might marry her. Of course the king does just that, as soon as he has discovered the truth.

Bilalang   See *Pa Bilalang*.

Bima   (or Bratasena) Second son of King *Pandu* in the *Mahabharata* as performed in the Javanese *wayang* plays. He was born wearing a helmet and armour, and possesses huge thumbnails with which to kill his enemies. See also *Dewi Nagagini; Gatutkaca; Werkudara*.

Bimbo   A Japanese peasant. See *Thunder Baby*.

Bimbogami   The Japanese God of Poverty, who is an obstinate companion of many families. Special rituals are performed to get rid of him. See also 'Gods of Japan' under *Gods*.

Bimbomushi   The Japanese word for the deathwatch beetle, literally 'poverty-bug'. It is believed that this ticking woodworm bodes poverty.

Bird of Paradise   A genus of *birds* belonging to the *Paradisaeidae* family with plumes of such beauty, variety and bright colouring that it was believed they had been given these *feathers* by the *angels* of Paradise, or that they themselves had escaped from *heaven*. Most species live on *New Guinea*.

Birds

1. In *Indonesia* the *souls* of the *dead* may become birds. The paddybirds, *gelatik*, are ancestors partaking in their descendants' food. When a child is seriously ill, its soul is called back by shouting '*Kuru! Kuru!*' the way one calls chickens. Spirit-shrines are decorated with chicken *feathers*.
2. A Japanese landowner loved shooting birds. Although he had two devoted daughters who loved them and often begged him not to kill any more of the innocent creatures, he could not stop shooting. One day a neighbour asked him to shoot two white storks who, he said,

were eating up all the *fish* in his pond. The two young ladies loved the beautiful white birds and decided to disguise themselves in white feathers and red bills. So dressed, they went and stood motionless near the fishpond. Soon enough their father spotted them from several hundred yards' distance. He fired his double-barrelled gun and did not miss. The two 'birds' fell dead. The girls had sacrificed themselves for the real storks who had a nest with young. Their father, contrite, buried his daughters and never shot another bird. *Buddha* forbade the harming of any living creatures.

For man-eating birds, see *Ngani-Vatu; Poukai*. See also *Antang; Bird of Paradise; Cassowary; Cockatoo; Dove; Garuda; Haida; Hornbill; Hototogisu; Indera Bayu; Khrut; Kinnara; Kiwi; Maori*(2); *Parrot; Pheasant; Pigeon; Radin; Raicho; Red Bird; Songbirds; Sparrow; Tevake; Toucan; Tui; White Raven*.

Bishamon One of the seven Japanese Gods of Good Luck, the giver of wealth. See also 'Gods of Japan' under *Gods*.

Bishamon Tenno See *Shi Tenno*.

Bismarck, Otto von See *New Britain; New Guinea*.

Biwa

1. The name of a lake in *Japan*, inhabited by a *dragon* king.
2. A four-stringed instrument played by a reciter of *epic poetry*.

Black The colour of mourning in *Indonesia*, because the *souls* of the *dead* are black, so the *spirits* who cause death will be misled into thinking that those who wear or make their faces black are already dead. The basic thought here is that death is contagious: if one relative has died, the others are susceptible to the same fate, as death hovers near. The custom of painting one's face black after a death in the family is also found in *New Caledonia, New Guinea* and *New Zealand*.

Black Monkey See *Lutung Kasarung*.

Blue Dragon The guardian of the eastern signs of the Japanese Zodiac.

Blue Rain Hill See *Fujiyama*.

Bluebottle In *Java*, this insect is believed by some to be an ancestor leading the *soul* of a recently deceased person to Soul Land. See also *Butterfly; Dragonfly*.

Boar

1. In the Thai *epic* of *Rama*, the god *Narayana* (Vishnu or *Wisnu*) assumes the shape of a wild boar, Varaha, to slay the demon *Hiranyaksa*.
2. In *Malaysia* it is said that the wild boar, *babi hutan*, is sometimes a man in disguise. Some wild hogs have golden chains hanging from

their tusks which must be gently taken off without killing the animal, while it is wallowing in the mud.

A man who knows the right incantations can change brass into gold by putting it in the stomach of a boar and burying it in the ground. It must be left there until the grass grows tall over it.

See also *Kamapua'a*.

Bochor An assassin. See *Senapati*.

Bodhisattvas See *Go-Chi Nyorai*.

Bomala The Melanesian word for *taboo*, prohibition, moral abstention.

Bommatsuri (or Bon, Bonmatsuri) The Japanese midsummer Lantern Festival (13–16 July), or the celebration of the *dead*, 'All Souls'. It is believed that the soul, after death, must travel a long time till s/he reaches the Sanzu no Kawa, the River Styx. There s/he must pay the fare for crossing and to that purpose the relatives will have placed a sachet with money round their dead loved one's neck. Sodzu Baba, the old woman on the riverbank, will take the money.

On the fifteenth day of the seventh month the people celebrate the 'Feeding of the Souls', for by that time the souls will have arrived in Gakido, 'Demon Road' or Purgatory, where they suffer hunger and other trials, doing penance for their sins. The living send food not only to their own dead but to all the lonely souls in Hades. Beautifully painted Japanese paper lanterns are hung outside and lit so as to guide the *spirits* to the house. The houses are decorated with fresh flowers and fires are lit. The people dance outside in light garments and set off fireworks. It ends with 'seeing off' the spirits with floating candles on the rivers.

See also *Death; Soul*.

Bomoh In *Malaysia*, the *medicine man* and exorcist who cures his patients of evil *spirits* causing diseases. He also sells charms and *amulets* for *magic* protection. A woman too, may be a *bomoh*; the *bomoh* Eisa in *Singapore* became famous when she cured a woman whose neighbour had bewitched her, as a result of which she kept having stillbirths and speaking in foreign tongues. See also *Fortune-Tellers*(2).

Bon See *Bommatsuri*.

Bon-Ten-O See *Footprint of the Buddha*.

Bonin Islands These small *islands* south of *Japan* are called *Mujinto* in Japanese. It is reported that a race of *giants* once lived there, the last of whom was nine feet tall and had lived alone on his island for 300 years when he died.

Bonmatsuri See *Bommatsuri*.

Borneo One of the world's largest islands, lying between *Sulawesi* and *Malaysia*, north of *Java* across the Java Sea. Its area is 751,900 sq km.

The northern quarter is divided between the states of Sabah and Sarawak and the Sultanate of Brunei. The southern three-quarters, called *Kalimantan*, belong to *Indonesia*. Malay-speaking people live in the towns. The coast-dwelling Sea-Dayaks (see *Dayaks*) are fisherman. In the rainforests of the interior live some of the earth's oldest races, the Punan or Penan.

See also *Basir; Buffalo; Creation*(6); *Dayaks; God*(2); *Illness; Indonesia; Kalimantan; Monkeys*(8); *Predestination*(3).

Bonze   A Japanese priest. See *Soryo*.

Borobudur   A great Buddhist monument in Central *Java* just north of Jogyakarta, the building of which commenced in 750 AD . Its base is square with sides of 173m. It is structured in seven terraces, the four lowest levels being square, the top three being circular. On the four sides, steps lead through ornamental gates, above which *makaras* (dragon-like monsters) keep guard, to the higher levels. The monument is built around a hill; though it can be called a *stupa*, there are no traces of any relics of saints. It seems to have been built solely for the instruction of the believers.

Along the walls of the square terraces the pilgrim can study 2,141 reliefs sculpted on the foot-long *stones*, depicting the history of *Buddha*'s life and that of his spiritual successors, ending with the 'history' of *Maitreya*, the future Buddha. The pilgrim is supposed to walk round studying the sculptures, then move up to the next higher level. In niches along the third and fourth levels, the pilgrim will also encounter seated statues of the Buddha. On the top three circular terraces are situated the majority of the 453 seated images of the Buddha, the 25 Bodhisattvas and all their philosophical emanations, as well as the 5 Manushi Buddhas, 18 Dhyani Buddhas, 12 Manjusris, 15 Avalokitesvaras, 19 Akshobhyas, 13 *Vairocanas*, 11 Amoghasiddhis, 24 Paramitas and Vasitas, etc.

Having studied all these statues (each one representing not a god but rather a philosophical concept for meditation and enlightenment), the pilgrim will finally emerge on the top level of the Borobudur where he will face the crowning *stupa*, 17m high, standing 43m above ground level. It has been structured into a bell-shaped dome of loose bricks fitted in such a way that a curious visitor can peer through the openings. Numerous other similar but smaller domes contain seated Buddha figures, but this *stupa* is empty. The reason for this has been variously explained. No statue seems to have been stolen from inside – though some others have been removed by 'collectors'. It should be remembered that 'emptiness', in Sanskrit *sunyata*, is an essential concept in Buddhist philosophy, one that is not easily grasped. It has been suggested, therefore, that the pilgrim is encouraged to contemplate 'emptiness', for which he has been prepared by the time he has reached the top. Emptiness is the result of the removal of all illusions (*maya*) from the mind. Desires, fear, indeed all thoughts, are illusions impeding the expansion of true enlightenment in the mind. Emptiness, not worship, is one of the goals of Buddhist philosophy. A second explanation is more in line with the concept of worship as represented by Mahayana *Buddhism*, of which the Borobudur is one of the finest monuments. The crowning *stupa* may be empty in expectation of the descent of Maitreya, the Buddha of the future, from his heaven, Tushita. A third theory asserts that the crowning *stupa* was intended to invite the presence of the *Adi-Buddha*, who cannot be represented in stone or any other substance, since he is the very essence of Buddha-character.

Boroka   On the *Philippines*, a cannibalistic *witch*. Boroka has wings like an eagle, four feet like a horse and the head of a woman. She loves children – to eat. See also *Spirit Woman*.

Boromakot   An eighteenth-century Thai king. See *Thailand*.

Bosatsu   The Japanese form of the Sanskrit *Bodhisattva*. A Bodhisattva is a manifestation of the *Buddha* in the past, present or future. Instead of entering nirvana, i.e. escaping the burden of individual existence, a Bodhisattva has decided to remain in this world for the benefit of humanity. See also 'Gods of Japan' under *Gods*.

Bottle-Imp   See *Polong*.

Brahma

1.   The great *Creator* of the Hindu pantheon, the ancestor of the gods, and the divine husband of *Saraswati*. See 'Gods of Bali' under *Gods*.
2.   In *Java*, *Bromo*, the God of the Great Volcano. See also *Volcano God*.

Brain Coral   Some Polynesian and Micronesian sailors secretly keep a piece of brain coral under their seat in the boat. It represents the Sea-God, whose help is invoked for a safe crossing.

Bratasena   See *Bima; Werkudara*.

Bratayuda   In Javanese mythology, the great war of the *Pandawas* and the *Korawas*; inspired by the Indian *Mahabharata*, it provides numerous tales for the *wayang* shadow play and *topeng* dances. See also *Ambiki; Arjuna; Bima; Dasamuka; Dewi Gandari; Drestarata; Duryudana*.

Breadfruit   *Artocarpus* of the *Moraceae* family, also called Jackfruit, breadfruit is indigenous to *Indonesia* but not *Polynesia*, having been brought there by the *Polynesians*. It is commonly used as victuals on long voyages, along with *coconuts*. See also *Kuru; Maori(2); Paliuli*.

Bridge   When a bridge was built in *Japan*, a man had to be buried alive under the central pillar to appease the *river spirits*.
   See also *Shodo Shonin*.

Bridge of Heaven   This floating bridge belongs to the Japanese Dance-Goddess *Uzume*, who is married to the God of the Paths, its guardian. The Bridge of Heaven leads from *heaven* through the clouds to Mount Takachihi, from where earth can be reached. See also *Ninigi*.

Bromo An active volcano in Central *Java*, which is part of the Tengger mountains and is surrounded by a desert.

In ancient Javanese mythology, Bromo was also the God of the Volcano. Bromo is the Javanese pronunciation of *Brahma*, the Sanskrit name of the Indian God of *Creation*, comparable with the Roman god Vulcanus. Bromo is worshipped by the people of the nearby villages, whose priests throw offerings down into the steaming crater, hoping for good health, good *rice* and good children. The sacrifice of a goat may induce Bromo to grant a son to a childless couple. He sometimes sends his own son, in the shape of a poor beggar or a handsome prince, to test the people and to reward them for their faithful prayers and sacrifices.

Bronze In Japanese, *seido*. The art of bronze casting was highly developed in medieval *Japan*. It was feared, though, that bronze warriors and *horses* might come to life in the night and ride noisily through the towns. It was said that other statues of animals (*tortoises*, *deer*, etc) could walk through the streets, so bronze horses and warriors were mutilated in order to prevent them from disturbing the citizens.

See also *Oho-Kuninushi*.

Brunei See *Borneo*; *Malaysia*.

Bua-Taranga In Samoan myth, Bua-Taranga was the mother of *Maui*, and the first person to cook her food. Every day she went to a certain black rock, pronounced her magic *karakia* and the earth opened. She had an oven in the *Underworld*.

Buata See *Monsters*(1).

Bubuli A woman of the island of Siar. See *Snake*(2).

Bubwayaita In Melanesia, the herb of oblivion. The *souls* of the *dead*, after arriving in *Tuma* (Paradise) will be given this herb. Its fragrance is so strong that they will forget life on earth and live happily ever after.

Buddha The Buddha is revered in all of continental South-East Asia (although in *Malaysia* only by the numerous Chinese Buddhists), in *Bali*, *Indonesia*, *Korea*, *Japan*, *Taiwan* and *Hong Kong*. In Balinese mythology Buddha is often identified with *Siwa* as the Supreme Lord of *Heaven* and the Great Teacher, *Batara Guru*, of all people. Like Siwa, he is believed to live on the summit of Mount *Mahameru*. Once a year Buddha flies on the Garuda Putih, his white eagle, down to the land of people. He is identified with *Yama-Raja*.

See also *Buddhism*; *Butsu*; 'Gods of Bali' and 'Gods of Japan' under *Gods*; *Naga Muchilinda*.

Buddhism See *Adi-Buddha*; *Aizen-Myoo*; *Akasa-Garbha*; *Amida*; *Arhat*; *Ashuku*; *Bishamon*; *Borobudur*; *Bosatsu*; *Buddha*; *Crystal*; *Daibutsu*; *Daimoku*; *Dainichi*; *Dandoku*; *Daruma*; *Dengyo*; *Dogen*; *Footprint of the Buddha*; *Fugen-Bosatsu*; 'Gods of Bali' and 'Gods of Japan' under *Gods*; *Hosho-Nyorai*; *Inga*; *Jizo*; *Jobutsu*; *Kannon*; *Kobo*; *Kongo-Kai*; *Lotus*,

Golden; Monju Bosatsu; Nembutsu; Shaka; Shugendo.

Buddhist Deities See *Colours and Compass*; also 'Gods of Japan' under *Gods*.

Budiman A king in Malay mythology. See *Indera Bayu*.

Bue In *Kiribati* there is a myth of the Sun-God in which he sent a ray of light to a woman on earth and so made her pregnant. She gave birth to a son whom she called Bue. She told her son who his father was, so he built a canoe and set out one night towards the east, hoping to meet his father. He wanted to receive wisdom, *rabakau*, and knowledge, *ataibai*, from the Sun-God. Hours before sunrise he set out and travelled east in his fast vessel until he saw the sunrise quite close. His father taught him the art of building boats and houses and gave him the power to call up the *winds* and soothe the *storms*, the knowledge to cure diseases, the secret of wealth and the art of poetry.

Buffalo Some Dayak tribes of north *Borneo* do not eat the meat of buffaloes because, they say, the buffalo is their ancestor. See *Dayaks*; also *Mahisa; Narayana*.

Bujang Sembelih The Throat-Cutting Demon. See *Spirits*(4).

Bujangga

1. In Sundanese mythology, the Bujanggas are the *angels* from heaven who may appear as human servants to serve *Lutung Kasarung*, who is the son of God. They can grow into giants to build a dam in a river, moving mountains if required. When they have completed what they have been asked to do, such as building a palace in one night, they bow and fly back to heaven by just moving their toes.
2. In *Malaya* and *Java*, a huge winged monster, a demon or a *dragon*, or a spirit with great knowledge, a genius.

Bukit Kaca In Malay cosmology, the Mountain of Glass, which is so high that its summit reflects the rays of the rising *sun* so that we see it red, orange and amber.

Bukit Seguntang A mountain, upstream from Palembang in Sumatra, where a palace called *Mahameru* was built by the god-king Sang Pertala Dewa of Palembang (see *Cow*).

Bulan See *Moon*.

Bulotu Tongan *Paradise*, where the *spirits* of the *dead* live amidst richly laden fruit trees and beautiful blossoms in eternal bliss.

Bulu The Land of the Dead in Fijian cosmology. See *Death; Hades*(4).

Bungisngis, the See *Monsters*(2).

Bunu See *Creation*(6).

Burisrawa A prince in the Javanese *wayang* play. See *Durga*.

Burotu The Fijian land of eternal life and joy. See *Dengei*.

Burung Une See *Dayaks*.

Buta In Indonesian mythology, an evil demon. Buta Cakil is a demon with hooked teeth.

Butsu (or Butsuda) The Japanese name for the *Buddha*.

Butsudan A family altar in a Japanese household, where the house deities are venerated with flowers and dishes of food.

Butsudo (literally, 'Buddha's Path') The Japanese word for *Buddhism*.

Butsugaku The Japanese word for Buddhist teachings and doctrine, *Buddhism*.

Butsuji In *Japan*, a Buddhist requiem or memorial service for the *dead*.

Butsuma In *Japan*, a room for the Buddhist altar for family services.

Butterfly

1. In Japanese mythology, butterflies carry the souls of human beings, some who have died and some still alive. On *Java*, it is said that a butterfly must never be killed because it may be carrying the soul of a sleeping person, and if the insect is killed, how will the soul rejoin its body? It is therefore believed in both countries that the arrival of a butterfly in the house of a sick person announces approaching death.
    In *Japan* it is also said that a butterfly may want to deliver a message. The one who follows the butterfly may be led to the solution of an old mystery. Sometimes the butterfly is a messenger of love which only a lover can understand. A flight of butterflies may announce a calamity like war or plague.
2. In *Indonesia*, the butterfly is a common image for the living soul of a person. When a butterfly enters the house, this can be regarded as the soul of a good friend who has predeceased the owner, anxious to visit his friends. If a butterfly alights on the head of a patient, it is a good omen that the illness will be cured, for the soul is said to be returning to his/her body.
3. The Kari Marupi of the lower Purari river in *New Guinea* relate that Pipi Korovu, 'Big Butterfly', used to watch the sea and watch the clouds sail past in the sky and longed to visit the country from which they came. He built himself a butterfly from cane and took off. He flew over the sea and arrived on an island where he perched on a tree. Below him he saw two lovely girls, Aro and Pora, the daughters of the local chief Marupi. He gave them a *betel* nut, which is symbolic of a proposal. They shared it, so he knew they liked him. He then took off for home where he prepared *magic* leaves and went to sleep on them. As a result he could speak to the girls in their dreams. He told them where he would meet them, namely near their well. Again

he flew over the water, singing, 'I am a butterfly, fluttering to the land of the dead, flying through the sky.'

He visited the girls regularly, and married them both, so they both became pregnant. It transpires in the tale that his 'butterfly' is a type of *mask* which transforms him into a butterfly spirit.

See also *Dragonfly; Hiku.*

Buwan   See *Moon.*

C

Canoe god (Cook Islands)

Cafre See *Monsters*(1).

Camellia See *Tsubaki*.

Canaque The French name for the inhabitants of *New Caledonia*. The word is not native and quite erroneous. It was James Cook who called all the 'natives' of the Pacific *kanakas* after his visit to *Hawaii*. *Kanaka* is the Hawaiian word for 'person, human being'.

Canoe (Malay, *perahu* (= *proa*, *pirogue*); Polynesian, *waka*; *Tagalog*, *bangka*) The vessel, sometimes 120 feet or longer which, sometimes with double, but always with at least one, outrigger, carried the Malayo–Polynesians across the ocean. Canoes have names because they are living spirits. Voyagers take wooden statuettes on board, called Canoe Gods, in Polynesian *Taringa Nui*, 'Big Ears', so they can hear danger. They stand in the bows, for good luck. See also *Atonga; Heron*(1); *Kat; Lata; Owl*(1); *Rain-Making; Rata; Spirit-Canoe; Talaipo; Waka*.

Canopus See *Atutuahi*.

Cargo The people of Orokolo (on the south coast of *New Guinea*) believed that their ancestors sent them many ships full of cargo – precious gifts from a distant island – but that the white men had such powerful *magic* that they turned the ships round and made them sail to

Australia. In the early 1920s 'prophets' appeared who said they had met the ancestors who had told them where the cargo was hidden. All that the people had to do was to collect money for a ship to go and find it. The people handed over the money and then the prophets vanished with it. See also *Evara; Germans.*

Carinae See *Atutuahi.*

The Caroline Islands A scattered chain of *islands* north of the Equator, now part of the Federated States of *Micronesia.*

See *Gora-Daileng; Icho; Lioumere; Lugeilan; Maihun; Naniumlap; Olofat.*

Carp This *fish* is revered in *Japan* and *Korea* as the symbol of youth, bravery, perseverance, strength and self-defence, qualities admired especially in warriors. In Korea it is also much loved by the people as a symbol of wealth. The *Dragon Carp* lived 1,000 years. In Japanese mythology there is a big carp, nine feet long, which devours people who are drowning in Lake Biwa. On 5 May, the Japanese people celebrate the Festival of the Boys, at which the carp is the most prominent ornament. It is hung on trees and walls. See also *Dragon Carp.*

Cassowary (from the Indonesian *kasuari*) A large running bird of the ostrich family. It is common in *New Guinea*, and also features in its mythology.

In the lower Sepík district they tell the following tale: a man wanted to bathe in the pond called Tuumbamuuta. Whilst he was there he heard voices so he hid in the shrubs. A group of cassowaries arrived, took off their feathered garments and became naked women. They plunged into the pond and commenced to bathe. The last woman to enter the water was the loveliest. While she was bathing, the man went quietly to the branch where she had hung her *feathers*, and took them away. When she came out of the water after the others, she could not find her feather dress and so had to stay behind when the others left as cassowaries. The man then emerged from hiding and invited her to his house, as it was getting dark. Now this man had a penis but the woman had no vagina, for she was originally a bird. But one day, as she sat down, a sharp stone cut open her bottom. She bled profusely: her first period. When the bleeding stopped, the opening remained, which the man then 'used'. She gave birth to many children, boys and girls, who later married one another because there were no other people on the earth. This is how people came into the world.

See also *Sumua; Tagaro; Woman*(2).

Cat

1. 'When the Lord *Buddha* did die, the cold-hearted cat did not cry.' In *Japan* cats are believed to be cursed and to possess witchcraft. They are malevolent *spirits*. Spectral cats can grow to gigantic size and terrorize whole villages, even though they are barely visible. Their gigantic faces with menacing grins may haunt people as they

slowly become visible though a wall, then fade away again.

It is also said that cats have power over the dead and the *demons*, especially the sea-spirits. Japanese sailors believed that the *souls* of the drowned never found peace, so they kept a cat on their ship to protect them against the invasions of the sea-spirits, the sad souls of the thousands of drowned sailors who want to rest in the *earth*.

2. In *Malaysia* they say that hidden in the cat's body there is an evil spirit, *badi*. Therefore a cat must never be permitted to touch the body of a dead person for the spirit would slip into the corpse and revive it, becoming a horrifying ghost.

3. On the Indonesian island of Lombok there is a myth about a white cat with yellow and brown spots. She was owned by Lo Aget, 'Mr Lucky', who had inherited her from his parents. She never went out and seemed to understand what her young master said. She turned out to be a princess who could resume her human form only when a young man told her he loved her. It was a *sorcerer*'s curse. Lo Aget told her he loved her and later married her.

See also *Dog*(1); *Monsters*(1); *Raiju*; *Rice*(2); *Sorcery*; *Vampire*.

Cave In *Tagalog* mythology there is a cave in which there lives a god who is invisible but very strong with a booming voice. If well served, the Cave-God will give generous rewards.

See also *Ama Terasu*; *Cibaciba*; *Dudugera*; *Glass-Man*; *Gora-Daileng*; *Lua-o-Milu*; *Ocean-Goddess*; *Sam Muk*.

Celestial Eagle See *Garuda*.

Centipede A terrifying, man-eating, mountain-sized monster that lived in the mountains of *Japan*. The famous hero *Hidesato* slew the centipede by shooting an arrow, on which he had put his own saliva, into its brain so that it died and subsequently fell into a lake. See also *Rice-Bag*.

Chaking The 'Tea-Bible' in *Japan*. An eighth-century book in which all the details of making good tea are described by Ru-Wu. Tea drinking became a religious ceremony among Buddhists. See also *Daruma*; *Dengyo*.

Chandi In *Indonesia*, a temple for one of the *gods*, usually *Siwa*. See *Prambanan*.

Chandra Kirana ('Golden Moon') In Indonesian mythology and in the *wayang*, the Princess of Daha, an incarnation of *Dewi Sri*, who is predestined to marry Prince *Panji* of Koripan.

Charon See *Topileta*.

Chatragiri See *Umbrella Mountain*.

Chaya Bulan ('Moonshade') A princess in Malay mythology. See *Indera Bayu*.

Chedi In *Thailand*, a temple complex with a place for worship and a monastery.

Chedu-Do This is one of over 3,000 *islands* lying off the coast of *Korea*. Because of the island's remoteness, *sorcery* is still relevant to the local people's way of life. An ever-present sight on Chedu are the primitive lava stone carvings made by early inhabitants; they are known as Tolharubang or grandfather statues. Some are seven feet tall. Once they were venerated as fertility gods and guardians of village gates.

Chekel Waneng Pati See *Panji*.

Cherry Tree (*Sakura*) In *Japan*, blossoming trees are widely revered as living beings, endowed with an individual spirit.

1. It is said that near Toba there once stood an ancient cherry tree. A Mr Matsui saw there, at night, a beautiful woman whom he perceived to be a ghost. Annoyed by these nocturnal visits of a cold apparition, he attempted to kill her with his sword. The only effect of his evil violence was that the tree died, but it took revenge. The spirit of the tree entered and animated a *kakemono*, a portrait of a beautiful woman which Matsui had hung in his room to contemplate during the night. Suddenly one night, at twelve, the face of the portrait changed, becoming distorted while blood trickled down its cheeks. Gradually the flesh wore off and it became a skull. The next morning the portrait was normal again, but Mr Matsui was a nervous wreck. After three nights he committed suicide. The bewitched painting, although worth a fortune, being an antique heirloom, could not be sold, for no dealer would touch it. See also *Horse*.

2. Another ancient cherry tree stood near a Shinto temple at Hirano. It was so beautiful that a rich samurai coveted it and offered to buy it from its owner, old Jirohei, a teashop manager. Jirohei refused. The samurai drew his sword, threatening to cut a branch off the tree, but Jirohei stood between the tree and its angry attacker. He received the blow and died on the spot. The samurai then took a branch from the tree to his family estate. There he discovered to his horror that his father had died moments earlier of a terrible wound. The tree spirit had taken its revenge. The samurai had to commit suicide, stricken with shame and disgrace. The tree died but no woodcutter would cut it, so it stands there still.

See also *Musubi-no-Kami; Tree-Spirit; Plum Tree; Willow Tree.*

Chichak The wall lizard, a common reptile in most houses in the tropics. In some parts of *Indonesia* it is believed to be an ancestral spirit.

Child Spirit On the *Trobriand Islands* it is said that before conception the spirit of the child is already alive. If you could see it, it looks like a beautiful baby but much smaller, no bigger than a mouse. It is said that child spirits emerge from the sea, attached to flotsam and jetsam, so that, if there is a lot of it in the ocean, girls will not go swimming for fear of becoming pregnant. See also *Reincarnation*.

Chomchaengi See *Fortune-Tellers*.

Chomjangi See *Fortune-Tellers*.

Chomphu Thawip In Thai mythology the continent of South-East Asia, of which *Thailand* forms part. It is the equivalent of the Sanskrit *Jambu Dwipa*, 'Fruit Island', a name for *India*.

Chong Yok ('Book of Change') See *Fortune-Tellers*.

Chonguita In the *Tagalog* tale, Chonguita was a monkey-girl. The Filipino folktale hero Prince Pedro was forced to marry her for fear of being bewitched by her mother. In the end she was changed into a lovely princess.

Chopstick In *Korea* it is said that the wife of a certain Taro prayed to the *gods* for a son, 'even if he were only as small as a chopstick'. Then, in a dream, she heard a voice: 'Put a bowl of rice with one chopstick near the hearth.'
  She did so and the next morning she found a baby boy no bigger than a chopstick in the bowl. Soon 'Chopstick' learned to walk and talk but he did not grow any bigger. One day he mounted his father's horse and dispersed a gang of robbers, freeing the three kidnapped daughters of the local landlord. The youngest, Uriko, married Chopstick in spite of his being only a foot long. One day he prayed to the river goddess, at the place of pilgrimage in the mountains near the river's source, and she gave him the size of a normal man.

Chrysanthemum *Kiku*, the national flower of *Japan*. The well-known symbol on Japan's national flag, a rising *sun*, was originally a chrysanthemum with 16 petals. The chrysanthemum also has a fairy in the shape of a pretty child. A tea is made from the leaves which cures colds.

Chujo Hime A Japanese nun, believed to be an *incarnation* of the goddess *Kannon*. She invented the fine art of embroidery. It is said the gods helped her to make the famous Lotus Thread embroidery depicting the flowers of Paradise at the temple of Toema Dera.

Chula Tupai See *Squirrel*.

Chulan A Thai–Siamese king. See *Malay Annals*.

Cibaciba With Drakulu, one of the cave entrances to the Fijian Land of the Dead. See *Hades*(4).

Cinderella This story is well known in *Indonesia*, usually as the tale of the two (step) sisters. In Halmahera, Cinderella is called Damura. Her stepmother tells her to go and wash clothes in the river. She loses one garment, so she has to go and find it. She meets a mother *crocodile* whom she greets politely, so the crocodile does not eat her, but agrees to look for the lost garment on the river bed. Meanwhile, Damura has to look after the baby crocodile. She does so, singing a nice song to the young reptile. The crocodile finds her garment and comes back with it, then says to Damura, 'Open your mouth!'

She does and the crocodile puts something in her mouth saying, 'Speak to nobody on the road!'

When Damura comes home and says, 'Hello, Daddy!' two golden coins fall out of her mouth. Of course then her stepsister has to visit the same crocodile. She 'loses' a garment and finds the crocodile, but when she has to hold its baby, she sings a wicked little song: 'Little reptile, you stink!'

When she comes home only stones fall out of her mouth. After this, the king invites everyone to a feast, but Damura has to stay home. She then goes to the crocodile, who gives her a sarong and jacket of golden silk, and golden sandals. At the feast the prince falls in love with her and when she has to run away at cockcrow, he catches hold of one of her sandals. The prince identifies Damura as the girl whom the sandal fits and marries her, but the stepmother throws her into the river. Fortunately the crocodile brings her to the surface and gives her back to the prince.

Cobra In *Malaysia* they say that this snake has a precious stone, *gemala*, in its head, which shines brightly at night. If a man succeeds in killing such a snake, the stone will ensure him victory over all his enemies. It is also claimed that it cures a snakebite when applied on the wound. See also *Yatim Nustapa*.

Cockatoo

1. In Melanesia, a spirit bird, who was born from a woman called Karawata. It steals food from women's ovens.
2. In *Indonesia*, *kakatua*, 'pincers', in folktales the bird whose chattering spreads news from the *gods'* world to the people's world.

Coconut

1. In eastern *Papua* the following tale is told about the origin of the coconut. A certain man was envied by his contemporaries because every evening he came home with baskets full of big fish. One day these men decided to spy on him. They hid in some bushes near the beach, early one morning. Soon they saw him standing on the seashore as dawn broke, taking his head off and hiding it under a shrub. He then waded into the sea and bowed. From all sides fish came swimming right into his gullet. When he had enough he returned to the beach and spewed all the fish out. By the afternoon there was a huge heap of fish on the beach. He then recovered his head and placed it carefully back on his shoulders. He started sorting the fish, throwing the little ones back into the sea and putting the big ones in his baskets. The next morning the jealous men spied on him again, but as soon as he had put his head away,

one of them sneaked behind him, picked it up and hid it in the sand. When the miraculous fisherman came back from his fishing he crept round in search of his head but he could not find it. Finally he waded into the sea, changed into a fish and swam away. Later the other fishermen searched for his head but it was gone. Instead they found a coconut tree. A woman was the first to eat of its fruits.

On Bougainville, this same story is also well-known; however, the story ends thus: as the instigator of the spying walked under the newly grown coconut palm, a coconut fell on his head, killing him.

2. On the island of Djaul near *New Ireland* the people relate that once upon a time there was an old man who lived with his two grandsons. The boys went fishing, but when their boat was full, Lumakaka the sea giant appeared. They threw him a fish and he vanished, but soon after he re-emerged from the sea and demanded more fish. Meanwhile the boys paddled furiously but their island was still quite far away. Again the giant appeared, growling for more food. The younger brother said, 'Cut off my arm!'

The elder brother cut off his brother's arm and threw it into the sea. Lumakaka caught it and quickly ate it. Then the younger brother's second arm had to be thrown to the giant. Now the elder brother had to paddle on his own. The younger brother's legs soon went the same way, one after another. Finally, the boat touched land and the elder brother carried what was left of his younger brother to their grandfather's house. Their grandfather said, 'Cut off the head and bury it!'

This was done. The trunk of the poor younger brother was buried separately. The next day the elder brother went to look and found a puppy. He brought it to his grandfather who said, 'Leave it alone: it will grow into a coconut tree which will give us food, drink and firewood.'

See also *Danger Island; Goddess*(1); *Lugeilan; Neititua Abine; New Britain; Niu; Rice-Goddess; Sina; To-Kabinana; Tuna; Vanuatu.*

Colours and Compass   The five old Javanese and Balinese *gods* of the Hindu pantheon are equated with the five Buddhist deities called Dhyani Buddhas (see *Pancha-Tathagata*). This process of harmonization of the Hindu and Buddhist divinities began in *India*, where it is known as Tantrism. It is widespread in South-East Asia. Furthermore, these five 'super-deities' are rulers of the four corners of the cosmos, with one in the centre of the earth, in accordance with the local astrology. Like the planets, each deity is also characterized by a colour.

Dhyani-Buddha	Japanese	Hindu God	Colour
Centre : Vairocana	Dainichi	Brahma	Yellow
East : Akshobhya	Ashuku	Vishnu	Blue
South : Ratnasambhava	Kosho	Yama	Red
West : Amitabha	Amida	Shiva = Siwa	White
North : Amoghasiddhi	Shaka	Indra	Black

The colours are not the same in all the traditions. See also *Dragon*.

The Cook Islands A Polynesian archipelago between *Tahiti* and *Tonga*, from where *New Zealand* was discovered and populated 700 years ago. The Cook Islands' area is 240 sq km, the population 20,000, the capital Avarua and the religion is 70 per cent Protestant. The biggest *islands* are Aitutaki and Rarotonga. The Cook Islands became British in 1888 and New Zealand territory in 1901. They are governed by a parliamentary democracy.

See also *Avaiki*; *Goddess*(4); *Ina*; *Miru*(1); *Motoro*; *Oro*(2); *Ru*(2); *Veeteni*.

Cook, James See *Canaque*; *Hawaii*.

Corpse-Eater In Japanese, *jikininki*, a demon who eats dead human bodies. Often these *demons* are the *spirits* of dead men or women whose greed prevented their *souls* from entering a more peaceful existence after *death*. They continue a half-life by devouring corpses.

A strong-willed priest called Muso Kokushi once kept watch near the body of a deceased person when a *jikininki* arrived to devour it. The priest's prayers liberated the demon's soul.

Coxinga See *Taiwan*.

Cow Prince Peri Dewa of Bukit Seguntang (*Sumatra*), saw a silver cow near a lake where he was bathing. After his bath he went in search of the cow, but found in its stead a beautiful girl with a golden skin. The prince asked his father, Sang Pertala Dewa, who was already in heaven, for advice by sending a messenger. The message came back that the golden girl was a gift from the *gods* to Prince Peri: a bride from heaven. Later, they had a son, *Maniaka*.

Creation

1. The Pareravo people who live near the Purari river on *New Guinea* relate that long ago a woman called Namora emerged from a lake named Eihovu where she swallowed a *fish*. It made her pregnant and in due course she gave birth to a son whom she called Maruka Akore. When he was fully grown he married his mother Namora, for who else should he marry? They had many children, who became the ancestors of a clan. Their descendants still sacrifice parts of every pig they slaughter to the spirit of Lake Eihovu. Maruka Akore is still venerated as the Great Protector in war as well as in peace.

2. The Elema of Orokolo in southern *Papua* relate that in the beginning there were neither mountains nor people nor land. There was only water, in which there lived one enormous turtle. She (for it was a female turtle) swam round for a long time until she wished to rest. With her huge forelegs she pushed sand up from the sea bottom until at last land appeared above the surface of the water (see also *Kamapua'a*). It grew and grew until finally the turtle crept out of the water and rested on the land. Then she dug holes in the beach, bigger than houses, and laid *eggs* in them. In due course two eggs hatched and out crept two people. The first man emerged and said to the first woman: 'I am Kerema Apo. This land is Kerema-Miri

[Kerema-beach], Huru-Kerema [Fertile Kerema].' It was. The turtle's other eggs appeared to contain trees and shrubs, vegetables and other plants which soon covered the land. The name of the first woman was Ivi Apo. The third person to emerge was Avo Akore 'Red Coconut'. He later transformed himself into a coconut palm, the red variety. The fourth person changed himself later into the black coconut palm, Ohare Akore.

3. On *Fiji*, the people tell of *Degei* the great *serpent* who had always lived, without companions. Only in the sky was there another being, Turukawa the *hawk*, wheeling around. It was a she-hawk. One day she made a nest and laid two eggs, which Degei kept warm. Out came two human babies, a boy and a girl. Degei created a banana tree to feed them on its fruits. When they had grown up, Degei created *yam* and *dalo* (*taro*) for them as solid foodstuffs, and he taught them how to make fire and cook their food. He also taught them to talk to him. Later they went away, lived together and had children who filled the earth. See also *Flood*.

4. In Polynesian mythology *Io*, the *Creator*, who has always existed, lived at first in a time when there was only dawnless darkness above the shoreless waters. It was Io who spoke first, calling light into existence so that day came. When he had contemplated the light for a while, he spoke again, calling darkness back, so *night* reappeared. The first day had ended. Then Io once more dispelled the darkness and established the rule of light. He raised the sky, separating it from the earth, then he separated the waters so that land became visible. Then he made *Ra* the *sun* and *Marama* the *moon*, and the bright Pacific *stars*.

5. The Samoan myth relates that Tagaloa, the Ocean-God, had a son who was born in the shape of a bird, named Tuli. Tuli hovered over the waters but found no place to nest, so Tagaloa pushed up a rock from the sea-bed called Papa Taoto, 'The Earth Reclining', which soon sprouted grass. In the mud between the grass, two grubs appeared which grew up, gradually becoming man and woman. Then Tagaloa ordered the rock to split so that two islands were formed which split again and so on until there were numerous islands in the ocean. Out of the rocks Tagaloa caused fresh water to spring forth. In man and woman Tagaloa created the Heart and the Will and Thought, and the Spirit of Life itself and they had children, two of either sex. They stood up and perceived the light.

In this mythology, Mamao, 'Space', is female; and Ilu, 'The Firmament', is male; together they formed the sky. The tallest rocks were placed by Tagaloa in such a way that they held the sky in position. The sky-couple had two children: *Po*, 'Night' and *Ao*, 'Day', who together had two children: Rangima, 'Bright-Sky' and Rangiuri, 'Night-Sky'.

6. According to the Ngaju (*Borneo*) mythology of the *Dayaks*, in the beginning of time there was only Mahatara, the Supreme God. His

other name is Sangiang Dewata; he lives in the heavens. Later in time he found a friend and helper called Jata, who lives in the cool waters of the deepest parts of rivers. In the course of time the Dayaks learned to invoke the names of 14 other *gods*.

One fine day Mahatara decided to create inhabitants for the empty earth. He took a stick from the *garing* tree and carved a male figure on one end, and a female figure on the other. When this wonderful work of art was completed the Creator dropped it to earth. It fell through the clouds and landed on a rock, where it broke into two halves. The half with the female statue lay on the land, while the half with the male statue fell in the water and floated downstream until it landed on an island. There it woke up and became a real man who took the name of Tunggal Garing Janjahunan Laut, 'Lonely Garing, risen from the Sea'. The female statue also came to life and she called herself Puteri Bualu Julah Karangan, 'Golden Princess from the Rock'.

The man made a boat and rowed to the mainland where he met the woman and lived with her. The woman had her first period in the water, where her blood became the wicked water sprites. The next month she had her period on land, her blood becoming the evil spirits on earth. The third time it happened in the forest and there her blood became the jungle demons.

Mahatara, upon seeing all these inauspicious beings growing up, became alarmed, so he descended to earth, where he taught the human couple how they should live as man and wife, so that these ominous events could not happen again. He instituted holy matrimony. After their wedding, the couple lived for many years in perfect happiness. The woman was always pregnant, and three of her sons, Sangiang, Sangen and Bunu lived long enough to have children of their own. Sangen was born with many seeds in his hand, so he spent his life sowing and planting, so that his children had enough both to eat and to store. Sangiang was born with a piece of iron in his hand, so he spent his life making tools and utensils of all kinds. Bunu was born with a bow and arrow, so he became the first hunter.

7. In pre-Islamic Bugi (*Sulawesi*) it was related that there were, in the beginning, two brothers, Sangkuruwira and Guru ri Seleng. The former had a son, *Batara Guru*, the latter a daughter, Nyilitimo. The two were sent to earth and married, becoming the ancestors of the rulers of Bugi. Note that the marriage is the ideal one, of parallel cousins.

8. The Torajas of *Sulawesi* relate the marriage between Ilai, 'Father Sun' and Indara, 'Mother Earth', who created stones which were given breath, i.e. life, by the *wind*. That is why people are mortal: they did not receive the heavenly life-breath from Ilai himself.

9. The *Bataks* believe in three major gods: Batara Guru (the Sun), Soripada (the Earth) and Mangala Bulan ('the Capricious Moon'). They relate the myth of Ompu Tuhan Mula Jadi, 'The Lord the Root of Becoming', who lived in heaven with his daughter, Si Boru Deak,

who was weaving the world. One day she dropped her shuttle and solemnly descended along the thread like a spider. She alighted on the sea where she dropped the earth which her father had given her. It became land. A nice young man from heaven joined her on earth and together they became the ancestors of humanity. No girl may marry 'below' her class.

10. In Nias they relate the myth of Latu, God, who lives in the sun. Latu has made and owns all human beings, whom he kills arbitrarily. So people sacrifice to him, hoping for a long life.

Lowalangi, the God of Good and Evil, is omniscient. He lives in heaven, but was born from a tree on earth. From the mist there emerged the Wind-God, Sihai, who created the wind from his breath. From this wind was born the Tree-God (from wind-blown seeds?) out of which various gods were born. From its only two fruits the first man and woman were born, to whom the wind gave life.

11. In the Minahassa (*Sulawesi*) they relate that the first human being was Lumimu'ut, a woman. She was born from a stone and when she was fully grown, the wind fertilized her (with pollen?), after which she gave birth to a son, Toar. He went out fishing and when he came back as a grown man he did not recognize his mother, so he married her and she gave birth to gods, demi-gods and the ancestors of the people of the Minahassa.

12. The Dayaks relate that Creation began with a spider descending from heaven. See further under *Dayaks*.

13. On the Luang Sermata Islands in *Indonesia*, people relate that in the beginning a woman descended from heaven to earth. She was fertilized by the south wind (which brings rain) and had many children.

14. On Tanimbar, near New Guinea, it is said that the first people emerged from the trees.

15. On Buru, near the *Moluccas*, people call the Creator Opo-Geba-Sulat, 'The Lord who Forms People'. Opo has written down our fate in his book. He also sent a messenger to earth, Nabiata, who taught people how to live.

16. On Bangka it is related that Ake Antak created mountains and trees, but the people were his children with the *Sea-Goddess*.

See also *Cassowary; In and Yo; Heaven*(1)(2)*; Idzumo: Kojiki; Loa; Mother-Goddess; Na Kika; Oya-Shima-Guni; Ta'aroa; Trinity; Vaitupu; Woman; Wulleb.*

Creator Most of the peoples of *Indonesia* believe in the Creator and Supreme God. The *Dayaks* of south-east *Kalimantan* call him *Mahatara*; the Sea Dayaks, Petara; the Balinese, Pintara. All three names are of Hindu origin. In *Java* and *Sumatra* many peoples call God *Batara Guru*, originally a praise name of *Shiva* as teacher of the Sacred Texts. In the *Moluccas* the Creator is addressed as Upu Lero 'Lord Sun'.

See also *Creation; Haronga; Izanagi; Izanami; Kahausibware; Kamapua'a; Kanaloa; Ndengei; Rua; Ta'aroa; Tagaro; Takami-Musubi; Tangaroa; Woman; Wulleb; Yalafath.*

Creese See *Keris*.

Cricket

1. The tree cricket is called *semi* in Japanese, *memmi* in Korean. Some people keep these insects in cages to sing for them. It is said that one species, the *minminzemi*, sing like the chanting of Buddhist monks, so they must never be killed.
2. In the New Hebrides (see *Vanuatu*) people say that in the beginning the sun did not set, so all people had to work round the clock. There were no crickets on earth, for they lived only in heaven. A man who lived in heaven collected crickets in a box. One day he suddenly stepped into a hole and fell down to earth. The box fell open and all the crickets were scattered. As soon as they began to sing, night fell.
3. On *Java*, the cricket is the insect which leads the dead to Deathland.

See also *Pelesit; Polong*.

Crocodile Several species of crocodile survive in South-East Asia, especially in *Thailand, Malaysia, Indonesia* and *New Guinea*. The frightening appearance of the crocodile and its reputation for grabbing and devouring swimmers has assured it a place in the myths of many peoples.

1. In *Sulawesi* it is believed that crocodiles are the *spirits* of the ancestors in a new *incarnation*, still wanting to protect their descendants. So crocodiles are sacred and are only killed when they have killed a human being.

   The Toraja of central Sulawesi believe that the crocodile may be an ancestor and address him as 'grandfather'. They say that crocodiles do no harm to anyone, except when Poe Mpalaburu (Vishnu, the Maintainer of Creation) commands a crocodile to kill a certain person. Certain wicked men, they relate, can reincarnate into crocodiles in order to settle an old score with their enemies.
2. In Malaysia it is said that a crocodile has two pairs of eyes, one pair for daylight and one pair for night and under water. It also has a special stomach in which it hides its human victims' clothes. A child which has fallen into a river may turn slowly into a crocodile, beginning by growing a tail. The head remains human longest. Some crocodiles are women from the waist up. If a young crocodile, just hatched from the egg, runs into the jungle instead of the water, it will turn into a *tiger*. If a crocodile is shot, its spirit will harm the hunter's family. It is said that the first crocodile was fashioned by Fatima, daughter of Muhammad.
3. In some parts of *Java* it is believed that crocodiles are related to people and protect them from illness. The people bring regular sacrifices to the riverside. After the birth of a child, the women of those regions will wrap the placenta up in leaves, place little lamps on it, and let it float downriver as an offering to the ancestors, whose spirits are now living in the crocodiles.

4. According to a Malay story, a ship's captain whose wife, when he tried to embrace her, stabbed him with his own *keris* (dagger), turned into a crocodile. (The moral of the story: wives, be grateful that you have a husband! Always let him do what he likes!)

5. In Indonesia, some men are said to possess the formula called *tiang maleh rupa* which, if intoned under the right conditions, will change them into crocodiles. Sometimes they will wait for bathers to arrive at the riverside and devour them. The usual motive is, however, to take revenge for humiliation, or to satisfy jealousy and grudges.

6. The Ngaju *Dayaks* in *Kalimantan* believe that the crocodiles are the servants of the Jata, the *gods* of the *Underworld*; down there they have the shape of men, but when they are sent to earth they assume the appearance of crocodiles.

See also *Cinderella; Crocodile-Wizard; Jaka Tingkir; Mahatara.*

Crocodile-Wizard In *Malaysia*, a magician who can call the crocodile-spirits together in order to discover a man-eater. When the guilty crocodile is found, its belly will be cut open to reveal its victim's clothes.

Crow In Selangor, *Malaya*, it was said that the crow was the *tiger*'s soul (*semangat*). A crow usually perches on the tiger, picking out its ticks.

Crystal (Japanese, *suisho*) It is said in *Japan* that in this precious stone, clear and transparent, can be seen the *Buddha*, riding a *white elephant*. See also *Moon*(3).

D

Dogaira mask

Daibosatsu (or Dai Bosatsu) In Japanese the Great Bodhisattva, the Buddha-Elect or the *Buddha* in his previous world appearance.

Daibutsu ('The Great Buddha') The gigantic statue of the meditating *Buddha* as world ruler near Kamakura in *Japan*.

Daikoku

1. One of the *Shichi Fukujin*, the seven Japanese Gods of Good Luck, the patron of farmers and God of Wealth. Daikoku's son is *Ebisu*. Daikoku is depicted seated on bags of *rice* and with a bag of jewels on his shoulder. He has a golden *sun* disk on his chest and the hammer which fulfils all wishes in his hand. His familiar is the *rat*; he is a friend of children. Sometimes the image is of a goddess, called Yasha.
2. Another god, Mahakara Daikoku, with the Wheel of Law and a *crystal*, *suisho*, represents *shindai*, 'fortune'. Mahakara is the Japanese form of Mahakala, a Sanskrit name for *Shiva* as God of Time, with whom Daikoku has been equated.

See also 'Gods of Japan' under *Gods*.

Daimoku The Japanese name for the *Lotus Sutra*, in Sanskrit *Saddharmapundarika*, one of the fundamental textbooks of Mahayana

Buddhism, containing *Buddha*'s famous parables.

Dainichi The Japanese form of the name of the Bodhisattva *Vairocana*, the Great Illuminator, the *Buddha* of Infinite Light, the Source of All Existence. He is especially venerated by the Shingon school of *Buddhism*, whose first monastery was built on Mount Koya. See 'Gods of Japan' under *Gods*.

Dainichi-Nyorai ('The Great Sun-Buddha') This is a name for the Bodhisattva Dainichi in his aspect of the element of *ether* in Japanese Buddhist cosmology. Ether signifies the understanding which becomes the nature-substance. See also *Elements*.

Daishi ('The Great Teacher') See *Kobo*.

Dakuwanga The Fijian Shark-God. See *Shark*(2).

Dalang In the Javanese *wayang* performances, the *dalang* is the director. He plays the puppets (made of leather in the *wayang kulit*), instructs the orchestra, and recites the narrative parts as well as the dialogues. Furthermore, he sings the hymns to the gods. He alone knows all the *gods* and heroes of Javanese mythology.

Damar Wulan In Javanese myths, as performed in the *wayang klitik*, a great hero and lover, Prince of Majapahit in East *Java*.

Damura See *Cinderella*.

Dan-no-Ura A Japanese sea battle. See *Epic Poetry*.

Dance In *Polynesia*, the dance, *kanikani*, is accompanied by the singing recital of the myths of the ancestors, like the original Greek tragedies. See also *Hula*; *Lizard*(6); *Wayang*.

Dandoku The mountain upon which *Buddha* performed his final meditation, according to the Japanese tradition, before starting to preach.

Dandomi The wife of *Sijobang*.

Danger Island An island 350m north-east of *Samoa*, called Pukapuka by its inhabitants. They relate that a man once went out to catch a *tuna* (eel) specially for his wife who was pregnant; pregnant wives' requests must be obeyed to avoid danger to the child. Just as he was going to cut the eel up, it began to speak and said, 'Cut off my *head* and bury it outside your front door.' The fisherman did so and out of the head grew a *coconut* palm.
  See also *Sina*; *Tuna*.

Dapie The Moon-Goddess in Seran mythology. See *Moon*; *Sun*(9).

Darma The Indonesian form of the name of the Indian deity Dharma, the God of Justice. He is reborn as *Yudistira*, the eldest *Pandawa*.

Daruma The Japanese name for the Buddhist *guru* Bodhidharma, an Indian sage who, according to legend, brought the tea ceremony to *Japan*, teaching Buddhist doctrine as well as the rituals of Zen tea drinking.

Many years previously he had been visited by temptations, like St Anthony, during his recitations. Once, instead of keeping his vigils, he fell asleep, dreaming that he met a temple girl whose mouth was like a lotus flower. Awakening, the saint felt so contrite that he did penance by cutting off his own eyelids so that he could never fall asleep again. These two eyelids became the first tea leaves. They grew into a teashrub where he had thrown them down, and later helped all the monks and saints to stay awake, for that was the original function of tea drinking: to keep the monks from sleeping.

In art, Daruma is represented without legs because they were lost after nine years of constant meditation; he had been sitting motionless for so long that an owl perched quietly on his shoulder and cobwebs surrounded his body. Three years after his death, Daruma was seen walking across the sea and over the mountains, perhaps on his way back to *India*.

Dasamuka In Javanese mythology, the enemy of the *gods* who incarnates (in the *Ramayana*) as Rawana and (in the *Pandawa* cycle) as *Duryudana* or Suyudana, son of King *Drestarata*. In order to defeat this powerful demon, *Wisnu*, son of the Supreme God, has to incarnate as Rama to slay Rawana, and as *Narayana-Kresna*, as well as in *Arjuna*, to defeat Duryudana.

Dasarata (or Dasharatha) The third king of the city of *Ayodhya* in the Thai *epic* myth. He had three queens but no son until his priest Kalaikota persuaded the god *Wisnu*, as *Narayana*, to incarnate himself as Rama and so become the king's eldest son and successor.

Dasheen See *Taro*.

Datu Jinn Hitam The King of the Black Jins. See *Spirits*(4).

Daughter of the Foam Puteri Tunjung Buih, the wife of the King of Palembang. See *Malay Annals*.

Dawn Like the Arabs and Romans, the *Polynesians* have several words and goddesess for the successive stages of dawn.

1. The goddess Atanua, wife of *Atea*, creates the *fire* of the morning. See also *Tangaroa*.
2. Another Polynesian goddess of the dawn is Atarapa, the first created being.

See also *Dawn Maiden*.

Dawn Maiden In *New Zealand* mythology, she is loved by the Sky-God *Tane*. Every morning she makes love to him, though he is her father. Then she gives birth to the *sun*, Ra, after which she vanishes.

Dayaks (or Dyaks) The Dayaks are the 'old' inhabitants of *Borneo*, which led to the assumption that they were there before Malay speakers arrived and 'pushed' them into the interior. This, however, is not a proven fact. In any case, there are the 'Sea-Dayaks' who live, and always have lived, on the coast; even the Dayaks of the interior may always have lived there and not been 'pushed'.

About the origin of mankind, the Dayaks have their own story:

From Heaven a spider descended at the end of its thread, down, down, down. There was as yet neither earth nor sea. The spider wove its web, but we do not know where it fastened the supporting threads, for only spiders know that. The web was ready, hanging empty in endless space.

From Heaven a piece of coral then fell, a red round stone. It landed on the web and lay there, growing flat and round like a mat. At last this round mat covered all the space under the skies.

From Heaven a slug and then a worm fell. They stuck to the mat with their sticky bodies, and from them the soil was formed, which grew and grew, until the whole mat was covered with the sticky brown stuff.

From Heaven then descended a sapling with its roots pointing downwards. It pushed its roots into the earth and grew into a tall tree. In its shadow other trees grew.

From Heaven a huge crab fell, which at once began crawling in the mud, making mounds and burrowing, digging rivers and throwing up hills and mountains.

From Heaven the rains fell, which filled the river beds, the swamps and lakes, the brooks, the ponds and puddles.

Up from the earth sprouted plants: bamboo shoots, pumpkins, maize stalks, rice, blades of grass, sweet potatoes and many more plants.

From Heaven two spirits descended, one male and one female. They could not have children because they were spirits. So they settled under a tree and made utensils out of wood. The man made a sword handle, the woman made a loom. The sword-handle fell into the loom, and some time later the loom gave birth to one human head, then another. The two spirits did not like their wooden offspring, so they flew back to Heaven.

The two heads married and had two children, heads with necks that could move. These two then married and also had two children, who looked a little more human: heads with necks and rumps, so they could crawl and even sit up. They in turn married and had two children with such long arms that they could reach the sky. They were Amei Awi and Burung Une, the gods of agriculture. They married and had twelve children, eight human and four lunar. These last four were the moons that appear in the sky every month: crescent and full moon, first and last quarter.

The eight human children were sent to climb a high mountain.

Those who reached the summit were to become the ancestors of the slaves because they were strong and prone to exertion. Those who stopped halfway up the slope became the ancestors of free men, and those who did not even begin to climb were to become chiefs and kings who prefer to sit and talk, and make others work for them.

Amei Awi cut some bamboo and built a house. He scraped bark from certain trees and scattered this around the house. The pieces of bark grew into chickens, dogs and pigs.

Burung Une gave birth to more children, but they were dumb. No presents or promises could make them speak until Amei Awi built a boat, went out fishing and came home with fish which he told his wife to cook. Having eaten the fish, the children could suddenly talk, but they spoke a different dialect, so they became the Bahau Dayaks.

Having populated the earth with their children, Amei Awi and Burung Une decided to retire below its surface. They withdrew underground and from there they still rule the grass, the plants and the trees. So the more sacrifices a Dayak brings to these two gods, the better his crops will be. At least once a year, therefore, a Dayak chief will order a great feast to be held, at which he will request the priestesses to say prayers and make supplications for abundant crops, vital to the people. Without these ceremonies there will be no harvest, only famine.

The full moon was the most beautiful of Burung Une's children; so lovely was her face that her brother, Crescent, became jealous. As they were having *bubur*, hot porridge, he suddenly threw some in his sister's face. As a result, dark spots can still be seen on the full moon where her shining face was burnt.

See also *Borneo; Buffalo; Crocodile(6); God(2); Illness; Mahatara; Night; Predestination(3); Radin; Shamanism.*

Dead, the

1. In Japanese cosmology, the ruler of the dead is *Emma-o*. He lives in a huge castle all covered in silver and gold, rosy pearls and other jewels. Emma-o judges the dead according to *Buddha's Law* so that anyone who has killed an innocent living being will be thrown into a boiling cauldron full of molten metal. If, however, they have made a pilgrimage to the 33 shrines of the *Goddess of Mercy, Kannon*, then all the evil they have done will disappear, and their afterlife will be peaceful and without any suffering.

   On the last day of the Festival of the Dead the sea is full of numerous *shoryobuni*, 'soul-ships', for on that day the high tide brings a flood of returning *ghosts* who go back to their spirit world. The sea is luminescent with the light that all those souls emit, and the whispering of the ghosts can be heard. While the ghosts are embarking, no normal human ship should come near. If one does stray into the soul-covered sea, the ghosts will ask for pails. The sailors should only give them pails without bottoms, otherwise the dead will sink their ship.

See also *Bommatsuri; Hotoke*.

2. In *Indonesia*, the soul after *death* has shape and colour, unlike the soul of a living person. The colour of the dead soul is *black*, which is the reason why the relatives of the deceased wear black or even make their faces black; they do this also in times of epidemics, *war* and other dangers. The reason is that the dangerous *spirits* who are wandering around at such times must be deceived into thinking that the living are actually dead too, for death is contagious. Kinsmen are so closely 'related', that if one dies, many may die, like the branches of a dying tree.

    The dead live under the earth in a less pleasant environment than the living, for which reason they envy the living, who, in turn, fear them. This fear explains the numerous funeral rites. Strict vigils are imperative during the first night lest the dead man should rise and strangle the living. The eyes, ears, mouth and nose of the corpse in the coffin are filled with mud so that the dead man cannot see, hear or smell, and so cannot find a victim. The coffin must be carried out of the house through a hole in the wall, and then carried three times round the house, so that the dead man loses his bearings and cannot return to haunt the living. For the rites concerning a woman who has died in childbirth, see *Puntianak*. Not all the peoples of Indonesia fear the dead: some fear the evil spirits who cause death.

3. The *Dayaks* fear the spirits of the dead, for the dead are jealous of the living and threaten to take their souls with them to Deathland. The bodies of the dead are lightly buried in the forest or on the beach. The fishermen of Buru look the other way when their boat sails past their graveyard for they are afraid of being recognized by the dead.

See also *Hades; Honey Tree Song; Kapuku; Monkey*(7)(8).

Death (Hawaiian, *make*; Indonesian, *mati*)

1. In *Polynesia* death is 'being eaten by the gods', especially *Miru*. There is the universal belief in all Pacific *islands* that the spirit survives the body and goes to *Hades* (*Reinga*). Dirges and elegies, *tangi*, are sung for the *dead*, often improvised. Fighting competitions were held by the young men to honour dead chiefs. The *spirits* of the dead are said to walk away along the path across the sea towards the setting *sun*.

2. Many peoples in *Indonesia* see death as the continuation of life in a different condition. The immortality of the soul is taken for granted by all. Indeed, if the body is mutilated then the soul after death will also be mutilated, so similar is the person's condition after death. Dr Bervoets, a Dutch physician, published an article about the care for the dead. When, *c.*1920, he asked the family of a

deceased Javanese man whether he could have his artificial leg back so that someone else could benefit from it, the family declined, saying that the deceased needed two legs in the next life.

See also *Ghosts; Hine-Nui-Te-Po; Immortality; Kahausibware; Merau; Rangi; Skulls; Spirits.*

Death-Stone An upright pillar standing on the lonely moor of Nasu in *Japan*. Inside it lives an evil spirit, called Hoji, which will kill the unwary traveller who lies down to sleep near the stone. See *Genno*.

Deer

1. In the ancient city of Phayao in *Thailand* there once ruled a king called Kham Daeng, the Golden Prince, because of the city's wealth. He was addicted to hunting and prided himself that he eventually caught every animal he pursued, but one day he was himself caught. That morning he saw, in the depths of the forest, a golden hind. He pursued her for many hours until she finally disappeared through a small opening in the sheer face of a rock. The prince dismounted and entered the cave through what appeared to be a door. Inside he discovered not a cave but a spacious palace. He walked past flower gardens surrounded by galleries where fountains sprinkled. There he was met by a lovely princess who spoke to him: 'O King, I have seen you many times and loved you for many moons. I changed myself into a golden deer in order to lure you to my palace. My name is In Lao, I am the ruler of this forest and these mountains. Please stay here.'

    The king was never seen again in his city. His servants found his horse in the middle of the forest but they could see neither cave nor door, only a sheer rock face. They concluded that their king had been bewitched.

2. The Bahau *Dayaks* of central *Kalimantan* (*Borneo*) believe that some people become deer after *death*. The Dayaks tell a tale of a hunter who fell asleep in a disused graveyard. He dreamt of a beautiful girl who spent the night with him. When he woke up at dawn, a hind who had been lying next to him, suddenly rose up and ran away. It was the spirit of the girl who had died there a long time ago and who had made love to him.

3. In Macassar it was said that once, long ago, two old people went into the forest to collect vegetables. Their children were the deer.

Degei (or Dengei) In Fijian mythology, Degei is the *Serpent-God* in the Kauvadra hills. After *death* the *soul* faces a long journey from the sunny land of the living to the cold, misty Land of the Dead (see *Hades*). Degei will interrogate the souls as soon as they arrive. Idle men, whose nails are long, will be punished. Industrious souls will be rewarded. After judgement the soul will be thrown into a deep lake. It will sink for a long time until it reaches Murimuria, a sort of Purgatory. There some will be rewarded and others will receive dire punishment. Only a few are chosen by the *gods* – arbitrarily, it seems – to go to Burotu, the land of eternal life and joy, where they will rest in the cool shade. See also *Creation*(3); *Flood; Sky-King.*

Deluge In Polynesian mythology, the Deluge was caused by a disagreement between the sons of *Rangi* (Ouranos) which started a war of the Titans, in which the Storm-God *Tawhiri-Matea* raged against all his brothers: *Tangaroa* the Ocean-God, Tane-Mahuta the Forest-God, and others. Ua-Roa, 'Long Rain', was one of the *gods* who caused the earth to be flooded. *Papa*, the Earth-Goddess, was entirely submerged, so that she remained hidden from the storm. Gradually she showed some of her beautiful parts above sea level and these are the *islands* of *Polynesia.*

See also *Flood; Hades*(2).

Demi-Gods (or *kupua*) In *Indonesia*, demi-gods have to help the people they protect to find the *souls* of ailing persons lingering on the brink of *death*. They give visions to priestesses and accompany them in the forest. They fly up to heaven to ask the *gods* for *rice* and rain on behalf of their people. See also *Hiku; Na Atibu; Sangiang; Tree-Spirit*(8).

Demons

1. In *Japan* in the reign of the Emperor Ichijo, there lived on the mountain Oye-Yama near Kyoto a gang of demons who from time to time came down to the city, picked up some boys and girls, took them back to their castle of iron and devoured them. One day even Kimitaka, the emperor's daughter, was caught and held captive. The emperor then invited the hero Raiko and his six gallant knights to slay the demons. The War-God *Hachiman* gave them a secret potion called 'Good for me, bad for demons'. Raiko persuaded the demons to drink it as a special treat. Soon they all slept, and were slain. Demons are of gigantic size and of bright red colour.

2. The Kyaka of western *Papua* tell of several types of demons. The *kiliakai* are small, ugly and entirely malicious. They steal *pigs* and maltreat them. They 'shoot' people who trespass their watery preserves, causing them to contract malaria. They steal babies from women's net-bags, if the mothers leave them unattended for a moment. In the place of the babies they will lay their own changelings, horrible-looking *dwarfs*, who will grow into savage *monsters*.

   Sky demons, called *yakirai* by the Kyaka, cause storms with thunder and lightning, with which they can kill people who are not protected by their ancestral *spirits* (through neglect of their worship). Magical ceremonies are needed to prevent such attacks.

   In the Kyaka language the word *kewanambo* denotes an ogre, a demon who devours human beings. He will disguise himself as a motherly woman and lure a child to his roost. An ogress who seduces men will be burnt by the fire in her vagina.

   Yama Enda is another female demon in the forests of the Kyaka.

She appears to men disguised as a beautiful girl, but when she has seduced one she devours him, like a tigress.

3. In *Indonesia*, demons are said to appear in many shapes. They may appear as *dragons*, pigs, *dogs*, *crocodiles*, night *owls*, hairy men or limbs. Numerous *snakes* are demons whose sight may cause barrenness in women. On Buru, seeing a *python* may cause cramp unless a pig's *head* is offered to it. In Sunda, a *jurik* is a type of demon who may be seen flying in the night sky looking like a fiery snake.

For the coastal peoples, sharks, sea snakes and sea-cows (*dugongs*) may be demons. On Kiser Island, demons appear as half people with one leg, one arm, one eye and one ear.

The *Dayaks* believe in the *jata*, sea demons who may cause cholera. *Crocodiles* are their servants.

In central *Borneo*, some demons look like little men with huge genitals; sometimes only the genitals are visible, floating in the air.

The *Bataks* say that a *begu* (ghost) may be a messenger of the *gods* bringing disease to punish sinners. The *hantu*, they say, are male or female spirits, very frightening, dressed in red or white. The *omang* are *gnomes* who live in the mountains, marry and have families. Their feet point backwards.

Some mountain demons in *Sumatra* look like people of both sexes but they are much stronger. Male demons will abduct human girls and female demons pick up young men whom they keep captive for years to have their pleasure with them. Some *hantu* may appear as visible demons, capture people and maim their victims, unless they receive substantial offerings.

See also *Digawina; Ganesa; Genno; Green Demon; Jin; Lioumere; Masalai; Mountain Man; Mountain Woman; Ngarara; Pahuanui; Pua Tu Tahi; Raiju; Raksasa; Spider; Spider-Boy; Spider-Woman.*

Dengei See *Degei.*

Dengyo A Buddhist saint who lived *c.*800 AD . He brought the tea ceremony to *Japan* where he was one of the founders of the Zen form of Buddhist meditation. It was a religious ceremony in which the monks would drink tea from a single bowl before the image of *Daruma.* Tea was regarded as a religious medicine.

Devata This Sanskrit word for the Deity is found widespread across the Indonesian *islands* in the meaning of 'god' and often 'Supreme God'. In Javanese *dewata*, in Dayak (*Borneo*) *jewata* or *jata*, in Batak (*Sumatra*) *leibata*, in Bisaya (the *Philippines*) *divata*, etc.

Devi Seri See *Dewi Sri.*

Devi Shri See *Dewi Sri.*

Devil In Tangu, a *language* spoken in Bogia district in northern *New Guinea*, the word *ranguma* (plural: *ranguova*) denotes a man who is essentially evil and tricky. The first *ranguma* was the last man who crept out of the hole in the earth 'from whence all men emerged'. He brought with him poison and the power to cause *illness* and *death*.

A *ranguma* can be recognized by his bloodshot eyes and by his hands – his fingers are, it seems, ready for strangling. While other men may commit adultery with other men's wives, both enjoying 'sin', the *ranguma* will lure a good woman away from her house and ruthlessly embrace her. He is to be feared at night, especially by women and children. He will kill the latter and rape the former. He will take what he can get from the community but he will not contribute his share of the work. He is a loner, usually sitting sullenly in his hut by the fireplace.

The people say that a *ranguma* is like a two-headed *dog*: a freak of nature. Like sudden dangerous squalls, lightning, huge *snakes*, *earthquakes*, man-killing *boars*, he is dangerous, different. He possesses charms, poison and other means of making people sick and even causing their death. He is a *sorcerer*, whose very presence causes men to fight. *Ranguma* men have a coven, with whom they eat dead babies and live toads, which will give them the desire, will and ability to kill others in cold blood.

See also *Sorcery*.

Dewa Laksana   See *Epic*(1).

Dewata   See *Devata*.

Dewey, Admiral   See *The Philippines*.

Dewi   In *Indonesia*, a goddess in general, but usually *Kali*, *Uma*.

Dewi Gandari   In Javanese mythology, the queen of the blind King *Drestarata*, daughter of King Tistawa. She gives birth, in one confinement, to 101 children: 100 sons, collectively known as the *Korawas*, and one daughter. See *Duryudana*, who is her eldest son.

Dewi Nagagini   The daughter and wife of the Serpent-King *Anantaboga*, by whom she has her son Anantaraja. Later she marries *Bima*.

Dewi Nawang Wulan   (lit: 'The Moon Goddess') In West *Java* she is identified by some people with the *Rice-Goddess Dewi Sri* in her appearance as a nymph. She flies down from heaven disguised as a swan to bathe in a Javanese river, where she is discovered by a young man, who steals her 'flying jacket' so that she has to stay on earth. Kyai Agung, the young man, marries her and they have a daughter, Roro Nawang Sih (Lady Large-Eye Love). Against her orders, Kyai Agung looks in the rice-pan where he sees only one ear of rice (which is symbolically the goddess herself). As a result of his curiosity it can no longer multiply in the pan as it used to do. Dewi has to go and pound rice every day until the rice in the shed is finished. She then discovers her magic jacket which her husband had hidden there. She puts it on and flies back to heaven, only returning once a day to breast-feed her daughter.

Dewi Parwati The Goddess of *Tapas*. See also *Uma*.

Dewi Pratiwi The Goddess of the Earth. See *Wijaya-Kusuma*.

Dewi Sinta See *Sinta*.

Dewi Sri (or Devi Shri or Seri) The equivalent of the Indian goddess Lakshmi, Dewi Sri is the *Rice-Goddess* of Indonesian and Thai mythology. She is also the Goddess of the Earth and the mother of the Javanese people. She is worshipped as the *Rice Mother*, and as the *Rice-Bride* in the Javanese harvest ceremony, and widely worshipped, even in semi-Islamized regions, as the great benefactress of the people who protects them against hunger. She brings the rain when the monsoon arrives and appears in dreams to give good advice.

In the Javanese myths of the *wayang* cycle, Dewi Sri is reborn as *Sinta* to marry her heavenly husband *Wisnu* in his incarnation as Rama (see *Dasamuka*). Reborn as Rukmini, she marries him in his new form as *Kresna*. Reborn as *Subadra*, she once again marries him, by then reborn as *Arjuna*, son of King *Pandu*.

See also *Dewi Nawang Wulan*; 'Gods of Bali' under *Gods*.

Dharma See *Darma*.

Dharmakara See *Amida*.

Dhyani Buddhas See *Pancha-Tathagata*.

Diamond Buddha Many years ago there lived in Lampang in *Thailand* a noble lady, Suchada (Sujata), who loved pious works. She once found a huge pumpkin in her garden which she offered to the abbot of the nearby monastery. The pumpkin changed overnight into a diamond. A stranger in white robes then arrived and carved an image of the *Buddha* out of the diamond, after which he disappeared. The mysterious white-robed diamond-cutter had made such a beautiful statue that pilgrims arrived from many countries to worship at the now famous temple of Lampang.

Alas! Good luck is always followed by envy, and envy by slander. Some people whispered that the pumpkin had been the accursed fruit of the sinful union of the faithless abbot and the lecherous Lady Suchada. When the king of Lampang learned of these tales, he believed them and declared Lady Suchada to be a *witch*. The credulous king ordered the good lady to be beheaded. When her head was severed from her body, however, it did not fall but rose up and flew to heaven. Her blood did not fall either, but drifted over the city like a vast cloud of red raindrops. Soon afterwards the king was thrown by his horse and died. The abbot disappeared a little later, leaving no trace, but the Diamond Buddha is still in the temple of Lampang. No one dares to touch it.

Diarsa A Balinese farmer. See *Siwa*.

Digawina In Melanesia, the name of a demoness with an enormous vagina, who steals food by stuffing it into this organ.

Divata　See *Devata*.

Djao Phraya　A Thai goddess. See *Maenam*.

Dodot　A royal robe. See *Jaka Tingkir*.

Dog

1.　On the island of Oki between *Japan* and *Korea*, it is related that centuries ago, the people had to sacrifice a girl every year to the Phantom Cat, a giant tom-cat. One night a brave knight brought to the island the courageous dog Shippeitaro, who tore the big cat to pieces. See also *Cat*.

2.　A Japanese dog, belonging to an old man, once dug up golden treasures in his master's garden. Wicked neighbours, becoming jealous, killed the dog. That night the spirit of the dog appeared to its master and told him: 'Take the pine tree on my grave and carve a mortar out of it.'

　　The owner did so, and all the *rice* pounded in the mortar became gold. Of course the neighbours, in their envy, took the mortar and burned it. Again the spirit of the dog appeared in his master's dream and told him: 'Take the ashes of the mortar and scatter it over dead trees.'

　　The owner did so and all the dead trees came to life, blossomed and bore fruit. The prince of that country, hearing of this, invited the man to his home and made him the royal orchard keeper.

　　In Japan, it is believed that dogs' *spirits* can leave their bodies and work miracles.

3.　In *Papua* the following is related: in the beginning men and women lived separate lives. There were very few men and they seldom saw women. The women were mated by the dogs who were big, powerful and numerous. When a woman gave birth to a boy, the dogs would devour him. Only girls were allowed to live on and were later mated by the dogs. Only some boys escaped the dogs and very few of them grew to manhood. One day a woman, searching for firewood, strayed from the other women who were being guarded by the dogs. In the deepest part of the forest she saw a handsome man who invited her to lie with him. She felt his penis inside her and it gave her pleasure, whereas a dog's penis never did. The man said, 'If you can get rid of the dogs, you can have this every day.'

　　The women dug a deep pit, telling the dogs it was for cooking meat. (In Papua meat is stewed underground.) The dogs believed there would be a big meat feast. The women lit a huge fire in the pit and when the dogs came close to smell the meat, the women pushed them into the pit. All the dogs were burnt except one puppy. Henceforth women married only men.

See also *Fire*(2); *Giant*(3); *Goddess*(1); *Momotaro*; *Monsters*(1); *Were-Dog*; *Yam*(3).

Dogaira　The malignant God of the Torres Strait Islands who has to be pacified by special masked *dances*. If not, he will cause high tides, rotting fish and blighted *coconuts*. He is also a war-god, to be propitiated with rich offerings.

Dogen Japanese sage (d.1253) and founder of the great monastery at Eiheiji, where Zen *Buddhism* was first taught. Dogen compared his teaching to the man in a boat which drifts along the shore. When he perceives that it is he himself that moves and not the coast, then he has discovered a part of the true condition of things. Dogen travelled extensively in China. See also *Za-Zen*.

Dolls See *Hina-Matsuri; Kojin; Replacement; Tokutaro-San; Wayang*.

Dolphin In *Indonesia* it is related that a woman had a husband who was a miser. One day her little son was hungry so she gave him a small *fish* from her husband's store. When he came home he missed the one fish and beat his wife with a shuttle. She fled to the beach to wash the blood off her body. There, she changed into a dolphin (*rujung*), from the navel downwards. Her children came to the beach begging her to come back, but she could no longer walk. She could only give the breast to her youngest child. She told the eldest: 'Take my tears and rub them softly on your father's back without his knowledge.'

This was done and suddenly the man realized how cruel he had been, and became a loving father. He often searched for his lost wife but in vain. In the end he became a porpoise, but still never found his wife. He was not worth her.

Dolphins' laments can still be heard.

See also *Sijobang*.

Dosojin See 'Gods of Japan' under *Gods*.

Dove In *Malaysia*, it is believed that the barred dove, *Turtur tigrinus* (*merbok*), brings good luck. Once upon a time all the houses in a village burned down except the one where the owners kept this bird. There are special rules for keeping it. See also *Hachiman*.

Dragon In *Japan* there are numerous dragons, most of them living in the seas, the rivers and the lakes. A dragon has scales like a fish, claws like a tiger, a crocodile or an eagle, and whiskers like a cat. Dragons can have heads like those of camels, antlers like deer and eyes like hares but with blazing fires in them. They have wings like a bat's but much larger, so they can fly, and often do so when assembling the clouds for an imminent storm. The breath of a dragon becomes a cloud which can fall down like rain or flare up like fire. They are also able to fly to heaven and back in a day. A dragon can be invisibly small but is able to grow to gigantic size in a few moments.

Most dragons live under water, guarding lakes, rivers and caves. Each of the four seas is ruled by a dragon-king of a different colour. The Yellow Dragon of the Middle brought the ancient system of writing from heaven to earth. The White Dragon of the West brought famine. The Red Dragon rules the south where the sun resides, and so is associated with summer and life (blood-red is the symbolic colour of life), with peach blossom, love and cherries. The Blue Dragon rules the east and is associated with scholarship, but also with marriage. The Black Dragon rules the north; it is associated with courage and honour.

Dragons are mostly guardians of virtue. The dragon Tatsu is one of the Japanese zodiacal signs. The Dragons of the Four Elements (air, water, fire and earth) reside under the feet of the goddess *Kannon*. See also *Monju Bosatsu*; *Naga*(1); *Pitaka*; *Ryujin*; *Taniwha*.

Dragon Carp In Korean mythology, a fisherman caught a gigantic *carp* but let it go when it begged for mercy. It turned out to be the son of the Dragon-King, ruler of the Ocean, who rewarded the fisherman richly.

Dragon-King's Palace See *Sea-King's Palace*.

Dragonfly This beautiful insect may be the soul of a dead person, according to some Japanese poets, returning to remind us of a vow or other obligation. It is said they 'play' above a pond.
See also *Butterfly*(1).

Drakulu With Cibaciba, one of the cave entrances to the Fijian Land of the Dead. See *Hades*(4).

Dreambook In the old Malay language there is a dreambook which interprets all the dreams anyone could possibly have. Here are some examples of dream-visions: if someone dreams of an animal it foretells madness; a sun eclipse foretells a king's death; blood foretells wealth; rain foretells mercy; children foretell pleasures; a comet foretells abundance; shaving foretells separation; a cool breeze foretells victory; thunder foretells slander; drizzle foretells trouble; a red cloud foretells disaster; a white cloud foretells plenty of rice.

Dreams

1. In Melanesia, the *spirits* of the *dead*, *baloma*, may often appear in dreams, especially those who died recently, because they still have an urge to communicate with their living relatives, often to announce another death. Dreams received from *Tuma*, the Island of the Dead, are especially memorable and are believed by all.

    Practical advice can be given by way of dreams, for example when a leader of fishermen whose ancestors were also fishermen is asked to give directions for successful fishing, his ancestors will appear to him in a dream during the night preceding the fishing trip. They will tell him where to place the nets, at what time, how many and when to haul them in. If they do not appear they must be displeased and must be propitiated. A leader of farmers will likewise dream that the spirits come and tell him when to plant which crops and where.

    The spirits will also predict the future of the villagers. If some *sorcerer* is bewitching a person, the victim will dream that he will fall ill, and who is causing that *illness* (since all diseases are caused by *sorcery*). If a man whose friend lives far away wishes to be remembered by him, he will 'send' a dream by *magic* means, so that the distant friend will dream about him and send him a present. Erotic dreams are the result of a person of the opposite sex 'sending' a dream by magic means, so the 'receiver' dreams that his sweetheart, or her lover, arrives in the night to make love and then disappears.

2. In *Japan* it is said that evil dreams are caused by evil spirits. There is one good spirit, however, called Baku, a monster with a *lion*'s head, *tiger*'s feet and a horse's body; it is the 'Eater of Dreams'. When a person awakens from a nightmare, he may cry: 'Baku, eat my dream.' Thus Baku may be induced to turn a bad dream into good fortune by eating up the evil.

See also *Dog*(2); *Dreambook*; *Mango*; *Reincarnation*(1); *Snake*(2); *Sumangat*.

Dress In *Japan* the spirit of a dead person, it is believed, may linger on in his or her garments.

Once the daughter of a rich merchant fell in love with a handsome young priest. Of course he spurned her, so the girl fell sick. Her father bought her a beautiful, very expensive dress to distract her, but she died all the same. The dress was given to the temple but was sold by the corrupt priest. However, it came back to the temple twice, always after its new owner had died of love. In order to appease the spirit of the dead girl, the priest decided to burn the garment ceremonially outside the temple. Alas! Just at that moment a fierce *wind* started blowing, spreading the fire over part of Tokyo, so that the temple burned down and thousands perished.

Drestarata A blind king in Javanese mythology, father of the Korawas. See *Ambiki*; *Bratayuda*; *Dasamuka*; *Dewi Gandari*; *Duryudana*.

Drum In Fijian mythology the drum of the king is highly valued. There is even a god of the drums, *Lingadua*, who, like the Germanic War-God Tiuz, is one-armed. If proper sacrifices are not offered to Lingadua he will punish the king by taking away the voice of his royal drum.

Drums were struck to announce war. See also *Ina*; *Tai-Moana*.

Drupadi In Javanese mythology, she is the wife of *Yudistira*, leader of the *Pandawas*. She is an expert archer and often joins in battle, dressed as a male warrior.

Dubois, Dr Eugene See *Indonesia*.

Dudugera In *Papua* there is a myth of a woman who was bathing in the sea when she saw a large fish swimming towards her (a *dolphin?*) They began playing together, during which the fish rubbed along her thigh repeatedly. Later the woman's leg became so painful and swollen that she asked her father to make an incision in it. Out came a boy whom they called Dudugera. When he grew up he became so strong that the other boys ganged up against him. So one night his mother took him to the beach and called the big fish, who arrived at once. Dudugera stepped into the mouth of the fish which it had opened as wide as a cave. It warned the mother to take shelter soon for the long night of the world would soon come to an end. The fish then closed its mouth and swam away towards the east. There it released the 'leg-boy' who rose up into the sky, rapidly brightening as he did so: he had become the *sun*. Soon he was so bright that the people had to seek shelter during the heat of the day. Deep in a cool cave his mother found lime (or loam) which she scooped up in big chunks and threw up into the sky where they became clouds. This is an apt description of the curious small globular grey clouds that drift over the Pacific and protect the people from the sun.

In Africa too, there is a myth of the young Sun-God, Lianja, who was born from his mother's thigh. The motif of the young Sun-God travelling in the belly of a fish is as old as the tale of Jonah.

Dugong In *Malaysia* they say that the dugong was once a pig. In *Indonesia* they say that the dugong was once a woman.

The people of the Manus Islands north of *New Guinea* relate that a green snake gave birth to a human girl. The girl grew up prosperously and one day she was seen by a man who lived alone nearby. He embraced her and though at first she was afraid, she later agreed to marry him, for she saw that he loved her. She worked with him in the fields until she gave birth to a son. They were very happy. One day the girl asked her mother the green snake to guard the baby while she went back to work in the fields. Her husband came home early that day and saw his son threatened by a green snake – or so he thought. He lost no time but killed the snake immediately. When his wife came home she was inconsolable over her mother's death at the hands of her husband. She left her home and walked into the sea, becoming a dugong: a woman who lives in the sea, wearing a sad expression.

Dukun A Javanese healer who recites *magic* texts to cure diseases. See also *Rice Soul*.

Durga (Batari, *Dewi*, *Kali*, Pramuni) The Balinese and old Javanese Goddess of Death and Disease; in *Java*, a goddess of certain sacred forests. She is the wife of *Kala-Siwa*, the God of Death, and is the horrifying queen of the cemetery *Gandamait*, where she lives, ruling ghosts and demons. She is the patroness of witches, *sorcerers* and other magicians of the black arts, *guna-guna*.

The jealous Prince *Burisrawa*, in the Javanese *wayang* play, sells his soul to Durga by promising to become her bodyguard in the *Underworld* after he has died. She, in turn, gives him a *magic* formula enabling him to have power over *Subadra*, whom he loves desperately.

See also *Ambu Dewi*; 'Gods of Bali' under *Gods*; *Lara Jonggrang*; *Waruna*; *Witch*(2).

Durna A Brahmin *guru*. See *Wilotama*.

Duryudana (Sanskrit, *Duryodhana*) In Javanese mythology, Duryudana or Suyudana is the *incarnation* of the demon *Dasamuka* as the son of King *Drestarata*. He is the eldest of the 100 Korawa brothers whom he leads into battle against the *Pandawas*. This is the great *epic* tale of the *Mahabharata* in Javanese *wayang*. See also *Bratayuda*.

Dwarawati In Thai mythology, a forest where the city of *Ayodhya* was founded for the young Prince *Anomatan*.

Dwarf See *Issunboshi*.

Dwarfs In the New Hebrides (see *Vanuatu*), dwarfs are *spirits* called *lipsipsip*. They live in trees or *stones*. If they feel offended by a man, they will devour him. See also *Fairies; Gnomes; Menehune; Mus; Ponaturi; Sukuna-Biko; Tipua*.

E

Easter Island statues

Ear Ornaments   It is related in *Thailand* that long ago a certain queen was so credulous that she believed anything that was whispered into her ear. On the advice of wise counsellors, the king had two elaborate ear ornaments made for his queen. He had her earlobes pierced, the first time that such a thing had been done in Thailand, and he told her: 'Always remember: no one must come near your ear. Believe little!'

Eare   A *witch*. See *Maori*(2).

Earth   (*Ashuku-Nyorai*) One of the *elements* in Japanese cosmology.

Earthquake   In Polynesian myths, an earthquake is caused by *Ruau-Moko*, the youngest child of *Papa*, the Earth-Goddess. Ruau has never been born but remains inside his mother, the earth. Whenever there is an earthquake – and this happens frequently in *Polynesia* – the people will say, 'The child Ruau-Moko is moving in his mother's womb.' See also 'Gods of the Pacific' under *Gods; Ligoupup; Sky*(2).

Easter Island   See *Rapanui*; also *Ahu; Hiro; Indonesia; Lizard*(6); *Pacific Peoples; Polynesia; Polynesians; Tangi'ia*.

Eau   See *Morning Star*.

Ebisu   One of the *Shichi Fukujin*, the seven Japanese Gods of Good

Luck, son of *Daikoku*, together with whom he is usually pictured. The patron of honest labour and especially of fishermen, he is depicted with a *fish* and a fishing rod. See also 'Gods of Japan' under *Gods*.

Ecstasis See *Oracles*(2).

Edao See *Loa*.

Eel

1. In *Thailand* there is a myth relating that long ago in the river Kok a white eel, an ancient totem animal, was caught that was as long as a palm tree is tall. The fishermen carried it to the palace and offered it to the king. The king then offered a slice of the eel to every citizen. That evening a youth was seen in the city. He was the God of the River. His visit was followed after nightfall by terrible *earthquakes* which totally destroyed the city. All those who had eaten a slice of the eel died, even the king.
2. *Tuna* in *Polynesia*, the god who created *coconuts* and taught the knowledge of *sex* to the first *woman*.
3. The Buginese people of south Sulawesi venerate freshwater eels as their ancestors. They neither catch them nor eat them, but feed them. Young women who want to become mothers will bring offerings of food to the fish, while ceremonial *drums* are beaten.

See also *Sina*.

Eggs In *Batak* land, *Sumatra*, it was said that out of seven eggs came all the plants, trees, animals and fish. Some of the animals became human beings. See also *Creation*.

Eisa See *Bomoh*.

Eisai A Buddhist priest. See *Rinzai*.

Eitumatupua See *Ahoeitu*.

Ekibiogami In Japanese myths, the God of Epidemic Diseases. See also 'Gods of Japan' under *Gods*.

Ele'ele The Samoan first *woman*. See *Adam and Eve*(4).

Eleio In Hawaiian mythology, a *kahuna*, a diviner who can see the *spirits*, cure diseases and return the *dead* to life.

One day, Eleio set out to find the root of the *awa* (*kava*) plant. Ahead of him he saw a lovely girl. He walked faster to catch up with her but so did she. He ran, but so did she. Over hills and woods she flew ahead of him. At last, on top of a high rock overlooking the ocean, by an old tower in which the kings of the past lay buried with their families, she turned to face him, saying, 'Leave me alone. I am a spirit. This is my home. Now go to that house there in the valley. My parents live there. Tell them you saw me and they will give you presents.'

After these words, the ghost vanished. Eleio entered the tower and there he saw the dead body of the girl. She had not been dead for long.

She was as beautiful as her spirit had been. Quickly, Eleio left the mortuary (you must never stay long near the dead), and went to the house she had indicated. There he found her parents mourning their beloved daughter. He told them that he had seen their daughter, and what she had told him. He ordered a pig to be slaughtered, a meal to be cooked and various objects to be brought. Then he went back to the old tower, accompanied by the dead girl's family. He chanted his *magic* incantations continuously. Suddenly he saw the girl's spirit again. This time he caught it. Bringing it back to the body, he held it there, pressing it against the insteps. It went in and up as far as the knees. There it stopped and only Eleio's untiring incantations induced it to go further and spread out into all the parts of the body. (See also *Hiku*.) The girl woke up and rose. Her parents, weeping with joy, helped her to place her first steps in her new life. Bringing her home in triumph, they offered the meal to the *gods*, after which they gave a feast. The girl, whose name was Aula, suddenly felt hungry. The parents spoke to Eleio: 'You have created our daughter anew. Without you we would have been inconsolable for life. Please take her as your wife.'

The leaves of the *awa* or *kava* plant are believed to have the power to revive the dead if administered with the right formulae.

Elements   In Japanese cosmology the elements are *water, earth, ether, air* and *fire*. See (respectively) *Amida-Nyorai; Ashuku-Nyorai; Dainichi; Fuku-Nyorai; Hoori*.

Elephant   In Thai mythology, when a queen dreams of a white elephant, she will give birth to a great ruler. When Queen *Maya* dreamt of a white elephant, she was pregnant with the *Buddha*, the future ruler of the world by right of the *Law*. When, after a dream in which a god instructed him, Prince Phrom-Kuman, 'Boy-God', captured a white elephant in the river, he rode it to victory over the kingdom of Khmer. The elephant is *Indera's* vehicle. See also *Elephant-Tiger; White Elephant*.

Elephant-Tiger   In Thai mythology it is related that in the dense forest which once covered most of *Thailand*, there lived a huge animal, having the body of an *elephant* but the head of a *tiger*. It had a very ferocious and irascible temper. Three intrepid hunters decided to catch it alive in order to offer it to their master, King Phan of Nakhon Pathom city. They succeeded in luring the elephant-tiger into a pit. They then tied it securely and led it to the city where it created panic. The grateful king used the elephant-tiger to breed a new race of war elephants which he fielded against the attack of his unfriendly neighbour, King Kong of Chaisi. The latter was defeated, suffering heavy losses. Still today, village people of Thailand celebrate this victory every year, for which they construct and animate a tiger-headed elephant.

Elixir   The *water of life*, which can be found in a stream on Mount Fuji. See *Fujiyama; Sengen; Yosoji*.

The Ellice Islands   See *Tuvalu*.

Emerald Buddha In *Thailand*, the most beautiful and most sacred image of the Holy Master, placed in the *chedi* at Bangkok.

Emma-o (The name is from the Sanskrit *Yama.*) The Japanese God of Death. He torments the *souls* of people who have sinned against the *Law* of *Buddha*. He lives under the earth in the *Yellow Springs*. See also 'Gods of Japan' under *Gods; Death*.

Enda Semangko Woman Spirit. See *Ghosts*(4).

Enggang A Sumatran prince. See *Hornbill*(2).

Enoshima An island off the coast of *Japan* where the goddess *Benten* first descended from heaven. It rose up from the sea to meet her feet.

Enua See *Papa*.

Epalirai Forest *spirits* of the Kyaka of the mountains of western Papua. See *Ghosts*(4).

Epic In Malay literature there are many sagas and legends in epic form called *shair* (*syair*). Altogether there are more than 100 long poems. Most of these deal with Islamic subjects such as the Day of Resurrection or the pilgrimage to the Holy City of Mecca; several describe the miraculous life of the Prophet Yusup or the words of Nabi Isa, who is the same as Jesus.

1. The best known, i.e. most popular, of these *shairs* are *Kin Tambuhan* and *Bidasari*. Equally romantic is the story of Selindung Dalima who was found in a box by her uncle's wives; she appeared to be the beautiful baby daughter of Princess Seri Bunian, whose husband Dewa Laksana had assumed the shape of a pomegranate. At that time, his kingdom had been destroyed by a *garuda* (Vishnu-eagle) who wanted to kill the king. So he disguised himself as a *dalima*, pomegranate, hoping she would 'pick' him. She did and ate the seeds (one only eats the red seeds of the pomegranate) and so she became pregnant.
2. Another tale relates how the hero *Yatim Nustapa* escapes poisoning and finds refuge with an old woman. When the Princess Indra Puspa in the land of Balantapura is poisoned, he cures her and receives her hand in marriage and her father's kingdom as a reward.

See also *Arjuna-Wiwaha; Lutung Kasarung; Mahabharata; Ramakien; Ramayana; Sijobang*.

Epic Poetry In *Japan* the famous priest Hoichi was a skilled reciter of epic poetry, especially that of the battle of Dan-no-Ura, where the Taira clan was annihilated together with the young emperor, Antoku Tenno. Their *ghosts* haunted the site of the sea battle, near the coast, for centuries.

The reciter of epic poetry plays a four-stringed *biwa*.
See also *Epic; Nana-Ula*.

Ether (*Dainichi*) One of the *elements* in Japanese cosmology.

Evara A prophet who lived in Vailala, *Papua*, around 1920. He prophesied that one day a steamship would arrive, carrying the *spirits* of the ancestors on board, who would bring presents for their living descendants. These heavenly presents would be the mysterious *cargo* which sparked off the cargo-cults in the Pacific, especially in Melanesia (see *Cargo*). Later, Evara prophesied that the ancestors would arrive in aeroplanes and bring guns. There would then be plenty of game for food, so life would be like heaven, like the 'millennium'. Wicked profiteers began to sell a telephone-like contraption by means of which, they told their innocent customers, they could speak to their dead relatives. Unfortunately, the relatives never replied and the presents never arrived.

Evergreen Land, the See *Sea-King's Palace.*

Expansion There have been several periods of expansion (known to anthropologists as 'swarming') of the people who now inhabit the Pacific coasts and *islands*. The most spectacular expansion was that of the Malayo–Polynesians before the beginning of the Christian era, from continental South-East Asia across the waters in all directions: north to the *Philippines* and Formosa (*Taiwan*), south to *Indonesia*, west to Madagascar and east to *Polynesia*. In all those areas even today clearly recognizable related *languages* are spoken.

How many waves of expansion there have been, and how long the intervals were, we do not know. We do know that those people had an amazing expertise in building ocean-worthy ships of any size and shape, with one or several outriggers, sails, one or more masts, and one, two or three hulks tied together so as to stay afloat on the huge waves of the Pacific.

It seems that the last wave of expansion took place around 1200 AD, to the farthest corners of the oceans, e.g. Madagascar and Easter Island (see *Rapanui*). By that time the Indonesian peoples such as the Javanese had been in their present habitat for over a millennium, had changed their religion three times, had developed writing systems for their languages, and built temples and the *Borobudur*, palaces and shrines.

See *Austronesia; Indonesia; Polynesians.*

F

Fox messengers with Inari

Fa'ahotu See *Atea*.

Fa'atiu The Samoan Wind-God. See 'Gods of the Pacific' under *Gods*.

Fables See *Panja Tanderan*.

Fairies (Japanese, *yosei*; Javanese, *apsari*; Malay, *peri*; Maori, *patupaiarehe*) A fairy is a member of a widespread species of sentient beings, always beautiful, usually friendly, often disguised or wrapped in mist or moonrays. They are most often seen as *birds*, cranes or swans. Sometimes they take human shape and seduce a man or a woman.

1. Kahukura, 'Rainbow', was a *Maori* fisherman. One night he took his *canoe* and his lines and sailed to the uninhabited island of Rangi-Aowhia. As he approached he heard a strange singing. The fairies were fishing with a net, something no human being had yet seen. They were singing: 'Drop the net in the sea, then haul it up at Mangakuku [Pigeon River].'
    The fairies seemed very happy, singing in the moonshine. They did not notice Kahukura, for his skin was almost as white as theirs. As dawn approached, the fairies made ready to sail home in their canoes but Kahukura managed to delay them by untying the strings they used to bind their *fish* together for transport. When the light

grew in the sky, the fairies suddenly saw that Kahukura was a man and not a fairy, so they immediately disappeared, leaving everything behind. Their canoes were only reeds which they could make into sailing vessels by *magic* whenever they wanted. Kahukura studied their net, noting that it was made by knotting long fibres across one another, thereby making hundreds of square meshes in which the fish got caught by their own gills. He took the fairy-caught fish home in his canoe. There, he taught his people to knot large nets with which they fished more successfully than with their lines. See also *Laufakanaa*.

2. Te Kanawa was another handsome young man, who went hunting in the forest one day. At nightfall he lit a *fire* and went to sleep between the roots of a tall tree. In the middle of the night he heard joyful singing: 'Climbing the Mountain of Tirangi . . .' He saw fairies, in the light of the dying flames, staring at him from the shadows with large beautiful eyes. Then suddenly they vanished.

3. If someone died in his sleep it was said that the fairies carried his *soul* away. Once, a man called Ruarangi found on his return from a fishing voyage that his wife had disappeared. He consulted a *tohunga*, an expert on unseen things, who told him the fairies had carried her away soul *and* body. It was true. The King of the Fairies had lifted her up from her garden as she was walking outdoors one moonlit night, and had flown off with her to his own palace. Once she was there, she was allowed to wander about freely, because, thought the king, she has already forgotten her home. That was true too. She listened to the singing of the fairies (the Maoris' singing is already absolutely entrancing) and to the king's flautist, and wished for nothing else. But one day she heard the singing of the *ngirungiru*, the white-breasted blue tit, the Maori lovebird, and suddenly she remembered her loving husband Ruarangi. This was the work of the *tohunga*, the priest who, with his *karakia*, magic incantation, had sent the lovebird to the Fairy King's palace to sing its song of remembrance. Even though the *love* of the fairies is infinitely more gentle and kind than the love of mortals, Ruarangi's wife now longed to be back with her husband. She hastened off into the forest, where she saw, in the distance, her husband, whom the priest had sent there to meet her. Quickly, Ruarangi took his wife home, as she felt cold and looked pale after her long sojourn with the fairies. Inside his well-built house he warmed her and fed her with well-cooked human food. The Fairy King had followed her footsteps and soon arrived at Ruarangi's house, but the *tohunga*, who could 'see' spirits, apprehended the fairy's presence and, by intoning his charms, induced the (in daylight) invisible king to go back to his fairy palace in the forest.

See also *Ati; Dwarfs; Gnomes; Menehune; Ponaturi; Tennin; Tipua*.

Falak   A divination system. See *Fortune-Tellers*(2).

Falcon See *Antang; Io.*

Fale-Aitu ('House of [the] *God*') On *Samoa*, a temple built on a stone platform. One such 'stone house' was built by the War-God *Fe'e* when he arrived from *Fiji.* It is still called Fale-o-le-Fe'e by the Samoans, 'House of Fe'e'. Like the Parthenon, it was surrounded by pillars, at least 20 in number, hewn of single blocks of stone touching 4m high (13ft). It now stands empty.

Familiar In Melanesia some *witches* have an invisible lover who is an evil demon and who teaches them the art of witchcraft (black *magic*). See also *Sennin; Tiger*(2).

Fan In *Japan*, the fan (*sensu*) is used as a symbol as well as a tool for fanning oneself, and a means to hide a shy face or to give oneself a pose. Princes also used their fans to command their retainers. The characters written on fans are often messages that cannot be pronounced, often *love* poems – in romantic tales that is. Lovers, before parting, exchange fans, hoping to recognize each other's fans, perhaps years later, if they ever meet again. See also *Morning-Glory.*

Farasul Bahri A sea-horse. See *Malay Annals.*

Fata Morgana See *Kuku Lau.*

Fatu-Titi See *Atea.*

Feathers If, in *Malaysia*, you suspect a man of being a were-tiger, watch him carefully. If he vomits up feathers, that is a sure sign he is one: the feathers are from the chickens he has devoured. See also *Macan Gadungan; Tiger.*

Fe'e In Samoan cosmology, he is the War-God, who is described as a huge octopus, living under the sea with his tentacles reaching to the far corners of the known world like a huge compass with eight hands. Fe'e was believed to cause thunderstorms in which his voice would be heard. The king's diviners would listen and if the god's voice was inauspicious, all war plans would be postponed.

Fe'e courted the daughter of the King of Upolu, and when the king refused him, he knocked a hole in the barrier reef protecting the island, where the city of Apia now lies. There he had a stone house built for himself, the ruins of which have been pointed out to researchers. Under the sea he had a palace called Bale-Fe'e.

Festival (Japanese, *matsuri*) See *Bommatsuri; Carp; the Dead*(1); *Hina-Matsuri; Hula; Inari; New Year; Pine Tree; Shaka; Songkran; Whale*(1).

Fetish A fetish is an object in which spiritual (metaphysical, *magic*) power resides or has been locked up. As a result such an object must not be touched by unauthorized persons such as children who would do themselves great harm.

An example from *Indonesia* is the *bezoar stone* (*guliga* or *mustika*), which is believed to contain a high concentration of 'soul-substance', so that, if held against the skin, it can heal wounds and infections. See also *Spirits*(5); *Stones*.

Fetu ('Star') A god of the night sky. See *Adam and Eve*(4).

Fig Tree (Indonesian, *waringin*) This sacred tree is inhabited by *spirits* and may not be felled without sacrifices. See *Ngabal*; *Sun*(2).

Fiji On the west central edge of *Polynesia* bordering on Melanesia, Fiji is an archipelago of 150 inhabited islands, Viti Levu and Vanua Levu being the biggest. The capital is Suva and the population, of mixed *Polynesians* and Melanesians, is 800,000. The *islands* were created, according to the Samoan tradition, by *Tagaloa* (see *Creation*(5)).

See also *Degei*; *Drum*; *Flaming Teeth*; *Flood*; *Ndauthina*; *Ndengei*; *Ngani-Vatu*; *Ratu-Mai-Mbula*; *Serpent-God*(1); *Shark*(2); *Sky-King*; *Tree-God*.

Fire (Japanese, *hi*; Malay, *api*; Polynesian, *ahi*)

1. In *Japan* it is said that *ghosts* may appear to be on fire. *Foxes* can emit flames, *badgers* may seem to be blazing in the night and of course *dragons* can spit fire. The blue heron may 'leak' fire through its skin. The *spirits* in the sea cause flames on the waves, and cemeteries can burn.

    Fire is also one of the *elements* in Japanese cosmology. See *Hoori*.

2. A myth told in *Papua* related that all the fire on earth was owned by the Fire-Goddess, who lived on top of a mountain (see also *Pele*(1)). The people saw smoke rising from an island in the sea, and messengers were sent to ask for some of the fire, until finally a *dog* succeeded in carrying home a stick that burned at one end.

3. In the lower Sepik area of Papua *New Guinea* the people relate that long ago folk ate their food raw. Only one old woman possessed fire, but she kept it secret. One little boy in the village used to go to the old woman and she would give him some cooked food from time to time. One day the boy took a cooked *yam* root home and showed it to his parents. There, two ants heard of it. They knew that the old woman hid her fire under a stone. They put dry leaves on it, so it began to flame. Soon the woman's hut was burning. People came and took the fire home.

4. According to the *Maori* tradition, in the oldest of times fire was guarded by Mahuika, an old mother of the clans. When *Maui* the Maori hero, heard of this, tired of tasteless raw *fish*, he decided to go and take some of that fire for his own people. Mahuika was, however, feared as a man-eating ogress and the people said of her: 'She eats human beings like the fire eats wood.'

    But Maui was called Maui-Tinihanga, 'Maui of the Many Devices', for good reason. Even though his mother Taranga refused to tell him where Mahuika lived, he found her house all the same, and stood there watching her until she noticed him. Mahuika had a terrifying appearance, but Maui showed no fear. She rose and came close to him as if she was going to devour him, but he said, 'Do not eat me, grandmother, I am Maui, your grandson.'

Then Mahuika questioned where he came from and who his parents were, and he answered her until at last he persuaded her to give him some fire. She pulled off one of her thick sharp fiery nails and gave it to him. He ran back with it but it burned his hands, so he dropped it into his boat. It then burnt its way through his boat and disappeared into the sea. So Maui had to go back to beg Mahuika for another nail. This happened several times until the old *witch*, finally losing her patience, waved her hands at him, exclaiming, 'Have it all!'

Immediately, Maui was surrounded by fire. To escape he had to change himself into a *hawk*, but the flames singed him even up in the sky. That is why the hawk is now dark brown. Maui then changed into a fish and plunged into the ocean, but it too was boiling hot. So, Maui leaped upon an island (which is still burning; it is called Whakaari) and resumed his own form again. He prayed to the *gods* that extinguish the fire: *Ua* (rain), Nganga (sleet), Whatu (hail) and *Apu Matangi* (storm). Only together were the gods capable of quenching the fire. Mahuika herself was almost drowned. Quickly, she placed her fire in the *kaikomako* tree, where it burned steadily. Maui carved firesticks from the wood of that tree so that henceforth people could make fire.

5. In Elema district on the south coast of Papua New Guinea, people relate of a man (or god?) called Oa Iriarapo, whose daughter was in labour. He put his hand on her belly and the child came out, placenta and all. Then, Oa Iriarapo raised his hand and fire came out of his palm, lighting the house. On the horizon, dawn appeared. After that, people cooked their food.

See also *Auahi-Turora and the Fire Children; Flaming Teeth;* 'Gods of Japan' and 'Gods of the Pacific' under *Gods; Goga.*

Fire Children See *Auahi-Turoa and the Fire Children.*

Fire-Face An exorcist once cured the wife of the governor of Nikaido district in *Japan*, but the governor refused to pay him, having him executed instead. The exorcist, whose name was Nikobo, went to live on top of a tree as a ball of fire. Inside the fire his face could still be seen. The governor died soon afterwards of a mysterious disease.

Fire Fade A Japanese prince. See *Ryujin.*

Fire-God In *Japan* his name is Kagu-Tsuchi, son of *Izanagi.*

Fireball In Lake Biwa in central *Japan*, the fishermen say they – or their grandfathers – have often seen a fireball. It shoots from one shore to another, and if it hits a boat, that boat will sink and the fishermen with it. They call it 'The Spider Fire of the Spirit of the Dead Akechi'.

Akechi once owned a castle, now in ruins; he died in a battle against a Shogun.

See also *Shito Dama*.

Firefly

1. Fireflies are believed, in *Japan*, to be the *souls* of the *dead*. Where a large number are seen together it is said there must have been a murderous battle centuries previously. See also *Butterfly; Dragonfly*.
2. In *Java* the firefly is called *nyawa*, 'soul'. If a firefly flies into someone's ear, that person will soon die, because 'the soul of an ancestor is fetching his soul', as they say.
3. On *Bali* it is said that certain people can turn themselves into fireflies at night, by *magic*. They devour the intestines of sleeping people. The latter will inexorably die. Such a person, called a *Leyak*, if discovered, will be sentenced and executed. They may also turn themselves into *tigers*; see also *Leyak*.

Fisaga   A soft breeze. See *Matagi*.

Fish   (Indonesian, *ikan*; Japanese, *sakana*; Polynesian, *ika*) Fish is the staple diet for all the Pacific peoples. Many *Polynesians* worship a fish-god. In Buddhist symbolism the fish signifies complete mental freedom. Just as the fish in the ocean is free to go anywhere, so the enlightened Buddhist needs no restraint. See also *Carp; Dugong;* 'Gods of the Pacific' under *Gods; Haumea; Hina-Ika; Narayana; Porpoise; Tangaroa*.

Fish-God   See *Dolphin; Dugong; Eel; Gods; Hine-Ika; Ika-Tere; Tangaroa; Tuna*.

Flaming Teeth   In Fijian mythology, this is the name of a giant who had teeth like burning logs from which flames flared up all the time. He used to go round the villages to capture people for his daily meal. Even those who had fled into the caves would be prised out by his long arms. Finally some young men banded together, raised a big rock and managed to smash the monster's skull. The giant died but the people brought branches to keep the *fire* going. So now they have fire.

Flood

1. In Fijian mythology it is related that when the young brothers of the first generation started hunting they killed Turukawa, the *hawk*, best friend of the *Serpent-God Degei*, the *Creator* (see *Creation*(3)), and so Degei decided to punish them. The brothers defied him by building a stockade, but Degei sent water which rose above their fortifications. At that moment the boys repented and asked to be forgiven, so Degei sent a big shaddock fruit on which they could sit as it floated on the waters. The flood swept away a tribe of people with tails. Some say they were all women. At last the waters subsided and the shaddock landed on another island.
2. There is a *Maori* myth about the flood which Maui caused by his prayers to the gods of rain and storm in order to quench the threatening *fire*. See *Fire*(4).

See also *Deluge; Nu'u*.

Flores On the Island of Flores stands Keli Mutu, a giant extinct volcano. Near the summit, on a vast plateau, there are three deep lakes of different colours: one is blood-red, one is milk-white and one is as green as fresh leaves. No scientist has told the people of Flores what causes the variation of colour in these three mysterious crater lakes. The Lio people, however, have the following explanation: in the red lake live the evil *spirits*, the *souls* of those whose sins were scarlet while they were on earth. These weird and wicked beings have a chief whom they all obey. Towards nightfall they wing their way up out of the lake and down into the valley of the living below. They are as dark as giant *bats*, but their eyes are fiery red, and their long hair waves and coils like black *snakes*. They cry 'Kri, kri!' like *owls*, and their purple flowing cloaks hide knives and daggers. As soon as their cries are heard, the Lio people hide inside their homes and lock their doors, for everyone knows that these spirits bring disease and discord.

In the green lake reside the souls of the children and other people who died before they were married. In the white lake live the souls of old people and those who lived to be married and have children. They have peace in the afterlife.

Some people do not receive the honour of a place in any of the lakes: those who did not have their teeth filed, nor their bodies tattooed, nor (worst of all) kept their noses clean. These negligent people will only sit under a banana tree when they die, and they may only eat soot and peel. The souls of the good people eat lizards, nuts and grass.

At the end of a long period in the lakes the souls are sucked downwards into a subterranean torrent which carries them under the earth and out into the ocean where they become fishes. Village chiefs become *sharks* and district chiefs become swordfish.

In this fine description of people's distinctive characters, *Indonesia* shows its true wisdom.

Flower See *Anta Kusuma; Asagao; Chrysanthemum; Fujiyama; Hades*(3); *Hasu; Idzumo; Ko-no-Hana; Love; Love-Magic; Mandala; Melati; Morning-Glory; Nilawati; Orchid; Peony; Predestination*(3); *Shaka; Tsubaki; Violets; Waterlily; Wijaya-Kusuma.*

Fly The *soul* of Tama, handmaid of a Japanese nobleman, who came back to his house as a fly and proceeded to buzz until he had given her money to go and pray for his soul in the temple.

Footprint of the Buddha In Japanese Buddhist cosmology, the *Buddha* as a cosmic deity stands above Bon-ten-o, i.e. the god *Brahma* in *heaven*. Under the Buddha's foot there lies Hoo-Kwan, the Crown of Treasures which emits eternal dazzling light, having the appearance of a radiating *wheel* with 1,000 spokes. It says in the Buddhist scriptures that whoever looks upon the footprint shall be freed from the results of thousands of faults. See also *Stones*(1).

Fortune-Tellers Fortune-tellers are numerous throughout the Pacific.

1. In *Korea*, *Chomjangi*, or *chomchaengi* is the usual word for diviners, although some 'future experts' deny that this term applies to their profession. There are horoscope readers who are the more scholarly type, like the interpreters of the Book of Change (*Chong Yok*); at the lower end of the scale there are the rice readers, those who interpret omens, portents or other signs of the spirit world, the palm, face and name readers and the bird diviners. Some have spent a long period of study or meditation, others are simply 'inspired'.

2. In *Malaysia* many people use divination – even *tigers* do so in order to ascertain the place and time when a fat human can be obtained. When a Malaysian child is born, the *bidan*, 'midwife', will tell the child's fortune from the contents of a pot which she has previously prepared. Rich people may secure the services of a *munajim*, an astrologer, who will read the child's future in the stars, or by *falak*, calculating the numerical value of the letters of the parents' names, or by observing the dripping of the wax of a candle into a bowl of water.

   Numerous events may be interpreted as omens by the *bomoh*, '*medicine man*', when a person is ill and wishes to know whether he will get better, or when a child is to be born and the parents want to know an auspicious place for its birth. Once born, if the child claps his feet together this is seen as a bad omen and is stopped . . . Praising the child's good health will bring ill luck. When a star is seen close to the moon, the Malays will say it signifies a wedding. If a bird or a reptile enters the house this is a very bad omen. medicine men are also consulted when a burglary has taken place; they will find, if not the thief, at least the hidden goods.

   Astrologers in Malaya also possess extensive tables showing the condition of the seasons in the near future, as well as the auspicious times for certain enterprises, such as voyages or weddings. These tables appear to be translations from Arabic or Urdu–Persian, or other Indian languages. There are other tables with Hindu deities or Muslim saints in which the diviner can read the answers to such questions as: where did my straying buffalo go? When is a good time to ask a favour from the prince? Will my business be successful? The main question is: what is a lucky time to do what I want to do? The seven planets or the twelve signs of the Zodiac, all known only by their Arabic names, will also help to answer these questions.

Fox A Japanese priest once found an old copper kettle in a corner of his temple. It was just what he needed. He rinsed the kettle, filled it with water and put it on the fire to boil. However, as soon as the water began to sing, the kettle grew a tail, two ears, four legs and a snout. It became a fox and started cavorting round the room. The priest ran out, locked the door and called a monk who lived nearby. Cautiously, they unlocked the door but heard nothing. There was no fox. The kettle stood innocently in a corner. The priest sold the kettle for a little money but after a few months it was brought back to him by the latest owner who begged him to pray daily for the disturbed *soul* so that it would find peace. It was believed that the fox was the appearance of a human soul who could only be laid to rest by a priest's prayers.

See also *Badger*(3); *Fire*(1); 'Kodomo-no-Inari' under *Gods of Japan*; *Inari*; *Kitsune-Tsuki*; *Possession*; *Tandanobu*; *Tanuki*; *Visu*.

Francis Xavier S.J. A Spanish missionary. See *Japan*.

Frog

1. In *Maori* mythology, the frog was a god of the waters, the rains and the rivers, and so no one would harm a frog. It was believed that killing a frog would cause downpours and floods.

   Once upon a time, they say, there lived only one gigantic frog, the mother of all the frogs, who had guzzled up all the water in the country. The animals met and decided that someone would have to make the frog laugh. Many animals tried their funniest jokes until the writhing dance of the sea-eel and his wife finally made the frog laugh so that all the water burst forth from her mouth.

2. A young Japanese man, who had inherited farmland and woods, sold all the land to pay for his pleasures. Finally, when he surveyed the woods for the purpose of selling them, he saw a squat person in a green coat, who spoke: 'I am the grandfather of all the frogs. We have lived in this pond where you played as a boy even longer than your ancestors have lived in the Manor House. Please do not sell these ancestral woods with this pond and this clear stream. The buyers will cut all the trees to sell them. Soon the stream will dry up and so will our pond. Where shall we live then? We shall all die.'

   The young man then changed his life and became a diligent farmer on his land. His descendants still live there and the frogs still live in their pond.

See also *Giant*(3); *Ramakien*.

Fudo

1. An ugly old Japanese god who resided in a temple on the summit of Mount Okiyama surrounded by fire. No one was allowed to see him seated in his sanctuary with sword and rope, on pain of blindness. His priest Yenoki lived on, after his death, in a tree, watching over the moral conduct of the country people.

2. Near Ohara in the province of Awa, *Japan*, there is a mountain, Shiratake. On its slope is a waterfall near which stands a shrine of the good god Fudo. Once a girl, O Ai San, prayed there hoping for the cure of her blind father. After 100 days standing naked under the waterfall, she found her father cured.

See also 'Gods of Japan' under *Gods*.

Fudo-Myoo The Guardian of Wisdom, the Unshakeable Spirit; in Japanese cosmology, the personified virtue of perseverance.

Fue On *Samoa*, a god, son of Tagaloa the Ocean-God, ruling the *Convulvulus* plant, the *sweet potato*.

Fugen-Bosatsu The Japanese name for the Bodhisattva Samantabhadra. He postponed his entering the condition of blissful nirvana in order to serve humanity, out of his divine compassion. He is depicted seated on a lotus adorned by a jewel in his crown, with a bunch of jewels in his right hand, symbolizing boon-giving. His left hand may hold a *bell*, a thunderbolt or a sword-lotus. In later artistic traditions he is represented seated on an *elephant* with six tusks, symbolizing the *Buddha*'s suffering for humanity.

Fuji-San See *Fujiyama*.

Fujin (also called Ryobu) A wind-god in Japanese mythology, painted as a terrifying dark demon wearing a leopard skin, the *winds* carried in a large bag on his shoulders. Yet he also has his benign aspect: he was present at the *creation* and when he first let the winds out of his bag, they cleared the morning mists and filled the space between earth and sky so the sun shone.

Fujiyama (or Fuji-San) The Immortal Mountain (though one could also translate it as 'The Mountain of Wisterias' or 'Blue Rain Hill'), Mount Fuji is regarded by faithful believers of *Shinto* as the central mountain of *Japan* and therefore as the centre of the world. This 'silent presence of eternity' is probably the most painted natural phenomenon in Japanese art. It has been called, like the earth-lotus, the seat of the Lord *Buddha* on earth. The snow of its cap has arranged itself into eight white sheets like the eight petals of the opened lotus, representing perception, purpose, language, conduct, life, exertion, concentration and contemplation, the eight forms of intelligence (see also *Lotus, Golden*).
   Mount Fuji rose up from the arid plain of Suruga in a single night, in one great eruption of fire. The place from which the earth was taken is now filled with water, forming Lake Biwa, according to Japanese myths.
   Mount Fuji is also the source of the *elixir*, the divine *water of life*. Whoever can find it will live in good health for 300 years. The Goddess of Fuji, *Sengen*, the Goddess of Blossom, administers the water of life from a stream on the slopes of Mount Fuji. She holds a flower, which may be a wisteria (*fuji*), an anemone (*okina*), or a camellia (*tsubaki*). The mountain is also inhabited by a god, Kuni-Toko-Tachi, whom numerous pilgrims worship every year by climbing the mountain after ritual purification, dressed in white robes. Thirdly, there is the God of the Crater, O-Ana-Mochi.

Fuku-Nyorai In Japanese cosmology, the element of *air*, signifying the wisdom of accomplishment. See *Elements*.

Fukurokuju One of the *Shichi Fukujin*, the seven Japanese Gods of Good Luck, giving wisdom. See also 'Gods of Japan' under *Gods*.

Furoshu Life-giving wine. See *Goddess of the Mountain*.

Futon Japanese for the quilt on which people sleep. If someone dies on it, his or her *soul* may linger in the quilt and lament until appeased by monks' prayers. See also *Dress*.

G

Garuda, modern woodcarving (Bali)

Gaetano A Spanish explorer. See *Hawaii*.

Gaki In Japanese cosmology there are 36 classes of *gaki*, ghosts. A *gaki* is a spirit suffering hunger and thirst in different degrees, depending on his way of life on earth and the preceding years of penance. The most unhappy *gaki* lives in hell, *jigoku*; the *gaki* who has almost completed his term of penance lives on earth, invisible, but at least able to eat, be it only impure substances (the worst sinners starve completely). To this end the *gaki* will enter the human body hoping to find warmth and nourishment. After a time he will be quite warm and will leave the body, but a day or two later he will return. The perceptive reader can recognize the pattern of attacks of malaria: first the patient shivers with cold, then he becomes hot. Suddenly the disease seems to be over, only to begin again a few days later. Meanwhile the patient becomes lighter and thinner until he is quite emaciated. Many *gakis* are identified with insects, e.g. *jiki-ketsu-gaki* 'bloodsuckers'. See also *Illness*.

Gakido ('Demon Road' or Purgatory) In Japanese cosmology the lowest form of existence.

Gama In Japanese mythology, the God of Longevity, pictured as a cheerful old man riding a stag and holding a scroll full of secret wisdom.

Gama-Sennin (also called Kosensei) A Japanese sage who is always accompanied by a *toad* and can change himself into a *snake*, or change his skin and become young again, for he possesses the secret of immortality. He has a benign nature. See also *Sennin*.

Gamelan The music of the *wayang* performances.

Ganas See *Ganesa*.

Gandamait A cemetery which is the home of *Durga*, the Balinese and old Javanese Goddess of Death.

Ganesa (Sanskrit, Ganesha; Japanese, Shoden or Sho Ten) On *Java* numerous statues have been found of this god, dating from the Middle Ages. Ganesa has an elephant's head. He is the God of Wisdom, the Remover of Obstacles. In old Javanese and Balinese mythology, he is also known as the Lord of the *Ganas*, or *demons*, belonging to *Siwa*'s entourage. Statues of Ganesa can still be found in *Bali*. He is depicted seated on a lotus and a ring of skulls, and is sometimes 'double-bodied', i.e. in eternal love-embrace with *Kannon*, in perpetual *creation/ generation*.

Ganesha See *Ganesa*.

Ganindo Ganindo was a great warrior of Honggo (Florida Island in the *Solomon Islands*). When he was killed in battle, his body was recovered by his clansmen and followers who brought it to Nggaombata, Guadalcanal. They buried their immortal hero on a hill called Bonipari, after having cut off his head. This they put in a basket which was placed in a specially built shrine. Now Ganindo had become a *tindalo*, an oracle-giving deity.

When they next went out on a punitive expedition, they took the basket with them. They let their ship drift along while 'listening' to their *tindalo*. When the bow pointed in the direction of the enemy's island, the ship trembled, demonstrating that their *tindalo* was indicating the direction which the expedition must take. They sailed on to the island, then, while the ship was becalmed, they enumerated the names of all the villages on the island, until the ship trembled again. This was another sign from Ganindo's spirit, of where he wanted the expedition to go. They landed on the beach near the village, stormed its palisades and after a brief battle the village was theirs. Back home, the men celebrated their dead hero-god with a fine thanksgiving feast.

See also *Oracles*.

Gareng One of the sons of *Semar*.

Garuda The Celestial Eagle, son of the Supreme God, vehicle of *Wisnu*, national emblem of *Indonesia*. Garuda is the messenger of the gods. He also functions in the Malaysian myth of King Merong Mahawangsa. By means of thunder, *storm*, hail and lightning, Garuda can defeat an entire fleet. His vast wings darken the ocean, their flapping sounds like thunderclaps. See also *Khrut*.

Garuda Putih   See *Buddha*.

Gatekeeper of Paradise   See *Topileta*.

Gatutkaca   In Javanese *wayang* myths, the son of *Bima* by the giantess Arimbi, a formidable warrior like his father. He possessed a magic jacket with which he could fly long distances.

Gecko   The gecko is believed to be an ancestral spirit by many *Pacific peoples*. It is 'grand totem' of the people of *New Caledonia*. Pili is the Gecko-God.

Gemala   A precious stone. See *Cobra*.

Gemini   In *Polynesia*, the twin stars, Castor and Pollux, are well known; they are called Hui Tarara. As in *India*, the Twins were human at first, but became gods later. When they heard that they would be separated, they fled, running away to the night sky. See also 'Gods of the Pacific' under *Gods*.

Genku   A thirteenth-century Japanese sage. See *Jodo*.

Genno   Genno was a Japanese Buddhist priest. One night, weary of travelling, he rested under a stone, but a spirit warned him that it was a dangerous spot. Unafraid, the intrepid priest heard the tale of many people dying while resting there. The culprit was an evil demon who lived in the stone. The Rev. Genno, knowing that the Lord *Buddha*, with his infinite mercy, would forgive even this wicked spirit, prayed long and earnestly for her (it was a female fox spirit). Finally the demon, contrite, swore that she would no longer harm the travellers.
  See also *Death-Stone*.

Gergasis   Brobdingnagians: quasi-human beings of gigantic size who live (we are told) on one of the Indonesian *islands*. Prince Merong Mahawangsa became their king and built a city called Langkasuka. See also *Monsters*(2).

Gerjis   In Malay mythology, a terrible monster, a colossal tiger-like man-eater. One day the animals convened to discuss the thinning of their numbers by the Gerjis. They voted to appoint the Mousedeer, the Kanchil, to be their delegate. The Kanchil convinced the Gerjis that the sky would soon fall down and offered to bury him in a pit for his own safety. The monster agreed and was duly buried. Later the Elephant crushed his skull with a tree.

Germans   In *Papua New Guinea* there was for a long time a belief that one day the Germans of before 1918 would come back as *spirits*, bringing precious gifts and prosperity. This is one of the many 'cargo' myths; see *Cargo*.

Gherkins   A delicacy in *New Guinea*. See also *Spirit Woman*.

Ghost-Mother   A pale haggard-looking woman came to a shop one night in a small town in *Japan* and bought some *mizuame*, malt-syrup, which in Japan is fed to babies whose mothers have died. When she came back the next night, the shopkeeper and his wife decided to follow her. She led them to a graveyard where they heard a baby crying. The woman disappeared into the tomb from whence the crying came. When the tomb was opened there was found the dead body of the woman, and a living baby, healthy but hungry. The mother had been buried prematurely and the baby had been born in the grave.

See also *Tomb*.

Ghosts

1. Japanese artists have painted ghosts, and story-tellers have described them, so that we know well how the Japanese people picture them. Ghosts may have very long necks so that they can appear inside a house through the window, their faces floating into the bedroom, attached to a snake-like neck. Some look like animals: toads, frogs and snakes. Others look like dead heads or skulls floating in the air, dead except for the eyes, leering around hungrily, yet others look like semi-human *monsters* with three eyes, or with only one eye, or with double faces, all white. Other ghosts are only a foot or two tall, have red hair and at night gnaw the bodies of the living with sharp teeth. Yet other ghosts are three feet tall, with very long ears; they devour the kidneys from dead bodies. Some ghosts look like 'normal', even attractive people, but most lack some essential parts, e.g. there are ghosts without feet or hands, without hair or ears. One type has no face, just a round bald head, without any features at all. See also *Fire*(1); *Shi-Ryo*.

2. On the isle of *Java*, ghosts likewise have many shapes. Particularly feared is the skull which pursues the lonely traveller at night by rolling along the path behind him. If the traveller starts running, the skull will rise up and overtake him. It then turns round and grins at the exhausted traveller, who by now is collapsing on the path. Its eyes beam a greenish light. It will drive the traveller mad.

3. In the New Hebrides people say that only human beings become ghosts after death. Most ghosts are malicious and have to be placated from time to time. They can cause illness in people, children and animals. They almost always appear in the shape of their former owners, but sometimes as *birds* or animals.

4. The Kyaka of the mountains in western *Papua* distinguish between the *demons* of nature, *kiliakai*; the *spirits* of the sky, *yakirai*; cannibal ogres, *kewanambo*; and forest spirits, *epalirai*. The ghosts of the *dead*, *semangko*, are in turn classified into six categories: i) the ghosts of the recent dead; ii) collective ghosts; iii) ancestral ghosts who are known by name individually; iv) the ghosts of previous owners of land or houses to whom sacrifices have to be made; v) ghosts of *sorcerers*, diviners and other *magic* experts for whom special circumspection is advisable; vi) finally, the most powerful ghosts of all: Enda Semangko, Woman Spirit, who is really a great goddess; Yama Enda, Sickness Woman, a forest spirit who is very dangerous;

and, most feared of all, Komba Ralingki, the Spirit of the Stranger. Ghosts can appear in human form or as animals, birds, insects or reptiles. They may help their living relatives or cause leprosy, yaws, blindness and madness.

5. Spirits of people who have died are numerous in the Malay countries. A girl who had died of *love* haunted her parents, who had forbidden her to meet her lover. Some ghosts show parts of their bodies to their victims: a hand, a leg, a face, a skull.

   Hantu Puteri is the ghost of a beautiful girl that drives her young male victims crazy. This happens, it is said, even to taxi-drivers in *Singapore*. One such young man was last seen on the cemetery near the grave of what had once been a beautiful girl, talking to himself (or to her?) Victims of the Japanese also still haunt the city in the shape of hairy monsters.

See also *Anshitsu; Badang; Cat*(2); *Cherry Tree*(1); *the Dead*(1); *Demons*(3); *Durga; Eleio; Epic Poetry; Fire*(1); *Gaki; Ghost-Mother; Hannya-Shinkyo; Kaseteran; Life After Death; Mauri; Oni; Puntianak; Shi-Ryo; Spirits; Treasure-Raining Sutra; Tree-Spirit*(2); *Tsuyu; Yuki-Onna.*

Giants

1. The first great *navigators*, according to Pacific mythology, were the original *Polynesians*, who called themselves *tangata* (= *kanaka*) 'people'. They were giants who were later revered as *gods* by their descendants. These gods married human women on the *islands* where they settled, and their descendants are the Polynesians of today. Those early gods possessed (we are told) *magic* science. They could sail for weeks without instruments, yet they never lost their way; they won *wars* without weapons and built boats without blueprints. They instituted *laws* of kinship and land rights for their descendants. Finally they re-ascended to *heaven*.

2. In *Java*, the King of the Giants was Wikramadatta, who demanded of King Jamajaya all the weapons in his entire kingdom. As a result, peace reigned in Java.

3. On the island of *Bali* lives a female giant who steals children. Once upon a time two little girls, Klodan and Klontjing, were put in a wooden case by the giantess. Their escape was effected by animals: mice gnawed a hole in the box, a *dog* carried the two girls home, while a pig danced to the *frogs'* music, distracting the giantess' attention.

See also *Bonin Islands; Bujangga; Coconut*(2); *Dog*(1); *Flaming Teeth; Gatutkaca; Gergasis; Kurangai Tuku; Malay Tales; Mary; Neititua Abine; Nether World; Phra In; Puteri Bualu Julah Karangan; Puteri Sembaran Gunung; Raksasa; Ramakien; Shodo Shonin; Spirits*(3); *Tengu; Tinoso; Tree-God; Tree-Spirit*(6); *Yoromitsu.*

The Gilbert Islands   See *Kiribati.*

Gimokodan   The Land of the Dead. See *Nether World.*

Ginger *Zingiber officinale*, of the *Zingiberaceae* family, a medicinal root from ancient *India*, ginger is well-known and loved in *Japan* and *Indonesia*, where it is used to cure sore throats, stomach pains and indigestion. The plant's name means 'horned man' in Sanskrit; it was believed to be a good spirit. In *New Ireland* a boy is given a ginger bath to make him a brave man.

See also *Ivo*.

Glass-Man On the South *Java* coast there is a huge cave system, a sanctuary of the *Ocean-Goddess*. In it 'lives' the glass-man, who is seen only at night when he appears transparent like shining crystal, emitting a faint blue light like early dawn. He was once a man but he disobeyed the goddess. Once every 100 years he is allowed to appear in the cave for one night to help one person rescue another from the Cave of Squids or the Cave of Lizards. See also *Ocean-Goddess*.

Gnomes The 'Little People' are widespread in *Indonesia* where they are known by different names. The *Bataks* call them *omang*, saying they are clever thieves. In the Minahassa in *Sulawesi* they are called *lolok*; they are so slippery that you cannot catch one. If you do, do not let him go before he has promised you plenty of rice and meat. In Halmahera these dwarfs are called *hoga*. They tease people – except those who put out food for them. For those good people they will fill the rice-sheds, at the expense of other people.

See also *Dwarfs; Fairies; Ponaturi; Tipua*.

Go-Chi Nyorai ('The Five Wisdom Buddhas') These are the five Bodhisattvas, viz. *Yakushi-Nyorai*, Taho, *Dainichi*, *Ashuku-Nyorai* and *Shaka*; in Sanskrit: Bhaishajya, *Amida*, *Vairocana*, Akshobhya Adarsanajnana and Shakyamuni (see *Shaka*).

Go-Shin Tai These are the Yasakani or Japanese crown jewels, divine symbols given to the first Japanese emperor by the Sun-Goddess. Prominent among them is the magic *sword* which *Susanowo* found in a dragon and the star-mirror Yata which the Sun-Goddess once used herself. These precious objects are still religiously kept in the royal shrine at Ise. See also *Mirror*(1).

Gobei A young impoverished Japanese nobleman. See *Willow Tree*(2).

Goblins See *Dwarfs; Fairies; Gnomes; Ponaturi; Tipua*.

God

1. The *Polynesians* believed in the Supreme *Creator* Atua (Hawaiian, Ke Akua) who was God the Father, progenitor of all living beings, protector of all people. His name was *taboo* so we only know Him as Atua, 'God'.
2. The Supreme God of the Olo Dusun, a branch of the *Dayaks* of *Borneo*, is called Hiang Piumbung, 'The Overshadowing God'. He lives in the zenith of the universe, which is represented as a large net thrown in the sea. Round his palace grow innumerable

garonggong flowers; whenever a flower wilts and falls, a human being on earth dies.

See also *Devata; Guriang Tunggal; Heaven; Indera; Siwa; Solanang; Tangaroa.*

Goddess The cult of the Goddess is widespread in western *Papua*. It is surrounded by secret ceremonies performed by or for important people. The cult usually spreads through adoption by relatives. The Goddess is represented or embodied in megaliths, and in stone 'artefacts', some of which are discovered after the Goddess appears in a dream (see also *Dreams; Fetish; Stones*). The participants in the ritual build a high wall around the sanctuary, where *pigs* are cooked and sacrificed to the Goddess, while priests chant. The Goddess is present during the ceremony, then moves to another clan.

When worshipped properly, the Goddess will protect her (mainly male) devotees against pollution by menstruating women and grant them success in warfare, good health to all clan members, fertility in their wives and proliferation of their pigs and fowl.

1. On the island of Nehan (Papua *New Guinea*) the following myth is told: in the beginning there were no people; only the great Mother Timbehes, 'Mother of Many', lived in the world, in Hohou, 'Place of Sleep'. She became the mother of all things. She had food but no children. One day she took a banana and put it in her vagina. After that she became pregnant and gave birth to a son whom she called Bangar. She liked him, so she used a second banana in the same way. In due course she had a second son, Lean. Then she used a third banana. This time she had a daughter, Sisianlik ('Songbird'?) When the children had grown up, Timbehes decided she wanted grandchildren, so she told Bangar and Sisianlik to lie together, and what to do further. In due course Sisianlik became pregnant, had one child and then another. She had numerous children who grew up to become men and women. Timbehes told them how to behave and how to marry together. They in turn had children and so Timbehes was very happy.

    One day she prepared a *singsing*, a picnic with singing and dancing, with as many baskets of food as there were guests. She told everyone to take food from each basket except one. The basket from which a person took no food was the one that contained the food he or she did not like and would never eat. So, if someone did *not* eat from the basket containing pigeons, he and his descendants should never eat any pigeons and they would be called the Pigeon Clan. Members of one clan were henceforth no longer allowed to marry each other.

    The unfortunate Lean fell in a fire and was burnt to ashes. Out of his skull grew a *coconut* and out of it the biggest coconut palm on earth, the mother of all coconut palms. Many tried to climb the tree to get coconuts, but only the flying *dog* managed to reach the top, which was above the clouds. He cut down coconuts and threw them to all the *islands*. The biggest nuts fell on Nehan, of course.

2. Among the Torajas of central *Sulawesi* it is related that God's youngest daughter was taken to earth by her brother and sister. They cut her into small pieces and scattered these across the fields of the earth, exactly as their Father had commanded them to do. The blood of the young goddess became *rice*, her bones became sugar cane while her flesh turned into cucumbers and pumpkins. Her brother and sister were married (for *gods* the rules of marriage are not the same as for people) and had a son.

The father went back to *heaven* but the mother brought her son up on earth. One day she hit him for stealing a cucumber. He ran away and after many years he came to a village where the people made him their chief and married him to a 'widow'. One day she discovered his scar and so she knew that her husband was her son. They had the people build a large reed hut around themselves, so that they were forever isolated, the son and his goddess-mother-wife. In the course of years, out of the reed 'basket' hut came cows, goats, pigs and chickens, so the people did not starve.

3. In *Bali*, four prominent goddesses are worshipped. Each one governs a region of the compass in the cosmos and is also associated with a colour:

Goddess	Durga-Kali	Lakshmi	Saraswati	Uma-Prawati
Region	West	North	South	East
Colour	Black	Yellow	Red	White
Husband	Kala-Rudra	Wisnu-Narayana	Brahma	Guru-Siwa (Shiva)

See also *Colours and Compass; Gods*.

4. According to the cosmology of Mangaia in the *Cook Islands*, Varima-Te-Takere, 'The Woman of the Very Beginning', was a goddess who lived inside an egg on the bottom of the primeval ocean, called the Silent Country. She gave birth to the first man called Vatea, who grew out of her left side. He was only half a man, the other half being that of a fish. He was given earth to live on, called 'Under the Bright Moon'. Later, Varima grew a child from her right side, who looked just like Vatea's dreams of a life companion. Her name was *Papa*, 'Earth'.

Goddess of Mercy   In *Taiwan*, it is said, there once lived a king, Miao Chuang, who had three daughters. The eldest two married handsome young heroes but the youngest, Miao Shan, insisted that she must become a nun: 'Only through self-sacrifice can I attain perfection.'

In the convent she performed the humblest tasks and cheerfully sounded the great bell, which was the heaviest work of all. Her father tried to have her killed for disobeying him as he wanted her to marry, but the Lord of Heaven had decided otherwise. The king fell ill, and the doctors declared that only the eyes and hands of a living human being could cure him. Miao Shan, upon hearing this, walked to the palace to offer her own hands and eyes for her father's healing. After this extreme sacrifice she died. The Lord of Heaven raised her soul to divine status, and she became Kwan Yin, the Goddess of Mercy.

See also *Kannon*.

Goddess of the Mountain Daimugenzan is a high mountain in Totomi province, *Japan*. On its slopes there used to be a shrine dedicated to the goddess *Kannon*. She protected the pilgrims against robbers and other villains by sending down an icy *wind* that rendered them unconscious. She gave her female devotees a phial of *furoshu*, life-giving wine, a *magic* medicine for eternal youth (see also *Elixir*), and sometimes appeared to her devotees in a cloud of cherry blossom petals.

Goddess of the Sky In Fijian mythology it is related that one day the goddess Adi Mailagu descended from the *sky* and plunged into a river, later emerging in the shape of a grey *rat*. She also appeared to men either as a beautiful woman or an ugly old hag with a yard-long tongue hanging out of her mouth. Sacrifices were offered to her and finally she answered the priests' questions about the future. If she visited an eager man at nightfall, in the guise of a lovely girl, he would surely die. She used to live in a tree in the shape of the grey tree-rat but when the tree was cut down she was never seen again. See also *Tree-Spirit*.

Goddess of the Southern Ocean See *Ocean-Goddess*.

Gods

Gods of Bali On *Bali* the ancient gods and goddesses of *India* are still worshipped. However, the Balinese gods are not completely identical with the Hindu gods of India. See *Colours and Compass; Goddess;* and under the names of the individual deities given below:

> **Brahma**, divine husband of *Saraswati*, rules the five southern rivers.
> **Dewi Sri** (Devi Shri in India, better known as Lakshmi) is *Wisnu's* divine consort. She rules all plants and trees. She is also the Goddess of Agriculture, so she is the revered and powerful *Rice-Goddess*. See also separate entry.
> **Iswara** 'The Lord' is the God of the Centre, the hub of the universe, around which all the heavenly bodies revolve. He is equated with *Indera* in the Balinese tradition.
> **Kali** is the fear-inspiring goddess who punishes sinners and evil *demons*. See separate entry.
> **Saraswati** is the Goddess of the Streams and freshwater pools. She rules the colour red and her domain is *bayu*, action and learning. See separate entry; also *Benten*.
> **Siwa** is the Mountain-God of the East; with him is *Prawati* or Dewi *Uma*, the benevolent White Goddess of Meditation and Modesty. See also separate entry.
> **Waruna** or *Mahadewa*, the Wind-God, and his spouse *Durga* or *Kali*, rule the west and are associated with yellow, the colour of sunset. See also separate entry.

Wisnu is the God of the North, who arrives flying on his faithful eagle *Garuda*, heralding rain. His colour is *black* or indigo, like the rainclouds. He is also known as *Narayana* or Narasinga. See also separate entry.

In Indian and Balinese philosophy the four gods of the four 'corners' of the world are identical: Siwa (east), Brahma (south), Waruna (west) and Wisnu (north) are worshipped in that order by the Balinese priest, *padanda*. Every morning before sunrise, the priest begins by preparing the holy water for Siwa by identifying himself with the great god.

The Buddhist priest, or *Padanda Boda*, does not disagree with this cosmology of the fivefold world; on the contrary, he considers it as the *Pancha-Tathagata* 'The Five Essential Walks of the Buddha'. The *Buddha* has divided his quintessence into five essences, each of them represented by one of his five manifestations as he 'walks' like a god-king to the extremes of the earth to spread enlightenment. The student of *Buddhism* will recognize the five major Bodhisattvas in these gods. In both philosophies the gods are visual representations of great spiritual concepts.

Further Balinese gods are *Yama-Raja*, the God of Judgement (in the Buddhist pantheon the god who judges *souls* after *death*), who is depicted in Balinese art as a terrifying monster with tusks and claws; and *Semar*, a Javanese–Balinese deity of pre-Hindu antiquity. He was once a benign earth god, represented in art as a rotund, smiling father figure. See also *Sumua*.

Gods of Japan   Here follow the chief deities of the Japanese pantheon:

Aizen Myo-o, the God of Love. See also separate entry.
Aji-Shiki, a shining young god who cut down his dead friend's mortuary house in *heaven* so that it fell to earth and became Mount Moyama.
Ama Terasu, the Sun-Goddess. See separate entry.
Amida, Amitabha or Amida Butsu, see separate entry. See also *Kannon*, as they are identical in essence, though not in appearance.
Anan (in India, Ananda), cousin, friend and loyal follower of the Buddha, widely revered in Japanese Buddhism as an immortal.
Benten, the goddess Saraswati. See separate entry.
Bimbogami, the God of Poverty. See separate entry.
Bishamon, the God of War and Wealth, one of the seven Gods of Good Luck. See separate entry; also *Shichi Fukujin*.
Bosatsu, Japanese form of the Sanskrit *Bodhisattva*. See separate entry.
Buddha, in Japanese Buddhism. See separate entry; also *Butsu*.
Daibutsu, the great bronze Buddha statue of Kamakura.
Daikoku, the God of Wealth, one of the seven Gods of Good Luck. See separate entry.
Dainichi-Nyorai, one of the Buddhist *Trinity*, the God of Purity and Wisdom.

Daishi, 'The Great Teacher'. See *Kobo*.

Dosojin, the God of the Roads.

Dragon-King, see *Dragons; Sea-King*.

Ebisu, the God of Good Luck and especially of the fisherman's luck. Anything found on the beach may be Ebisu, even a ghost or its corpse. See also separate entry.

Ekibyogami, the god (*kami*) of *ekibyo*, plague, pestilence. See also separate entry.

Emma-o, the God of Death, judge of the *dead* and Lord of *Hades*. See also separate entry.

Fudo, the God of Wisdom (in that function identified with *Dainichi*); the God of Fire. See also separate entry.

Fukurokuju, from *fuku*, 'good luck', a 'catch', the God of Good Luck. See also separate entry.

Gaki, a demon, an evil spirit, often associated with the dead. See separate entry.

Go-Chi Nyorai, 'The Five Wisdom Buddhas'. See separate entry.

Gonge, an *incarnation* of the Buddha as a mountain deity. See *Gongen*.

Gongen, a mountain spirit. See also separate entry.

Hachiman, the God of War, the deified Emperor Ojin. See separate entry; *Tide Jewels*.

Hoderi, 'Fire Shine', son of Ninigi (see below). See *Hoderi and Hoori*.

Hoori, 'Fire Fade', brother of Hoderi (see above). See *Hoderi and Hoori*.

Hoso-no-Kami, the God of Smallpox.

Hotei, one of the Gods of Good Luck and the wisdom of being content. See separate entry.

Hotoke, the spirits of the dead, including the saints and all the Buddhas.

Iha-Naga, the Princess Live-Long. See separate entry.

Inari, the *Rice-Goddess*, also the Vixen-Goddess. See separate entry.

Isora, the God of the Seashore. See *Tide Jewels*.

Izanagi and *Izanami*, the *Creator* and Creatress. See separate entries.

Jizo, the God of Children. See separate entry.

Jurojin, one of the seven Gods of Good Luck. See separate entry.

Kagu-Tsuchi, the Fire-God, son of Izanagi and Izanami, whose birth caused his mother's death. See *Izanagi* and *Izanami*.

Kami, deity or spirit of any sort which may live in an object or in a natural phenomenon such as a *rainbow*, or may be an ancestral spirit. See separate entry.

Kaze-no-Kami, 'Wind-God', the God of Wind, Storm and Bad Colds.

Kenro-Ji-Jin, 'Solid-Earth-Being', the deity of the *earth*.

Kishi-Bojin, the goddess who protects children, a goddess of Indian origin. See also separate entry.

Kobo Daishi, a Buddhist sage whose spirit still wanders on earth. See separate entry.

Kodomo-no-Inari, the fox deity of the children.

Kojin, the ancient good-natured deity of the kitchen. See also separate entry.

Koshin, the God of the Roads, of Travelling and Progress. See also separate entry.

Kuni-Toko-Tachi, an earth deity, one of the Creators, who inhabits Mount Fuji (see *Fujiyama*).

Kannon (Kwannon), the *Goddess of Mercy*, the Chinese Kuan Yin. See separate entry.

Marishi-Ten, the Queen of Heaven, Goddess of Light, of Sun and Moon.

Maya Bunin, Buddha's mother.

Miroku, *Maitreya*, the future Buddha. See separate entry.

Monju Bosatsu, the Bodhisattva of wisdom and knowledge. See separate entry.

Musubi-no-Kami, the God of Marriage. See separate entry.

Nikko-Bosatsu, the Bodhisattva of smiling sunshine and good health.

Ninigi, Prince-Ear-of-Rice and Plenty, grandson of *Ama Terasu*. See separate entry.

Nioo, a fierce-looking spirit guardian of the temple gates.

Nominosukune, the patron deity of the Japanese wrestlers.

Nyorai, the esoteric term for all the Buddha's appearances. See also separate entry.

O-Ana-Mochi, 'The Owner of the Crater' of Mount Fuji (see *Fujiyama*).

Oho-Yama, the Great Mountain God, whose daughter *Uzume* married *Ninigi*.

Okuni-Nushi or Onamuji, son-in-law of the Storm-God, *Susanowo*, King of *Izumo*, identified with *Daikoku*. See separate entry.

Oni, evil spirit(s), ogre, devil, demon, ghost. See separate entry.

Otohime, the beautiful daughter of the Sea-King; the immortal bride. Her other name is *Toyo-Tama*; she marries Hoori.

Raiden, the God of Thunder. See separate entry.

Rakan, a personal disciple of the Buddha, a perfect saint, worshipped as a god.

Rinjin, 'Luminous Being', the Sea-King.

Sengen, the Goddess of Mount Fuji. See *Fujiyama*; also separate entry.

Shaka Muni, the Silent Sage, the embodiment of perfect virtue, the first appearance of the *Buddha* on earth in bodily form. See *Shaka*.

Shi Tenno, the four Heavenly Kings who protect Japan against evil spirits. See separate entry.

Shichi Fukujin, 'Seven Happiness Beings', the seven deities of good fortune. See separate entry.

Shoden or Shoten, the Japanese name for the Indian Elephant-God of Wisdom, *Ganesa*.

Shotoku, a prince who was deified as the reincarnation of Siddhartha. See separate entry.

Susanowo, the Storm-God, dark brother of the Sun-Goddess. See separate entry.

Taishaku, the Japanese name for the Indian god Indra. See *Indera*.

Tanabata or Shokujo, daughter of the God of the Firmament. See separate entry.

Ten, the *sky*, *Paradise*, heaven, Providence, *God*.

Tenjin, the God of Calligraphy, who taught men to write their *language*.

Tennin, a heavenly being, a fairy, an angel. See *Angels; Fairies*.

Toyo-Tama, 'Luminous Jewel', the daughter of the Sea-God *Tangaroa*. See separate entry; *Hoderi and Hoori*.

Toyouke-Omikami, the Goddess of Grain. See separate entry.

Toyo-Uke-Bime, the Goddess of Earth and Food.

Tsuki-Yumi, the God of the Moon. See *Ama Terasu*.

Uzume, the Goddess of Dancing. See separate entry.

Yakushi-Nyorai, the Healing Buddha. See separate entry.

Yofune-Nushi, the Japanese Serpent-God.

Yuki-Onna, the Snow Queen. See separate entry.

Gods of the Pacific Here is the Polynesian pantheon, arranged by function, alphabetically:

Ancestors – *Ao* was sometimes called 'The Father of the Ancestors'. Many ancestors were worshipped, especially those of the chiefs and certainly the powerful spirits of the kings of the past in *Hawaii, Tahiti* and *New Zealand*.

Birds – Pouakai was a giant bird-god who devoured people. See *Poukai(2)*.

Clouds – Ao, the God of the Clouds (white, grey, black or red), was of vital importance to the Polynesian *navigators*, because they could discern the presence of land from the shape of the clouds on the horizon, and also used them to predict rain.

Comets – *Rongo-Mai* ('Water-Food'), who is also God of Whales, is the God of Comets.

Creation – Haronga is praise-sung as the father of sun and moon, and of Atarapa, 'Daybreak'. He is also called a son of *Rangi* the Sky-God, whose embrace with his wife *Papa* was *Creation*. In a famous *Maori* creation myth the poet rhapsodizes:

Io the God dwelt in space immense, the firmament of darkness
He spoke the words that darkness must be light, and light
appeared.

Dawn – Atarapa and Atanua are goddesses of the dawn. See *Dawn*.

Death – In Maori myth, the Goddess of Death is *Hine-Nui-Te-Po*, 'Great Lady of the Night', a goddess whom the hero *Maui* could not overcome, because a *songbird* laughed. So Maui became the first man to die (see separate entry). In another myth it is the Moon-God Marama who does not permit man to return to life after death, as the moon itself does. Merau is the Goddess of Death and the *Nether World*.

Earth – The earth is also a goddess, Papa, the *Mother-Goddess* who lives in constant love-embrace with her husband Rangi the Sky-God, during which epoch Creation takes place. See *Rangi; Sky*(2).

Earthquakes – Mafui'e (Samoan) or Ruau-Moko (Maori), is the God of Earthquakes. Ruau was never born but still stirs inside his mother Papa, the earth. See separate entry.

Father – the Father of the Gods is Rangi the Sky-God, also called Hanui-o-Rangi, the Father of the Winds. See also *Sky*(2).

Fire (*ahi*) – On Hawaii, *Pele* is the Goddess of the Fire in the Volcano, the Mother of Eruptions, ravishing, whimsical. In New Zealand, Maui is the hero who persuaded *Mahuika*, the guardian of the fire, to give him some. In another version, the Sun-God, Tama Nui-Te-Ra, gives some of his fire to humanity as a boon, for life. Hine-i-Tapeka was the Goddess of the Fire in the Earth. See also *Goga*.

Fish (*ika*) – Tangaroa as Ocean-God is often represented as a huge *fish* giving birth to all the sea creatures, including mermen and mermaids. From these latter sprang humanity, so people are really fish who have lost their fish-like appearance. There is a school of biology which holds that human beings were once aquatic, hence their hairlessness. *Ika-Tere* is the most common name for the Polynesian Fish-God. Ika-a-Maui, 'Maui's Fish', is the name of North Island, New Zealand, since Maui 'fished it up' from the bottom of the ocean.

Food (*kai*) – Rongo (Lono, Ono) is the God of Cultivated Plants, especially *kumara*, the *sweet potato*. His brother Haumia Tiketike is the God of Uncultivated Food, i.e. wild berries and roots. Maui introduces cooked food (see *Fire*(4)).

Forest – Tane-Mahuta is the God of the Forests. He is co-Creator when he raises trees on his mother Papa.

Goddess – See *Goddess; Mother-Goddess; Moon; Night*.

Hades – *Reinga* is the Abode of the Dead. *Milu* or *Miru* is 'Owner of the Land of the Spirits', *Lua-o-Milu*, 'Milu's Cave'.

Health – *Waiora*, the '*water of life*' is the Goddess of Health, (like the Greek Hygieia). See separate entry.

Heavens – The God of the Heavens is the south *star Atutuahi* or Autahi. See separate entry.

Light – The god *Tane* was the first son of Rangi and Papa the Creator god and goddess. Tane was the God of Light who after his birth settled in the sky. At *dawn* he 'splits open the world' by lifting up the seam of the sky off the earth, so that a part of the outside world becomes visible. The *Dawn Maiden* is his daughter.

Lightning – Uira, also called Kanapu, an ancestor of *Tawhaki*, out of whose armpits lightning flashes.

Lizards – *Moko* is the Lizard-God. *Lizards* possess great *magic* powers. Pili is the *gecko*.

Milky Way – See separate entry.

Mirage – The goddess who deludes voyagers by showing them non-existing countries on the horizon is called Kuku Lau.

Mist or fog – The deities of mist are Hau Maringi, son of *Ua*, the God of Rain, and Kohu (see *Tane*).

Monsters – The God of the Sea-Monsters is *Paikea*, son of Papa.

Moon – There are many myths about *Marama* the Moon-God and *Ina* his wife, also called Rona, the Moon-Goddess. Ina taught the women on earth the art of plaiting baskets. In Hawaii her name is Hina or Ma-Hina, the Goddess of Fish. She makes barkcloth which she also taught to earthlings. She is the mother of the island Molokai. *Hina-Keha* is the bright moon. *Hina-Uri* is the dark, invisible moon. Sina or Ma-Sina is the Samoan name of the Moon-Goddess. She had relations with *Tuna* the Eel-God.

Morning Star – Kopu or Malara (Venus), whose rising beauty is much admired. See separate entry.

Mother-Goddess – Papa, the Earth-Goddess, wife of the Sky-God Rangi. She gave birth to all living things: the gods, the birds, the animals, the trees, the plants and the people. See *Mother-Goddess; Papa*.

Nether World – Milu or Miru is the God of the Nether World, the world under the earth where the spirits of the dead live in a vast cave, *Reinga*.

Night – The Goddess of the Night, Darkness and Death is *Hine-Nui-Te-Po*.

Ocean – Tangaroa is the Sea-God who separated the sky from the earth. He may appear as a huge fish, father of all fishes. See separate entry; *Sky*.

Rain – The God of Rain is Ua. See separate entry.

Rainbow – *Kahukura*, an appearance of the god Rongo. See separate entry.

Sea – See Ocean, above.

Sky – The Polynesian Sky-God Creator is Rangi (Langi, Lagi), in Indonesian and *Tagalog* it is Langit. See also separate entry; *Rangi; Tane*.

Stars – Several stars are gods. See *Atutuahi; Milky Way; Morning Star; Star; Star Spirit*. Rehua is the Star-Goddess.

Storm – There are many storm-gods, including *Tawhiri-Matea* of New Zealand; *Apu-Hau*, 'Fierce Squall', of Hawaii; the Maori *Apu Matangi*, 'Howling Rainfall', and Awha; and the Samoan Afa. See also Rain, above.

Sun – The sun is snared by Maui. The Sun-God is Ra. The sun and the moon are brother and sister, as in Greek mythology. Sunset shows the path to Spirit Land. See separate entry; *Sun*.

Sweet Potato – See separate entry; *Rongo*.

Taro – See separate entry.

Triad – Three prominent gods, *Kane*, Ku and Lono (Hawaiian; Tane, Tu and Rongo in Maori), form a triad. See *Trinity*.

Twins – Hui Tarara. In the South Pacific two stars in *Scorpio*, are called Na Ainanu. Castor is called Pipiri; Pollux, *Rehua* in Polynesian. See *Gemini*.

Underworld – See *Hades; Lua-o-Milu; Milu; Miru; Nether World; Papa; Pare; Reinga; Tapairu*. Miru or Milu is the ruler of the Underworld; the *Tapairu* are the nymphs of the pool that leads there.

Venus – Kopu is the name given to Venus as the rising Morning Star.

War – The Polynesian War-God is the co-Creator of man and a member of the triad (see *Trinity*). He is the initiator of quarrels, envy and friction. His name is *Ku* in Hawaii. See *Maru*.

Whirlwind – The deity of the tornado is known as Ara Tiotio or Awhiowhio. He is much feared by seafarers. See also *Storm*.

Wind – There are several names for the Wind-Gods of the Pacific: Hanui-o-Rangi the Sky-God is called 'Father of Winds' (see *Rangi*; also *Storm*).

Hau is the Maori name for the Wind-God. He is the son of Rua-Tapu, 'The Forbidden Path', who was murdered, so the Wind-God Hau is howling for revenge.

The name Matagi in Samoan, Makani in Hawaiian, is connected with the Maori Apu-Hau or Apu Matangi, a storm-god, because any wind can grow into a storm.

The Great Wind-God is known as *Raka Maomao* (Maori), *La'a Maomao* (Hawaiian) and Fa'atiu (Samoan).

A benign wind-goddess is Hine-Tu-Whenua, who blows the sailors gently to their destination.

See also *Aizen-Myoo; Ambu Dewi; Ananta Thewi; Assembly of the Gods; Awabi; Bagaspati; Bato; Darma; Dasamuka; Demi-Gods; Dogaira; Fujin; Gama; Goddess of Mercy; Goddess of the Mountain; Goddess of the Sky; Grass-God; Haikili; Haumea; Hema; Hiiaka; Ira; Kahoali; Kala; Karaeng Lowe; Kishijoten; Kishimo-Jin; Kohara; Kompera; Koya-No-Myoin; Kukailimoku; Laufakanaa; Lugeilan; Matagaigai; Matariki; Miyazu-Hime; Motoro; Nakatsu-Hime; Namiumlap; Nevi Yanan; Ndauthina; Neititua Abine; Oa Rove; Ocean-Goddess; Olofat; Ono; Paikea; Paka'a; Raeit Ngabal; Rati; Ro'o; Ru(1); Shichi Fukujin; Sparrow; Tikokura; Waitiri; Weaver.*

Goga In the mythology of the Massim people of *Papua*, Goga was the Goddess of Fire. She was pictured as an old woman guarding her fire against the persistent rains which were sent by the Rain-Goddess, her rival. Then, one day, a man came and stole the fire. He carried it to the Land of People where it soon lit all the homes. Now the Fire-Goddess had to ask the Rain-Goddess to quench all those illegal fires in the people's homes, because the fire belonged exclusively to her. The rain extinguished all the fires except one, which a *snake* kept in its tail. See also *Fire*(4).

Gokuraku Jodo ('The Pure Land') See *Amida; Jodo*.

Golden Dragon Naga Mas, in Malay mythology, is a gigantic sea monster, brother of Prince Lela Muda, son of Raja Budiman, King Wise.

Golden Flute See *Magic Flute*.

Golden Tortoise See *Green Demon*; *Magic Flute*.

Gondoriah See *Sijobang*.

Gonge See 'Gods of Japan' under *Gods; Incarnation*.

Gongen In *Japan*, a mountain deity, an incarnated living spirit, a *Shinto incarnation* of the *Buddha*. Mountain climbers hope to gain spiritual enlightenment on the summit of those mountains which have such a spirit. See also 'Gods of Japan' under *Gods*.

Gora-Daileng He was the God of the Nether World in the Carolines' myths. He would punish the sinners by pushing them in to his river which carried them down into a cave from whence they never returned. See *Nether World*.

Grail See *White Raven*.

Grass-God This god is invoked in *Japan* to give a rich harvest of *taima*, hemp, for rope-making.

Grasshoppers In Japanese mythology, the *horses* of the *dead*.

Green Demon In *Annam* it is related that in the marshes lives a monster with a *snake's* head. His body has the shape of a man but it is no more than a green vapour. He is the demon of the plague, a disease which covers the body with sores and causes certain *death*. It can only be cured when the king blows a golden flute, which is in the possession of the Golden Tortoise who lives in the waterfall of Ma Cho. The pure tone of the flute will cause a soft breeze to blow from the ocean which will dispel the green vapour and the disease with it. See *Magic Flute; Tortoise*(3).

Grubs In some Polynesian myths the first man and woman were created from two grubs by *Tangaroa*. See also *Creation*.

Guna-Guna The 'black arts' in *Indonesia*. See *Durga; Kahuna; Magic; Ngelmu; Sorcerer; Sorcery; Tohunga; Witch*.

Guriang Tunggal The Supreme God in Sundanese mythology. His son is *Guru Minda* who descends to earth as *Lutung Kasarung*.

Guru

1. Indonesian sage, teacher and counsellor who knows the future.
2. In Balinese mythology, the benevolent god-teacher *Siwa*. See also *Mahayogi*.

Guru Minda The son of *Guriang Tunggal*, the Supreme God of Sundanese mythology in West *Java*, and *Ambu Dewi*. Guru Minda lives on earth as *Lutung Kasarung*, the Black Monkey, to protect Princess Purba Sari against the whims of her wicked elder sister the queen.

Guru ri Seleng See *Creation*(7).

H

Hanuman, Bali stonecarving

Hachiman In the cosmology of popular Japanese religion, Hachiman is the God of War. He is worshipped not only by soldiers but also by peasants as a god of agriculture, and by the fishermen, who hope he will fill their nets. He is also a protector of children. His messengers are *doves*. An alternative name for him is Yawata, the God of the Eight Banderoles. In *Shinto*, Hachiman was identified with the Emperor Ojin, son of the Empress Jingo (fourth century AD) and in the Buddhist pantheon (eighth century AD) with the great Bodhisattva *Daibosatsu*.

See also 'Gods of Japan' under *Gods; Tide Jewels*.

Hades

1. *Milu* is, in Hawaiian mythology, the God of the Land of the Dead, the equivalent of Hades. *Lua-o-Milu*, 'Milu's Cave', is the abode of the *dead*. The dead know what the living are doing but not vice versa. They have the power to turn the living into stone by simply staring at them. Strong-willed *spirits* may come back to earth, and the living may visit Hades, but should eat nothing there, otherwise they will have to stay there forever.
2. According to another description, Avaiki, or Hades, is a huge oven or fireplace for roasting all the dead who will subsequently be devoured by *Miru*, the fierce Goddess of the Underworld. She had

some beautiful daughters, *Tapairus*, whom she would send out to lure seducible men away from the earth. Once she had them in her palace, she would give them *kava* to drink, and when they were stupified she would lightly roast them and eat them. One day, two Tapairus succeeded in luring the Polynesian hero *Ngaru* himself to Miru's palace, in spite of his grandfather *Moko*'s warnings. However, as soon as Miru placed him on the glowing hot stones, hoping to roast him, the heavens opened and a *deluge* came pouring down, extinguishing the fires of hell. Miru was swept away and the two nymphs saved themselves by holding onto Ngaru's arms. In this myth a natural disaster is mythically described. Ngaru is himself the God of the Waves. From time to time the ocean penetrates the interior of a volcano through a crevasse in its structure, while at other times volcanoes spew out fire onto the waves, causing a storm of steam to blow up, or the waves touch hot volcanic rocks and so produce steam. See also *Volcano God*.

3. In Thai, Hades is Patal, from the Sanskrit Patala. The *epic* of *Ramakien* gives a vivid description of the *Nether World* when *Hanuman* visits it. One can enter the World of the Dead (if one knows the right incantations) by penetrating the stalk of a lotus flower, which rises up from the lake bed to the water's surface. Down through its centre glides whoever can make himself small enough to enter a flower. Down there on the dark and slippery path to the kingdom of King Maiyarab one meets terrifying *demons*. Divine power is needed to protect the traveller against those numerous *monsters*, including mosquitoes as big as chickens. Machanu, half-fish, half-god, guards the lake which all wayfarers have to cross. None will survive who have not received special instructions from one of the *gods*. Wailing can be heard from the victims who are being boiled. The traveller has to be (morally) weighed before being judged worthy of entering the deeper compartments. Heaviness betrays corruption.

4. In Fijian cosmology, the *soul* of a dead man has a long journey ahead of him on the way to Bulu, the Land of the Dead. First he walks to the coast where the goddess Lewalevu awaits him. During his lifetime he should have sacrificed to her. Souls of bachelors are smashed against the rocks by Nangananga, Goddess of Punishment, who also awaits the souls on the cliffs. All men ought to marry, for it is the only good way of life. Between the sheer rock and the seething ocean the path leads down to the caves of Drakulu and Cibaciba, the entrance to the Land of the Dead. Only the men who can walk with their wives through the bleak boulder-strewn landscape reach the last Stepping Stone. There, a boat will await the souls and carry them to Nabangatai, the silent village of the invisible souls. The warrior souls have to do battle with Samulayo, the God of War and Death in Battle. Finally they appear before the *Serpent-God Dengei* who will interrogate and judge them.

5. *Banoi* is the Land of the Dead in the cosmology of the *New Hebrides*.

See also *the Dead; Death; Eleio; Emma-o; Hawaiki; Hiku; Jigoku; Milu; Miru; Nether World; Other World; Pare; Reinga; Sangiang; Shamanism; Underworld.*

Hadir See *Kilir.*

Hahau-Whenua ('Searching for Land') This was one of the first names of *New Zealand*, when *Maui* had just magically raised it up from the bottom of the ocean, and when only gods lived on it. It was compared to a huge fish, full of good nourishment. The earth, the Holy Mother, was the daughter of *Tangaroa*, the Ocean-God.

Haida The Haida people live on the Prince of Wales Islands and the Queen Charlotte Islands off the Pacific Coast of British Columbia and Alaska. Like the Koreans, they have in their mythology ancestral links with the Bear-Mother. Long ago the bears wore their fur coats only in public. Inside their houses they took them off and became people. Later some of the bear-beings kept their fur on all the time, whereas others lost their coats and were condemned to run about naked, even in public and out in the cold. They became human beings, but the Bear-Mother still protects them.

The Haida people also relate myths of the Thunder-Bird, whom they represent in colourful wood carvings with a huge bill and a second face on its stomach. It is such a big bird that it can fish *whales* out of the ocean. When it flies, its flapping wings sound like thunderclaps, while its gold-coloured bill emits flashes of lightning.

Haikili In Hawaiian myth the God of Thunder.

Hakawau In *Maori* myth it is related that there were once two powerful *sorcerers* who possessed an idol in the shape of a large wooden head which they kept inside a spirit-house. Whoever came close to the outer gate of that spirit-house would surely die. By means of its evil power, the two sorcerers, Puarata and Tautohito, could bewitch all their enemies.

Eventually the people appealed to the old shaman Hakawau, who was known for his magical powers as well as for his goodness. Hakawau summoned his many familiar *spirits* to come and help him. They arrived and accompanied him to the palisade which surrounded the spirit-house. On the way they passed the many corpses of the brave men who had tried to defeat the Head before them, but had failed. As Hakawau approached the dangerous evil spirit of the Head, it radiated its destructive beams, but Hakawau was constantly reciting his protective incantations (see *Karakia*), assisted by the *magic* power of his many familiar spirits, and so was protected. Finally the spirits entered the enclosure and penetrated the house of the Head, which could no longer bellow, only moan. Puarata and Tautohito appealed to the once powerful spirit of the Head but it had expired or fled. Finally Hakawau himself penetrated the sanctuary, still reciting his enchantments, and threw the Head down from its pedestal. Then he clapped his hands, which caused the two sorcerers to fall down dead. Thus Hakawau is still remembered as the good shaman who delivered his people from a dreaded demon and its two evil priests.

Hakumele A songmaster. See *Kilu*.

Halau A Hawaiian temple. See *Hula*.

Halulu See *Spirits*(5).

Hambei An old Japanese gardener. See *Plum Tree*.

Hammer In *Japan*, the Princess Sanjo found a hammer which had once belonged to a demon. It could fulfil any wish. You only have to wish something, tap it on the ground and your wish will be fulfilled. It is probably still in the imperial palace.

Hana-Matsuri ('Flower Festival') See *Shaka*.

Hanagaki Baishu See *Benten*.

Hang Tuah Hang Tuah is the Malay national hero. Son of Hang Mahmud, shopkeeper on the island of Bintang near *Singapore*, Hang Tuah chose four friends, Hang Jebat, Hang Kasturi, Hang Lekir and Hang Lekiu, and together they became the equivalent of the Four Musketeers for the kings of Bintang and Singapore, and later for the King of *Melaka*. They defeated a fleet of pirates at sea, and also defeated five madmen who attacked the vizier. Hang Tuah also studied with the saint *Adi Putra*, who had lived in the mountains since time immemorial.

Hannya-Shinkyo (Sanskrit, *Prajna-Paramita*) A Buddhist text of great power. The Sanskrit title means 'The Highest Wisdom'; the Japanese title means 'Freedom of the Spirit for Wisdom'. In *Japan* they say that if a person is harassed by evil *spirits* he should be stripped and these verses should be written all over his body, leaving no blank space at all. Then the *ghosts* who come to kidnap him will be unable to see him.

Hantu A word widespread in *Indonesia* denoting any type of invisible, frightening being, a spirit, ghost or demon.

Hantu Air The Malaysian Sea-God. See also 'Gods of the Pacific' under *Gods*; *Phosphorescence of the Sea*.

Hantu Ayer See *Water Spirit*.

Hantu Kuang The Ghost with a Hundred Eyes. See *Spirits*(4).

Hantu Puteri See *Ghosts*(5).

Hantu Uri The Placenta Spirit. See *Spirits*(4).

Hanui-o-Rangi See *Rangi*.

Hanuman A Hindu god, a manifestation of Vishnu (*Wisnu*) in the shape of a rhesus monkey, often depicted as a man with a monkey face. Made tremendously popular by his exploits in the *epic* of *Ramayana*,

Hanuman's fame spread to *Thailand* and *Indonesia*. Even in the mythology of *Japan* and China 'Monkey' is a divine hero.

South of the Javanese port of Bantam (Banten) rises a mountain range where the Badui people live. They say that Hanuman can be seen in the forest in the shape of an orang-utan, the ancestor of all monkeys. See also *Lutung Kasarung; Ramakien*.

Hapopo A priest of the *Maori* chief Tawheta. See *Uenuku*.

Haoumea See *Pere*.

Harae See *Harai*.

Harai (Harae) In Japanese religion, a variety of ceremonies intended to purify the *soul* of sins and other evil influences by means of prayers and payments to temples or priests. This often involves exorcism, i.e. the casting out of evil *spirits*. See also *Hannya-Shinkyo*.

Hare The old Indian myth that there is a hare in the *moon* is commonly found in Japanese tales as well as on *Java* and *Bali*. See *Mochi*.

Hari See *Wisnu*.

Haronga A Polynesian god, son of *Rangi* the Sky-God, and father of the *sun* and *moon* and of Atarapa, 'Daybreak'. See 'Gods of the Pacific' under *Gods*.

Hasu The Japanese lotus flower, *Nelumbo nucifera*, or *Nymphaea tetragona*. Dedicated to the *Buddha*, this flower signifies the world, resting as it does on the *water*, as the earth was believed to be floating on the surface of the primeval ocean. The Buddha is seated on it, in profound meditation, signifying the universal spirit ruling the earth and all matter, by virtue of his *Law*.

Hasu-Ko ('Lotus-Child') In Japanese mythology, a girl who died of *love* for her betrothed, whom she had never seen. When he finally arrived, her spirit 'stole' her sister Kei's body for a year so she and her fiancé could live as lovers. Kei became ill 'like one dead'. At the end of a year Hasu-Ko brought her lover home and told her parents that she was content to die 'definitively', on condition that they would marry Kei to him. They had to promise that in order to give her *soul* peace. When she faded away, Kei revived suddenly and was happy to marry her sister's fiancé, not knowing that he already loved her body. They lived happily ever after.

Hati See *Liver*.

Hau

1. The *Maori* name for the Polynesian Wind-God. See 'Gods of the Pacific' under *Gods*.
2. See *Hautupatu*.

Hau Maringi The Polynesian God of Mist or Fog. See also 'Gods of the Pacific' under *Gods*.

Hau-o-Tawera A hero. See *Poukai*(2).

Haumea A *mother-goddess* in Hawaiian mythology. She had many sons. When the eldest had become a handsome young man, she died and was reborn so she could marry him. When finally he too died, she also died and was again reborn to marry her youngest son. Later again she died and was reborn to marry her great grandson. She was the goddess who attended women at the birth of their children, but she was also a goddess of *death*. She possessed an orchard full of magical trees, some of which she gave to her children on earth. Whenever the owner needed something, he could order the tree to produce it for him. Haumea also owned a *fish* tree. In those times there were no fish in the ocean yet. She gave her fish tree to one of her sons, who was the first fisherman. It had to be placed in the sea, where its fruits became fish. However, its owner became greedy, so he shook his fish tree, whereupon the fish fruits swam away instead of falling into his hands. So now fish have to be caught by fishing.

Haumia Tiketike The Polynesian God of Uncultivated Food. See 'Gods of the Pacific' under *Gods; Sky*(2).

Hautupatu A *Maori* myth tells of Hautupatu (or Hau for short), who was the youngest of three brothers. When he fell out with them he went off into the forest on his own. There he saw the ogress Kurangai Tupu. She was busy catching *birds* by shooting out her lips at them. She saw him as he ran away and took off, easily catching up with him, for she had wings on her arms. Though she was very big and heavy, she was strong and could run fast. She caught him and carried him to her *cave*. She ate the birds she had caught, giving some to Hautupatu, but he was not hungry and did not like raw food. The next morning the ogress left the cave to go hunting. Hautupatu cooked some of the birds she had given him, and so stilled his hunger. Then he climbed out of the cave. The exit had been blocked by the ogress to prevent him from escaping, but Hautupatu knew a *karakia* for opening rock and other walls, so he made his way out. Alas! there was a little bird in the cave, which flew out to where the ogress was, singing: 'Kura, Kura, Kurangai, your prisoner has escaped!'

Although she was far away, Kurangai could step over mountains as if they were molehills, for she too had a *karakia*: 'Stretch out, stride along!' This made her legs longer than the trees were tall, so she could walk over the forest as if it was a grassy field. Soon she had caught sight of Hautupatu, crying, 'I'll catch you!'

But Hautupatu had learned another *karakia* from his grandmother. It went like this: '*Matiti, matata*', which means roughly: 'Rock open, rock close.' He recited this *karakia* and a door opened in a rock wall. Hautupatu went in, and it closed behind him leaving no trace. He came out on the other side of the mountain and ran to his house, but Kurangai

Tuku spotted him again. Hautupatu then hid near the other side of a bubbling hot spring and when Kurangai Tuku alighted she did not look where she put her feet, so she fell into the boiling water and died.

Havoa See *Morning Star*.

Hawaii The Hawaiian *islands* were discovered by the Spanish explorer Gaetano in 1542, and were again visited in 1567 by one of his officers, Mendona, who fixed their position on his maps. The islanders are reported to have known the use of iron since that time.

After the visit of Cook in 1778, the Hawaiians enter into world history. In those times the islands were described as a flourishing archipelago peopled by 400,000 inhabitants (according to Captain King) or by 242,400 (according to Mr Bligh). Once informed about the use of firearms, they started a sanguinary war, led by local princes, which lasted from 1780–91 and eliminated an estimated 15 per cent of the population. One of the local rulers emerged triumphant and established himself as Kamehameha ('monarch'), the first king to rule over the entire archipelago.

In his reign, the first merchandise of the country, sandalwood, was sold to Canton, although as early as 1830 not a single tree was left. In 1804 the first of many epidemics swept the country, a kind of pestilence, one of the causes of the eventual ruin of the nation.

When Kamehameha died in 1819, he was succeeded by his son Liholiho, who ascended the throne as Kamehameha II. He was an intelligent but dipsomaniacal young man and did not want to obey the traditional *taboos*. He broke them by dining with his wives, a famous act which marked the end of paganism. The priests felt their social status threatened and started a revolution, but they were defeated by the king's troops, and eventually their wooden idols were destroyed.

In 1820 the first missionaries, two congregational Americans, landed in Hawaii, but had no success until members of the royal family agreed to be baptized. In the same year, the first whaler entered the harbour of Honolulu, which had been founded by Kamehameha I. This marked the beginning of the harbour industry and of prostitution. The Hawaiian girls, having no cultural objection to sexual licence, indulged in contact with foreign sailors, ignorant of the imminent dangers. Doubtless we must search here for the cause of both the venereal diseases in the country and of its romantic reputation in the outer world. Needless to say, the missionaries fought this 'evil' in vain; however, they succeeded in Christianizing the whole population and in teaching them to read and write.

In 1823 Kamehameha II and his wife died while on an official visit to England. His brother succeeded him as Kamehameha III, still under the tutorship of the old queen, Kaahumanu, wife of the first king. She firmly maintained what the whalers considered 'stupid morality' and was, in 1829, congratulated on this by the President of the United States. She died in 1832 however, and the young king was unable to keep up the moral standard of his mother. But in spite of his lascivious life, he was an honourable statesman who in 1840 issued the constitution of his state, which made it a democratic monarchy. As such it was recognized in its sovereignty by the United States, France and England in 1843, though in the same year an Englishman, Paulet, annexed the country temporarily for England. In 1849 the French followed suit, Admiral Tromelin and his crew occupying the fort. When they left they took the king's yacht with them. However, internal turmoil in France between the revolution of 1848–52, when Napoleon III became emperor, caused the annexation to be dropped.

In 1848 the people died in their masses from a measles epidemic and in 1853 from an epidemic of Asiatic smallpox.

In 1852 all legal subjects of His Majesty received the right to vote, and the representative and legislative bodies were reorganized so that the constitution was now a very liberal one. However, in 1854 the king, intimidated by the arbitrary actions of foreigners in his state, and under the influence of American missionaries, some of whom had become his ministers, was ready to sign a document asking for Hawaii to become a protectorate of the United States. While the American ships anchored in his harbour to receive the document that only waited for his signature, the king died of asthma. He was nicknamed 'The Good', for he did no evil.

As he died childless, his successor was Alexander Liholiho Kamehameha IV, son of Kinau, a daughter of Kamehameha I. The new king annulled the cession. He also gave orders for a new code of law to be composed, including a penal code, which was issued in 1859 in both Hawaiian and English. He erected a hospital and a prison. He died in 1863 from asthma; his son had died the year before, so his brother Lot ascended the throne as Kamehameha V. His first act was to order the composition of a new constitution, which was issued in 1864.

King Kamehameha V died in 1872, in the midst of the intrigues of foreign residents, who had an interest in the annexation of Hawaii by the United States. He was 43 years of age. The new king, elected by the legislative assembly, was Lunalili, a cousin of the late king. He cancelled a proposal of the United States to exchange the free sale of Hawaiian products in all US territory against Pearl Harbour as a naval base and coaling station. He died childless in 1874, at 39 years old. The next king to be elected was David Kalakaua. The first thing he had to do was to quell a revolt of the party of the other pretender, Queen Emma, with the assistance of two American and two British battleships that happened to be present.

In 1876 a treaty was concluded which allowed both nations mutual import and export of all products to all harbours of both states free of duty. This important treaty guaranteed to the Hawaiian Islands the vast market of the United States.

King Kalakaua died in 1890 and was succeeded by his sister Lydia Kamakacha Liliuokalani. She was the last indigenous ruler on the Polynesian islands, except for *Tonga*. She died in 1917.

Hawaii had finally been annexed to the United States in 1898 after five years of negotiations. During the Second World War it served as the US Naval Headquarters. After the war, it developed peacefully, becoming a state of the US in 1959.

See also *Adam and Eve*(1); *Apu-Hau*; *Awa*; *Canaque*; *Eleio*; 'Gods of the Pacific' under *Gods*; *Hades*; *Haikili*; *Haumea*; *Heiau*; *Hiiaka*; *Hiku*; *Hula*; *Incest*; *Io*; *Kaha'i*; *Kahiki*; *Kahoali*; *Kahuna*; *Kamapua'a*; *Kanaka*; *Kanaloa*; *Kane*(2); *Kane Hoalani*; *Kilu*; *Ku*; *Ku-Kau-Akahi*; *Kukailimoku*; *Kumu-Honua*; *Kaka*; *Lohiau*; *Lono*; *Mahina*; *Make*; *Menehune*; *Milu*; *Moikeha*; *Nana-Ula*; *Nu'u*; *Oracles*; *Paka'a*; *Paliuli*; *Papa*; *Pele*; *Polynesia*; *Trinity*; *Uhi*; *Wahie Loa*; *Wakea*.

Hawaiki   The 'Old Homeland' of the *Polynesians* where their *spirits* will return, after they have died, to join their ancestors. See also *Hades*.

Hawk

1. In *Hawaii*, the hawk is personified as *Maui*, who, in taking fire from the Earth-Mother, was singed by the flames. This is why the hawk's *feathers* are brown. See *Fire*(4).
2. The *Dayaks* of the Sarawak pray to the hawk before weeding the *rice* fields, to protect the weeders from falling ill. Before harvesting they thank the hawk, hoping that all the *taboos* have been observed.

See also *Creation*(3); *Flood*; *Io*.

Head

1. In Fijian mythology they relate that in the beginning the *gods* waged *war* against one another. These wars were terrible. In one of them, the head of the god Ulupoka was severed and fell to earth. It did not die because the gods are immortal, so their parts too survive, even if severed from the main body. Since Ulupoka was a god of evil, his head brought disaster and disease to earth. The head used to travel from village to village at dusk. A cold breeze would announce its arrival. The head would come rolling along the beach, then bounce into a village, and jump into the hut of a doomed man. In his sleep, the head would bite his foot and he would never rise again.
2. Many people of *Indonesia* take extreme care that their heads are well protected, so they keep them covered. They are never seen in public without an *ikat* (folded headcloth) and they are deeply indignant when an outsider touches their heads. It is believed that the *mana* of a person is concentrated in his head. This also explains the head hunting which, in prehistoric times, seems to have been widespread in Indonesia and Melanesia. The head hunter acquires, with the head, the *mana* of his enemy.

See also *Ganindo*; *Hakawau*; *Tuna*.

Head-He-Go-Round-Man   In *Papua New Guinea*, a seer or prophet who tells the people that he can see the *spirits* of the *dead* and tells them what the dead have told him. Many of these 'dreamers' are either crooks or madmen.

Heaven

1. For the Malays and the other Islamic peoples in *Indonesia* and the *Philippines*, the shape of the heavens is described in the story of *Creation*. In the beginning, it says, God created the earth in the shape of a tray (on which food is offered) and the *sky* above it like an umbrella, *payung*, such as pages hold up for their kings. (The implication is that the Great Light, i.e. God Himself, is above that umbrella, outside our sky; without that umbrella we would all perish in His fierce light.) God suspended the stars inside this dome, much like the lamps suspended from the ceiling of a mosque. He sent the *sun* and *moon* on their orbits in such a way that when the sun rises it is morning everywhere on earth at the same time, so when the *angels* in heaven say their prayers, all people should say their prayers at the same time. God created the heavens in seven layers, like the upper floors and balconies in a mosque, all under the same dome. Each 'floor' is ruled by one of the seven prophets: Adam, Jesus, St John, Enoch, Joseph, Moses, Aaron and Abraham. The seventh heaven is where God created *Paradise* for the good *souls* of the believers. In it there are palaces for the saints and martyrs; there are clear streams and trees bowing down with fruit. Above this is the mosque where the angels pray (70,000 at a time). Far above that is the Tree of the End, whose leaves are the death records of all people. When a leaf falls, a person dies on earth, the one whose name is on the leaf that is falling from the tree. Far above that is the Throne of God, bathing in divine light.

2. The *Polynesians* relate that the sky is a male god, *Rangi*, who is hovering above the earth, *Papa*, his goddess, like a seagull hovering above the waters. The sky can be seen as a blue or grey dome over the earth, so the two are seen to fit together like the two valves of an open oyster. Inside, just as the mother of pearl is glowing in the oyster, so the light from heaven is shining over the ocean and the clouds. All things have come forth from the conjunction of heaven and earth. When people die, their souls will walk east towards the rising sun.

See also *Ama Terasu; Amida; Aneka-Warna; Bridge of Heaven; God; Kami; Nga-Atua; Rehua*(1); *Tane; Te Toi-o-nga-Rangi; Ten.*

Heduru A god of *New Guinea* who lived in *heaven*. See *Sky*(1).

Heiau In *Polynesia*, especially *Hawaii*, a large space for worship, one to five acres in size. It was surrounded by a stone wall of up to 10 feet thick and 20 feet high. Within this enclosure there was usually a temple in front of which stood the altar on a large raised platform up to 14 feet high, up to 40 yards long and 20 broad. Up to 12 statues of the *gods* stood in a circle or semi-circle at one end of this platform, which were regularly worshipped. The priests stood there while they were delivering *oracles* from the gods, whose influence was naturally strongest inside their circle at the sanctuary. All these sites are now in ruins.

Heitaro   See *Willow Tree*(1).

Heitiki   See *Amulet*.

Hema   Hema was the son of the goddess *Waitiri* and Kai Tangata in *Maori* myth. He married the goddess Urutonga ('South-West'); they had three children, two boys and a girl. The youngest was *Tawhaki*, the God of Thunder and Good Health. Hema was killed by the *Ponaturi* sea-spirits, and his two sons took revenge for his death (see *Tawhaki*).

In Hawaiian myth, Hema was the son of *Mahina*, the Moon-Goddess.

Hensho Kongo   See *Kobo*.

Hero-Day   Hero-Day is 23 October, when the Japanese people honour the spirits of the heroes fallen in the Second World War.

Heron

1.   In one of the myths of Aitutaki, the hero *Rata* rescues a heron from the jaws of a *sea-serpent*. The grateful heron, really an elf, shows him how to dig out a tree trunk to make a *canoe*.
2.   In *Malaysia* the *ruwakruwak* is a heron whose nest makes its owner invisible by its *magic* power whenever it wishes.

Hevehe   A great feast. See *Mask*.

Hi   See *Fire*.

Hi Haela   ('String Man') See *Yam*(2).

Hiang Piumbung   ('The Overshadowing God') See *God*(2).

Hidari   The most famous Japanese sculptor, who once saw a woman of such exceptional beauty that he made a sculpture of her. It was such a perfect image of the woman that the sculpture came to life.

Hideyoshi   A sixteenth-century Japanese dictator. See *Japan*.

Hidesato   A famous fearless hero of Japanese legend. He killed the *Centipede*, amongst other *monsters*.

Hidetada   A seventeenth-century Japanese ruler. See *Japan*.

Hiiaka   In Hawaiian myth, Hiiaka, daughter of the Sea-God *Kane*, was the Goddess of Hawaii, of the *islands*, of the hills, the lands, the cliffs and caves. She was a benign goddess, much praised in song during music festivals. See also *Pele*(2).

Hikayat Bayan Budiman   See *Parrot*.

Hikayat Hang Tuah   See *Hang Tuah; Malaya*.

Hikayat Pandawa Jaya   See *Mahabharata*.

Hikoboshi   A Japanese cowherd. See *Tanabata*.

Hiku   Hiku was a *kupua* or demi-god in Hawaiian mythology, the son of the Mountain-Goddess Hina, who forbade him to visit the world of the people until he finally persuaded her to let him travel. He took his *magic* arrow Pua-ne and set out. His arrow was his guide: he would throw it up into the air and it would fly in the direction he had to go. One fated moment, it landed at the feet of a queen, Kawelu. She picked it up and hid it. Then Hiku appeared, tall and handsome, calling: 'Pua-ne!'

The arrow replied from the queen's bosom: 'Ne!' (Here!) So the queen had to give up the speaking arrow. She fell in love with Hiku and in her turn, using magic, she detained him in her palace, like Calypso holding Odysseus. But after a time he grew wings and flew away over the ocean. Inconsolable, the queen died.

When the news reached Hiku, he decided to try and bring back her unhappy *soul* from *Milu* (*Hades*). He rubbed his body with *kukui*, an oil that smells like a corpse, and told his friends to lower him, by means of the long tough stem of the *kowali* (Convulvulus), into the *Lua-o-Milu*, the Pit of Hades, an abyss leading to the *Nether World*, where the *spirits* of the *dead* are gathered. No living man is allowed to visit Hades but, deceived by his cadaverous odour, even the god Milu did not become suspicious. Kawelu's spirit soon recognized Hiku and sat down on his *kowali* 'swing' with him. At once Hiku's friends, receiving his secret signal, began to pull the 'rope' up. But Kawelu did not really want to leave the dead-land. She changed her appearance to a *butterfly* in order to escape. Quickly, Hiku imprisoned her in an empty *coconut* shell he had brought for the purpose.

As soon as he was above earth again, Hiku travelled back to the queen's palace where her body was still lying in state. He knelt down and with his arrow made an incision in the big toe of the left foot. Then, with his magic songs he persuaded the soul to re-enter the cold body through the wound. After that he bandaged the wound and began to rub the foot, massage the leg, and so on, until the soul had spread throughout the body and reached the heart so it became warm again. (See also *Eleio*.) Kawelu opened her eyes, smiled at Hiku and asked, 'Why did you leave me?' She did not remember her journey to the Nether World, nor her return.

Himaphan In Thai cosmology, a mountain range where fruit trees grow which bring forth fruits whose juice cures all *illnesses*. See also *Mango*.

Hina (Ma-Hina, Mahina or Hine) A universal goddess with many functions. As the first woman, she is represented with two heads, i.e. night and day. She is Guardian of the Dead in the *Underworld* as well as patroness of arts and crafts. She loved *Tuna*, a fish-man, out of whose head grew the first *coconut* palm.

See also *Adam and Eve*(3); 'Gods of the Pacific' under *Gods*; *Hiku*; *Hina-Ika*; *Hina-Keha*; *Mahina*; *Sina*.

Hina-Ika ('Lady of the Fish') Hina-Ika was one of the sisters of the Polynesian Sun-God *Maui*. Maui used her hair to make a strong net by means of which he pulled the *sun* into the world. He then he released it, whereupon it flew across the *sky*. In the west, in the land of *Avaiki*, Maui used the net again to lower the sun gently into the sea.

Hina-Ika's husband was Ira-Waru, an ancient fish-god, half-man half-fish. It was believed that male fish could mate with women if they went swimming too far out to sea. Ira-Waru could fish better than Maui. It was one or other of them who invented the *hinaki*, the eel-trap, and other fish nets as well, all woven from Hina's strong hair, moon-hair, the silver threads of moonrays.

Hina-Keha ('Bright Lady') The Polynesian Goddess of the Moon in her full phase. As the sister of the Sun-God *Maui* she is comparable to Artemis–Diana the 'Radiant Goddess', sister of Apollo.

In one of the versions of the *Maori* moon mythology, it is related that in her 'dead' phase (see *Hina-Uri*) the Moon-Goddess drifted into the sea and was covered by weeds. She was washed ashore and a man discovered her in human form under a tangle of kelp and seaweed. In another version she saw him first and seeing that he was a handsome prince, as in Andersen's tale, she rose from the water and changed from her fish form into a beautiful maiden. The prince's name was *Tini Rau*, or Rupe in another version of the myth. She fell in love with him, like Artemis in Endymion falling in love with a mortal man. However, like the prince in Andersen's tale, he was already married. Nevertheless they loved each other on the shore of a lagoon, and in due course Hina gave birth to a son, Tuhuruhuru. It was a very difficult birth so she composed and recited a powerful *karakia* which made the child come out easily. This *magic* formula was still used by the women in *New Zealand* earlier in this century. Thus Hina-Keha is also the Goddess of Childbirth, like Diana. Also like Diana, she is often seen in the company of a dog.

Hina-Keha also has many names, e.g. Hine-Te-Iwa-Iwa. *Iwa* means 'nine', so this may be a reference to the 'nine moons of carrying' preceding childbirth. In this appearance Hina is the patroness of women and the arts and crafts. She is the one who received the first *amulet*, *heitiki*, from her father *Tane*. Another name is Hine-Te-Ngaru-Moana, 'The Lady of the Ocean Waves', when she is in her fish-like form. See also 'Gods of the Pacific' under *Gods; Hina-Uri; Kae; Moon*.

Hina-Matsuri In *Japan*, the Doll Festival for girls, on 3 March. It is a feast for girls, who learn to make dolls in preparation for motherhood. Some Japanese dolls have a *soul*. See also *Tokutaro-San*.

Hina-Te-Iwa-Iwa See *Hina-Keha*.

Hina-Uri ('The Indigo Lady') Hina-Uri is the Goddess of the Moon in Polynesian mythology, the sister of *Maui*. She may be identical with *Hina-Ika* ('Hina Under Water'). She represents the moon in her dark phase, hence the reference to her colour. As Hina-Uri is the moon at the time when she will soon be reborn, she possesses the secret of new life. See also 'Gods of the Pacific' under *Gods; Hina-Keha; Tini Rau*.

Hinaki An eel-trap. See *Hina-Ika*.

Hine See *Hina*.

Hine-i-Tapeka The Goddess of the Fire in the Earth. See 'Gods of the Pacific' under *Gods*.

Hine-Kau-Ataata ('Lonely Gentle Woman' or 'Lady of the Early Gentle Floating Shadows') See *Woman*(1).

Hine-Kaikomako See *Kaikomako*.

Hine-Nui-Te-Po ('Great Lady of the Night') In *Maori* myth, she was the Goddess of Death and Decay (note that *death* is feminine in Maori myth, just as the Roman Mors was a goddess). Hine-Nui-Te-Po was black with green eyes which a man could see staring at him in the night when his time of death was approaching. A dying man was said to be 'creeping into the womb of the Sleeping Mother Death', meaning he went to sleep in the darkness of the earth. The end of a man's life was thus a return to the womb.

When *Maui* the great Maori hero perceived that his moment of death was approaching, he stalked the sleeping Death-Goddess. If he could have succeeded in creeping through her body and coming out at the other end without her waking, he would have overcome death and would rise to new life. But just as he was almost inside, the fantail, a chattering, twittering *songbird*, laughed, waking the goddess. She closed her hips and Maui was a prisoner forever. The songbird went on singing merrily.

See also 'Gods of the Pacific' under *Gods*; *Pare*.

Hine Piripiri The wife of *Tawhaki*. See *Tawhaki*(1).

Hine-Tu-Whenua A Polynesian wind-goddess. See 'Gods of the Pacific' under *Gods*.

Hirantayaksa See *Hiranyaksa*.

Hiranyaksa (Hiranya-Aksa, 'Gold-Eye'; in Thai, Hirantayaksa, although a *yaksa* is a different demon) Hiranyaksa was a demon of the Hindu pantheon who caused a great flood which completely drowned the earth. The god Vishnu (= *Wisnu*) had to change himself into the great boar Varaha in order to shovel up the earth with his snout, so that its muddy hills rose out of the water again. The earth, Lakshmi, Vishnu's own wife, is seen on sculptures embracing her husband gratefully for saving her and destroying the demon. Hiranyaksa is known in old Javanese and Balinese mythology.

Hiranyapakasura A demon. See *Narayana*.

Hiro A Polynesian hero who lived during the *expansion* of the twelfth century. He explored the western Pacific, the reputed home area of the *Polynesians* (*Indonesia*?) from which he returned with the art of writing. He (or his successors?) introduced the script on *Rapanui*.

Hiroshige A Japanese artist. See *Skulls*.

Hituhitu See *Spirits*(5).

Hiyoyoa In the mythology of the Wagawaga people of *Papua*, Hiyoyoa is the *Nether World*, to which the soul, *arugo*, will travel after death. The Lord of the Dead rules there; his name is Tumudurere. He is the God of Plants who puts the *arugos* to work on the vast gardens where he cultivates plants. Very rarely, a human being is allowed to travel back to earth with a plant that will feed humanity.

Hizen A Japanese prince. See *Vampire*(1).

Hnang See *Ramakien*.

Hoa-Tapu The son of *Oro*. See *Oro*(1).

Hoderi and Hoori ('Fire Shine' and 'Fire Fade') These were two sons of *Ninigi* and his wife *Ko-no-Hana*, in Japanese mythology. Hoderi became a fisherman, while Hoori became a hunter and eventually the ancestor of the Japanese emperors. After Hoderi quarrelled with his brother over a lost fishhook Hoori descended to the bottom of the sea to look for it and he met the Sea-God's daughter, *Toyo-Tama*. They fell in *love* and were married. The Sea-God summoned all his *fish* until one of them found the missing fishhook.
See also 'Gods of Japan' under *Gods*.

Hoga See *Gnomes*.

Hohou ('Place of Sleep') See *Goddess*(1).

Hoichi A famous Japanese priest. See *Epic Poetry*.

Hoja Maimoon A rich merchant. See *Parrot*.

Hoji The spirit of the *Death-Stone*. See also *Fox*.

Hom The woman who adopted and brought up Phan. See *Oedipus*.

Honen A thirteenth-century Japanese sage. See *Jodo*.

Honey Tree Song A song sung by the young men of the Bidayuh people in Sarawak when climbing a tree where *bees* have a hive. Their hero, Sibauk, in the beginning of time, climbed up the first tree on earth to where the roots were fixed upside-down in the sky-ceiling. In the Sky Land, he met Grandfather Moon and the souls of the dead, who are like bees.

Hong Kong An island in the Pacific, 20 minutes by ferry from the New Territories on the Asian mainland, forming with some two dozen other islands, not all inhabited, the Colony of Hong Kong, 1842–1997. The population of almost 6 million speaks very good English, as well as Cantonese, the language of almost 100 million people in Guandong province to the north. Other languages are spoken by various sections of the population, such as Pu Tong Hwa (formerly known as Mandarin), and Hakka, a distinct language, as well as others.
There are a dozen Asian religions commonly practised in Hong Kong, including various forms of *Buddhism*, Taoism and ancestor worship, as

well as Confucianism, Hinduism, Islam, Judaism, and Parseeism. There is also Protestantism, Catholicism and Russian Orthodoxism. Every religion has its own places of worship. Shrines for the *Buddhas* and ancestors can be seen in many places.

Ho'o Ipo   The daughter of King Puna of Kaua'i, wife of *Moikeha*. See *Moikeha*.

Hoo-Kwan   The Buddhist Crown of Treasures which emits eternal dazzling light. See *Footprint of the Buddha*.

Hoori

1. The ancestor of Japan's emperors. See *Hoderi and Hoori*.
2. In Japanese cosmology, the element of *fire*. See *Elements*.

Hornbill

1. In *Malaysia* it is related that the hornbill, an ugly bird with a huge horn on its bill and a call like cynical laughter, was once a man who chopped down his mother-in-law's house, after which misdeed he laughed cynically. She turned him into a hornbill.
2. In *Sumatra*, in the province of Padang, there once lived a prince called Enggang, who was so jealous that whenever he went on a journey he shut his wife, Rangkong, up in a tree, without food. One day she was liberated by the groom Sidin. She fled to her mother's palace on Mount Singalan, but the prince followed her and destroyed the palace. For his punishment he was changed into a hornbill. The faithful Princess Rangkong changed into a female hornbill, Enggang Papan, and the two birds are always heard calling 'Enggang!' This shows the ideal of Oriental faithfulness.

See also *Radin*.

Horse   The Japanese painter, Kanasoka, once painted a horse that was so realistic that it broke out of its painting, ran into people's gardens and started eating the vegetables. When the farmers complained, the able Kanasoka painted in a strong rope, tying it to a solid post, thereby resolving the problem.
   See also *Cherry Tree*(1); *Grasshopper*; *Kakemono*; *Kobo*; *Koshin*; *Tipaka*.

Hosho-Nyorai

1. The 'Gem-Birth Buddha'. In Sanskrit, Ratnasambhava, who presides over virtue and happiness, because he makes no distinction between persons or things, for he has *samatajnana*, 'equality-wisdom'. See *Colours and Compass*.
2. In Japanese cosmology, the element of fire.

Hoso-no-Kami   See 'Gods of Japan' under *Gods*.

Hotei   ('Cloth Bag') In Japanese mythology, one of the *Shichi Fukujin*, the seven Gods of Good Luck. He is depicted in sculpture with a round belly symbolizing generosity. He carries a cloth bag containing precious things, including children. He may sit in an old cart drawn by boys, as the Wagon Priest. See also 'Gods of Japan' under *Gods*.

Hotoke   The Japanese *spirits* of the *dead*, including the saints and all the *Buddha*s. See also 'Gods of Japan' under *Gods*.

Hototogisu   The Japanese cuckoo, whose sad cry is explained by the country people as the melancholy longing of a dead *soul* to return to the land of her loved ones.

Hotu-Hiva   A Tahitian princess. See *Tai-Moana*.

Hotu-Papa   See *Papa*.

Houtman   Dutch explorer brothers. See *Indonesia*.

Hui Tarara   The twins, Castor and Pollux. See *Gemini*.

Hula   A religious *dance* festival celebrated on *Hawaii* in the *halau* or temple which contained the shrine, *kuahu*, of the goddess *Laka*, the patroness of the dance. Hymns were sung in her honour during the dance, while her altar was adorned with flowers, leaves and branches, each one known by name. She was addressed as the bride of *Lono* (*Rongo*), the God of Agriculture and protector of the *kumara* (sweet potato).

Human Sacrifice   See *Kahoali; Motoro; Oro*(1)*; Pyramids; Volcano God*.

Huru-Kerema   See *Creation*(2).

Hutu   A *Maori* chief. See *Pare*.

I

Izanagi and Izanami (Japan)

I Tsing A Chinese pilgrim. See *Indonesia*.

Iao The Polynesian name for the Supreme Being. See *Io*.

Ibrahim ibn Rahmatallah Nyakrawati See *Sunan Bonang*.

Ichiko In Japanese religion, a sibyl or medium, a maiden serving at a temple who may become spontaneously possessed by the deity of the shrine, or by other *spirits*, who will predict the future. Later these women diviners began travelling across *Japan* as *fortune-tellers*. See also *Miko*.

Icho (also called Icho Kalakal) A legendary hero in the mythology of the *Caroline Islands*, who led his people to the Carolines from the south.

Icho Kalakal See *Icho*.

Idamidam See *Pregnancy*.

Idzumo ('The Central Land of the Reed Plains') In Japanese mythology, the first part of the earth inhabited after the *Creation*. In those days the trees and even the flowers could still speak, so that the earth was full of voices.

Iesada The sixteenth Japanese shogun. See *Japan*.

Iha-Naga ('Princess Live-Long') She was the rock-strong daughter of

Oho-Yama, the Japanese Mountain-God, who wanted to marry her to the Rice-God *Ninigi*. However, Ninigi preferred her younger sister, *Ko-no-Hana*, so Iha-Naga cursed him. See also 'Gods of Japan' under *Gods; Ko-no-Hana*.

Iho-o-Kataka A mysterious tree standing on North Island, *New Zealand*, whose *magic* qualities have been known for 20 generations. Childless women used to approach this tree to pray for children, clasping the tree in their arms. If they stood on the eastern side of the tree they would be asking for a boy, if on the west, for a girl. Their husbands too, would be there, accompanied by a *tohunga* who would perform the required rites. For Oriental peoples there is nothing more important than having children and no greater suffering than infertility.

Ihova

1. In Orokolo (south *New Guinea*) the word for a sign from the *spirits*, identified with Jehova of the Bible.
2. One of the 'new' *gods* of the followers of 'modern' religious movements in *Papua*. He is pictured dressed in hat, coat, trousers and shoes.

I'i The first settler on Savai'i. See *Sava*.

Ika See *Fish*.

Ika-Roa See *Milky Way*

Ika-Tere In Polynesian mythology, Ika-Tere is the Father of Fish, grandson of the Ocean-God *Tangaroa*. He begat all the animals that live in the sea and rules them with wisdom. See also *Fish*; 'Gods of the Pacific' under *Gods; Tangaroa*.

Ikan See *Fish*.

Ikat An Indonesian folded headcloth. See *Head*(2).

Iki-Ryo In Japanese myth, a spirit of anger and envy which does harm to other people. It may be just the result of a person's hatred radiating towards its object and causing that person to fall ill and die.

Iko In the mythology of *New Guinea*, the first man to die. See *Mirage*.

Ila The name of the first woman on the island of Tutuila, according to Samoan myth. See *Islands*.

Ilaheva See *Ahoeitu*.

Ilai ('Father Sun') See *Creation*(8); *Sun*(4).

Ilha Formosa ('Beautiful Island') See *Taiwan*.

Illness The *Dayaks* of *Borneo* regard every disease as an individual being, an evil spirit which threatens the lives of their loved ones. These spirits are ruled by the Raja Hantuen, the King of the Ghosts. They make a person ill by stealing his *soul* and torturing it, after which they go and live in the patient's body. The priestess is called, who has to sing her *magic* hymns to the *sangiang*, the *demi-gods* or spirits of the air, to try and retrieve the soul.

See also *Crocodile*(3); *Gaki; Green Demon; Indera Bayu; Lioness; Lizard*(3); *Magic Flute; Mango; Nini Muni; Predestination*(3); *Replacement; Ro'o; Toucan; Tree-Spirits*(3)(4)(7).

Ilocano The Ilocano people live in the north-west corner of Luzon in the *Philippines* in the provinces of Abra, Ilocos Norte and Ilocos Sul. They speak Ilocano, a language related to, but quite distinct from, *Tagalog*. They number under a million. They are of Malay ancestry, according to their traditions. Before 200 BC they arrived via *Borneo*, Palawan and Mindoro. Before they were converted to Christianity the Ilokano had a complex pantheon of *gods* and *spirits*.

See also *Monkeys*(2).

Ilu ('The Firmament') See *Creation*(5).

Imo See *Taro*.

Immortal Mountain, the See *Fujiyama*.

Immortality

1. The Japanese Gulliver, Shikaiya Wasobioye, arrived one day at an island where *death* was unknown. The people there lived for their pleasures but they were all bored. They were unable to die even though many tried to commit suicide. After living there for a long time, Wasobioye sailed away again, because to all the immortals life had become a burden.

2. There once was a man called Sentaro who wished to learn the secret of eternal life on Mount Fuji (see *Fujiyama*). He went to pray at the shrine of Jofuku, and suddenly saw a gigantic crane. On its back he flew to the land of Perpetual Youth. It appeared that the people there were so tired of their endless life that they ate poison in the vain hope that they would die. Seeing this, Sentaro returned home, content with a short life.

In The Thai Lord of Heaven. See *Phra In*.

In and Yo The Japanese equivalent of the two Chinese elemental principles, ying and yang. In is the female material element, associated with night. Yo is the spiritual aspect, the light element in both meanings of 'bright' and 'floating upwards'.

At one time in the beginning of history there was no distinction, only one fluid, indistinct chaos, so that the universe resembled an egg – the primeval Creation-egg. Gradually the limpid, transparent, light liquid rose to the top and became the sky, whereas the heavy, thick, opaque substance sank down and became the earth. See also *Creation*.

In Lao See *Deer*(1).

Ina (or Rona) A moon-goddess in the mythology of Mangaia in the

Cook Islands who was born in the land of Nunu-Tere, 'Swift Pigeons'. Her two brothers Rupe and Tangi-Kuku also had pigeon names. Ina travelled on the backs of fishes, even sharks, to find the famous chief *Tini Rau* on Motu Tapu, the 'Forbidden Island'. She found the chief, who came when she struck his *drum*, and they married. They went up to live in the sky, where the moon lived. They had two children, a daughter, Aroture, and a son, *Koro*.

On the island of Aitutaki (Hervey Islands) it is related that when her husband began to show signs of advancing age, Ina proudly said to him: 'You are stooping down towards the earth, therefore I will send you back to die on earth.' She created a *rainbow* and sent him down it to the earth.

See also *Tapa*(1).

Ina Moe-Aitu See *Tuna*(2).

Inari The God of Food or the Goddess of Rice in Japanese religious tradition, Inari is one of the most mysterious deities of *Japan*. Both male and female, s/he is sometimes kind, sometimes malicious, appearing like a beautiful woman, then suddenly changing into a fox. In every Japanese village there is a shrine dedicated to Inari as the giver of food and prosperity. Even in many houses s/he is venerated as the bringer of wealth and friendship. At shrines s/he is guarded by statues of foxes, divine messengers. Inari is also sometimes identified with Uga-no-Mitama, the Goddess of Agriculture. Inari's central temple is Fushimi-Inari in south-east Kyoto city, built *c.*700 AD . As *Rice-Goddess*, she is celebrated in a festival held during the first days of spring, when cultivation begins, and may be identified with the Indian Lakshmi and the Javanese *Dewi Sri*.

See also *Fox*; 'Gods of Japan' under *Gods*; *Kitsune-Tsuki*; *Possession*; *Spider*; *Tanuki*; *Yeta*.

Incarnation In Japanese *gonge* means 'incarnation', 'avatar'. A god, *kami*, or even the *Buddha* himself may decide to descend to earth in a human or animal form, or even in a stone.

In *Indonesia*, *jelma* is 'incarnation, coming to life'. In folktales a spirit, human or other, may enter the body of a dead man or animal. So the body has to be burnt lest an evil spirit enter it. This 'purifies' the body, so that no spirit may enter. Ancestors' *spirits* may come back as *birds* or butterflies (see *Butterfly*).

In Hindu myth, a man can be both a god's son and his incarnation, as *Arjuna* is of *Indera*.

See also *Awatara*; *Jobutsu*.

Incest In *Hawaii* it was considered a good thing if a chief married his sister, his niece or his daughter. Among the *Maoris*, however, this was illegal. See also *Oedipus*; *Sinta*.

Indalas (also Andelas) The ancient indigenous name of *Sumatra*. See *Malay Annals*.

Indara ('Mother Earth', 'The Maiden') See *Creation*(8); *Sun*(4).

Indera   The Indonesian form of the name of the Indian god Indra
(Japanese, Taishaku). In *Indonesia*, Indera is now only invoked in *Bali*,
but in *Java* there are still numerous tales told about Indera's power and
miracles. On Java and in the Malay-speaking areas, Indera still plays a
prominent role in the myths that are performed during the *wayang*
shadow plays. Indera is often called *Batara Guru*, 'Worshipful Master',
as he plays the part of the wise senior god who resolves conflicts in *heaven*
and on earth. He lives on the mountain *Mahameru* in Central Java. He
wields the lightning-weapon *vajra*.

Indera is also found in pre-Islamic Malay literature, as the Supreme
God. He may, whenever he wishes, incarnate in a prince, whose name
will then be Indra Kamajaya, 'Victory of Love', his parents having
learned in a dream that it has pleased Indera to become a man. The
handsome hero *Arjuna* is an *incarnation* of Indera. As a prince, Indera
will always marry the princess who is destined for him, but only after
numerous encounters with dangerous *demons*.

Indera Bayu   ('Divine Wind') In Malay mythology, a magical pet bird
owned by Princess Chaya Bulan, 'Moonshade'. Indera Bayu is a female
bird who knows all things and so, in the end, she becomes Prime
Minister to King Budiman and his son Lela Muda. She can cure all
*illness*es by her singing.

India   According to some scholars, India is the land of origin of the
Polynesians, who left it in early historic times, at least 3,000 years ago,
taking the Indus script with them.

Indian Gods   See 'Gods of Bali' under *Gods*.

Indonesia

History   In 1894, Dr Eugene Dubois discovered, on the island of *Java*,
remains of a primate which he named *Pithecanthropus erectus*, the erect
apeman, also called Java-man, one of the oldest species of apeman ever
found. This find proved that Java was inhabited by some type of human
being a million years ago.

It is 'only' 50,000 years ago – very roughly – as palaeontologists now
assume, that the *Australids* (the first people to populate Australia) lived
in Indonesia, in transit, as it were, from South-East Asia to Australia.
Gradually spreading out towards Australia, they were superseded in
Indonesia by later arrivals.

After them came the 'Proto-Malays', displaying a markedly different
appearance from the later Malayo–Polynesians as we know them in
western Indonesia, the type normally associated with the Malays. It
should be noted that some of the Javanese display features of a yet more
advanced human type. It has been said that such Javanese people
descend from Indian Brahmins.

The Malayo–Javanese brought with them *rice* and the system of its
cultivation: the submergeable field surrounded by a dam, the *sawah*.
*Sawah*s are the most characteristic aspect of the landscape in South-East
Asia.

The Malayo–Polynesians were also great seafarers, inventors of the *perahu*, the sea-worthy canoe which can be fitted with one or two outriggers. With these they sailed to the far corners of two oceans, to Madagascar, *Taiwan*, the *Philippines*, *Hawaii*, *Rapanui* and *New Zealand*, where closely related *languages* are still spoken. That great expansion may have begun in the second millennium BC.

The oldest surviving Indonesian *race*, the Weddids, are found today in the darkest forests of *Sulawesi* (the Toalas, Tomunas, Tokeas) and in southern Sumatera (official Indonesian spelling of *Sumatra*) are found the Kubus.

From an early date the Indonesian peoples were influenced by the great cultures of *India* and to a lesser degree, China. Statues of the *Buddha* have been found in places as far apart as Sumatera and Sulawesi, dating from the third century AD , sculpted in the Indian style.

The oldest known inscriptions in Indonesia, found on *Borneo* and Java, both datable at *c.*400 AD , are composed in the Sanskrit language. In the seventh century, the Chinese pilgrim I Tsing, on his way to India, praised the high standards of Buddhist scholarship in the South-East Asian islands. In that century there existed a kingdom in eastern Sumatera called Sriwijaya (Shri-Vijaya). Further north there was the kingdom of Malayu, with its capital where the city of Jambi now stands. The people of Malayu were great seafarers. They gave their name to the language which they spread to the far corners of the archipelago and to the Malay peninsula, which is named after them. The first inscriptions in an Indonesian language, in a Sanskrit-derived script, are composed in Malay.

Great temple complexes were built for the worship of the Hindu god *Siwa* (Shiva) on the Dieng plateau and in the valley of Prambanan in Java before 900 AD. The splendid Buddhist centre of pilgrimage called *Borobudur* was built not far from Jogyakarta *c.*800 AD by the kings of the Shailendra dynasty of Mataram. Learning and literature flourished as the old Javanese language was cultivated, with its own script. Powerful kings ruled Java, bearing Sanskrit names, from Purnavarman, *c.*415, to Vikramavardhana, 1389–1429, 1,000 years later.

By the late Middle Ages, Islam had begun to spread in the Indonesian cities, apparently arriving from India, carried by merchants from Gujerat. When a local ruler on Sumatera was converted, he would style himself henceforth Sultan, and the inscription on his tomb (many of which can still be seen today) would be composed in Arabic, and later in Malay in Arabic script.

In 1511, the Portuguese captain Gomes d'Abreu visited the Moluccas, the first European in Indonesian waters after Marco Polo stayed on Sumatera in 1293. The next Portuguese captain visited Halmahera. He was Magellan (Fernao de Magalhaes), who in 1521 sailed along the Moluccas, having traversed the Great Ocean, which he called *Oceano Pacifico* (because it was calm then), on his way to the *Philippines*, where he would later be killed. The Portuguese built a fortress at Ternate (1522) near Halmahera and by 1540 had established their authority over the Moluccas (Amboina).

Meanwhile, Islam gained ground in many towns of Indonesia, including Jacatra, now Jakarta. *Senapati* (d.1601) was the last great Hindu king of Java. The next great ruler was Sultan Agung Abdur Rahman, 1613–45, a Muslim.

The first explorers to arrive from Holland were the brothers Houtman (1596). One of them perceived the relationship between the Malay, Achinese and Madagascar languages. Gradually the Dutch merchants expanded their power over what was to become Indonesia. They were not interested in conquering land, since the Republic of the Netherlands had no king to conquer for, unlike the Spaniards and Portuguese. The Dutch were determined, however, to protect their commercial interests at sea. They interfered in the *wars* between local rulers only if their lines of transport and their port facilities were threatened. By so doing however, they had to occupy the Moluccas and most of Java. As Sumatra and Borneo were of only peripheral interest, only the port cities were occupied.

This commercial empire ended when Holland was occupied by Napoleon (1795), and Java by Thomas S. Raffles for the British East India Company (1811). After the Napoleonic wars, a series of treaties between the British and Dutch governments settled the numerous claims of both parties, some justified, some less so. In this way, the British acquired all the territories which now form part of *Malaysia*, although its population is ethnically identical with most of the western Indonesians. On the eastern side, the Netherlands retained western *New Guinea*, even though its population is ethnically and linguistically completely distinct from the Indonesians.

During the second half of the nineteenth century, the Dutch East Indies prospered, becoming one of the richest countries in the world, with the cultivation of coffee (since *c.*1700), quinine (since 1815), tobacco (since 1863), sugar cane (since 1870), tea, cocoa, rubber, oil palm and groundnuts.

The last 20 years of Dutch rule were marked by the evolution of the Indonesian peoples' political consciousness.

Modern History After the liberation from the Japanese (late 1945) and the colonialists (late 1949), Indonesia was faced with a task for which the government was ill prepared: keeping the country together. There was no national coherence in a country speaking over 200 languages using 6 alphabets, living on 300 islands, belonging to all the world's great religions: *Buddhism*, Christianity, Hinduism, Islam and the original local Indonesian religions. So the government had to send troops to all the districts outside East Java to impose its will by force, so that some people whispered that one bunch of colonialists had replaced another.

Sukarno, well known for his anti-Europeanism and his sympathies for the new communist China, became president. He sought to create unity by his slogan: *Tanah satu, rakyat satu, bahasa satu* (One country, one people, one language!) A vigorous campaign was organized to teach the people the national language and to use it, even at home, instead of Javanese, Sundanese, Madurese and the rest, including Dutch, which many educated people still spoke. This campaign succeeded: today the *Bahasa Indonesia*, the national language, based on Malay, is spoken on all the islands except in the remote forests of Borneo and New Guinea. In 1972 a final agreement was reached with the Malaysian government, to unify the spelling of the two Bahasas, the two national forms of Malay, which now has well over 200 million speakers, making it the seventh language of the world. Out of this, an entirely new literature arose.

Less easy to achieve was the revival of the economy, ruined after years of warfare and Japanese rapaciousness. The old plantations were overgrown, and the demand for their products had been satisfied by other countries. It was only the rising oil price after 1973 that lifted the nation out of its poverty. Tourism only became gradually a top industry. Sukarno pursued a policy of 'guided economy', a sort of semi-nationalization, and 'guided democracy', permitting only agreement. By 1964, after 15 years in power, he made himself president for life and styled himself the 'Great Leader of the Revolution'. This revolution was being prepared by the PKI, the Indonesian Communist Party, with his full cooperation. It would remove the last vestiges of democracy and of the free economy, and align the country with North Vietnam and North Korea into an Asian Axis. On 1 October 1965, the Communists kidnapped six of the seven leading generals of the army and murdered them. (The one who escaped was General Nasution, the defence minister.) The army quickly regrouped under General Suharto, then commander of the Army Reserve, and mounted a counter-attack across the country. In the fighting of the next few weeks half a million people are said to have died. This abortive coup is known as the Gestapu Affair.

After the failure of the coup, Sukarno's position became untenable, so he had to retire. Suharto has ruled the country ever since, gradually improving the economy, which was dangerously inflationary, by admitting foreign experts to rebuild the means of production.

Indonesia is an incredibly rich country. It has everything, from oil and tin to tea and timber, rice and rubber. It can feed itself, in spite of a population increase of four per cent annually. The last Sumatran elephants are having to give way to expanding fields for cultivation. The nation as a whole still needs more schools, more textbooks, more teachers, more colleges, more science and more technicians. At heart the Indonesians are gentle and friendly people, though the majority are still poor. Only the militant Achinese have not been integrated. The proud natives of New Guinea do not wish to be 'Islamized', which is a process that some government officials equate with Indonesianization.

See also *Adat; Amulet*(5); *Aneka-Warna; Austronesia; Avaiki; Bali; Batara Guru; Betel; Birds*(1); *Black; Breadfruit; Buddha; Buta; Butterfly*(2); *Cassowary; Cat*(3); *Chandi; Chandra Kirana; Chichak; Cinderella; Cockatoo*(2); *Creation*(13); *Creator; Crocodile*(5); *Darma; the Dead*(2); *Death*(2); *Demi-Gods; Demons*(3); *Devata; Dewi; Dewi Sri; Dolphin; Dugong; Expansion; Fetish; Fig Tree; Flores; Garuda; Gergasis; Ginger;*

Gnomes; 'Gods of the Pacific' under *Gods*; *Guru*(1); *Hanuman*; *Head*(2); *Heaven*(1); *Incarnation*; *Indera*; *Islands*; *Jin Laut*; *Kancil*; *Kaseteran*; *Kay Islands*; *Keramat*; *Keris*; *Kesna*; *Kraton*; *Ladder of Heaven*(2); *Lang Kasuka*; *Liver*; *Melati*; *Moluccas*; *Monkey*(5); *Moon*(1); *Mother-Goddess*; *Nini Muni*; *Oracles*(2); *Pancha-Sila*; *Panja Tanderan*; *Papa*; *Parrot*; *The Philippines*; *Predestination*(1); *Pregnancy*; *Puntianak*; *Raksasa*; *Rasa*; *Rice*; *Rice-Bride and Bridegroom*; *Rice-Goddess*; *Rice Mother*; *Rice Soul*; *Semadi*; *Semangat*; *Shamanism*(1); *Shiva*; *Si Junaha*; *Si Lunchai*; *Snake*(3); *Soul*; *Sulawesi*; *Sun*(3); *Sweet Potato*; *Tangi'ia*; *Tapa*(2); *Tapas*; *Taro*; *Tiger*; *Tree-Spirit*(3)(8); *Turmeric*; *Volcano God*; *Wali*; *Waterlily*; *Wayang*; *Wisnu*.

Indra   See *Indera*.

Indra Kamajaya   ('Victory of Love') See *Indera*.

Indra Puspa   A Malay princess. See *Epic*(2).

Indraditya   A Thai king. See *Thailand*.

Infanticide   This was once a well-known custom in *Polynesia*, as it was in Australia. In Vaitupu it was *law* that two parents were allowed only two children. In Nukufeitau (*Tuvalu*) only one child per couple was permitted. This was the only way in which famine could be prevented.

Inga   (also *ingwa*) In Japanese Buddhist philosophy, fate, which is the inevitable result of the *law* of cause and effect. It translates the Sanskrit *karma*. *Ingwa-no-Ko* is a child of fate, a child with some defect.

Ingwa   See *Inga*.

Intelligence, Eight Forms of   See *Fujiyama*.

Inthra   See *Phra In*.

Inuvaylau   In the myths of the *Trobriand Islands* he was a man with a penis as long as a snake with which he could fecundate the women in their gardens while standing at the edge of their fields. When the women's husbands finally found him out, they tried to kill him, but he left their village voluntarily, weeping and cutting off pieces of his penis which petrified and can be seen there to this day.

Invisible City   In *Thailand* they relate that in the forest of Phetburi there was once a city whose citizens could make themselves invisible. Once a poor woodcutter had to spend the night in a tree and saw people come out of a hole in the ground. Later, he saw them come back and spoke to the last one to go back through the hole. It was a young woman. He fell in love with her and asked her to become his wife. She agreed and took him down into the hole with her. There he lived with her in a big city. They had children and were very happy. However one day he lied, and his mother-in-law told him: 'This is the City of Truth. Since you have lied, you must leave us.'

The man's wife wept, but obeyed her mother. She gave him a bag full of *ginger* roots and took him up to the hole in the ground, where she said goodbye to him. Then she vanished. He never saw her again, nor could he (or anyone else) ever find his way back to that secret city. In those days, ginger was unknown on earth and so the man sold it for much money.

Io (pron. 'ee-o'; or Iao) One of the Polynesian words for *God*, the Supreme Being. In Hawaiian the word *io* means a *hawk*, a bird whose name is in many languages not distinguished from the falcon. This may suggest that Io was once a sun-god, since the falcon was a universal symbol – or an identification – for the Sun-God. Also, it is quite possible that Io is the original name for God the *Creator*, but that later this holy name became *taboo* and so, the word *Atua*, 'The Old One', was used instead. Thirdly, it is possible that *Io* is related to *io*, Hawaiian for 'truth' or to Iao, the name for the planet Jupiter, but that is speculation.

The *Maoris* worshipped Io as the God of the House and of Knowledge. The combination of these two subjects is not as far-fetched as it seems. 'Knowledge' in many cultures meant knowledge of life, that is, of living in peace and having many children. For most peoples there is no more important knowledge than that which prolongs life and produces offspring. To that end a good marriage is necessary and, of course, a good house for the family to live in. So the god Io was invoked during the inauguration ceremony of a new house. It was he who selected *Tane*, the God of the Forests, as the one who would receive his secret knowledge, *wananga*, by which men live.

Io was praised in hymns as Io the Wise, Io of all Holy Knowledge, Io-Nui 'Io the Great', Io-Roa 'Io with the Long Tail' (like the falcon), Io-Taketake 'Io who Stays the Same', Io-Te-Wananga 'Io the Source of Knowledge', Io Matua 'Io the Parent', Io Mata-Ngaro 'Io of the Hidden Face' (referring to secret lore), Io Mata-Aho 'Io the Invisible', Io-Te-Waiora 'Io the Source of Life', Io Tikitiki-o-Rangi 'Io the Highest', Io Mata-Kana 'Io the Vigilant', Io-Te-Kore-Te-Whiwhia 'Io the Withholder' and Io-Matua-Te-Kore 'Io who has no Parents'. This last epithet suggests that he was the original Creator, himself uncreated. All things flowed from Io where he dwelt above the *sky* in Te Toi-o-nga-Rangi, the highest *heaven* of the 12 upper worlds. Indeed, Io was the Creator of 'the heavens and the dawn, which gave birth to light between the waters below and the sky above which Io had raised up'. (See also *Creation*(4).) He was known as Te-Io-Ora, 'The Living God', but also as Te-Io-Mate, 'The God of Death', because he creates our lives, at the end of which our *spirits* travel back to Io in the sky.

See also *Mareikura; Tangaroa*.

Ipomavea See *Taro*(1).

Ira In *Polynesia*, the Mother of the Stars, the Sky-Goddess.

Ira-Waru An ancient Polynesian fish-god. See *Hina-Ika*.

Ise-Jingu In *Japan*, the great shrine of *Ama Terasu* at Uji-Yamada.

Ishvara See *Iswara*.

Iskandar The Malay form of the name of Alexander the Great. Alexander, after his conquest of *India*, married its ruler's daughter. Their descendants became rulers of India. One of these princes travelled to *Malaya* where his descendants became, also by marriage, ancestors of the rulers of *Malaysia*, *Sumatra* and *Kalimantan*. See *Malay Annals*.

Island of the Blessed See *Tuma*.

Islands (Polynesian, *motu*; Indonesian, *pulau*) Here is the Samoan myth of the *creation* of the islands: Tagaloa the *Creator* sent his messenger, Savali, to the surface of the ocean. Savali first called up the eastern group of islands, the Tuamotu or Old Islands. They rose to the surface and began to grow like the leaves of waterlilies. Then he called the western islands, and *Fiji* (Viti) and *Tonga* rose up and spread out like flowers. Then Savali went to the centre, where he watched Tagaloa who was creating the most beautiful of all the new islands – Savai'i. Tagaloa appeared on the horizon in a black cloud, observed the islands and was pleased in his heart upon seeing their loveliness. Then he created a pair of human beings, called Atu and Viti, whom he charged Savali to accompany to Viti (Fiji) where they landed and settled. After this Tagaloa created another human couple, called Atu and Tonga, whom Savali conducted to Tonga. Thus a man and his wife were sent to every island in the ocean: Tele and Upolu were sent to the island of Upolu; Tutu and Ila to the island still called Tutuila.

(The larger islands, such as *New Zealand*, are not perceived as islands.) See also *Creation*; *Izanagi*.

Isora The Japanese God of the Seashore. See 'Gods of Japan' under *Gods*; *Tide Jewels*.

Issunboshi In Japanese mythology, a sage or priest of one inch in height. He travelled on water in a rice bowl, paddling with a chopstick. He defeated two *demons* with a needle.

Iswara The Thai form of Ishvara, the Supreme God, *Siwa*. (The Balinese tradition is very different because of long isolation: see 'Gods of Bali' under *Gods*.)

Iva In Polynesian dirges, Spirit Land, where the *souls* live.

Ivi Apo See *Creation*(2); *Sex*.

Ivo In the mythology of south *New Guinea*, Ivo was the first man born from the earth who visited *heaven*, where he learned the knowledge of the first ritual practices. His wife Ukaipu was born from a wild *ginger* root and they are the ancestors of the Orokolo people.

Iware-Biko The first Emperor of *Japan*, also known as *Kamu-Yamato*. *Jimmu Tenno* was his later given name. See also *Tenno Heika*.

Iwazaru See *Monkey*(4).

Izanagi The first of the Japanese *gods* to descend to earth, arriving with his sister *Izanami*; down here they became man and wife. Izanami gave birth to the gods, and her last child, the Fire-God *Kagu-Tsuchi*, was the cause of her *death* (see *Izanami*). She went down to Yomi, *Hades*. Izanagi was disconsolate, so he went in search of her. She asked him not to look at her, but he lit a flame in the darkness anyway and saw his wife as an ugly corpse. Then he was pursued by the terrifying *monsters* of dark Yomi-land. He threw down his head-dress, which became a bunch of grapes. The monsters paused to eat the sweet fruit, enabling Izanagi to escape from Hades. See also 'Gods of Japan' under *Gods; Izanagi*.

Izanami   The first Japanese goddess and the first human being to die, twin-sister of *Izanagi*, whom she married. They descended to earth. At that time there was only the primeval ocean. Onogorojima was the first island; Izanami gave birth to the other *islands*, the trees, streams, mountains, plants and gods. Her firstborn was *Ama Terasu*, the Sun-Goddess, the 'Great Deity who Illuminates Heaven'. The Moon-God was born next, Tsuki-Yumi, who, it was decided, should become Ama Terasu's husband, so he too was sent to heaven, but the Sun-Goddess quarrelled with him and banned him to the night sky. Next, Izanami gave birth to *Susanowo*, the Storm-God, a young man of impetuous temperament. Her last child was Kagu-Tsuchi, the Fire-God, who hurt his mother during his birth so badly that she died and went down to live in the land of Yomi, *Hades*. Her husband found her there, lit a flame, against her wish, and saw that she had become an ugly corpse, surrounded by the gods of the *Nether World*, the deities of the earth, fire, mountains and thunder. He escaped but Izanami remained in Hades.
     See also 'Gods of Japan' under *Gods; Izanagi*.

Izumo   Izumo is a small but very old country town on *Japan*'s west coast where there is a great temple in which the *gods* meet annually in October to discuss the fate of humanity and the love affairs of individuals.
     See also *Assembly of the Gods*; 'Gods of Japan' under *Gods; Omitsunu; Sukuna-Biko; Susanowo*.

J

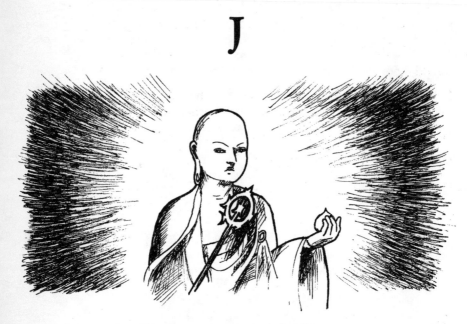

Jizo Bosatsu, protector of children

Jackfruit See *Breadfruit*.

Jaka Tingkir (or Mas Krebet) The Sultan of Pajang, *Java*, who may have lived in the sixteenth century. Many miraculous tales are told about him, such as that he could walk on water and command the *crocodiles*, and that on the darkest nights his face would shine brightly with divine light.

One night while Sultan Pajang was asleep with his four wives, covered only by his royal robe, four murderers sneaked in, sent by his enemy, Prince Panangsang. The assassins raised their daggers and stabbed the ruler, but the royal skin would not let the steel pass. The daggers flashed in the moonlight as they came down yet again, but in vain, for the Sultan's body remained as smooth as marble. Not even a scratch was visible. The women then woke up and screamed. The *dodot*, the royal robe, flew up like a giant bat, attacking the murderers and scattering them on the floor so that their daggers fell clattering on the stones. The Sultan rose and his murderers fell with their faces on the ground before him, exclaiming, 'Shadow of God! Have mercy! We are only tools, eunuchs of Prince Panangsang.'

Jaka Tingkir dismissed them, saying, 'If God wishes to keep the skin whole, no steel can cut it; if He wishes to keep the blood in the body, it will not flow. It is not the knife that cuts the flesh, it is God. So go in peace. Here, have some money.'

After this, his intended murderers became his loudest admirers. Later he had Panangsang killed in battle and became king of the whole lovely island of Java. Prince *Senapati* ruled after him (see *Prambanan*).

Jalatunda A well. See *Underworld*.

Jamajaya A Javanese king. See *Giants*(2); *Keris*.

Jan See *Spirits*(4).

Janaka

1. In Javanese *wayang* tales, this is another name for *Arjuna*.
2. In the *Ramayana*, King of Mithila, father of *Sita*, Rama's wife.

Janszoon, Willem A Dutch explorer. See *New Guinea*.

Jantam The King of *Kalimantan*. See *Kilir*.

Japan Officially, Japan's history begins in November 660 BC, when *Jimmu Tenno*, the 'Son of Heaven', ascended the throne as the first emperor. The Japanese call their country Ni-Hon-Go, 'The Rising Sun Country'; the emblem of the *sun* is also found on the Japanese flag (but see also *Chrysanthemum*).

Modern historians do not feel confident about Japan's history until 1,000 years later, even though the chronicles record a continuous line of 17 emperors, who averaged 100 years of age each. In the late fourth century AD , the first empress, *Jingo*, invaded *Korea* and colonized its southern tip. This had two beneficial results for Japan: the introduction of *Buddhism* and the art of writing, in Chinese characters. Korean and Chinese craftsmen settled in Japan, bringing their skills, arts and techniques (such as metal work and silkworm culture) with them. Buddhism developed its own unique cultural form in Japan, based on Chinese rather than Indian models, and has given Japan its national religion, *Shinto*, with its colourful rituals, its moral philosophy.

The essence of mainstream Shintoism is that Japan belongs to the *gods* and its people are their descendants. Male heirs were once considered essential to worship the ancestors and continue their lineage (for this reason in the century following 1890, the Japanese population trebled from less than 40 million; polygamy was permitted until 1945). Ancestors are worshipped at a shrine in or near the family home; its size depends on the importance of the family. The head of the clan speaks to the ancestors to announce important events, such as births and deaths in the family. Even the emperor speaks to his ancestors at their shrine in Ise, Kyoto. These ancestors include *Ama Terasu*, the Sun-Goddess, the Mother of the Nation, for all Japanese people are cousins: the nation is one family. Every morning, many Japanese housewives place bowls of rice before the family ancestors, whose spirits are alive and present, as well as before their husbands. Buddhism is not inimical to Shinto and never replaced it, but many Japanese belong to both religions. Many of the Shinto deities were also integrated with Buddhist deities.

Japan first learned artistic splendour and luxury from the T'ang dynasty in China (618–906), while Japanese literature became established during the Heian period (794–1185), in which both poetry and political life were rigidly conventionalized.

Though in Japan only one imperial dynasty has reigned for the last 15 centuries, the majority of the monarchs were 'rois-fainéants', leaving the affairs of state to a *kampaku*, 'civil dictator', a sort of *major domus*, usually belonging to one of a small number of clans such as the Fujiwara family, later the Taira military clan. The latter was overthrown by the Minamoto family in 1185. The leader of this new dynasty of regents was the first to receive, from the emperor, the title of *tai-shogun*, 'great general'.

In 1274 and 1281 the Mongol Emperor of China, Kubilai Khan, launched two attacks on Japan with enormous armadas. Both invasions ended when sudden *storms* wrecked the enemy's fleets. Even today this providential interference of Heaven is still remembered as *kami-kaze*, 'divine wind'. The term is associated with suicidal defence because the Japanese warriors of 1274 fought to the death and it was believed that it was for this bravery that the gods rewarded Japan. The priests, however, attributed the victory to their constant prayers and vigils. It was hoped that a similar sign from the gods would keep the Americans away in 1945, but nothing happened.

The period of the shogunate of the Ashikaga family at Muromachi, 1339–1573, was a time of great development of the·arts and the philosophy of Zen, which stressed the need to seek unity with nature. Thus landscape painting flourished. So did trade: the Japanese sailed to the coasts of Asia as merchants and pirates, and Osaka became a leading port city. Money replaced rice as the exchange currency. These contacts increased China's influence on Japan's art and thought.

Even more portentous, however, was the arrival of the first Spanish missionary, Francis Xavier S.J. in 1549. The most important technical novelty then to come to Japan was gunpowder, as used in the Spanish musket. This new weapon enabled the Daimyo (feudal Lord) Oda Nobunaga to defeat his neighbours and become Japan's leading nobleman in 1578. Oda Nobunaga conversed with the Jesuits and showed them respect, which was mutual.

Japan then showed inclinations toward imperialism by two expeditions to Korea (1592, 1597), which were intended to open the way for a conquest of China. They met with little success, however, owing to the Korean invention of the first armoured battleship.

At this time, the peasant Hideyoshi (d.1598), who became a *kampaku* of Japan, not only dealt effectively with the divisive nobility, the *samurai* class, but also succeeded in reconstructing Japanese society after a century of civil strife among the '60 kingdoms of Japan'. Tokugawa Ieyasu (d.1616) then completed the pacification of the country.

In 1614 the spread of Roman Catholicism made the Spanish priests too overbearing in the eyes of the Japanese nobility, so Ieyasu had them expelled, their churches demolished and the Christian religion prohibited. His son Hidetada besieged the last Christians in Hara castle near Nagasaki and massacred them in 1638. However, since the Second World War, Shinto has no longer been the state religion and there are now a large number of Christians in Japan.

The Japanese nobility rightly saw their position threatened by foreign ideas, so after 1638, only Dutch traders were permitted to trade with the Japanese government. All other foreigners were banned from the country and no Japanese were permitted to travel overseas. Japan locked its doors for 230 years, except for the scientific instruction the Japanese constantly requested, and received, from the Dutch doctors at Deshima, where the Dutch 'consulate' remained operative for three centuries. The new scientific knowledge was adopted by the nobility, who took care that the common people should not learn such dangerous wisdom.

From 1616 to 1867, the government of the shoguns of the Tokugawa family continued in power, a remarkable achievement. It was finally brought down by the following factors:

a) Pressure from Europe and America;
b) An attack by an alliance of the feudal lords whom the shoguns had kept out of the government;
c) A challenge from the reawakening imperial court at Kyoto;
d) The over-conservative structure of the government itself, which made it incapable of resisting the gradual evolution of Japanese society, as a result of the inevitable 'seeping' of scientific knowledge and the ideas of the Enlightenment.

In spite of several peasant risings, it was not the rise of a middle class or a working class that changed Japan. These uprisings did indicate, however, that the shoguns could not adapt to economic changes precisely because they were always intent on maintaining stability. Yet the shoguns did encourage learning, although this included Chinese philosophy, which in its Confucian form taught loyalty to the emperor, ultimately leading some intellectuals to wonder if the shoguns were not usurpers!

After 1716, Dutch scientific books were allowed to be imported, and were painstakingly translated into Japanese, especially books on medicine, geography, astronomy, etc. Very slowly some of this vast body of knowledge percolated through to the governing class, the functionaries and the merchants. This included a knowledge of overseas countries and their power. Contrast this Japanese curiosity with the Chinese disdain for all knowledge about foreign countries. In this way the Japanese knew about the Russian penetration to the Siberian east coast and to the islands north of Japan and Alaska.

In the nineteenth century Japan was forced to open up to outside influences. The British defeated China in 1842, and 'surveyed' the Ryu Kyu Islands, which were Japanese territory, in 1846. The Americans opened a door on the Pacific coast in 1850 by making California a state. Finally, in 1853 Commodore Matthew Perry sailed into Yedo Bay (now entirely surrounded by Tokyo City) and demanded that the shoguns

open Japan to international trade, similar to the trade with China. If the
shogun government refused they knew Japan would be occupied and
become a colony, yet if they yielded they would lose face. So they
procrastinated. Meanwhile they requested, and were given, a ship by the
Dutch government, the first steamship owned by Japan. Dutch officers
were sent with it to teach modern navigation methods. So, naturally, the
first foreign treaty signed by the sixteenth shogun, Iesada, was with the
Netherlands, in 1855. It was only in 1857 that the American Consul
Townsend Harris concluded a treaty with, and saw, Iesada, who agreed
that 'Intercourse shall be forever.'

For a decade, however, Japan still hesitated between repulsion and
admiration of the foreigners. Finally, though, it proved inevitable to
imitate them, because Japan wished to remain a military power. The first
clan to organize a Western-style militia was the Choshu family, so that
from 1866 until 1945 that clan dominated the military establishment;
similarly, the Satsuma clan dominated the navy, after their city, Satsuma
on South Kyushu, was bombed by the British Navy in retaliation for
attacks on British officers.

In 1867 the imperial dynasty was restored to its original position. At
the age of 15, Prince Meiji ascended the throne, and presided over the
rise of Japan as a world power. (He died in 1912.) In the 30 years between
1867–1897, Japanese imports of raw materials quintupled while Japan's
exports rose 20 times. In 1872, compulsory education was instituted,
making Japan in 50 years the most literate nation of the world.

In 1875 a Japanese force was sent to Formosa to 'deal with' the natives
who had maltreated some Japanese fishermen, and in the same year the
first conflict over territory arose, with Russia, which coveted Sakhalin
(in Japanese, Karafuto). Japan agreed to give up Sakhalin, but claimed
the Kurille Islands, which have only strategic value. For the first time
a foreign power dealt with Japan on an equal footing. Thirty years later
the balance had shifted: Japan sank the Russian fleet, beat the Russians
at Mukden and so regained half of Sakhalin and half of Manchuria.
(They took the other half of both in 1931.)

In 1879, Japan incorporated the Ryu Kyu Islands. In 1889 the emperor
instituted Parliament and, in 1890, a constitution. The war with China
of 1894–5 netted Japan Formosa, the Pescadores and Port Arthur, which
it had to give up under Russian pressure, the cause of an enmity which
was to last for a century. The Japanese victory of 1905 was the first
setback of a European power in Asia. The Russians took revenge in 1945.

In 1900 Japan concluded an alliance with Great Britain that was to last
till 1921. In 1910 Korea was annexed. During the Great War Japan
mopped up German resistance in *Micronesia*. The Great War was a boon
for Japanese industry, especially shipbuilding. In 1931 all of Manchuria
was occupied. In 1945, Japan had to give up all its acquisitions. In the
same period, the emperor disclaimed any form of divine ancestry. The
myth had ended.

See also *Aizen-Myoo; Akasa-Garbha; Ama Terasu; Amida; Angels;
Anshitsu; Asagao; Assembly of the Gods; Auahi-Turoa and the Fire Children;*

Awabi; Badger(1); Bato; Bees; Bells; Benkei; Benten; Bimbogami; Bimbomushi; Birds(2); Bishamon; Biwa(1); Blue Dragon; Bommatsuri; Bonin Islands; Bosatsu; Bridge; Bridge of Heaven; Bronze; Buddha; Butsu; Butsudan; Butsudo; Butsugaku; Butsuji; Butsuma; Butterfly(1); Carp; Cat(1); Centipede; Chaking; Cherry Tree; Chrysanthemum; Chujo Hime; Corpse-Eater; Cricket(1); Crystal; Daibutsu; Daikoku; Daimoku; Dainichi; Dainichi-Nyorai; Dandoku; Daruma; the Dead(1); Death-Stone; Demons(1); Dengyo; Dog(2); Dogen; Dragon; Dragonfly; Dreams(2); Dress; Ekibiogami; Elements; Emma-o; Enoshima; Epic Poetry; Fan; Fire(1); Fire-Face; Fire-God; Fireball; Firefly(1); Fly; Footprint of the Buddha; Fox; Frog(2); Fudo; Fudo-Myoo; Fugen-Bosatsu; Fujin; Fujiyama; Futon; Gaki; Gakido; Gama; Gama-Sennin; Genno; Ghost-Mother; Ghosts(1); Ginger; Goddess of the Mountain; 'Gods of Japan' under Gods; Grass-God; Grasshoppers; Hachiman; Hammer; Hannya-Shinkyo; Harai; Hare; Hasu; Hasu-Ko; Hero-Day; Hidari; Hidesato; Hina-Matsuri; Hoderi and Hoori; Horse; Hotoke; Hototogisu; Ichiko; Idzumo; Iha-Naga; Iki-Ryo; Immortality; In and Yo; Inari; Incarnation; Inga; Ise-Jingu; Issunboshi; Izanagi; Izanami; Jigokomushi; Jigoku; Jingo; Jingu; Jizo; Jobutsu; Jodo; Joshi; Kaguya; Kakemono; Kami; Kamidana; Kaminari; Kane(1); Kannon; Kappa; Ki; Kintaro; Kirin; Kishi-Bojin; Kishijoten; Kishimo; Kitsune; Kiyo; Ko-no-Inari; Koan; Kobo Daishi; Kodomo-no-Inari; Kojiki; Kokutai Shinto; Kongo; Kongo-Kai; Koromo; Koshin; Koya-no-Myoin; Ksitigarbha; Kuruma; Kuya-Shonin; Ladder of Heaven; Liver; Lotus, Golden; Migration of Souls; Miko; Miro; Mirror; Misogi-Kyo; Miyazu-Hime; Mochi; Momotaro; Momoye; Mondo; Monju Bosatsu; Monkey(4)(5); Moon(3); Moon-Bird; Morning-Glory; Mountain Man; Mountain Woman; Musubi-no-Kami; Mijo-Jo; Natatsu-Hime; Namu-Amida-Butsu; Nara; Nembutsu; New Year; Nichiren; Ninigi; Nyorai; Oho-Kuninushi; Omitsunu; Omokage-no-Ido; Oni; Otter; Oya-Shima-Guni; Peach; Pear; Peony; Pheasant; The Philippines; Pillow; Pine Tree; Plum Tree; Possession; Predestination; Raicho; Raiden; Raiju; Red Bird; Reincarnation; Rice; Rinzai; Ryujin; Sanganichi; Satori; Sea-King's Palace; Sea-Serpent; Semebito; Semmai-Doshi; Sengen; Senju; Sennin; Shaka; Shi-Ryo; Shi Tenno; Shichi Fukujin; Shinden; Shinju; Shinto; Shinto-Shrines; Shito Dama; Shodo Shonin; Shojo; Shotoku; Shugendo; Singapore; Skeleton; Skulls; Snow-Spirits; Soryo; Soto; Sotoba; Sparrow; Spider; Spider-Boy; Spider-Woman; Stones(1); Suijin; Sukuna-Biko; Susanowo; Sword(1); Tadanobu; Takami-Musubi; Takara-Bune; Tanabata; Tanuki; Taro; Temmu; Tendai; Tengu; Tenjin; Tennin; Tenno Heika; Tenrikyo; Thunder Baby; Tide Jewels; Toad; Tokoyo-no-Kuni; Tokutaro-San; Torii; Tortoise(1); Toshogu; Toyo-Tama; Toyouke-Omikami; Toyouke-Bime; Treasure-Raining Sutra; Tree-Spirit(1); Turtle; Uba; Ujigami; Urashima; Uwabami; Uzume; Vairocana; Vampire(1); Violets; Visu; Waterlily; Weaver; Whale(2); White Tiger; Will o' the Wisp; Willow Tree; Witch(1); Yama-Uba; Yamato Take; Yamoto; Yasha; Yegara-no-Heida; Yeta; Yofune-Nushi; Yomi; Yorimasa; Yoromitsu; Yoshitsune; Yosho; Yosoji; Yuki-Onna; Za-Zen; Zushi.

Japanese Gods   See 'Gods of Japan' under *Gods*.

Jata

1. In the *Dayaks'* mythology, the son and helper of *Mahatara*, the Supreme God. See *Creation*(6).
2. The Dayak word for 'God'.
3. Sea *demons* who may cause cholera. See *Demons*(3).

Jataka In *Buddhism*, the previous existences of the *Buddha*. Over 500 Jataka tales are circulating in *Thailand* alone. These are moralistic legends of the Bodhisattvas (see *Bosatsu*), comparable to the parables of Jesus. The Thai collection of these tales is known as *Panyasa-Jataka*.

The best known Jataka tale is that of the burning house. The Buddha said: 'I am like a man who knows that a certain building is on fire, Inside, people are feasting, unaware of the danger. I have to persuade them to leave the building quickly to escape imminent suffering.' The burning building is the image of this world, full of hot desires which will cause pain later. Those who perceive this will abandon this world and overcome all desire.

See also *Monkey*(3).

Java The Javanese have always been a very religious people. They have an ancient culture in which Hinduism blended with the religion of the original Malayo–Polynesians or Austronesians. Later, during the Middle Ages, *Buddhism* was introduced and the Javanese learned to worship the Bodhisattvas side by side with Shiva and Indra (see *Siwa* and *Indera*). In the late Middle Ages Islam was introduced by merchants from the western Indian Ocean and began to spread slowly across the island. In many parts of Asia, Islam was imposed by the sword so that the people were completely Islamized in one generation, but in Java the expansion was more peaceful, so that the Javanese retained many features of their ancient culture and so preserved their unique Javanese identity. As a result they created a singularly Javanese Islamic culture in which mysticism played a much greater part than in the Arabian countries. Their Islam still reflects, in a way, the spirit of Buddhist pacifism. Their lives are not motivated by the keen mercantilism of the Arabs. Indeed, the Javanese peasants have always been the victims of the Arab money-lenders, who often pretended to be members of the Prophet's family.

The Javanese mind is reared in the warm valleys of what has been described by many travellers as the most beautiful island on earth. Grace and gentle beauty surround the children of Java so that they imagine a divine world without conflict, a dreamy heaven that could hardly be more colourful than their own island. Their relationship with God is, likewise, one of gentle trust and benign providence, quite different from the total submission demanded by the Allah of the Arabs, whose aggressive concept of Islam has led to numerous conflicts. Javanese Islam, on the contrary, is tolerant. People are permitted, even now, to bring food and flowers to the worn statues of gods and Buddhas, or to the graves of famous saints and ancestors. Javanese religion is all-embracing rather than proudly exclusivist. Since the Javanese now number over 70 million, they are one of the two most numerous Islamic peoples on earth, with Bangladesh.

See also *Abdul Ra'uf of Singkel; Abiasa; Aji Saka; Ambiki; Ambu Dewi; Anantaboga; Anta Kusuma; Arjuna-Wiwaha; Asmara; Awatara; Bagawan; Bairawi; Bale Kenchur; Bantam; Basuki; Bherava; Bima; Bluebottle; Borobudur; Brahma(1); Bratayuda; Bromo; Bujangga; Burisrawa; Butterfly(1); Creator; Cricket(3); Crocodile(3); Dalang; Damar Wulan; Dasamuka; Death(2); Devata; Dewi Gandari; Dewi Nawang Wulan; Dewi Sri; Drestarata; Drupadi; Dukun; Durga; Duryudana; Firefly(2); Gandamait; Ganesa; Gatutkaca; Ghosts(2); Giants(2); Glass-Man; Guru Minda; Hanuman; Hare; Indera; Indonesia; Jaka Tingkir; Janaka(1); Javanese Mysticism; Jin Laut; Joshi; Kala; Kali Jaka; Kalong; Kancil; Karna; Kayon; Keris; Kesna; Korawa; Kraton; Kresna; Kyai Blorong; Lakon; Lara Jonggrang; Lutung Kasarung; Macan Gadungan; Mahabharata; Mahameru(1); Maitreya; Makara; Manjushri; Manyura; Melati; Migration of Souls; Monkey(6); Moon(1); Naga(2); Narada; Navel; Nilawati; Ocean-Goddess; Pancha-Tathagata; Pandawa; Panja Tanderan; Panji; Pata; Prambanan; Pratiwi; Python(3); Raden Rahmat; Ramakien; Ramayana; Rangsang; Rasa; Ratna Dumilah; Ratna Jumilah; Rice-Bride and Bridegroom; Rice-Goddess; Rice Mother(2); Sadono; Said of Kalijaga; Sakti; Sanghyang Tunggal; Sangiang; Sarong; Semar; Sembadra; Senapati; Singapore; Sinta; Sita; Snake; Star; Subadra; Sunan Bonang; Sunan Gunung; Swine; Topeng; Tresnawati; Underworld; Vasudeva; Volcano God; Wajera; Wali; Wall Oil; Watu Gunung; Wayang; Werewolf; Werkudara; Widyadari; Wijaya-Kusuma; Wilotama; Yudistira.*

Jayanagara   One of the Dhyani Buddhas. See *Pancha-Tathagata*.

Jayawardhana   One of the Dhyani Buddhas. See *Pancha-Tathagata*.

Jelma   See *Incarnation*.

Jewata   See *Devata*.

Jigokomushi   In Japanese mythology, 'hell-insect', the ant-lion, *myrmeleon*, of the suborder Planipennia, order Neuroptera, class Insecta. The larva digs itself a small conical pit in the sand and buries itself at the bottom. Ants falling into the pit are seized and eaten. The adult becomes the ant lion fly.

Jigoku   (or Jugokudo; also Naraka) In Japanese *Buddhism*, one of the many hells, the lowest form of existence.

Jiki-Ketsu-Gaki   ('Bloodsuckers') See *Gaki*.

Jikoku   See *Shi Tenno*.

Jilted Lover   In *Malaysia*, a girl must be very careful about whom she rejects. The resentful lover might well change himself into a *tiger* one night and devour her.

Jimmu Tenno   The first Emperor of *Japan*, also known as *Iware-Biko* and *Kamu-Yamato*. See also *Tenno Heika*.

Jin In *Malaysia* and western *Indonesia*, *jins* are a race of *demons*. See *Malay Annals; Sang Gala Raja Jin*.

Jin Laut An Indonesian sea demon; in Javanese mythology, a servant of the Goddess of the Southern Ocean (see *Ocean-Goddess*), who can kill a person by sitting on his chest.

Jingo The first Empress of *Japan* and the first monarch to initiate a policy of aggressive military expansion, hence the term 'jingoism'. See *Japan; Tide Jewels*.

Jingu In *Japan*, a shrine where a *Shinto* deity is worshipped.

Jinn See *Spirits*(4).

Jirohei See *Cherry Tree*(2).

Jizo In Japanese *Buddhism*, Jizo is the male counterpart of *Kannon*, the Goddess of Mercy, the Bodhisattva who is depicted as a wandering monk, to whom many miracles are attributed. His proper title is Jizo Bosatsu, the Japanese name for the Bodhisattva *Ksitigarbha*. He is a god of little children, a divine father, a Buddha-god who, instead of meditating eternally, walks upon earth to console mothers who have lost a child. Jizo also cares for fishermen by soothing the ocean's waves. If a statue of Jizo is carried to a house, its owner must give generously to those who carry it lest he be called a miser.

Jizo is also the graveyard keeper who protects dead *souls* against *oni*, evil spirits. To this purpose the mothers of dead children who are buried in graveyards build towers of stones, praying all the time to Jizo for protection. He hides the small souls in his sleeves and drives away the red-eyed *oni* with his staff, also guarding his charges at night while they play in the dry bed of the River of Souls. Jizo regularly visits the horrible halls of the Buddhist hell where the sinners live, the souls who could not contain their greed. He alleviates their pain and works for their salvation; he may even plead with the Death-God, *Emma-o*, for their release.

See also 'Gods of Japan' under *Gods*.

Juan A Philippine hero. See *Monsters*(3).

Jo and Uba See *Pine Tree*.

Jobutsu (Japanese for 'The Living Buddha', Jobutsu can also be translated as 'The Loving Buddha') This concept is based on the belief that at any time in history there will be at least one human being alive on earth who is at least a partial *incarnation* of the *Buddha*. It is not always easy to find him! This living Buddha looks like a normal man – though more modest and gentle than most – but inside that body there will be the absolute knowledge of the Bodhisattvas. One of the first masters to teach this doctrine of 'The Buddha Within' was Saicho (see *Tendai*); it has become immensely popular.

Jodo (or Gokuraku Jodo) The 'Pure Land' (see *Amida*) in Japanese

Buddhist cosmology, the equivalent of *Paradise*. There is also a sect of that name, founded by a sage called Genku or Honen, *c.*1200. He taught his followers to practise a simple faith and kindness, and to have faith in the *Buddha* Amida who will save all men in his mercy. All those who invoke Amida with a sincere heart will gain access to the 'Western Paradise of the Pure Land'. Honen had been charged by his dying father to forgive all sinners and lead all people to salvation.

Joshi ('Love–Death') In old *Japan* it was believed that if two lovers could not marry, it was a punishment for not keeping their promise to marry in a previous life. Lovers prevented from marrying by class or custom might tie themselves together and jump into a river or into the sea. They believed that they would be reborn and finally be permitted to marry each other in a following life. The belief that virtuous couples will rediscover one another and marry at last in a subsequent existence on earth goes back to ancient *India*, and is also common in Javanese myths. See also *Love; Reincarnation; Violets*.

Jugokudo See *Jigoku*.

Jurojin In Japanese myths, one of the *Shichi Fukujin*, the seven Gods of Good Luck, giving longevity. He is painted riding a white stag, smiling like a friendly old gentleman, accompanied by the *tortoise* (symbol of old age) and the crane for good luck in travelling. See also 'Gods of Japan' under *Gods*.

Juru The wise uncle and prime minister of *Senapati*. See *Senapati*.

K

Kannon, Goddess of Compassion, with the gem and wheel which satisfy desire

Kaahumanu A Hawaiian queen. See *Hawaii*.

Kabu A *soul* with a visible form. See *Life After Death*.

Kadzutoyo A wise young man. See *Badger*(2).

Kae The *Maori* name of a *tohunga* or priest who presided over the name-giving ceremony of the son of *Hina-Keha*, the Moon-Goddess. He travelled by riding a *whale* across the ocean, but succumbed to the wiles of a beautiful nymph, as did the Celtic priest Merlin.

Kaehehe See *Vailala*.

Kafar See *Monsters*(1).

Kagu-Tsuchi The Japanese Fire-God. See 'Gods of Japan' under *Gods*.

Kaguya A girl who was found in a bamboo field in *Japan* by a bamboo cutter. She was no taller than a hand at that time, but soon grew up to become the fairest in the land. Princes and dukes wooed her, but she set them difficult tasks, such as finding the *Buddha*'s own begging bowl, or a branch of the jewel-tree of Mount Horai, whose fruits are precious *stones*, or a fur robe made of the skins of the fire-proof rats who live in the land of Morokoshi. All her suitors deceived her by bringing counterfeit treasures. Eventually even the emperor heard of her beauty and travelled to the bamboo field in a litter to transport the lovely lady to his palace. When the litter arrived, however, she had disappeared. In the middle of the night the King of the Moon, *Tsuki-Yumi*, had sent down a silver throne for her, since he had long contemplated her beauty. Earthly weapons had no effect on the moon-men: the emperor's guards shot their arrows in vain at the moon-host. The moon-men simply ordered Lady Kaguya to make herself ready to depart with them at once to join the immortals and marry Tsuki-Yumi. She was never seen on earth again.

Kaha'i In Hawaiian myth, the God of Lightning. See also *Tawhaki*, the *Maori* god.

Kahausibware In the mythology of the *Solomon Islands*, a female spirit or goddess who created people, animals and trees. She made trees which gave fruits in such abundance that the people never had to work. Alas! With life, she also created *death*. It happened as follows: when the first *woman* had given birth to her first baby, she entrusted her child to the goddess, who had appeared to her in the form of a *snake*. The snake looked after the child until it began to cry and would not stop. Finally, confused by the noise, the snake coiled itself around the baby and strangled it. When the mother came back and saw what had happened, she took a stone and killed the snake. Enraged, Kahausibware left the people, who then had to work to eat.

Kahawali See *Pele*(1).

Kahiki In the Hawaiian tradition, the island from which the Hawaiians first sailed to *Hawaii*. It is identified with *Tahiti*. There is an ancient Hawaiian song which recalls the memory of Kahiki:

O Kahiki, land of the far-reaching ocean . . .
Indistinct are the land and the sun while we are approaching.

During the first few centuries after landing and settling in Hawaii the sailors remained in regular contact, as many Hawaiians sailed back to Kahiki to trade or even to marry, but by the time Cook arrived – in 1773 he watched a regatta of over 300 double *canoes* off Tahiti – all contact was lost.
See also *Nana-Ula; Navel of the Earth*.

Kaho Short for Kahomovailahi, a legendary blind old navigator from *Samoa* who could tell the exact location of a craft by feeling the sea with his hand. The King of Samoa knighted him for correctly predicting landfall. Kaho's descendants inherited his skill and were known as Fafaki-Tahi, 'Feelers of the Sea'. *Birds*, too, indicate the distance from land. See also *Navigators*.

Kahoali In Hawaiian myth, the God of Sorcerers to whom human sacrifices had to be offered, such as eyeballs with *kava*. See *Sorcerers*.

Kahomovailahi See *Kaho*.

Kahukura ('Rainbow') The symbol of man's mortality, a pathway from *heaven* to earth; an appearance of the Polynesian god *Rongo*, God of Agriculture and Cultivated Plants, also the name of a *Maori* fisherman (see *Fairies*(1)). See also *Ina*.

Kahuna A priest in the religion of the Hawaiians, a wise counsellor who also functions as a medicine expert. There are two types, the low-order *kahuna* who prays people to *death* by black *magic*, and the high-order priest who heals the sick with prayers and knows the art of white magic and herbal medicine. The priest will, during therapeutic ceremonies, pray to the *gods* of his own ancestors as well as to the national Hawaiian gods, who favour good health as soon as proper ceremonies are held.
   See also *Eleio; Tohunga*.

Kai The Polynesian word for food. See 'Gods of the Pacific' under *Gods; Kumara*(2); *Rongo; Sweet Potato; Taro*.

Kai-n-Tiku-Aba ('The Tree of Many Branches') This is the sacred tree of *Samoa*. It grew on the back of *Na Atibu*, the father of the *gods*, but one destructive man broke the tree down. His name was Koura-Abi. With the tree broken, the people became violent and scattered over the earth so that sorrow became their companion. Thus the people of *Kiribati* explain the cause of their long migration from Samoa.

Kai Tangata A *Maori* man, husband of *Waitiri* and father of *Hema*. See *Waitiri*.

Kaidu See *Malay Annals*.

Kaikomako When *Maui*, the great Polynesian Ulysses, extinguished all the fire on earth, the 'longheads' (flames) took refuge in the *kaikomako* tree, *Pennantia coymbosa*, which is still used to make fire by friction, because the tree harboured the fire inside itself. Hence the tree's name, Hine-Kaikomako, 'Mother Kaikomako', since all men and women have to carve a piece of her body to make fire (*hika ahi* = to beget fire). See *Fire*(4).

Kailasa See *Krailasa*.

Kaiser Wilhelmsland See *New Guinea*.

Kaitalugi A mythical island in Melanesia where ships are wrecked on the reefs and the sailors are washed up on the beach. There, they are awaited by a crowd of naked women who at once seize the men and rape them. As soon as one woman has 'had' a man, the next one will take him. The men are soon exhausted and die.

Kaitangata The son of *Rehua*. See *Rehua*.

Kakaluk See *Amulet*(3).

Kakemono In Japanese, a painting intended to be hung on the wall. A famous painter called Sawara painted a portrait, from memory, of the beautiful Kimi, who had loved him so much that she had cut her throat when she learned that she could not marry him, and died. When the portrait was complete, the painter hung it on his wall, but that night it came to life and there stood Kimi, with a large wound in her throat, which Sawara had not painted. This happened every night, so Sawara had to give the painting to the temple at Korinji where the priests prayed for peace for the spirit and her lover.

See also *Cherry Tree*(1); *Horse*.

Kala In Javanese and Balinese mythology, the ancient God of Time, the Kronos of Asia, and so the Death-God, whose appearance to a person was inexorably the sign of his approaching end. He gave wealth to young men on certain conditions, then, at the appointed time, reappeared to claim his due, punishing any defaulters. He was thus pictured as a terrifying Demon-God. Kala was identified with *Siwa* (Shiva), and 'Kala-heads' in Javanese sculpture are the heads of demoniac *monsters* associated with death and retribution. He may also be the Ocean-God; see *Sea-King*; *Waruna*. See also *Kalong*; *Kyai Blorong*.

Kalaikota A priest. See *Dasarata*.

Kalakaua A Hawaiian king. See *Hawaii*.

Kalamainu and Kilioa In Polynesian myths, two *lizard* women who keep the *soul* of the deceased imprisoned.

Kalamakua A cousin of the King of Oahu. See *Kelea*.

Kali Kali is the dreaded Hindu–Javanese and Balinese Goddess of Time, spouse of *Siwa* – *Bairawi* in Hindu–Javanese myth. She is another manifestation of *Durga*, the Goddess of Death, but is also the Goddess of Magic and Love-Potions and of Wealth. She is sometimes identified with Ratu Lara Kidul (see *Ocean-Goddess*) and *Lara Jonggrang*.

One day in the cosmic history an evil demon called Mahisura (see *Mahisa*), with his fellow devils, took the shape of a wild *buffalo* of titanic size and stormed heaven, chasing the gods from their own palaces. The Supreme God *Brahma* then assembled the gods for consultation on how to defeat Mahisura. The gods were so furious that as soon as they opened their mouths to speak, jets of divine wrath-fire streamed out. These rays of cosmic anger united and were formed by the divine will into unison, into a goddess of radiant beauty whom they called Kali, 'Black Female' (originally Kali was an Earth-Goddess, hence her black colour; the fire is, in all ancient mythologies, hidden in the earth, whence it emerges through the volcanoes, and in the wood of trees where it remains hidden until the wood is lit. Thus all fire can be seen to come ultimately out of the earth; see also *Fire*). Kali thus became the mightiest of all the goddesses and was given the divine energy of all the gods together in order to combat evil. This she did with great success. Her long war against the demons of the Evil World is sung in *epic poetry*.

See also *Ambu Dewi*; *Durga*; 'Gods of Bali' under *Gods*; *Ocean-Goddess*; *Sakti*; *Uma*.

Kali Jaka   A legendary Javanese king who may have lived during the late fourteenth century. He is credited with having promulgated and organized the establishment of Islam on *Java*. In this meritorious work he was assisted by eight learned sages, so that together they are known as the nine wise men who founded Islam on Java. Many miracles accompanied their good work.

Kalila and Damina   See *Panja Tanderan*.

Kalimantan   It is written in the *Chronicle of Kutai* that the first King of Kalimantan (southern *Borneo*) was a grandson of Alexander the Great (see *Iskandar; Malay Annals*) who married the daughter of the Raja of Dipa Negara, 'Island Country', the capital of which is Kota Waringin, 'Fig Tree City'. The young Prince Lembu, acting upon a dream, sailed down the river to where Banjarmasin now stands. In a waterfall he saw a lovely maiden whose name was Tunjung Buih, 'Lily of the Foaming Water'. Out of the sunrise, Suryananta, the Sun Prince, approached, married Tunjung Buih and became King of Kalimantan. See also *Dayaks*, who live in Kalimantan; *Puntianak*.

Kalong   In Javanese, the word for a 'flying fox' or large bat. It is said that when a man dies, the god *Kala* comes flying along in the night and takes the man's *soul*, disappearing with it.

Kalpavriksha   A wish-giving tree. See *Ksitigarbha*.

Kalulu   See *Spirits*(5).

Kama   The God of Love in Hindu cosmology.

Kama-Hua-Lele   A Polynesian bard and astrologer. See *Nana-Ula*.

Kamapua'a   The Great Boar, one of the *Creator* divinities in Hawaiian mythology. With his enormous snout he pushed up the earth from the sea bottom so that the *gods* and the people had a place to live and land to cultivate. He wielded a huge mace in battle against the enemies of the gods and the people, capturing their feathered helmets. He was a good god in spite of his fierceness for, amongst other things, he dug wells so the people had fresh water. He wooed the Goddess of Fire, *Pele*, but at first she was too proud to consider him. However, in the contest against her other suitors that followed, Kamapua'a won by extinguishing nearly all her fires with mud, so Pele yielded and they were married.

Kamapua'a may be compared to the Indian god Vishnu, who also had a mace and who, as *Varaha* the Boar, dug up the land.

Kamehameha   The name of five Hawaiian kings. See *Hawaii*.

Kami   *Kami* is often translated as 'heaven' because of its association with nature, the sky, rocks and mountains, waterfalls, rivers and the ocean. In Japanese dictionaries, it is rendered as 'God, the Almighty, the Lord', also 'a god, a deity, a goddess', and, as an adjective, 'divine, heavenly'. It may also have the plural meaning of 'gods, *spirits*'; this may include the *gods* of *Buddhism*, i.e. the Bodhisattvas, and the celestial gods of *Shinto*, first and foremost *Ama Terasu*, as well as the earth deities of nature, the Snow-Goddess and the deified ancestors whose shrines are venerated in the homes. Some scholars distinguish *amatsu-kami*, celestial *spirits*, and *kunitsu-kami*, terrestrial spirits.

Each *kami* has a symbolic representation, which may be a tablet with a Chinese character signifying the spirit's original name, or a statuette. These are placed in a shrine in the inner sanctuary. At shrines in the country, picnic meals may be consumed, signifying the new vigour which the freshly worshipped *kami* grants.

See also *Incarnation*.

Kami-Kaze ('Divine Wind') See *Japan*.

Kamidana In *Japan*, a family household altar, where the deity is worshipped with offerings of food.

Kamiko ('Child of the Deity') See *Miko*.

Kaminari ('Heaven's Noise') In Japanese mythology, Thunder Woman. She has been seen by some people in the shape of a heavenly queen.

Kampaku ('Civil dictator') See *Japan*.

Kamu-Yamato The first Emperor of *Japan*, also known as *Iware-Biko*. See also *Jimmu Tenno*, his later given name; *Tenno Heika*.

Kanaka The Hawaiian form of the Polynesian word *tangata*, 'human being(s), people'. It is the word by which the Hawaiians refer to themselves and has thus become the word for 'native' or Polynesian. In its French form, *canaque*, it is now used as far away as *New Caledonia* to refer to the original populations. See also *Polynesians; Race; Tangata*.

Kanaloa In Hawaiian myths, the *Creator*, the equivalent of *Tangaroa* in *Maori* mythology. He is also the God of the Underworld, who can teach *magic*. He appears in the shape of an octopus. There is a hymn to the Creator in which Kanaloa is addressed as *Kane*:

> O Kane, raising up continents
> Bringing forth the sky and the land
> Spreading out the rippling ocean
> Quickening the waves all restless
> Multiplying little fishes
> Fixing rows of stars in heaven . . .

See also *Tangaroa; Underworld*.

Kanapu See *Uira*.

Kanasoka A Japanese painter. See *Horse*.

Kanchil (Javanese; Pelandok, Malay; Pelanduk, Kancil, Indonesian) The smaller chevrotin, pygmy antelope or mousedeer, *Tragullus kanchil*. This shy forest animal, standing around two feet high, is extremely popular in Indonesian and Malay folklore. With its serious eyes, white goatee and grave mien, it reminds the hunter of the saintly scholar who, by his gentle persuasion and *magic* incantations, can influence men and spirits to obey the Law of Scripture. There are numerous fables in which the Kanchil outwits the Crocodile, the Panther and other predators. One day the Kanchil even persuaded the Tigers to live in peace with the other animals, by convincing them that it possessed powerful magic.

See also *Gerjis; Malay Tales*.

Kane

1. A bell which is struck at dawn in every *tera* (temple) in *Japan*.
2. In Hawaiian myths, the God of Procreation and the Sea. He was the maker of the three worlds, the *sky*, the earth and the 'upper' *heaven*, the ancestor of all human beings. He lived on earth for a time with his children, then withdrew to heaven. He is called Kane-Hekili, 'Thunderer', 'Lightning Breaking the Sky'. See also *Adam and Eve*(2); 'Gods of the Pacific' under *Gods; Heaven; Hiiaka; Kanaloa; Tane; Trinity*.

Kane-Hekili   See *Kane*.

Kane Hoalani   (or Kane Milohai) An ancient Polynesian god and father of the goddess *Pele* in the Hawaiian myths. Kane owned a seashell so small that a man could hold it in his hand. If placed on the ocean waves it would quickly grow into a splendid sailing ship, larger than any owned by man, with sails the colour of mother of pearl. The owner only had to name his desired destination and he would be carried there in no time. See also *Pele*(2).

Kane Milohai   See *Kane Hoalani*.

Kane-Oi-E   See *Trinity*.

Kangaroo   In west *New Guinea* there is a myth about Amori, a female kangaroo who followed the first human couple to where they lay down together. When they had left, Amori licked up the surplus sperm left behind on the beach. She did this several times until she was pregnant, as was the woman. They both gave birth to a human boy. Amori's son was called Sisinjori; Maniwori was the human mother's son.

Kanikani   See *Dance*.

Kannon   (or Kwannon, Japanese; Chinese, Kuan Yin) In Japanese and Chinese mythology the Goddess of Love and Mercy, the Far Eastern equivalent of the Virgin Mary as Saintly Mother. In Buddhist philosophy, her equivalent is Avalokiteshvara, or rather his Shakti, the white goddess Tara. She is represented in many forms, for instance: Sho-Kannon, 'Wisdom Kannon'; Nyoirin-Kannon, 'Omnipotent Kannon'; Senju Kannon, 'Kannon with a Thousand Hands' (to help people). As Goddess of Creation she is the deity who gives children to families. She is also the patroness of embroidery, an art which is very highly developed in *Japan*, in her *incarnation* as the humble nun *Chujo Hime*. The Dragons of the Four Elements reside under her feet.

Kannon's presence is so radiant and beneficent that she once turned hell into *Paradise*. So the God of Hell sent her back to earth, because hell should remain gloomy.

Thirty-three shrines are devoted to the worship of Kannon in Japan. In Nigatsu-Do, 'February-Hall', there is a copper statue of the goddess which at certain times becomes warm like a living body. On Mount Nariai there is a wooden statue of Kannon. The goddess once changed parts of it into cake to feed a starving monk.

Sometimes Kannon is represented as a male god, as indeed Avalokiteshvara was a manifestation of the *Buddha* and so, male. This 'confusion' can only be understood by the fact that the Japanese language, like Chinese, distinguishes no gender, and by perceiving the essence of Buddhist philosophy in which male and female merge, as all contradictions in life are united. By this very unison one living soul can feel the pain of another. This universal compassion is embodied by Kannon.

There is a tale of a pure golden statuette of Kannon which the emperor once gave to the Lord of Kii as a gift. A thief burgled the palace of Kii and stole the golden statuette. He should have known better than to touch the goddess with impure fingers. He was in a hurry to cross the bay in a boat, when a storm arose suddenly, overturned the boat and threw the thief overboard. His dead body was dredged up; the golden goddess was also discovered, and returned to the Lord of Kii.

See also *Goddess of Mercy; Sison; Shinju*.

Kanzakura   A sacred *cherry tree*. See *Musubi-no-Kami*.

Kanzo   See *Liver*.

Kappa   A Japanese water monster with long hair, the body of a tortoise, scaly limbs and an ape face. It attacks travellers and fights them. It sucks their blood under water as they wade through a river. It attacks animals too, including horses. A *kappa* travels on a cucumber, its preferred food. These cucumbers can fly like dragonflies. *Kappas* may once have been wise *monkeys*. They can be befriended by wise men, to whom they will teach the art of setting bones.

Kapu   See *Taboo*.

Kapuku   In *Polynesia*, the secret art of reviving the *dead*.

Karaeng Lowe   ('The Great Lord' in the Macassarese *language* of south-west *Sulawesi*) This translates Mahaiswara or Shiva (see *Siwa*). This god is venerated in a cave in the shape of a big phallus or *linga* by priestesses, when the *moon* is full. He is an almighty sea-god who determines people's good and bad luck. See also *Stones*(7).

Karakia   In *Polynesia*, a *magic* formula in poetic form, so it can be sung, hummed or softly intoned; an incantation to put a spell on people or animals, to escape from wild beasts or *demons*; a charm to protect the reciter against *illness*, drowning or fatigue. A *karakia* may put people to sleep or help a woman in labour to give birth without pain. It may make a cool heart fall in love with the singer. There are many different *karakias* for special purposes. Some are long, some are only a few words, but not a word must be omitted or disaster will strike. They are inherited from the elders, and are usually kept a family secret.

See also *Hautupatu; Pitaka*.

Karara-Hu-Ara See *Ngarara*.

Karawata See *Cockatoo*(1).

Karihi The brother of *Tawhaki*. See *Tawhaki*(2).

Karna In Javanese mythology, a warrior, son of the Sun-God Suria, who was born from the ear of his mother *Kunti*. He joined the *Korawas*.

Kartanagara One of the five Dhyani-Buddhas. See *Pancha-Tathagata*.

Kaseteran In Malay–Indonesian mythology, the Land of the Ghosts. Kaseteran is a dense, dark forest where the god *Siwa* reigns. There, the *spirits* dance before the eyes of trembling visitors. Only the heads with their luminous eyes are visible. Some *ghosts* creep along the ground, licking the travellers' feet in the dark with long cold tongues.

Kasuari See *Cassowary*.

Kat The Good God of the Banks Islanders, who taught the people how to hollow out a tree trunk and make a *canoe*.

Katwanga A mace. See *Siwa*.

Kaurava See *Korawa*.

Kava (also *awa, kawa*; literally 'bitter') An intoxicating beverage brewed from the roots of the *kava* plant, of the *Piperaceae* family. The peeled roots of the *kava* plant, *Piper methysticum*, were chewed by women and children. They would eject the pulp into a vessel where it was diluted with water and allowed to ferment. It is used as a sedative and narcoticum by Hawaiian healers, and is also used in Polynesian ceremonies.

The oldest function of *kava* may have been to quieten hunger. It was said that centuries ago the King of Tonga visited a distant island plagued by famine. The people had nothing to offer him, so one woman, in her zeal to offer the king good food, sacrificed her baby, cooked it and wrapped it in leaves as if it were a suckling pig. The king perceived in time that this food was *taboo* and ordered that the child should be given a princely burial. Out of the grave grew the *kava* plant which alleviates hunger.

See also *Hades*(2); *Kahoali; Miru; Tonga*.

Kawao An island king. See *Kelea*.

The Kay Islands (or Key Islands) These *islands* are located in Eastern *Indonesia*. It is related that the inhabitants are all descended from one man and his wife who once lived on the island of *Bali*. The man was chosen by the *gods* because he was the only virtuous man they could find. They built a magical ship for him and his family which overnight transported him and his sons, together with their wives and children, to Great Kay. The gods said, 'This is the best land on earth. Live here in peace with your offspring.'

The people thanked them, giving offerings to Nevi Yanan the Sea-God for a safe voyage, and to Raeit Ngabal, the Forest-God, to propitiate him prior to cutting down trees for building houses and clearing fields.

See also *Ngabal*.

Kayon (from *kayu*, 'wood') In the Javanese *wayang*, a stylized tree representing the Tree of Life and *Creation*, growing from earth to *heaven*.

Kaze-no-Kami The Japanese God of Wind and Bad Colds. See 'Gods of Japan' under *Gods*.

Ke Akua See *God*(1).

Kei See *Hasu-Ko*.

Keiko A Japanese king, the father of *Yamato Take*.

Kelana The pirate in the *wayang* performances. See *Topeng*.

Kelea The beautiful sister of Kawao, King of the Hawaiian island of Maui. She refused to marry and preferred to ride the waves on her *onini* (surfboard). The god *Lono* had said in an oracle that 'in riding the surf Kelea will find a husband'. But how?

On the island of Oahu there lived at that time a handsome prince, Lo-Lale, brother of Piliwale, King of Oahu. The latter had only daughters so he was anxious that his brother should marry and beget an heir to the throne. So a *canoe* was readied to travel in search of a wife for the prince. Kalamakua, the king's cousin, an adventurous young man, was put in charge of the expedition. He sailed to Molokai first, but, finding no suitable princess there, he set sail again in the direction of Maui. A mile or more from the beach they spotted Kelea, who was swimming. Kalamakua invited her on board and hauled her out of the waves, but just as they were turning towards the land, a sudden storm arose and blew them far away into the ocean. As soon as the wind calmed and became stable again, Kalamakua, an accomplished navigator, set his course not to Maui but to Oahu. Kelea too, was familiar with the seas and observed that they were not sailing to her home island. She remarked, 'If you are taking me away, my brother will make war on you.'

'He will have work for his spears,' retorted Kalamakua, but with a captivating smile. 'I want you to meet my cousin the King of Oahu, and his brother, who needs a bride.'

After a night, a day and another night, they landed in Oahu, where Kelea was received with all the honours due to a sovereign's daughter.

When Lo-Lale met her he fell in love with her at once, and she consented to marry him before consulting her brother, which of course was an affront to the King of Maui. So, immediately after the wedding, Kalamakua was dispatched to Maui, to use his diplomatic skills in the interests of the dynasty. He succeeded in convincing King Kawao that he had not, owing to adverse winds, been able to land in Maui with Kelea, but had been forced to sail home instead, and also that she, King Kawao's sister, was now married to a prince and that, if she had a son, he would one day be King of Oahu. Indeed, Kelea had three children. Yet later she divorced Lo-Lale and married Kalamakua, that Lancelot of Hawaii. They had a daughter who married her cousin, King Kawao's son. All this happened 16 generations ago.

Ken Tamboehan See *Kin Tambuhan.*

Kenro-Ji-Jin The Japanese deity of the earth. See 'Gods of Japan' under *Gods.*

Keramat (from the Arabic *karama*, 'generosity') Originally 'a gift from God', in *Indonesia* as in other Islamic countries, the word *keramat* came to mean 'the power to work miracles', usually ascribed to saints and other 'friends of God'. Even some animals can have *keramat*, e.g., a friendly *tiger* must not be shot. A thief desecrating the tomb of a saint may be struck dead by the saint's *keramat.*

Keraton See *Kraton.*

Kerema Apo See *Creation*(2); *Sex.*

Kerema-Miri See *Creation*(2).

Keris (or kris; also spelled creese, but pronounced 'keris' or 'kiris') A *keris* is a long dagger with a wavy blade, like the emblem of Asclepios. It is the typical weapon of the Indonesian and Malaysian people, and is found only in these areas of South-East Asia. The princes of *Java*, *Bali*, *Sumatra* and *Malaya* used to have very special *kerises* with magical power, *sakti*, so that the mere touch of the weapon killed the enemy. A *keris* is usually *pusaka*, a sacred heirloom, the last thing an impoverished nobleman would pawn. He would rather starve than let others touch his father's *keris*. It is related that the first *keris* was given to King Jamajaya by the goddess *Durga.*

Kesakten See *Soul.*

Kesna In Indonesian mythology, the Malay and Javanese form of the name of the Hindu god Krishna. See also *Kresna; Narayana.*

Kewanambo Cannibal ogres. See *Demons*(2); *Ghosts*(4).

The Key Islands See *The Kay Islands.*

Khadir See *Kilir.*

Kham Daeng ('The Golden Prince') The King of Phayao, the ancient Thai city. See *Deer*.

Khrut In Thai mythology the magical bird called *Garuda* of Indian and Indonesian mythology. It is often seen sculpted in temple precincts.

Khuna In Thai mythology, the realm of the good, *Paradise*.

Khwan See *Soul*.

Ki (Japanese; Qi, Chinese) This mysterious but important character can best be translated by 'spirit', in the sense of the English 'to be in high spirits', 'the team has a good spirit'. *Ki* is a series of forms of energy, spiritual and therefore also physical, which must be allowed to operate at all levels of the mind-and-body complex. It is primarily a mental state which influences the body's condition.

A person whose *ki* is in a poor state will also feel in 'low spirits' and this will affect his health. Bad *ki* is caused by having few friends, neglecting one's relatives, being uncaring, having poor relations at work. A man should have fatherly feelings towards all younger people, including his personnel, a woman should have motherly feelings and so, be in a caring relationship with all other living beings, also at work. This can only be done after all feelings of pride, enmity and dissatisfaction have been abolished, otherwise *ki* has no room to be effective.

A good *ki* is achieved by mental exercise, by relaxing (first relax the mind, then the body will relax itself). Next, worries must be removed. This is done by abolishing wishes, desires, jealousies, hatreds and all other forms of egotism, as the *Buddha* has taught.

Ki is a whole-person philosophy, it does not advocate mortification of the body by domination of the mind as in *Buddhism*, nor does it favour Western hedonism which saturates the body's wishes but starves the mind. On the contrary, say the Far Eastern scholars, one should listen to soft music, contemplate flowers and trees, read poetry and reflect about it. Beauty relaxes. First of all, we should learn satisfaction with what we have. This does not mean we should not work or be ambitious. The philosophy of *ki* encourages normal work, as much as the body and the mind need to feel useful. Too much hard work is, however, just as harmful as idleness. Striving to achieve something is just as much part of our normal needs as food and drink. But nothing too much. There should be harmony, which is the condition for beauty. There should be beauty in the way we live, symmetry between mind and body.

Kiavari The Orokolo word for the *spirits* of the *dead*.

Kida See *Malay Annals*.

Kidir See *Kilir*.

Kidul See *Ocean-Goddess*.

Kijo An ogre living in the Japanese woods. See also *Mountain Woman*.

Kika The first octopus. See *Nareau*.

Kikazaru   See *Monkey*(4).

Kiliakai   See *Demons*(2); *Ghosts*(4).

Kilir   (Kidir, Hadir, Khadhir, Nabi Khadir, etc.) The 'Green One', whose footsteps make the desert green. The immortal preceptor and minister of Alexander the Great, who accompanied him to the Malay countries.

In *Kalimantan*, the king, Jantam, who had just given his daughter in marriage to Alexander, asked Kilir how he could bring wealth into his poor kingdom. Kilir told him to build a big *gudang* (storehouse) and when it was ready, he filled it with gold and silver, silken fabrics, precious *stones*, porcelain and copper vessels, by *magic*.

See also *Malay Annals*.

Kilu   A song competition in *Hawaii*, a kind of eisteddfod, where the legends of the past were recited as well as the *mele-inoa*, praise songs for *gods* and kings, led by the *hakumele*, the songmaster.

Kimat   The lightning-dog of Tadaklan the Thunder-God. See *Tinguian*.

Kimi   A beautiful Japanese woman who loved a painter. See *Kakemono*.

Kimitaka   The daughter of the Japanese Emperor Ichijo. See *Demons*(1).

Kin Tambuhan   (or Ken Tamboehan, 'Lady Unknown') This Malay princess was given her name since she was discovered in the forest by the King of Kuripan, the famous Javanese city which has long since disappeared. She had been kidnapped from the garden of her own palace by a *garuda*, 'eagle'. The king who found her gave her a pavilion of her own in the garden of his own palace, and ladies to wait on her. The king's son, who had dreamed that the moon smiled at him, discovered her and recognized the moon's face in her features. They fell in love and were married at the king's orders. But the queen wanted to destroy poor Kin, because she had another bride in mind for her son. So she had Kin taken to the forest by her own huntsman, and killed. The corpse floated down a river where it was discovered by the prince, who was swimming with his friends.

Kinau   The daughter of *Kamehameha* I. See *Hawaii*.

King   In *Polynesia* the king, *ariki rahi*, was revered as a divine being as soon as he was crowned; his word was *law*. Anyone who offended the royal person would be executed at once because a dangerous *taboo* adhered forever to him. See also *Star*.

Kinnara   In Thai mythology, a creature which is half-man, half-bird.

Kintaro   ('Golden Boy') A strong hero in Japanese mythology, son of Princess *Yaegiri*. He lived alone in the forest where he talked to the animals. He was so strong that he could bend *pine trees* like twigs. He once confronted a demon in the shape of a poisonous spider as big as an elephant. Kintaro uprooted a tree and felled the monster with it. He later joined the suite of the hero *Yoromitsu* and became a great warrior too, renamed Sakata Kintoki.

Kiore Ti and Kiore Ta See *Ngarara*.

Kirata-n-Te-Rerei See *Taburimai*.

Kiribati A group of 33 *islands* straddling the Equator just west of the dateline of 180 degrees (east or west of Greenwich). Their land area is 900 sq km, spread out over 5,000,000 sq km. Geographically, Kiribati is part of *Micronesia*, but ethnically it is closer to *Polynesia*, like the Phoenix Islands to the east which belong to the same state, and *Tuvalu*, formerly the Ellice Islands, to the south. Kiribati is the Polynesian pronunciation of the name Gilbert.

The Gilbert and Ellice Islands were placed, by an Act of Parliament of 1893, under the Western Pacific High Commission, together with *Tonga*, *Samoa*, the Solomon, Marshall, Caroline, Phoenix and other islands, provided they were not 'already within the jurisdiction of a civilized power'. The Gilberts became a colony in 1916. They were occupied by the Japanese in 1942 and recaptured by the Americans in the brutal battle of Tarawa, the capital, in November 1943. In 1979, the Gilberts became independent and renamed themselves Kiribati. The islanders' staple food is fish, but they depend heavily on aid.

See also *Bue; Kai-n-Tiku Aba; Na Atibu; Na Kika; Nareau; Neititua Abine; Taburimai; Te-po-ma-Te-Maki; Tuvalu.*

Kirin In Japanese myths the unicorn, sometimes identified with a giraffe, an animal-god who punishes the wicked with its single horn, protects the just and grants them good luck. If one sees a *kirin* this is an omen of extreme good luck – if one is a virtuous person.

Kishi-Bojin The Japanese goddess to whom women pray when they want children. Her image is treated with great care and reverence in the house. See also 'Gods of Japan' under *Gods*.

Kishijoten The Goddess of Good Luck and Wealth in Japanese mythology, patroness of song and *dance*, protectress of the geishas.

Kishimo-Jin In Japanese *Buddhism*, the protectress of children, identified with the Indian goddess Hariti. She represents the *Buddha*'s appeal to compassion, and his devotion to the welfare of the weak. She is depicted as a mother suckling her baby, with a pomegranate in her hand, symbol of love and fertility.

Kitap Ngelmu The Javanese book of magic. See *Ngelmu; Pigs*(6).

Kitoka A type of *devil*. See *Sorcery*.

Kitsune-Tsuki In Japanese mythology, a *fox* spirit, a demon who appears in the shape of a fox. *Kitsune-tsuki* is *possession* (mostly of women) by such a demon. See also *Fox; Inari; Tanuki.*

Kiwa In Polynesian mythology, the mother of all shell-fish.

Kiwi A big bird in *New Zealand* which could not fly. It was created by *Tane* from a calabash.

Kiyo The beautiful waitress of a teahouse on the Hidaka riverbank in Japan. A priest fell in love with her but after a time he overcame his passions and refrained from further meetings. Kiyo, furious, sought revenge. She went to the temple of *Kompera* and was taught the *magic* arts. She then turned herself into a *dragon* and flew to the monastery where the priest was hiding under the temple bell. The dragon melted the bell with her fire, thereby killing the priest. Thus the priest was punished because he should not have permitted his desire to guide him in the first place.

Klodan and Klontjing Two Balinese girls imprisoned by a giantess. See *Giants*(3).

Ko A human spirit. See *New Caledonia*.

Ko-no-Hana ('Child-Flower') The Japanese symbol of this delicate earthly life, the goddess who makes the flowers blossom, daughter of the Mountain-God Oho-Yama. On the seashore she met Prince *Ninigi*, grandson of the Sun-Goddess, *Ama Terasu*. They fell in love, so Ninigi went and asked Oho-Yama to give him his daughter in marriage. Oho-Yama proposed that Ninigi should marry his elder daughter *Iha-Naga*, 'Princess Live-Long'. She was not beautiful but so strong that she would surely live forever, like the rocks. With her Ninigi would have a stable, long life. However, Ninigi loved and chose the lovely Ko-no-Hana and with her, a fragile existence. They lived together happily for some time and had three sons, including *Hoderi and Hoori*, but the marriage ended in disaster. Ko-no-Hana retired to the woods because her husband was unreasonably jealous. She set fire to her hut and perished. See also *Sengen*.

Ko-no-Hana-Saku-ya-Hime See *Sengen*.

Koan In *Japan*, a confusing riddle by which the Zen masters educate their students. See also *Mondo; Rinzai*.

Kobo (Kobo Daishi, Great Master Kobo) In Japanese legend, Kobo, an eighth-century Buddhist priest, is the subject of many tales of wonder and wisdom. He was the founder of the school of Shin-Gon, 'True Words'. Kobo means 'Spreader of the Lore'; his original name was Kukai. Kobo was given yet another praise name, Hensho Kongo, which is normally translated as 'Shining Diamond of the Universe' but which, with different characters, could be read as 'Book-Writing-Collection', i.e. one who has a complete knowledge of all books.

Kobo was born with his hands in the gesture of Dainichi Mahavairocana, so he may have been a *reincarnation* of that great Dhyani *Buddha* (see also *Vairocana*). While still a boy, it is said that Kobo, then still called Totomono, 'Respected Person', stood on the top of a steep cliff and vowed that he would throw himself into the ocean if *heaven* did not give him total enlightenment immediately. *Angels* then came winging down from heaven to prevent him from falling.

Like a Japanese St Anthony, Kobo, during his long periods of fasting, had visions of *dragons* and other *monsters*. The giant *sea-serpents* were pacified when he spat into the ocean, because his saliva was fortified by the radiation of the planet Venus. A crippled man was cured when Kobo gave him a page from his book with one of the Buddha's sacred names on it. Once, while praying, Kobo saw no water for his offerings to the Buddha. So he pushed his staff into the ground and fresh water sprang up there and flowed forever after. The well is still there, at Kashima. One blind man was cured by water from a well which Kobo had created. When Kobo needed shade he would plant his staff in the ground. Immediately it would sprout roots and grow into a big leafy tree.

One year there was such a severe drought that the Emperor Tencho sent for Kobo to ask him what could be done. Kobo went up to the lake at Shinsenen, which was dry, sat down and prayed for many days on end. Finally the Dragon-King, the God of the Lakes, relented and filled the lake and all the other lakes in Japan as well.

One day Kobo asked a woman for water. She said the water in her well was muddy because she was too lazy to fetch some for him. So, ever since then, that water *was* muddy. One day Kobo asked another woman for some water, but she said she had none. However, her maid quickly fetched water and gave it to the saint. In return he gave her a handkerchief. When she wiped her face with it, she suddenly became so beautiful that a rich young man who happened to pass by asked her to marry him. When her mistress was told what had happened, she too wiped her face with the kerchief. She, however, became a horse.

One day an *oni*, a man-eating devil, suddenly appeared to Kobo and demanded a human being every day from the district which Kobo administered as abbot of the local abbey. Kobo agreed on condition that the demon create 1,000 fertile valleys out of the ocean floor for the people to live on. The demon agreed and started building the rocks that would surround the valleys. When the valleys were ready, Kobo caused one valley to disappear so, when the *oni* came for his human victim, Kobo made him count the valleys again. When he discovered that one was missing, the demon, in his rage, spat rocks at Kobo. Rocks with the dents of demon's teeth in them are still pointed out by the local people.

Once Kobo prayed in front of the leaning tower of a temple (a pagoda). After long prayers, the tower finally became straight. Kobo, it is said, was so skilled at writing that he could wield five brushes at the same time, one in each hand, one in each foot and one in his mouth, writing different characters with each.

Kobo died in deep meditation in 835, but the people say he did not truly die, he still sits there meditating. The cave where he sits has been sealed off but for some seekers of knowledge it will open, they say.

See also *Angels; Momoye; Monju Bosatsu; Omokage-no-Ido; Stones*(1).

Kodomo-no-Inari The Japanese children's *fox* deity. See also 'Gods of Japan' under *Gods*.

Kohai See *Ahoeitu*.

Kohara In Polynesian mythology, the mother of all tuna fish.

Kojiki (*Records of Ancient Matters*) Written in 712 AD , this is the oldest Japanese literary work and the standard ancient history book. It begins with *Creation*:

> First there was Chaos, when nothing was named. Then Heaven and Earth parted. The Three Gods began to create. The Passive and Active Essences developed. The Two Spirits became the ancestors of all things. Sun and Moon were revealed when the Primeval Being washed his eyes. He floated in the ocean while the gods of heaven and earth emerged from him. The earth was conceived and the islands were born.

Kojin A Japanese goddess with many arms who lives in an *enoki* or nettle-tree. (All gods have at least four arms, and as Kojin is a tree-deity, she has many 'branches'.) She is the Goddess of the Kitchen. Old dolls may not be thrown in the dustbin in *Japan* but must be dedicated to Kojin, by being placed at the roots of the *enoki* tree. See also 'Gods of Japan' under *Gods*.

Kokutai-Shinto (literally, 'National-Government-God-Worship') This is a common term for the form of Japanese religion usually referred to as 'emperor-worship'. It is part of Shukyo-Shinto (see *Shinto*). A distinction should be made here from the concept of infallibility of the living emperor as head of the Shinto state; this divine nature of the emperor was officially abolished in 1945. On the other hand there are several shrines dedicated to the memory of semi-mythical emperors such as *Jimmu Tenno* and *Ojin*; these rulers of the dim past are worshipped by the people as deities.

Kokuzo Bosatsu See *Akasa-Garbha*.

Komba Ralingki See *Ghosts*(4).

Komoku See *Shi Tenno*.

Kompera (or Kompira) A Japanese god. Probably the Indian Kubera, the Lord of the Demons, Master of Magic. Often identified with *Susanowo*, the Impetuous Male, who sometimes aids people in mischief, Kompira taught Kiyo the secret of changing herself into a dragon or serpent, to take revenge on her lover for being jilted. See also *Kupera*.

Kompira See *Kompera*.

Kong The Thai kings of Chaisi and Si Wi Chai. See *Elephant-Tiger*; *Oedipus*.

Kongo ('Diamond') In Japanese mythology this is a trident-shaped staff which emits a bright light in the darkness. It gives a man wisdom and insight. Its original owner was the Mountain-God *Koya-no-Myoin*. It is the equivalent of the Sanskrit *vajra*, the lightning-jewel of the Mountain-God *Indera*. The trident-shape actually represents the three flames of the sacrificial *fire*, part of the image of the *vajra* wheel.

Kongo-Kai ('Diamond-Wonder') In Japanese cosmology, the Buddhist Vajra-Dhatu, the Diamond-Element, the Essence of Wisdom.

Konui The thumb, one of the Fire Children. See *Auahi-Turoa and the Fire Children*.

Kopu See *Morning Star*.

Korawa (Sanskrit, Kaurava) The collective name of the 100 sons of the blind King *Drestarata*, son of *Abiasa* and *Ambiki*, in Javanese mythology. They belong to the 'left hand party', i.e. the wicked, in the *wayang* plays. See also *Bratayuda*.

Korea Korea is a peninsula protruding from the East Asian mainland into the Pacific Ocean, between the Yellow Sea and the Japanese Sea, bordered in the north by the Yalu and Tumen rivers and high mountains. Since 1945 it has been divided into two states, North Korea and South Korea, respectively with 15 and 25 million inhabitants. All these people speak together one homogeneous language which shows remarkably little dialectal variation, in spite of the fact that during much of its history Korea was divided into two or more states, the northern one often subservient to China. In spite of this constant intervention by the Chinese, or perhaps because of it, Korean culture is remarkably homogeneous and entirely *sui generis*. The dominating religion is *Buddhism*, but this has partly arrived directly from South-East Asia rather than from China. What did arrive from China was the Chinese script, which is still in use, though only partly. The vast majority of books, magazines and papers are printed in the Korean alphabet, which was invented by a team of scholars at the king's behest in 1440–6, and is exclusively used for the Korean language.

Many aspects of Japanese culture and kingship were introduced from Korea, as archaeology has revealed. The Korean language is not related to either Chinese or Japanese, but isolated, although many words have been adopted from Chinese literary usage, especially word for Buddhist philosophical concepts, e.g. *ki*.

The Korean people are very religious and are much more Buddhistic than the Japanese. On ceremonial days, the temples are crowded with worshippers bowing down and praying to the Buddha. Side by side with this, and without conflict, as is typical in Buddhist countries, there is a lively practice of the autochthonous Korean religion, which is based on the veneration of the family ancestors. The officiants for this religion are often called *shamans*, i.e. specially gifted persons who have the ability to receive messages from the spirit world and reveal them to the people for their benefit.

See also *Bells; Buddha; Carp; Chedu-Do; Chopstick; Cricket*(1); *Fortune-Tellers*(1); *Japan; Kut; Miruk; Migration of Souls; Shaman*(2); *Sudo; Tide Jewels; Tolharubang; Weaver.*

Korero The wife of *Tangaroa*, in Polynesian mythology, the *Creator.*

Korinchi (Korinci or Korintji) A tribe on *Sumatra.* They are said to possess the power of changing themselves into *tigers.*

Korinci See *Korinchi.*

Korintji See *Korinchi.*

Koriro ('Bright, cheerful') The epithet of the *Maori* god *Maui. Koriro* may also mean 'reciting' like someone repeating *magic* formulae, as Maui did when he obtained *fire* from the *Creator* goddess Mahuika (see *Fire*(4)) and in creating his many inventions.

Koro (in full: Koro-mau-Ariki) Koro was the son of *Tini Rau*, chief of Motu Tapu, and *Ina*, the Moon-Goddess. He learned from his father the secret art of attracting *fish* and of making them assume human shapes. On moonlit nights they watched the mermaids dancing and joined them, travelling far away.

Koro-mau-Ariki See *Koro.*

Koroa The index finger, one of the Fire Children. See *Auahi-Turoa and the Fire Children.*

Koromo A priest's or nun's outer robe, a black habit, in *Japan.*

Koropanga Short for Tu-Te-Koropanga, the Paris of *Maori* mythology who elopes with *Rukutia*, wife of chief *Tamanui*, sparking off a great war. See also *Tattoo.*

Korwar In *Kalimantan, New Guinea* and the surrounding *islands, korwars* are wooden statues, busts or just heads, placed on pedestals, of the ancestors. On Biak, there is a real skull inside the ancestral image. The function of the *korwar* is to serve as an *oracle*, which may answer questions from the living.

Kosensei See *Gama-Sennin.*

Koshin The Japanese God of Roads, to whom little straw horses are offered, with prayers for a safe journey, by all travellers. See also 'Gods of Japan' under *Gods.*

Koura-Abi See *Kai-n-Tiku-Aba.*

Kowali The convulvulus flower. See *Hiku.*

Koya-no-Myoin In Japanese mythology, the Mountain-God of the sacred Mount Koya. He is represented as a hunter with a red face and two hounds. See also 'Gods of Japan' under *Gods.*

Krailasa (or Kailasa) In Thai mythology, a high mountain where Shiva (see *Siwa*) lives.

Kraton (Javanese; Keraton, Indonesian) The 'inner' quarters of the palace of a Javanese ruler. Surrounded by a wall, the palace court included gardens, queens' rooms and even a library. No common man would dare to enter the gate.

Krengjai (Thai, 'Consideration for Others') The Buddhist virtue of patience and tolerance towards one's neighbours.

Kresna (or Krisna) In the Javanese *wayang* myths, King of Dwarawati. He is originally an *incarnation* of the god *Wisnu* (also known as *Narayana* or Narasinga). See also *Vasudeva*.

Kresna Dwipayana See *Abiasa*.

Kris See *Keris*.

Krishna See *Kresna*.

Krisna See *Kresna*.

Krut See *Garuda; Khrut*.

Ksitigarbha (Chinese, Ti Tsang) One of the Bodhisattvas who is not so well known in *India* but very popular in *Japan*, where he is known as *Jizo* Bosatsu. Ksitigarbha is represented in sculpture seated on a lotus, the world symbol, since the name Ksitigarbha means 'Whose Womb is the Earth'. By the side of the sculpture there is the wish-giving tree Kalpavriksha, all coloured light green.

Ku (also *Ku-Kau-Akahi*) A Hawaiian *Creator* and war-god. See *Trinity; War;* also 'Gods of the Pacific' under *Gods*.

Ku-Ka-Pau ('Ku the Constructor') See *Trinity*.

Ku-Kau-Akahi ('Ku Standing Alone') The Master of the Universe in Hawaiian cosmology, the head of the Triad or *Trinity*. See *Ku; Trinity*.

Kuahu See *Hula*.

Kubera See *Kupera*.

Kubilai Khan The Mongol emperor. See *Japan*.

Kukai See *Kobo*.

Kukailimoku The Hawaiian God of War. His image has been preserved: a fierce-looking head covered skilfully with blood-red bird *feathers*, topped by a Roman-type helmet crest. The eyes are two gleaming shells.

Kuku Lau (or Fata Morgana) The Polynesian goddess who deludes voyagers by showing them non-existing countries on the horizon. See also 'Gods of the Pacific' under *Gods*.

Kukuhae A magician. See *Vailala*.

Kukui An oil. See *Hiku*.

Kumara

1. 'Young Man', the Hindu War-God, Mars. See *Ku*.
2. In Polynesian, *kumara* means the *sweet potato*, one of the foods that kept the explorers alive on their long voyages. See also *Rongo*, the God of Cultivated Foods.

Kumo See *Spider*.

Kumokomba The God of Fate of the Tontemboan people. See *Predestination*(2).

Kumu-Honua (Hawaiian, 'The Origin of the Land') Kumu-Honua was the first man in Hawaiian myth. His wife was Lalo-Honua, 'Lowland'. They were given a fine garden by *Kane* where they lived happily. See also *Adam and Eve*(1).

Kuna See *Tuna*.

Kuni-Toko-Tachi The god who inhabits Mount Fuji. See *Fujiyama*.

Kunitsu-Kami See *Kami*.

Kunti Kunti was the daughter of King Surasena, of the Yadava dynasty, and married *Darma*, the God of Justice. She was the mother of the *Pandawas*. See *Karna*; *Mahabharata*; *Yudistira*.

Kupe According to legend, a man named Kupe was fishing near his home on Raiatea when an octopus stole his fishhooks with its many arms. Enraged, Kupe jumped into his *canoe* and pursued the beast for 35 days. By that time he had covered 2,400 miles to the south-west and there he sighted an island larger than any he had ever seen before: North Island, *New Zealand*. He sailed back and invited his compatriots to follow him to the new found land. They did and so became the *Maoris*.

Kupera (Thai; Indonesian, Kuwera; Japanese, *Kompera*) In Thai mythology, the Indian God of Wealth and Ruler of the North, Kuvera or Kubera.

Kupua See *Demi-Gods*.

Kurando A Japanese officer of the guards. See *Yaegiri*.

Kurangai Tuku A ogress in *Maori* myth. See *Hautupatu*.

Kuripan A famous Javanese city. See *Kin Tambuhan*.

Kurma A *tortoise*. See *Narayana*.

Kuru In *Maori*, the *breadfruit* which was brought down from *heaven* by the Moon-Goddess.

Kuruma

1. ('Wheel') In Japanese *Buddhism* it is said that the pain follows the sin just as the *wheel* follows the foot of the ox. This is the kernel of Buddhist philosophy.
2. (From Sanskrit *Kurma*) A name for *Wisnu-Narayana* in his *incarnation* as the *tortoise* who lives on the bottom of the ocean in the Hindu myths, the symbol of the earth.

Kusanagi-no-Tsurugi ('Grass Cutting Sword') See *Susanowo*.

Kushinada A young Japanese girl menaced by a monster. See *Susanowo*.

Kut In *Korea*, the elaborate ceremony of purifying the house and garden of a family after a severe *illness* or a *death*. The *mansin* (*shaman*) will be invited, with her assistants bringing *drums*, cymbals and costumes to impersonate some of the powerful *spirits*. If they are evil aliens, they have to be driven out; if they are family spirits, they have to be propitiated with offerings, usually money.

Kuvera See *Kupera*.

Kuwatawata The guardian of the Gate of Heaven. See *Turehu*.

Kuwe See *Mother-Goddess*.

Kuwera See *Kupera*.

Kuya-Shonin In Japanese myths, a miracle-working Buddhist saint who built a temple (Rokuharamitsu-Ji) in Kyoto in 963. This good act ended the epidemic which was then ravaging *Japan*.

Kwan Yin See *Goddess of Mercy; Kannon*.

Kwannon See *Kannon*.

Kwega See *Betel*.

Kyai Agung See *Dewi Nawang Wulan*.

Kyai Belorong See *Kyai Blorong*.

Kyai Blorong (or Kyai Belorong) In East Javanese mythology he is a servant of the *Sea-Goddess*. He is represented with a *fish* tail, 1,000 arms and legs, and is covered in golden scales. His servants are lovely mermaids. He lives in a palace on the sea-bed. Its roof is made of skeletons and it is held aloft by pillars who are living men, the worst sinners, who have become prisoners of their own greed. Kyai Blorong possesses gold without limit. Any man may get as much as he can carry but after seven years he will die. Kyai Blorong also has a palace in the forest where his bonfire makes gold from *stones*.

Kyaka A people in the mountains of western *Papua New Guinea*. See *Demons*(2); *Ghosts*(4).

L

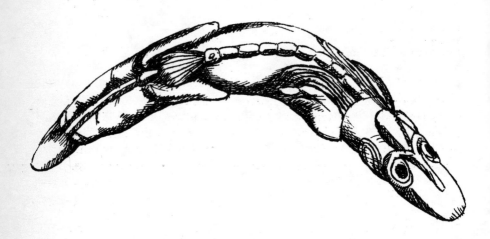

Lizard man necklace for dances (Easter Island)

La'a Maomao The Polynesian God of the Winds. See 'Gods of the Pacific' under *Gods; Moikeha*.

Laa The adopted son of King Olopana of Oahu, son of Ahukai, great grandson of the famous Pau-Makua, chief of eastern Oahu Island. Laa was first adopted by *Moikeha*, then by his brother Olopana. Laa married three wives so that all three leading chiefs of the kingdom were pleased to become his fathers-in-law. He had a son by each wife.

Ladder of Heaven

1. In Japanese mythology, the *moon, Tsuki-Yumi*, as soon as he was born, climbed up the Ladder to Heaven and rose majestically.
2. In *Indonesia* and *Malaysia*, they relate how the Prophet Muhammad climbed up the Ladder of Heaven in the night when *God* had called him to give him His revelation. This night is still celebrated annually; it is called *miraj*, 'ladder'.

Lagi See *Rangi*.

Lahatala The God of Heaven in Seran mythology. See *Sun*(9).

Laka The Hawaiian Goddess of Plenty and the Dance. See also *Hula; Lono*.

Lakon   In Javanese literature, the 'script' for the *wayang* performances, in which the chief characters are the gods *Wisnu*, *Siwa*, Wayu and *Indera*, incarnated in the heroes Rama, Krishna (see *Kresna*), *Arjuna*, *Bima*, et al.

Lakshmi   See *Dewi Sri; Rice-Goddess*.

Laksmi   See *Dewi Sri*.

Lalo-Honua   See *Adam and Eve*(1); *Kumu-Honua*.

Langi   See *Rangi*.

Langit   See *Rangi*.

Langsuir   See *Puntianak*.

Langsuyar   See *Puntianak*.

Language   In the lower Sepík district of *New Guinea* it is related that a man called Noa went into the forest one night with his son and strangled him. He then stood on a hill, carved up the boy's body and threw a piece in the direction of every future village. Each time he threw out a piece of his son's flesh, he pronounced a different language. That is how each village has its own language. Out of the pieces of the boy's flesh grew the populations of the villages. Thus Noa created all the villages; he is the ancestor of all the people.
   See also *Indonesia*.

Lanka   The island of Sri Lanka, cradle of Theravada *Buddhism*. See also *Ramayana*.

Langkasuka   A mythological Indonesian city. See *Gergasis*.

Laos   See *Thailand*.

Lapa   Te Lapa is a phenomenon of electric rays deep under the ocean surface, quite distinct from phosphorescence or other bioluminescence. This 'lightning' of the sea radiates out from volcanoes so that *navigators* can find their way about at night.

Lara Jonggrang   ('Lady Jonggrang') A tall statue of *Durga* (see also *Kali*) in the main temple of the Prambanan complex in Central *Java*. The local people believe that she was the daughter of the legendary King Ratu Baka, who is none else but Shiva (= *Siwa*). See also *Ambu Dewi; Sakti*.

Lara Kidul   See *Ocean-Goddess*.

Lares   See *Atua*.

Lata   A Samoan hero who once sailed to *Samoa* from *Fiji*. He was the first to build large double *canoes* connected with a deck. Lata is no doubt identical with the *Maori* hero *Rata*, and Kupolu, where the latter received his canoe from the *fairies* or wood elves, may be originally Upolu, one of the Samoan *islands*.

Latu   See *Creation*(10).

Lature　A god who lives in the sun. See *Sun*(7).

Laufakanaa　In the mythology of Ata, one of the Tongan *islands*, Laufakanaa is the God of Winds. The heavenly god Tamapo sent Laufakanaa down to earth to rule the winds. He landed on Ata and became its ruler. The skippers of all Tongan vessels would pray to Laufakanaa for favourable winds and would even visit Ata with offerings of bread and *coconut* oil to appease the god's stormy temper. Laufakanaa brought the banana tree from *heaven* and taught the Tongans the art of fishing with a net and of making the nets (see also *Fairies*(1)). His name means 'Speaking' (*lau*) and 'Peace', just as the wind in the Pacific is quiet one moment and roaring the next.

Law　For *Polynesians*, the laws of the nation were the rules of the patrilinear clan system, the greatest clan providing the kings. See also *Adat; Pancha-Sila*.

Lean　See *Goddess*(1).

Lebai Malang　('Reverend Bad Luck') He is a character in Malay folklore who is always dogged by misfortune. Nothing ever goes right for him, and numerous anecdotes circulate about his misadventures. When he goes sailing the wind is against him. When he takes his oars, the current will sweep him where he does not want to go. When he is called to perform a *magic* ceremony, he cannot find his habit (white tunic). When he comes home for his dinner, a dog has eaten it, etc.

Legaspi, Lopez de　A Spanish captain. See *The Philippines*.

Leibata　See *Devata*.

Lejo　A chief of the *Dayaks*. See *Night*.

Lela Muda　A prince in Malay mythology. See *Indera Bayu; Oil of a Thousand Charms*.

Lembu　A prince. See *Kalimantan*.

Lewalevu　A Fijian goddess. See *Hades*(4).

Leyak　On *Bali*, a *Leyak* is a person who lives a seemingly normal life, except that at night he wanders on the cemetery where he collects the entrails of the corpses. With these ingredients he can make a concoction whereby he can change himself into a *tiger*. If the need arises he will even take the entrails from sleeping people.
　　See also *Firefly*(3).

Lidah Bumi　('Tongue of the Earth') A mysterious plant in Malay mythology through which the earth (Bumi) speaks; you can hear her if you hold the plant to your ear, and the earth knows everything, even the future.

Life After Death　The Ngaing people of the northern *Papua* coast believe that a person's breath and his shadow are manifestations of his living *soul*, which after the body's *death* continues life as an immaterial being, unless it wishes to appear as a *kabu*, a being with a visible form, either human, i.e. a ghost, or animal, i.e. a bat, a rat, a *snake* or a glow-worm. In the old days, bodies were left in the forest, in an old *drum*.

The *spirits* of the *dead* travel to the sanctuary of the War-God or to the pool of the Water-Deity. They sometimes visit their relatives, appearing in *dreams*, looking as they were when still alive, wearing clothes and ornaments; they can also appear to a relative who is fully awake. The spirits of the dead protect their living descendants. They are always around, they do not go away to *heaven* or the *Nether World*. They bring messages about the future to the living, so they have superior knowledge. They accompany their male descendants into battle or on the hunt. They cause their kinsmen's arrows to hit their enemies, but the enemies' arrows are deflected by them. They drive the game towards their kinsmen, and protect their plantations from wild pigs.

At the Harvest Festival, the spirits of the dead, having helped to bring the crops to maturity, must be thanked. They are formally invited to the village and offered a share of the first fruits. The men lead the spirits from the sacred pool to the cult house by playing the spirits' individual tunes on the 'Trumpets of the Dead'. The invisible spirits are ushered in, are shown the dishes and invited to eat.

Ligoupup In Micronesian mythology, she is the great goddess who was never born. She created the world and all that is in it. She lies on her back beneath the sea and when she stirs, it is an *earthquake*. Her son became the ruler of the ocean and the *Underworld*; her daughter rose up to *heaven* where she married the Sky-God. They had a son, Aluelap, who is the possessor of all knowledge.

Liholiho A Hawaiian king. See *Hawaii*.

Lilang See *Sangiang*.

Limdunanji The first woman. See *Loa*.

Limu The Polynesian God of the Dead. See *Reinga*.

Lingadua A Fijian god. See *Drum*.

Lion There is a myth in *Thailand* which seems to suggest that its oldest royal family traced its descent from the lion, the King of the Animals. In religious terms this may indicate how strong the influence of Hinduism still was in those days, for the lion is one of the *incarnations* of Vishnu (see *Wisnu*), whose manifestation as Nara-Simha, 'Lion-Man', symbolizes divine protection against evil. There are different variations of the myth, the nucleus of which is as follows: a lion elopes with the king's daughter, or takes her from the park behind the palace. He persuades her to live with him in the wilderness, where she gives birth to a human son who is also called Singh, 'Lion'. The son escapes and is accepted at court. Later he kills the lion during a hunt when the lion, who recognizes his son, does not fight back. The mother finally arrives and reveals that the young man is her son and so he ascends his grandfather's throne. In a later version he is not the lion's son but the king's. Apparently by that time the totemic significance of the leonine ancestor was lost: it had become embarrassing. The young prince is advised by the Buddhist priests to build a temple on the spot where he killed the lion. By that time there is no trace left of Hinduism. In the ancient Middle East, the young king had to kill a lion to prove his bravery before he could ascend the throne.

See also *Lioness; Malay Annals; Narayana; Singa.*

Lioness   The milk of a lioness can cure the illness of a queen, according to a Philippine myth. See also *Lion.*

Lioumere   In the myths of the Caroline Islanders, a terrifying female demon with iron teeth, which possessed great magical power, if a man could get hold of one.

Lipsipsip   See *Dwarfs.*

Liver   In *Japan* the liver, *kanzo*, is believed to cure blindness (see *Morning-Glory*; see also *Monkey(5)*). In *Indonesia*, the liver, *hati*, is the seat of feeling and deciding.

Lizard

1. In *New Zealand*, James Cook was told of lizards of enormous size who dwelt in caves and devoured people. Others say that the big lizards only stare at you, but that still signifies that you will soon die.
2. In *Malaysia* it is said that a *bajang*, an evil spirit which takes the shape of an animal, in this case a lizard, can be seen escaping from the nose of a drowning man condemned to die in the water for witchcraft.
3. In Melanesia, if a lizard is seen walking towards the house of a sick man he will get better.
4. On *Bali*, the lizard is called *Saraswati*, the name of the River-Goddess, wife of Brahma. Its chirping is a confirmation of what a person has just said.
5. The Polynesian god *Tangaloa* regularly changed into a green lizard, signifying fine weather.
6. On Easter Island (see *Rapanui*), there was a society of Lizard Men who performed ritual *dances*, wearing special lizard necklaces.

See also *Chichak; Flores; Kalamainu and Kilioa; Miru(2); Moko; Mother-Goddess; Whiro.*

Lo Aget   ('Mr Lucky') See *Cat(3).*

Lo-Lale   A prince. See *Kelea.*

Lo Thai Dharmaraja   A Thai king. See *Thailand.*

Loa   According to the myths of the people of the Marshall Islands, Loa was the name of the *Creator*. Living alone in the primeval ocean, he created the colourful reefs and barriers which gradually filled up with sand. Then he made the plants, trees, *birds* and colourful *fish*. He placed a god as guardian over each of the *islands*. Then he created, from between his legs, *Wulleb* and Limdunanji, the first man and woman. They had many children who, when they had grown up, conspired to kill their father. Wulleb fled and landed on an uninhabited island. There, out of his leg, he gave birth to two more children. The youngest son was called Edao; he became the first magic-worker.

Lohiau In Hawaiian myth, a prince of Kaua'i whom *Pele* loved. See *Pele*(2).

Lolok See *Gnomes*.

Lona The Moon-Goddess in north Polynesian mythology, who fell in love with a mortal man, Ai Kanaka, and married him. She carried him on her wings to the White Kingdom she ruled. They lived very happily until Ai Kanaka died because he was an earthling.

Lono In Hawaiian mythology, the God of Song and Agriculture who descended on a rainbow to marry a Hawaiian girl who was the goddess *Laka*. See also 'Gods of the Pacific' under *Gods*; *Hula*; *Rongo*; *Trinity*.

Lo'o See *Rongo*.

Losi In Samoan mythology, the son of the *Creator*, *Tangaloa*. He was sent to earth with the *taro* as a present to the people, and is its protective god.

Lotophagoi See *Reinga*.

Lotus, Golden It is said in *Japan* that the Lord *Buddha* met a *dragon* who promised to give him words of profound wisdom on condition that he, Buddha, fed the dragon human meat. The dragon said, 'All appearance is deceptive. All living beings deny Buddha's Law. Peace comes only after death.'

Since it was against Buddha's principles to slaughter for food, he then gave himself to be eaten by the dragon. At that moment the dragon changed into the Golden Lotus of Eight Petals, Buddha's Law. See also *Fujiyama*.

Lotus Sutra See *Daimoku*.

Love In the Thai myth of King *Sison* and Princess Thewi Suthat, love is described as twofold, being both the effect of destiny and of the needs of this life. Like the lotus flower rising from the dark bottom of the pond and living thanks to the clear water, love is originally caused by the mutual recognition of two *souls* who have loved each other in their previous lives. From that moment it is fed by the mutual needs of the lovers' hearts and bodies. The flower of love will remain pure as long as it is allowed to grow undisturbed.

See also *Asagao*; *Asmara*; *Jilted Lover*; *Joshi*; *Kannon*; *Love-Magic*; *Moon*(1); *Musubi-no-Kami*; *Orchid*; *Rati*; *Shinju*.

Love-Death See *Joshi*.

Love-Magic In Bokairawata (Melanesia), there is a myth relating how
a boy invented the art of brewing *love* potions in the village of Kumila-
bwaga. He boiled aromatic leaves in *coconut* oil and put the pot
containing the finished love-potion on a high shelf in his mother's hut.
His sister later upset the pot so that its contents flowed all over her face
and into her mouth. Suddenly she felt her insides burning with love for
her brother. She asked her mother where he was.

'In the sea,' her mother replied. She then asked, 'Have you become
mad?', showing that she perceived there was something wrong with her
daughter.

Heedless, the girl ran to the beach, plunged into the sea, and there
in the surf, she made her brother make love with her. They were later
found lying side by side, dead, in the cave of Bokairawata, with the magic
flower of mint growing around them. Mint, *Mentha venerea*, was believed
to be a plant with aphrodisiac properties. The 'aromatic leaves' in the
love-potion were probably mint leaves. The seeds were also used in
potions.

See also *Oil of a Thousand Charms*.

Lowalangi See *Creation*(10).

Lu Thai A fourteenth-century Thai king. See *Thailand*.

Lua-o-Milu ('Milu's Cave') The Polynesian Land of the Dead. See
Hiki; Mahiki; Milu; Miru.

Lugeilan In the mythology of some *Caroline Islands* peoples, Lugeilan
was the God of Knowledge who descended from *heaven* to teach the
people on earth how to cultivate crops. He is associated with the *coconut*
palm.

Lumakaka A sea giant. See *Coconut*(2).

Lumimu'ut See *Creation*(11).

Lunalili A Hawaiian king. See *Hawaii*.

Lutung Kasarung The title of an *epic* poem in the Sundanese language
of West *Java*. Lutung is the name of a black forest monkey, a disguise
of *Guru Minda*, son of *Guriang Tunggal* the Supreme God. He is sent
down from *heaven* by his mother Queen *Ambu Dewi*, to find a princess.
She is Purba Sari, who is however oppressed by her wicked sister Purba
Rarang. The latter demands a palace, a fishing lake and a golden bull,
all of which are supplied by the Black Monkey, who for the purpose
changes back into his heavenly shape and borrows *bujanggas*, gigantic
angels, from his mother in heaven. These angels can build palaces, dams,
clear forest, plough rice fields, sow and harvest rice, all in one night.
Finally Purba Rarang wants a competition: who has the handsomest
bridegroom? At that moment Lutung Kasarung changes back into Guru
Minda, the shining Prince of Heaven, son of the *Rice-Goddess* Sunan

Ambu whose *incarnation* on earth is Purba Sari herself. She marries the prince, who is the incarnation of her heavenly husband, identified with Siwa Mahayogi or *Batara Guru*.

Lu'ukia See *Rukutia*.

Lydia Kamakacha Liliuokalani A Hawaiian queen. See *Hawaii*.

M

Maitreya-Miro (Horyuji temple, Nara, Japan)

Ma-Hina See *Hina*.

Ma-Sina See *Sina*.

Ma Muang See *Mango*.

Maapita See *Mother-Goddess*.

Macan Gadungan In Javanese, the 'were-tiger', a *tiger*'s body with the spirit of a man. It is said that a man's *soul* can leave his body during sleep. If a man has a smooth upper lip without the 'dimple' in the middle, he must be a were-tiger. Some men do not know that they become tigers at night, but others change themselves into the nocturnal animal by *magic, ngelmu gadungan*. See also *Feathers*.

Machanu In Thai mythology, the half-fish, half-god guardian of the lake which must be crossed to reach the *Underworld*. See *Hades*(3).

Maenam (or Menam) The great holy river of central *Thailand*, ruled by the goddess Djao Phraya, 'The Mother of the Waters'.

Mafui'e The Samoan God of Earthquakes. See 'Gods of the Pacific' under *Gods*.

Magala Bulan ('The Capricious Moon') See *Creation*(9).

Magellan (Fernao de Magalhaes) See *Indonesia; The Philippines.*

Magic In Melanesia, magic power is concealed in certain fixed traditional formulae which are believed to have existed since time immemorial. These words have to be carried to the object of the ritual by the magician's breath. Magic is used to ensure good crops, a good catch for the fishermen, favourable winds for the sailors, success in *love* and *war*, and good health. See also *Guna-Guna; Karakia; Love-Magic; Makutu; Medicine Man; Ngelmu; Sanguma; Sorcerer; Sorcery; Tohunga; Witch.*

Magic Flute In *Annam* it is related that a golden flute has been given to the king by the Golden Tortoise. Whenever the king blows the flute, a cool ocean breeze will arise, curing all the people's diseases. If anyone else blows it, it will lose its magic power. See *Green Demon; Tortoise*(3).

Maglawa The ancestral *soul*. See *Tinguian.*

Mahabharata (Javanese, *Bharatayuda*) In Malay and old Javanese mythology this great Hindu *epic* has left a powerful literary heritage. In Malay it is called *Hikayat Pandawa Jaya*, 'Pandawa Victory'. See also *Arjuna; Arjuna-Wiwaha; Bima; Bratayuda; Pandawa; Phrot; Wayang.*

Mahacabatara See *Siwa.*

Mahadewa See 'Gods of Bali' under *Gods; Waruna.*

Mahameru

1. A mountain in Javanese cosmology, on whose summit the *gods* live, including *Indera.*
2. A holy palace built on a mountain on *Sumatra*, above Palembang, where the Malayu river rises, which gave its name to the Malays.

Mahatara The Supreme God of the *Dayaks*. He remains aloof from human life and whenever sacrificial food is put ready for him, he sends *Antang*, his falcon, to pick it up and bring it to the High Heavens, where Mahatara enjoys only the spirit of the sacrifice, the 'soul of the food'.

Mahatara has seven daughters, the Santang Goddesses. They descend to earth by turns, seated on golden brooms. On earth, the Santang Goddesses direct the fate of men: they reward some and punish others.

One of Mahatara's sons is *Jata*, who has a red face and a head the shape of a *crocodile*'s. That is why the Dayaks consider crocodiles to be sacred, and will only kill them when one of their number has eaten a person. The Dayaks will then search the reptile's guts for relics of the dead, and when they find a piece of cloth or other remains they will kill no more crocodiles.

See also *God; Siwa.*

Mahavairocana See *Vairocana.*

Mahayogi The Great Ascetic, epithet of the god *Siwa* in Sundanese myth. Siwa was the first ascetic and teacher (*guru*) of the yogis. See also *Batara Guru*.

Mahiki In Polynesian cosmology, the path along which the *dead* must walk, alone or in procession, to the Spirit Land, *Lua-o-Milu* (Milu's Cave), in a deep cavern, abyss or seaside cave. Others relate that the dead walk towards the rising *sun*.

Mahina (Hawaiian, 'moon'; literally, 'The waning, wasting away woman') One tale relates that she was the wife of Ai Kanaka (literally, 'Man-Eater'). They had two children, *Hema* and Puna. However they had such unclean habits that Mahina left in disgust. Her husband tried to retain her, but she just faded away, as the moon does. Every month, though, she comes back to rejoin her family.

Mahisa (or Mahisha, Mahisura) In Javanese mythology, an evil demon who had taken the shape of a wild *buffalo*. The goddess *Kali* or *Uma*, wife of *Siwa*, at the gods' request, took on her terrifying form as *Durga*, Goddess of Death, to destroy the monster. See also *Bairawi; Death; Kali*.

Mahisha See *Mahisa*.

Mahisura See *Mahisa*.

Mahu-Fatu-Rau The daughter of *Oro*. See *Oro*(1).

Mahuika

1. The Polynesian Fire-Goddess. See *Auahi-Turoa and the Fire Children*.
2. The old *Maori* mother of the clans and man-eating ogress. See *Fire*(4).

Maihun In the *Caroline Islands*, this is a reef where evil *spirits* live who eat sailors.

Maitreya The *Buddha* of the Future. He is the last of the Bodhisattvas (see *Bosatsu*) who has agreed to incarnate at the end of human time, when he will return to earth to establish the *Law* (*dharma*), instituting the Age of Justice. Until then, he will reside in Tushita, his own *heaven*.
  In *Korea*, in the Pop Chu San Temple, built in 553 on Mount Song Ni San, there is a huge statue of Maitreya or *Miruk*. In *Japan*, Maitreya is venerated as *Miro*. There is a famous statue of him in the Horyuji temple at Nara. There is also a beautiful early medieval statue of Maitreya, seated like a king, in the Central Javanese temple complex of Mendoet (Mendut) where he is now, however, no longer worshipped.

Maiva See *Rotuma*.

Maivia Kivavia A *fish*. See *Taro*(1).

Makara A dragon-like monster, sometimes described as a 'fish-elephant'. It is seen sculpted over the gateways of Javanese, Balinese and

Thai temples and shrines. Its bulging eyes and numerous teeth frighten away evil *spirits*.

Make　See *Death*.

Makea-Tutara　The father of *Maui*, Makea was chief of the *Underworld*. Maui first saw his father in that world when his mother Taranga visited her husband there. She presented Maui to Makea. Makea predicted a great future for his son, then dedicated him to the *gods* in a solemn ceremony, sprinkling water over his head, as baptism, *tohi*. But he could not give Maui immortality, in spite of his incantations. Sadly, he sent Maui back to his life in this world.

Makutu　In *Polynesia*, the art of witchcraft, which can be acquired by years of study. The candidate's first test is to reduce to powder a stone in his hand. If successful, he moves on to causing a green tree to wither by merely looking at it. The third test is killing a bird in flight with his will. At a higher level, a *tohunga* (magician) can cause a dried up tree to sprout new green leaves. See also *Karakia; Love-Magic; Magic; Medicine Man; Sanguma; Sorcerer; Sorcery; Witch*.

Malacca　See *Melaka*.

Malae　See *Marae*.

Malanggan　In *New Ireland*, a ceremony for the commemoration of the *dead*, and at the same time the initiation ceremony for young men. It is attended by the spirits of the ancestors, who solemnly arrive in visible form in a fish-shaped, 12 foot long boat. They are often sculpted in wood seated in their boat.

Malara　See *Morning Star*.

Malay Annals　A number of chronicles in Malay in Arabic script, written *c*.1600, collectively known as *Sejarah Melayu*, 'The Malay Dynasties'. The earlier chapters of these works contain the myths of origin of the ruling Malay families.

Here are the main motifs: Alexander the Great (*Iskandar* in Malay) conquered *India* and married Syarul Baria, the daughter of its ruler, Kida or Kaidu (= Puru or Poros). She gave birth to Alexander's son Arisatun Shah, whose descendants ruled India for many generations. One of these, Raja Suran or Sulana, conquered the Malay town of *Melaka* by defeating its ruler Shah Jahan, whose sister he married. Later he defeated the Thai–Siamese King Chulan, whose daughter Onang Kiu he also married. Later still he visited the ocean, where he married the Sea-Princess Muhtabul Bahri ('Beloved of the Ocean'), daughter of the *Sea-King* Aftabul Ardi. She gave him three sons. Suran is pictured as the successor of King Solomon, the only king who could rule the jins (see *Jin*). He ordered Raja Jinn Peri, the King of the Fairies, to bring him three crowns from the Solomon in the *magic* land of the jins. Suran then returned to Malaya by riding Farasul Bahri, the sea-horse.

In Part Two of the Malay Chronicles the three sons of King Suran and the Sea-Princess descended from the mountain of the gods, *Mahameru*, and met three farmer's daughters near Palembang on the island of Andelas (or Indalas), now called *Sumatra*. The eldest brother, Mencha Terim, became King of Sumatra at Minangkabau. The god Batara sent a sign from heaven to confirm him in this new kingship as King Sapurba, 'The First'. He killed a *serpent* which had devoured many people; he also caused a freshwater well to arise near Kwantan. A lovely princess, 'Daughter of the Foam' (Puteri Tunjung Buih) (the name is identical with Aphrodite) was washed up on the shore, adopted by King Sapurba, and married off to the Chinese ambassador, who was made King of Palembang. King Sapurba is still honoured as the ancestor of the kings of Pagar Ruyung, the legitimate dynasty of rulers of all the Malay peoples.

Part Three of the Malay Chronicles describes the foundation of *Singapore* (= Singapura, 'Lion City') by Sapurba's younger son, Nila Utama, 'Excellent Blue' ('Blue' is an allusion to Vishnu). The island was previously called Bambam or Tumasik, 'surrounded by sea'. Prince Nila saw a *lion* (*singa*) there, according to the traditional etymology, but it is probably named after Nara-Simha, i.e. Vishnu. According to this, later, tradition, Prince Nila Utama became the first ruler of Singapore under the new name of Seri Turi Buwana. He lies buried in a hill on the island.

Thus ends the third of the 38 sections of the Malay Annals. The following chapters contain few myths and are mostly historical.

See also *Malay Tales*; *Malaya*; *Singapore*.

Malay Tales In Malay, *penglipur lara*, 'Dispeller of Worries', is the praise-name for the story-teller who possesses the art of enthralling his listeners. In the course of centuries, the Malay story-teller developed and refined his art until it became the very expression of the swift movement of the prince's horse; the snake's winding coils; the heavenly nymph flying through the sky, bright and golden. Inimitable are the images that are strewn across Malay tales. The strongman's moustache hairs are compared to steel needles, the enemies' armies to heavy rainclouds when the wet season breaks. The appearance of a princess to her lover is described as the approach of dawn on the beach. A burning hatred is called 'a tar fire inside the hull of a ship at sea', and as for stillness at sea: 'It was so quiet that one could hear a fly fly from one island to another and back.

Besides stories about princes and princesses – all very intelligent, beautiful and artistic – there are the tales of *Tom Thumb* and how he was eaten by the giant, and the many farcical adventures of a moronic man, whose various names sound something like 'Stephen Stupid', 'Stanley Stumble', 'Dave Dumb' and 'Donald Donkey' (see *Lebai Malang; Pa Pandir*). In addition, there is Old Daddy Grasshopper, Pa Bilalang, who has a series of lucky strokes, but is wise enough to retire on the proceeds before his good luck runs out on him. The Malay taste for stupid adventures may differ from our own, yet it is fascinating to realize how all nations have their crazy characters who are as much part of the oral tradition as the great heroes and *demons*. These are the stories for the common people, in contrast to the heroic tales of princes and princesses which are set in the royal palaces, and the mercurial histories of rich merchants and their adventures during their business voyages, which are evidently composed for and told to the middle classes. There is a tale for every taste! In this way, the study of the Malay story-teller's art makes the listener familiar with the life of all classes of Malay society, from the prince to the peasant. The clever peasant may even become king, like *Si Lunchai*, whose powers of persuasion are such that he made the king lay down in his coffin of his own free will!

The moral of these stories may be that one must not believe anything without seeing it, and that a clever talker can always make a good living in the world. *Si Junaha*, perennially in debt, seems to illustrate this: he sells worthless objects for good money to those who do not know him well enough to beware of his easy lies.

All the Malay tales contain some grain of wisdom. This is also true of the cycles of fables, the stories of the two jackals, Kalila and Damina (see *Panja Tanderan*), as well as those about the *Kanchil*, the astute mousedeer.

Malaya Now part of *Malaysia*; according to one tradition, the Malay peninsula is the original homeland of the *Polynesians*, who first travelled east past *Sulawesi* and Seran in the late sixth century. The southern route through the Torres Strait may have led directly to *New Zealand*, the northern route to *Kiribati*, Tokelau and *Samoa*.

The first Malays we know of must have lived around what is now Palembang, the first town mentioned in their oral traditions, which were written down long after their original composition. It seems that the *Hikayat Hang Tuah* is the oldest of the Malay prose traditions; it tells us how the Malays swarmed out from Palembang to Bintan and from there to *Singapore* (= Singapura, 'Lion City'). From Singapore, the town of *Melaka* was finally founded.

The tradition stresses that the dynasty of the Malay rulers of Palembang, who descended from the gods Batara and *Dewi Sri*, were responsible for these successful settlements. It is, of course, well-known that in the oldest Malay and Javanese traditions, kings and queens are descendants of *Wisnu*, *Siwa* or *Indera*; in the Islamized traditions, the ancestor of the Malay kings was usually Alexander the Great, Iskandar-Shah (see *Iskandar*).

Stripped from its dynastic mythology, we may accept the following points as facts in the Malay traditions:

a) The Malay people originated in the province, *daerah*, of Palembang in south *Sumatra* and developed a nautical culture.
b) They expanded in a mainly northern direction along the Riau archipelago, and through and across the Straits to form fishing settlements on both sides. By the beginning of, or rather even before, the twelfth century, they had reached northern Sumatra, where

Perlak (now Peureulak in Acheh) was, it seems, at that time a Malay settlement, which was only gradually drawn into the Achinese ethnic expansion. The tradition of dynastic leadership is supported by one point: the choice of settlements cannot have been left to the accident of winds and currents. Each of the towns of the early Malays is strategically positioned, and all of these cities are ideally situated to attract trading vessels on their way from South Asia to the Far East. It may be that there are good fishing grounds in those waters, but they are certainly all along the trade route.

See also *Bujangga; Crow; Iskandar; Keris; Malay Annals: Malay Tales; Malaysia; Pacific Peoples; Polynesians; Spectre Huntsman; Sun*(8); *White Elephant*(2).

Malaysia A nation of post-war formation with great geographical and ethnic diversity. Peninsular Malaysia, previously *Malaya*, is 720km long and 320km wide. Sabah, the state on the north coast of *Borneo*, lies 1,360km east of peninsular Malaysia; Sarawak, to its west, is 'only' 640km from the mainland. In between lies Brunei. Together they have a coastline of well over 2,000km, all along northern Borneo. Malaysia has 13 states; the total population is about 18 million and rising fast; fewer than 3 million live in the 3 northern Bornean states. The Peninsula comprises 10 states with traditional sultans who rotate the chairmanship of the federation. The capital of Malaysia is Kuala Lumpur, with 2 million people. Indians form 10 per cent of the population, Chinese 33 per cent; the rest are Pakistanis and Arabs. Just over 50 per cent are Bumiputras, 'Autochthonous', the vast majority of whom are Malays, with in the inland forest areas scattered groups of Penan, Bajau, Murut, mostly in Sabah. In Sarawak there are Ibans, Dayaks and Malanau, Malays and Chinese.

All these peoples have their own languages, but the four chief languages are Cantonese, Tamil, English and, of course, Malay, which is everybody's language. Since 1972 its spelling has been unified with that of Indonesian, so that the two languages are now identical except for word usage, like British and American English. All four languages are literary idioms, but most writers use English. The four languages also represent culture groups in the sense that the Tamils are Hindus and the Malays are Muslims, while the other peoples have their own religions. The Chinese are of different backgrounds, and so have diverse forms of worship.

From the ninth to the fourteenth centuries, peninsular Malaysia formed part of the huge Sumatran Hindu empire of Sri Vijaya. Islam was introduced by Muslim traders from *India*, who congregated in Malacca (*Melaka*) as the *entrepôt* city for the trade between China and Egypt, via India. The first Muslim rulers appeared in the fifteenth century, styling themselves sultans (see *Malay Annals*).

The Portuguese arrived in 1511, on their way to China; the Dutch in 1641, the British in 1824. The worst ever disaster for Malaysia was the Japanese conquest and occupation lasting from 1942–5. Many people were killed.

Independence was granted in 1957.

See also *Bajang; Batara Guru; Boar*(2); *Bomoh; Borneo; Buddha; Cat*(2); *Cobra; Crocodile*(2); *Crocodile-Wizard; Dove; Dugong; Feathers; Fortune-Tellers*(2); *Garuda;* 'Gods of the Pacific' under *Gods; Heron*(2); *Hornbill*(1); *Indonesia; Iskandar; Jilted Lover; Jin; Keris; Ladder of Heaven*(2); *Lizard*(2); *Malay Annals; Malaya; Merong Mahawangsa; Owl*(2); *Pelesit; Penanggalen; Phosphorescence of the Sea; Pigeon*(1); *Polecat; Polong; Porpoise; River Spirit; Sang Gala Raja Jin; Singapore; Spirits*(4); *Squirrel; Tioman; Vampire*(2); *Wali; Wayang.*

Malayu A kingdom in *Indonesia.* See *Mahameru.*

Malik Ibrahim A Islamic preacher on *Java.* See *Raden Rahmat.*

Mamao ('Space') See *Creation*(5).

Mambang Kuning The Spirit of Sunset. See *Spirits*(4).

Mana In Polynesian and Melanesian cosmology, the possession of vital strength, as an expression of divine favour, resulting in success with one's enterprises, influence among one's peers, power in one's nation, an extensive family, wealth and good health, courage, endurance and perseverance. *Mana* is measured by a person's success in life, which may be caused by his oratory and eloquence, by his bravery in war or by his influence on others, his 'charisma'. This concept is widespread. It was first mentioned in Europe by Robert Marett in 1909 in his book *On the Threshold of Religion*, published in London.

Mana is the *gods'* favour, grace poured down on someone's head. It has been explained as an impersonal invisible force, but also as spiritual energy, or as a divine being who always accompanies his or her favourites so that they have good luck all the time. The *tohunga* (priest) has *mana* when his chanted prayers cause the gods to fulfil the people's wishes. The warrior has *mana* when the enemies' arrows miss him, while his own hit their targets. The chief has *mana* when his retainers obey him and his wives bear him many children. The farmer has *mana* when his crops are abundant and his pigs multiply. A woman has *mana* when she has many healthy sons and her handicraft is admired by all. See also *Head.*

Manawa

1. In the Malayo–Polynesian *languages*, heart, mind, spirit; also the ring finger, one of the Fire Children. See *Auahi-Turoa and the Fire Children.*
2. In Polynesian cosmology, the *soul* as the principle of life, born from the *fire* in the earth.
3. A *Maori* chief. See *Tahua.*

Mandala A sacred circle representing the earth (often drawn as a lotus flower resting on the Eternal Water) or even the celestial orbit, the hub of which is the primal hill, the receptive sanctuary upon which the deity is invited to descend, like a bee onto a flower. The deity, recognizable in iconography as Vishnu, Lakshmi, *Brahma*, *Buddha* or a Bodhisattva, resides on the flower, representing the spiritual principle living in the physical principle, like the *soul* in the body. See also *Borobudur*.

Mang A goddess in Dayak mythology. See *Night*.

Manga The mother of *Veeteni*.

Mangaroa See *Milky Way*.

Mango In *Thailand* there is a myth about the divine origin of the mango fruit, to which medicinal powers are attributed. In the early days of the Thai kingdom, it is related, there lived a king who fell ill one unlucky day. His physicians prescribed fruit juices but none had any effect. One night, in a dream, the king heard a god's voice telling him that in the mountains of *Himaphan* (probably the country that is now called Assam) there grew a tree, the fruit of which would certainly cure him. The king sent out all his woodsmen to find the tree, which the god's voice had described as the Mother of Mangoes. They found the tree, but when they tried to pick one of its fruits, the tree cried like a mother, so a priest had to come and pray to the Mango-Goddess to part with one fruit for the sick king. The Mother of Mangoes then consented. The fruit is still called Ma Muang, 'Mother of Mangoes').

Mango-Roa-i-Ata ('The Long Shark at Dawn') In *Maori* cosmology, this is the *Milky Way*. *Maui* (as *Koriro*) caught this shark when he was fishing *Creation*. He threw it up into the night sky.

Mangrai (or Mengrai) A Thai king. See *Thailand*.

Maniaka The son of Peri Dewa and the 'Golden' Princess (see *Cow*), grandson of *Indera*, the first king of the *islands* of Bintang and *Singapore*.

Manikesara See *Ajapal; Anomatan*.

Maniwori See *Kangaroo*.

Manjushri (or Manjusri) The first of the Bodhisattvas; in late medieval *Java* the Bodhisattva of victories. His statue with an inscription (dated 1343) still stands in East Java, and there is one on *Bali*. See also *Monju Bosatsu*.

Manjusri See *Manjushri*.

Mansin See *Kut; Shaman*(2).

Mansur Shah A fifteenth-century ruler of the Malay Peninsula. See *Needles*.

Mantri A Javanese minister. See *Star*.

Manyura In *Java* and *Bali*, a peacock, a royal symbol of *Saraswati*.

Maohi The original name of the oldest *Polynesians*, according to their own traditions; sometimes identified with *Maori*.

Maori

1. The Maoris are culturally among the most advanced and important
    of the Polynesian peoples. They arrived in *New Zealand* more than
    1,000 years ago; it is not known exactly when, nor from where. Their
    own traditions seem to indicate they came from the east, but others
    maintain that their homeland was in the north. We do know that
    all the *Polynesians* must originally have sailed out from what is now
    eastern *Indonesia* (though not *New Guinea*).

    Of all the Polynesian languages, Maori is the most conservative;
    it has remained closest to the original Malayo–Polynesian common
    language of the ancient mariners from the times before Christ.
    Malayo–Polynesian belongs to the wider phylum of Austronesian
    languages; Maori is perhaps the most beautiful among a family of
    exceedingly melodious languages.

    The Maoris have a very elaborate system of rituals in their religion,
    which forms part of their highly refined culture, matched by their
    strikingly developed language. Maori mythology is one of the richest
    in the Pacific area, although it is not, of course, on a level with
    Japanese mythology. The gods of the Maoris, whose exploits are
    reminiscent of those of the Greek gods, still have names that are
    clearly related to those of the Hawaiian gods, 7,000km away!

    See also *Adam and Eve*(3); *Ao; Avaiki Tautau; Fairies*(1); *Fire*(4);
    Frog(1); 'Gods of the Pacific' under *Gods; Hakawau; Hautupatu;
    Hema; Hina-Keha; Hine-Nui-Te-Po; Incest; Io; Kae; Kai Tangata;
    Koropanga; Kupe; Kuru; Mango-Roa-i-Ata; Maohi; Maru; Matuku;
    Maui; New Zealand; Nganaoa; Ngarara; Ngirungiru; Pare; Pia; Pitaka;
    Polynesia; Ponaturi; Poukai*(1); *Raka-Maomao; Rata; Rohe; Rongo;
    Scorpio; Spirits*(1); *Sweet Potato; Tahua; Tamanui; Tangotango; Taro;
    Tane; Tangaroa; Tattoo; Tekoteko; Tipua; Tohunga; Tonga; Tuna*(3); *Tu-
    Te-Wehiwehi; Ua; Uenuku; Uwhi; War; Whiro; Woman*(1).

2. The Maori of the Pulari river of *Papua New Guinea* (who are not
    related to the Maori of New Zealand) descend, according to their
    myth of origin, from the 10 birds who were driven away by the *witch*
    Eare. The birds flew west to the Pulari river and hid in a *breadfruit*
    tree on the riverbank. The witch pursued them so the birds chose
    a bad fruit to hide in, lest she should find them. She cut the tree
    down and the breadfruit with the birds in it fell in the river. It floated
    towards the delta where 10 girls were bathing. One of them saw the
    fruit floating, picked it up, opened it and found 10 handsome men
    inside. They married the girls and each pair became the ancestors
    of a clan. Maori was one of the 10 brothers.

Mapere In Polynesian, the middle finger, the one who is like a dart.
One of the Fire Children. See *Auahi-Turoa and the Fire Children*.

Marae (or *malae* or *morai*) A public square in front of the temple or
chief's mansion in *Polynesia*, a *marae* is enclosed by stone or coral rock
walls, with a shrine for the deity at one side, where the *kings* were

crowned (see *Maro*). Thus *marae* came to mean the centre of royal power, the most sacred meeting place of the nation. See also *Pyramids*.

Marama   The Polynesian Moon-God, first made by *Io* the *Creator*. His wife was *Ina* or Rona. See *Creation*(4); 'Gods of the Pacific' under *Gods*; *Tapa*(1).

Marawa   In the myths of the people of the Banks Islands in Melanesia, Marawa is the Spider-God, the Trickster-God who tricked man out of his immortality.

Mareikura   Heavenly nymphs in the cosmology of *Polynesia*. They are attendants of *Io* the *Creator*, acting as messengers to earth and guardians of *souls*.

Marikoriko   The first *woman*, according to *Maori* mythology. See *Woman*(1).

Marishi-Ten   The Japanese Queen of Heaven, Goddess of Light, of Sun and Moon. See also 'Gods of Japan' under *Gods*.

Maro   In Polynesian this means government. Originally the word meant 'belt' as a symbol of kingship. During the enthronement ceremony, the new king fastened around his person the *maro ura*, the 'scarlet belt', as a token of becoming *ariki rahi*, the 'paramount chief'.

Maru   (South Island *Maori*; Tu Matauenga, North Island Maori)

1.   The Polynesian War-God, commander of the heavenly hosts. When a great man, a war-leader, prays to Maru with the right *karakia* (hymn) the god may be persuaded to join him in battle and so decide the day in his favour. Maru possesses a huge fire in which the evil *demons* he has vanquished are burnt. See also 'Gods of the Pacific' under *Gods*.

2.   A Polynesian chief who married his daughter to Tuakeka, although she had been betrothed in infancy to the son of Te Rangi Whakaputa. The latter felt so insulted by this breach of promise that he went up to Maru's compound and killed a servant of Maru's in broad daylight. Of course, Maru could not let this heinous act stay unavenged, since his honour as a chief was in jeopardy. He rallied the clan of the Ngai Tahu, who were allied to him, they came and together with his own men they stormed one of Whakaputa's enclosures, and took it. They captured Hinemaka, a noble maiden, whom Maru married to his son. She bore him grandsons and so gave Maru men for the loss of his man-servant.

Maruka Akore   See *Creation*(1).

Mary

1.   In an *epic* tale in the Pampanga language of the *Philippines*, the Virgin Mary becomes the nurse of a young prince (after he has been baptized) in order to protect him from the voracity of a heathen giant cannibal.

2. According to another Philippine epic, the Virgin Mary gave a *magic* whip to her foster-son Juan. With it he drove all the armies of the infidels out of his country and made it Christian again. Later, the whip built a royal palace for Juan with lions and tigers in the garden.

Mas Krebet See *Jaka Tingkir*.

Masalai In Melanesian mythology this is the generic term for animal *spirits*. Some of these become *demons* and haunt human beings. They can also look like human beings if they want to, changing their shape at will. Some *masalai* are men, some are women and some are children. Some are kind and help people, some are vicious and do harm, or even eat people's flesh. These spirits do not have a spirit world of their own, they just live in the bush or in old houses. *Masalai* men may appear to women in the form of male hounds and mate with them, while *masalai* women may appear in attractive physical shapes to human men, marry them and have special children. Some *masalai* women appear in the form of cassowaries, yet they seem to attract some men in that shape and marry them (see also *Cassowary*).

In the Manus Islands they tell the tale of Pokop who saw a *fire* on the path ahead, so he decided to roast the *fish* he had caught for his lunch. When he had finished he threw the bones back into the fire. He did not know that the fire came from an invisible *masalai*, one of the spirit men, whose behinds can produce flames. Suddenly the fire exploded, for the *masalai* was angered by the fishbones. Pokop fled and the *masalai* pursued him, wishing to devour him, but Pokop was too clever and managed to escape.

Mask Masks are used in religious rituals by many peoples in *New Guinea* and some of the Melanesian *islands*. Their function is to express in ritual the people's expectations, hopes and fears, and to revive the ancestors and to re-tie the bonds with their friendly *spirits*. Among some peoples the ritual meaning of masks has faded so they only function for prestige or as ritual presents or as art objects.

Every mask of the Orokolo people on the south-west coast of *Papua* is decorated in five colours (pink, black, white, yellow and grey) and each decorative design is a symbol known only to the clan. Rectangles represent the clan's cultivated fields and a coloured area at the top of the mask represents the 'empty' land which the clan hopes to find in the future when their present land is exhausted. Thus a mask, which has the oval shape of a shield, is an image of the known world as well as the future world. An ancestor's face will occupy the lower half of a mask; it may be surrounded by his 'cap of clouds', showing he is a world spirit. The line down the centre of a mask is the *magic* rope which links *heaven* and earth.

A boy may wear a mask for the first time after his initiation (girls may not wear masks). Every mask is animated by a powerful spirit so that people will be highly agitated upon seeing the mask, even though they know that it is a boy wearing it. At the moment when the boy has the mask on for the first time, he has to jump over his mother and sisters while they lie flat on the ground.

Masks 'are danced' for a month. The people say the mask dances, for the mask is the spirit. At the end of the great feast (*Hevehe*) the ancestors have to be sent (or driven) back to Spirit Land and so the masks have to be destroyed. They are burnt and the ashes are thrown ceremonially into the sea, where the great spirit resides who swallows all others.

Masora See *Mother-Goddess*.

Mata Upolu The East Wind. See *Matagi*.

Matabiri In *Papua*, malevolent *spirits* of the swamps.

Matagaigai In the mythology of the Papuans, the God of Trees, who is the teacher of the herbalists.

Matagi (pron. 'matangi'; *wind* in Samoan) It is related that *Maui* the Sun-God brought the winds under control, one after another, beginning with Tua-Uo-Loa, the South Wind, then Matuu, the North Wind, then Mata Upolu, the East Wind, and finally the South-West Wind, *Tonga*. Only the Fisaga, a soft breeze, was allowed to remain free. Each wind is described in detail by the narrator, who thus teaches the young generation the art of sailing.

Matakau See *Amulet*(5).

Mataora A mortal prince who married a fairy princess. See *Turehu*.

Matariki (Literally, 'Little Eyes') The seven *gods* of the Pleiades who supervise agriculture and guide the Polynesian *navigators*. See also *Atutuahi*; 'Gods of the Pacific' under *Gods*; *Milky Way*; *Morning Star*; *Ru*(2); *Star*; *Star Spirit*.

Mati See *Death*.

Matianak See *Puntianak*.

Matsu In *Japan*, the *pine tree*, often drawn by artists for its fine dark needles shown against an autumnal sky. It is a symbol of stability, since it stays green through the winter. Hence it is also a symbol of a stable marriage. Married people pray to the Pine-God for long life together. See *Pine Tree*.

Matsui See *Cherry Tree*(1).

Matsya A *fish*. See *Narayana*.

Matuku ('Bittern') A *Maori* demi-god, son of *Tawhaki*. He was a cannibal of harsh character, brought up by one of his sea-ancestors who taught him the art of making and flying kites. He also taught him to walk along the bottom of the sea. In this way Matuku could escape from all his enemies, living under water.

Matuu The North Wind. See *Matagi*.

Maui The great Polynesian Ulysses. In the *Maori* tradition he is the fifth son of *Makea-Tutara* and Taranga. One day Taranga was walking along the seashore when suddenly Maui was born prematurely, an unformed child. She took some of her hair, wrapped the body in it and put the bundle down in the waves. The sea-fairies found the child and cared for him. They hid him in some kelp but a storm tore it to pieces and cast him back onto the beach. There he was found by his own ancestor, Tama-Rangi, 'Son of Heaven', who 'woke' him back to life, and taught him the lore of his fathers, their tales and songs. Soon, Maui went off wandering around until one night he heard the noises of a feast in a meeting house. He went in and recognized his brothers, who were standing in front of their mother. She called their names: 'Maui-Taha, Maui-Roto, Maui-Pae, Maui-Whao.'

Quickly Maui took his place at the end of the row but his mother did not recognize him until he reminded her that she had thrown him into the sea. At last she embraced him and gave him a *hongi* (nose-kiss), calling him Maui-Potiki, Maui-Tikitiki ('Maui the Last-Born, Maui the Top-Knot'). When his brothers expressed their jealousy, they were told: 'It is better to make a friend than an enemy, so live in peace.'

Maui, being the youngest, slept in his mother's bedroom. At dawn he found that Taranga had disappeared, but when he asked his brothers they did not know anything about it. Later she returned, but the next morning Maui awoke early and when his mother left at first light, he followed her secretly. She disappeared under a clump of thick reeds in the bushes. Maui lifted the clump and saw the *Underworld*: trees moving in the wind. He told his brothers but they showed no interest. So he took his mother's apron and wrapped himself in it. By this means he took on the shape of a wood pigeon and descended, through the clump of reeds, into the *Nether World*. There he soon found his mother, who was resting under a tree with her husband Makea-Tutara. Maui took his feathery disguise off and stood staring at them with his flaming red eyes, as if he were *Tu Matauenga*, the God of War. At last his mother recognized him (he had grown big in a few days) and presented him to his father.

One evening Maui decided that the days were too short for work, and the nights too long. So he went with his brothers to catch the *sun* in a snare, but the ropes were too dry, so the sun burnt them and broke free. Then Maui used ropes made of wet flax and this time the sun was trapped. Maui beat the sun, who exclaimed: 'Why do you beat Tama Nui-Te-Ra ['The Great Son of the Sun']?' That was the sun's true name! Maui demanded that the sun must travel more slowly through the sky, to make the days longer, and the sun agreed. (In the original myth, Maui used the hair of his sister, *Hina-Ika*. Later, he was made into a culture hero rather than a sun-god, so he was represented as the inventor of ropes for fishing and sailing.)

After lengthening the day, Maui went fishing and taught his brothers to make fishhooks and fishspears with barbs so the *fish* could no longer slip away. He also invented the fish basket for catching eels, invented kite-flying and dart throwing and created the *dog*, the only domestic animal of his people.

One day the brothers sailed out without him, or so they thought, unaware that he was hiding in the bilge, as small as a shrimp. As soon as they wanted to stop sailing and start fishing he persuaded them to sail a little farther and then farther yet. Finally he told them to start fishing with their lines. They soon filled their boat with fat fish and wanted to go home, but Maui persuaded them to wait until he had done his fishing: 'I will bring up the biggest fish you have ever seen,' he boasted.

The brothers refused to let him use their bait, so he hit his own nose and used his blood as bait. He chanted an incantation and lowered his line deeper than it had ever been. Finally he hauled up a fish that was hundreds of miles long. It rose to the surface and stayed there, becoming earth and beaching the boat. The *Maoris* called it Ika-a-Maui, 'Maui's Fish', but when Captain Tasman arrived in 1642, he called it *New Zealand*, after his homeland, Zeeland in the Netherlands. The city now called Wellington stands on what the Maoris call Whanga-Nui-a-Tara, 'The Great Bay of the Goddess Tara'. This, they said, was one of the eyes of Maui's great fish. Thus Maui was the *Creator* of the Maoris' homeland. His 'hauling up' of the land as a great nutritious fish, from which the people can eat for a long time, is no doubt symbolic of the mystery of a great navigator, who by his secret knowledge of the ocean, can discover land for his people to live in.

See also *Fire*(4); 'Gods of the Pacific' under *Gods*; *Hawk*(1); *Hina-Ika*; *Hina-Keha*; *Hine-Nui-Te-Po*; *Kaikomako*; *Matagi*; *Rehua*(1); *Rohe*; *Scorpio*; *Tuna*(3).

Mauleon   A giant. See *Tinoso*.

Mauri   In Polynesian cosmology, the *soul* or ghost, the principle of life, that which survives the deceased.

Mavu   The daughter of Maivia Kivavia. See *Taro*(1).

Maya   The queen who dreamt of a *white elephant* and gave birth to the *Buddha*.

Meanderi   A Papuan goddess. See *Taro*(2).

Medicine Man   On *New Guinea* there are two types: the death-makers who will lay *magic* traps for enemies whose attack is expected, so that the attackers will become blind or sick when passing these 'charms'; and the life-makers who will make 'good' charms to protect their own people against enemy attacks, *snakes*, sickness and *fire*. They can also make them invisible. See also *Bomoh*; *Fortune-Tellers*(2); *Karakia*; *Love-Magic*; *Magic*; *Makutu*; *Sanguma*; *Sorcerer*; *Sorcery*; *Tohunga*; *Witch*.

Meiji   The first active emperor of *Japan* in 400 years. He reigned from 1867 to 1912, supervising the great expansion of the Japanese empire. See also *Japan*.

Melaka (Malacca) This old Malay fishing town was first Isalmicized by Sultan Muhammad Shah, 1424–44. Under his successors it became a centre of learning, but the Portuguese destroyed it in 1511. It was taken by the Dutch in 1619 and by the British in 1811. Melaka was made a partner of the Federation of Malaya in 1896. See also *Hang Tuah; Malaysia*.

Melanesia See *Austronesia; Baloma; Betel; Beyawa; Bomala; Bubwayaita; Cockatoo*(1); *Digawina; Dreams*(1); *Evara; Familiar; Head; Kaitalugi; Lizard*(3); *Love-Magic; Magic; Mana; Marawa*(1); *Masalai; New Guinea; Pacific Peoples; Pigs*(2); *Reincarnation*(1); *Sanguma; Shark*(1); *Sorcerer; Spirit-Canoe; Stingaree; Vanuatu; Witch*(5).

Melati In *Indonesia, Jasminum sambac,* a very fragrant flower which young women wear in their hair. The love flower in Javanese myths.

Mele-Inoa Polynesian praise-songs for *gods* and *kings*. See also *Kilu.*

Memmi See *Cricket.*

Menak See *Amir Hamza.*

Menam See *Maenam.*

Menari A *dance.* See *Oracles*(2).

Mencha Terim (or Menca) The King of Sumatra. See *Malay Annals; Sumatra.*

Mendicant A rich man in *Thailand* had a son whom he betrothed at an early age to a merchant's daughter, by contract, as was the custom in those days. One day a mendicant monk arrived, a holy pilgrim, who was on his way to Bodhigaya. The rich man gave him not only food and clothes, but also a room in his house, and asked him to stay for as long as he wished. The monk and the rich man's son took to each other and the monk taught the young man many gems of wisdom. When he departed he gave the young man a bag full of pebbles, telling him to put it under the floor. With him luck went. The rich man soon became poor and died. His son then went to see the merchant, asking him for the hand of his daughter who was betrothed to him. The merchant refused to give his daughter to a pauper, but the girl escaped and ran off. After many vicissitudes she arrived at the house of her betrothed. They were married and decided to repair the old house which was, by then, in ruins. Under the floorboards they found the bag of pebbles, but they discovered that the *stones* had since turned into diamonds.

Mendana, Alvaro de A Spanish explorer. See *The Solomon Islands.*

Mendona A Spanish explorer, an officer of Gaetano. See *Hawaii.*

Menehune In Hawaiian, the brownies, *gnomes,* 'little people' or *fairies* who are, just like people, divided into tribes with different names. They will help us mortals with difficult labours if we approach them in the right way. They live in the mountains of Pu'ukapele, 'Hills of *Pele*'. They hear the voice of the magical expert who prays to them. He will promise them food, an abundance of *fish*, if he wants them to work for him. They are little men and women, but very numerous, and each one is stronger than a human man. They are invincible experts in the arts of *magic* and witchcraft. If a man breaks his promise with them, he will surely die.

See also *Dwarfs; Fairies; Ponaturi; Tipua.*

Menezes, Jorge de A Portuguese sea-captain. See *New Guinea.*

Mengindera The King of Indrapura. See *Bidasari.*

Mengrai A Thai king. See *Thailand.*

Merau The Polynesian Goddess of Death and the Nether World. See *Death;* 'Gods of the Pacific' under *Gods; Nether World.*

Merong Mahawangsa A king in Malaysian myth. See *Garuda; Gergasis.*

Miao Chuang The King of Taiwan. See *Goddess of Mercy; Taiwan.*

Miao Shan See *Goddess of Mercy.*

Micronesia ('Small Islands') With Melanesia and *Polynesia,* one of the three major divisions of the Pacific. Micronesia is the name for a few thousand *islands* situated in the western Pacific, north of the Equator between Belau and *Kiribati.* It is in turn divided into three major groups: the Marianas in the north, the Carolinas in the south and the Marshall Islands in the east. The most prominent islands are Belau (Palau), Guam, Yap, Truk and Kwajalein. The islands now form the Federated States of Micronesia.

See also *Brain Coral; Caroline Islands; Japan; Ligoupup; Loa; Wulleb; Yalafath.*

Migration of Souls On *Java* many people still believe in the migration of souls even though that belief is incompatible with Islamic doctrine. Everyone hopes to be reborn in a higher social position than he occupies at present, even if only a little higher. There is even a special *magic* rite to effectuate this.

In Buddhist countries like *Japan, Korea* and *Thailand,* metempsychosis is universally accepted. See *Reincarnation.*

Miki Nakayama The founder of the *Shinto* sect of *Tenrikyo.*

Miko A virgin who is assigned to the lifelong service of a Japanese deity. These maidens are chosen from specific traditional families. The *kamiko* ('child of the deity') girls have to assist the *Shinto* priests with certain rituals. They are chosen from certain Japanese families, make a vow and subject themselves to a rigid daily regimen. See also *Ichiko.*

Milk See *Narayana.*

Milky Way In *Polynesia* this shining vehicle of the Night-Goddess Po is called Ika-Roa, 'The Long Fish, who Gave Birth to All the Stars', or

Mangaroa, 'Long Brook' or 'Flour River'. The Milky Way was of vital importance to navigators as a beacon. According to myth, it was fished up by *Maui* as *Koriro* and placed in the night *sky*. Some relate that the Light-God *Tane* gathered heaps of small stars together and put them in a *canoe*. Others say that Ika-Roa is the mother of the other stars, the ornaments of the Sky-God.

See also *Atutuahi*; 'Gods of the Pacific' under *Gods*; *Mango-Roa-i-Ata*; *Matariki*; *Morning Star*; *Ru(2)*; *Star*; *Star Spirit*; *Tanabata*.

Milu   ('Owner of the Land of Spirits') Milu is the Polynesian *Hades* or Pluto, God of the Nether World, the *Lua-o-Milu*, 'Milu's Cave', where the *souls* live. See also 'Gods of the Pacific' under *Gods*; *Miru(2)*; *Nether World*.

Minahassa   A region of north *Sulawesi*. See *Sulawesi*.

Mirage   In southern *New Guinea* people relate that Iko, the first man who died, went on to the dead-land, but he left a mirage behind him so that no living person could ever find his way there, except a seer or prophet. See also *Woman(1)*.

Miro   (or Miroku) The Japanese name for *Maitreya*, the living *Buddha*. See *Maitreya*; also 'Gods of Japan' under *Gods*; *Shotoku*.

Miroku   See *Miro*.

Mirror

1. In *Japan*, the *Jata-Kagami* mirror is one of the Go-Shin Tai or divine symbols given by the Sun-Goddess to the first emperor.
2. Also in Japan, it is said that a mirror which a dying mother gave to her little daughter reflected the dead mother's face as often as the daughter looked in it. A mirror has a will of its own and can reflect any face, even a dead person's. A mirror spirit may forecast the future by showing it when asked what will happen. A mirror can even kill to punish a sinner who looks in it.

Miru

1. In *Polynesia*, a demonic goddess who lived in *Avaiki*, in the *Nether World*, below the island of Mangaia in the *Cook Islands*. She devoured the *souls* of men after stupifying them with *kava*, of which she possessed cellars full. She had a large oven which burned eternally, where she used to cook her victims. The *Tapairus* were her daughters. See also *Hades(2)*.
2. **The God of the Dead who collects souls in his cave,** *Lua-o-Milu*. His servants are large *lizards* who live on the flies in the *Underworld*. See also *the Dead*; *Hiku*; *Mahiki*; *Milu*.

Miruk   The Korean name for *Maitreya*. See also *Miro*.

Misogi-Kyo   In Japanese *Buddhism*, the doctrine that purification ceremonies are periodically needed to cleanse the self of lust and anger.

Miyazu-Hime   In Japanese mythology she was the Goddess of Royalty, spouse of Susa-no-o (see *Susanowo*) the Storm-God, brother of *Ama Terasu*. Her shrine is at Atsuta. See also 'Gods of Japan' under *Gods*.

Mizaru   See *Monkeys*(4).

Mizuame   Japanese malt-syrup. See also *Ghost-Mother*.

Moaro   In the language of *New Caledonia*, the word for 'clan'. It also means house, just as in England 'the House of York' refers to a family, a dynasty. Thirdly, *moaro* means 'altar, shrine'. Behind each family dwelling there is such a shrine on a hillock where the ancestors have been laid to rest (originally they were not buried but laid out on the bare ground). The image of the ancestor is there, in wood, near the *moaro*.

Mochi   (Japanese, 'full-moon') The ardent observer, we are told, will perceive that on the *moon* there lives a *hare*, who is constantly busy preparing cakes from rice flour, *mochi*.

Moikeha   One of the early heroes in Hawaiian mythology, Moikeha was a son of Muliele Alii, King of Oahu, and descended from a long line of illustrious rulers (*alii-nui* = 'paramount chief'). Being the third son, he had little hope of succeeding to the kingship, so he set out in a small outrigger *canoe*, in search of his fortune.

One of his voyages led him to Ra'iatea in the Society Islands, where he had the good fortune of meeting La'a Maomao, an old man who offered his services as astrologer, adviser and navigator. La'a Maomao was the Wind-God in disguise. Returning in the direction of *Hawaii*, Moikeha landed on the island of Kaua'i, where King Puna had just announced that a great sailing contest would be held. The winner would receive the hand of King Puna's only child, Princess Ho'o Ipo. Chiefs and princes arrived in sleek and fast sailing boats, and bowed to King Puna to pay him homage and recite the lineage of their ancestors, demonstrating that they were worthy of marrying a king's daughter. Early the next morning they set out, riding the surf in their slender canoes. Their aim was to reach the island of Kaula, 100 miles away. One of the king's officers was waiting there and would hand over a finely decorated ornament to the first prince to arrive. The winning prince would sail back and offer the ornament to the king's daughter and so become betrothed to her.

The chiefs and other princes sailed with great art and ability, but Moikeha's navigator was the god who ruled the winds. He held a large calabash in which he had locked up all the winds. Thus, while the other princes were becalmed, Moikeha's sail was filled with a favourable wind, let out of the calabash by La'a Maomao. What skipper needs a crew if he has the Wind-God on board? Naturally, Moikeha arrived in Kaula a day before the others and arrived back in Kaua'i with the ornament which he offered to Princess Ho'o Ipo, who gladly accepted him as her bridegroom. When Puna died, Moikeha became King of Kaua'i. Ho'o Ipo bore him seven sons.

The princes' contest for the hand of a princess seems very similar to the *svayamvara* of ancient India. Also the god disguised as a humble guide is reminiscent of Indian fables. The Greek Wind-God Aiolos likewise holds the winds together in a container.

See also *Laa*.

Moko (also Tu-Te-Wehiwehi) The 'Great Lizard', the King of the Lizards in Mangaian mythology. Moko was half man in appearance but he had human descendants, including his grandson *Ngaru* whom he constantly protected with his *magic*, though he rested on the rocks.

See also *Lizard; Whiro*.

Mollusk A woman of Tanimbar once found a mollusk on the beach. She took it home and put it in a pot to cook it. Lo and behold! Out of the pot crept a little baby boy whom she fed and brought up as her own child.

The Moluccan Islands See *The Moluccas*.

The Moluccas (or the Moluccan Islands or the Muluka Islands) Set in eastern *Indonesia*, these were once called the Spice Islands and their possession was hotly contested. Each of these islands has its own language and folktales, though Malay–Indonesian is widely spoken. The population is mainly Christian. The Moluccas may have been, if not the cradle of Polynesian civilization, at one stage the starting point of the great maritime migrations towards the Polynesian islands, even to *Hawaii* and perhaps to *New Zealand* and the *Fiji* islands as well. The three main islands are Buru, Ceram (Seran) and Amboina (Ambon), the biggest nutmeg producer.

See also *Creator; Indonesia; Mother-Goddess; New Guinea; Papa; Replacement*(1); *Sun*(2).

Momotaro A hero in *Japan* who was born from a *peach*. He was joined in his adventures by a dog, a monkey and a pheasant. They sailed to an island ruled by *demons* whom they slew, liberating two princesses.

Momoye A Japanese pseudo-scholar who said mockingly that one of the calligraphed characters which *Kobo* had written resembled a wrestler. That same night, a wrestler arrived, jerked Momoye from his bed and beat him up until *dawn*. Only then did Momoye see that the character he had mocked was missing from the written text.

Mondo The way of teaching Zen in *Japan* by questions and answers. See also *Koan; Rinzai; Soto*.

Monju Bosatsu The Bodhisattva *Manjushri* in Japanese *Buddhism*, the Bodhisattva of wisdom and knowledge, the oldest of the Bodhisattvas. He is depicted with a bow and arrow, an association with later Zen Buddhism, symbol of 'hitting' the right conclusion.

Monju once appeared to *Kobo* in the shape of a dashing young man. He took a brush and painted a fiery *dragon* with such *magic* concentration that the dragon came to life and flew up into the *sky*. Thus

Kobo knew who his visitor was. Monju then ascended to *heaven*, surrounded by lightning.

There are several myths about Monju and the art of writing on water. See also 'Gods of Japan' under *Gods; Manjushri*.

Monkeys

1. In *Tagalog* mythology, the origin of monkeys is related as follows:

> Bathala was the only living being in the world before there was anything on earth. Feeling lonely, he decided to make some friends. He went down to earth to fetch some clay, but the earth was bone-dry. So, Bathala ordered the rain to fall, which it did for the first time ever. Bathala created mountains, rivers, plants, trees, animals and birds. Then, Bathala decided to make a man, but when he had almost finished shaping the clay, the lump slipped from his hand. He held it by the lower end of its back, but it stretched into a rope of clay. Finally the lump fell in a tree and stayed there. Bathala said, 'You will become a monkey and live in the trees forever!'
>
> The rope of clay became the monkey's tail. Bathala then made a man.

See also *Batala*.

2. In *Ilocano* mythology, they narrate that long ago there was a human girl who lived in the forest. One day the Goddess of Weaving arrived, wanting to teach her weaving so that she would have clothes to wear. The goddess gave the girl cotton and told her what to do. 'First it must be cleaned, then it must be beaten, then it must be spun, then it must be woven, then it must be cut, then it must be sewed,' said the goddess.

   But the girl was too lazy for all this work, so she just sat there in the forest, not interested in a proper dress. At this, the goddess condemned her to be a monkey. Humans must dress properly.

3. In Thai mythology, in 11 *jatakas*, previous existences, the *Buddha* was a monkey, helping fellow animals or poor, misguided people on the way to salvation.

4. Monkeys have a reputation for sagacity because they resemble wise old men. That is why the monkey outwits the *crocodile*. However, the *turtle* always outwits the monkey, because he is even older.

   The three famous wise monkeys often depicted in Japanese art have names as follows: 'Mizaru has his hands over his eyes, Kikazaru covers his ears and Iwazaru lays his hand on his mouth.' In Western culture they seem to act like fools, since Westerners want to know everything, especially if it could be dangerous or naughty. The Buddhist, however, is neither afraid nor interested in gossip or any other news. He hopes to keep his mind pure, free from slander, seduction, desire and sin.

5. The fable of the monkey and the *fish*, of Indian origin, is well known from East Africa to *Indonesia* and even in Japan. A monkey is invited

by a fish (*shark*, crocodile or *Sea-King*) to see the wonders of the ocean or enjoy a sumptuous dinner. He sits on his host's back; the latter swims away, then tells the monkey that the fish's wife (sea-queen, she-crocodile) needs a monkey's *liver* to be cured of some *illness* (or to give birth). Quickly, the monkey asks to be taken back to the shore because he has left his liver at home. Once home, he no longer wants to see the palace of the Sea-King! The moral of the story is: Turn down invitations from sharks, crocodiles and other strangers. In the Japanese tale the fish is a jellyfish.

6. In *Java* it is said that the *souls* of true scholars will reincarnate as the black *budeng* monkey (see *Lutung Kasarung*) whereas the souls of dilettantes and posers become the brown *keteh* monkey. It is believed that the head of a *budeng* may grow into a complete monkey again.

7. In the Minahassa (north *Sulawesi*) it is said that the souls of the *dead* migrate to the island Manado Tua, where a species of monkeys live who are believed to be the ancestors, so they are left in peace.

8. In *Borneo*, near Banjarmasin, there is also an island of monkeys; these are believed to be the souls of people who were lost in the jungle. The Bahau people in central Borneo believe that the souls of the dead transmigrate into grey monkeys, so they eat these monkeys only in times of famine.

See also *Chonguita; Hanuman; Kappa; Momotaro; Ramayana; Sijobang; Sinata; Witch*(6).

Monsters

1. In *New Britain*, people relate that there lives in the forest a *buata*, monster which is bigger than a wild *boar* but has similar tusks. It can talk but is stupid. It eats people and is terribly strong. In the *Philippines*, such a monster is called *pugut* or *pugot*, also *cafre* or *kafar*. It is black, walks on its hind legs and also eats people – but only secretly. A *pugut* is much taller than a man but it can change itself into a black *cat*, with fiery eyes or into a wild dog. It is nocturnal and sometimes appears without a head, emitting fire and smoke.

2. The Bungisngis also haunts Philippine myths. He looks like 'a big man who is always laughing'. That is explained by the fact that as soon as he sees you he is happy to have found his next meal! His name means 'showing his teeth'. His upper lip is so large that when he throws it back, it covers his face completely. He can lift up a *buffalo* and throw it. The hero Suac steals his huge club and is then able to kill all his enemies. In *Indonesia*, the *Gergasi*, a giant with a spear, has a similar role (see *Gergasis*).

3. The Philippine hero Alberto meets several monsters. One has seven heads and lives with a princess. Made invisible by his magic hat, Alberto cuts off all the heads with the monster's own sword. He then travels on to another castle where the princess' sister is held captive by a monster who has 10 heads. It too, can be killed only after all its 10 heads have been cut off by its own sword. Next, Alberto travels

to the third sister who is a captive of a monster with 12 heads. This monster's sword is so heavy that only after drinking three pails of magic water can Alberto lift it. He cuts off the 12 heads one by one until the monster falls dead.

4. The Philippine hero Juan, son of Tetong, also kills monsters who guard beautiful girls. They were *giants* with a taste for human flesh. In another tale Juan (perhaps not the same one) meets a black monster that lives in a tree. It sings a song to Juan in which it promises him 'a happy life and a pretty wife' if he does not kill it. It has a magic stone under its tongue which builds palaces. Juan lets it live and it fulfils its promise to him.

See also *Badang; Bujangga(2); Centipede; Demons; Dreams(2); Gerjis; Ghosts; Golden Dragon; Green Demon; Hades(3); Izanagi; Kappa; Kintaro; Makara; Paikea; Pear; Pitaka; Samebito; Spirits(5); Susanowo; Taniwha; Tuna; Yofune-Nushi.*

Moon (Hawaiian, *mahina*; Indonesian–Malay, *bulan*; Javanese, *wulan*; Maori, *marama*; Samoan, *masina*; Tagalog, *buwan*)

1. The Moon-Goddess, on *Java, Dewi Nawang Wulan*, is venerated widely as the Goddess of Love (*asmara* or *cinta*) and Fertility. It seems that centuries ago the worship of the moon, especially by women, was widespread in *Indonesia*.

2. Some peoples in *Papua New Guinea* relate that a man once saw a beautiful white princess standing on a tree above his head. He climbed up to catch her but she flew away, shining brightly. She became the moon; the *stars* are her maidens.

3. In Japanese mythology, the moon is a vast circular palace of white *crystal*. Thirty princes live in it, fifteen wearing white robes, fifteen wearing black robes, each ruling the moon for one day. The moon also had a king who once courted the Lady *Kaguya*.

4. The Tomori people of central *Sulawesi* relate that the deity Omonga lives in the moon. They perform sacrifices for this divinity in their *rice* barns. Without such a ceremony there would be no rice the following year. They sing a hymn to the Mother-Moon, in which she announces herself as a queen rising from the *Nether World* to help her people. She has 10,000 children, the stars.

5. The women of the Nuforese fishermen (Irian Jaya) sing to the moon, hoping she will keep their husbands in good health during their voyages.

See also *Ama Terasu; Creation(4)(9); Dayaks; 'Gods of the Pacific' under Gods; Hare; Hina-Ika; Hina-Keha; Hina-Uri; Ina; Kaguya; Ladder of Heaven(1); Lona; Mahina; Marama; Mochi; Moon-Bird; Moonstone; Owl(2); Sun(9); Tsuki-Yumi; Yam(2).*

Moon-Bird A Japanese fisherman once found a robe of white feathers on the beach. No sooner had he picked it up than a beautiful shining girl emerged from the sea, begging him to restore her property, for:

'Without my plumage I cannot go back to my home in the sky. If you give it back to me I will sing and dance for you.'

The fisherman returned to her the lovely robe of feathers. She put it on, took her lute, and sang a hymn to the *moon*, where she had her palace. Gradually as she danced, she rose up into the *sky*, then she unfolded her white wings and flew away to the full moon.

Moonstone   In Malay legend, one of the Seven Precious Stones owned by the Seven Sages at the court of King Kukul. Each stone represents one of the seven planets (a ruby for Mars, a diamond for the Sun, an emerald for Venus, a sapphire for Mercury, etc.), so that by means of these seven stones the sages can predict the future. The moonstone has the property that an accurate portrait of a conqueror whose victory is imminent will appear on it, enabling King Kukul to avoid defeat by not provoking a battle against a powerful ruler.

Morai   See *Marae*.

Morning-Glory   (*Ipomoea*; Japanese, *asagao*) A delicate blue flower of the *Convolvulus* family, also a name given to a famous blind singer who had exchanged her *fan* with her lover and stayed faithful to him. An old servant who had once wronged her father committed *seppuku*, suicide, so that his *liver* could be taken out and applied to Asagao's eyes. She regained her sight and went in search of her lover. When she found him, all was happiness.

Morning Star   (Kopu or Malara) In Orokolo (south coast of *New Guinea*) it is said that Malara the Morning Star was looking for wives. He went and found the daughters of Maelare, the Sun-God, Eau and Havoa, and married them.

See also *Atutuahi*; 'Gods of the Pacific' under *Gods*; *Matariki*; *Milky Way*; *Ru*(2); *Star*; *Star Spirit*.

Moro   Daughter of Maivia Kivavia. See *Taro*(1).

Mother-Goddess   On the island of Seran (Ceram) in *the Moluccas* in *Indonesia*, the Alfurians relate that in the beginning there lived Patinaya Nei, 'Queen-Mother', the mother of all people. It seems that in the beginning there were only women on earth. She had the shape of a banana tree; people grew out of her bananas.

A variant of the myth relates how the two first people were young men, Maapita and Masora. They went in search of fire. Masora discovered an old woman who told him to pick her lice first. This he did obediently, though her lice were as big as caterpillars. Then she told him he could get his reward by picking the ripest fruit in her *langsap* tree. While he was climbing the tree, the other fruits cried with girls' voices: 'Pick me first, may I come with you?' But Masora obeyed the old woman and brought down only the ripest fruit. The woman turned it into a lovely girl for him.

Of course, Maapita wanted his own girl when he saw the beauty that Masora came home with. So he too went to the old woman, but he was lazy and impatient. He was frightened by the big lice so he did not pick them properly. Nor did he pick the ripest fruit, for he was confused by all the voices. So his girl squinted and was snub-nosed. He later took revenge and killed Masora, but the old woman made him live again with elaborate magical rites. The woman appears to be a monitor lizard goddess called Kuwe.

See also *Creator; Haumea*.

Mother Timbehes ('Mother of Many') See *Goddess*(1).

Motoro Name of a god worshipped on Mangaia in the *Cook Islands* as the living god, Te-Io-Ora, because he did not wish human sacrifices. However, if someone offended him, that person would have to die. See also 'Gods of the Pacific' under *Gods*.

Mount Fuji See *Fujiyama*.

Mountain of Wisterias, the See *Fujiyama*.

Mountain Man A Japanese demon, living in the forests, described as very strong and resembling a hairy ape. Woodcutters offer him rice to pacify him. See also *Demons; Mountain Woman*.

Mountain Spirit In the Saraburi mountains of *Thailand* a princess once travelled in a litter. While she was being carried across a bamboo *bridge* it broke and she fell into the ravine. She became the Mountain Spirit and whoever wishes to travel through the mountains has to pray to her first or he will perish.

Mountain Woman A mysterious demoness living in the wooded hills of *Japan*. She can fly like an insect but she is bigger than a man and very strong. She can pick up an unwary traveller and devour him. See also *Demons; Mountain Man*.

Mouse The Toraja of *Sulawesi* relate that a man saw a mouse emerge from the nose of his sleeping friend. The mouse ran toward him so the man hit it with a stick. The mouse was dead and so was his friend. See also *Bajang*.

When a mouse nibbles a sleeping person's hair at night, the Toraja say, it is a dead relative announcing his death.

Mousedeer See *Kanchil*.

Mu (pron. 'moo') In *Papua New Guinea* the *mus* are a race of *dwarfs* only two feet high but immensely strong. They will avoid 'big' people but not out of fear. They can make themselves suddenly invisible. However, they will help little children who are lost in the forest, comfort them and give them nuts.

Mudang See *Shaman*.

Muhtabul Bahri The wife of Raja Suran, ruler of *India* and *Malaya*. See *Malay Annals*.

Mujinto　See *Bonin Islands.*

Muliele Alii　See *Moikeha.*

The Muluka Islands　See *The Moluccas.*

Munajim　A Malaysian astrologer. See *Fortune-Tellers*(2).

Muntu-Untu　The Sun-God in the Minahassa. See *Sun*(6).

Muso Kokushi　See *Corpse-Eater.*

Musubi-no-Kami　In *Japan,* the God of Love, Cupid. He has his old shrine in Kagami in the province of Mimasaka. He may appear to girls in the shape of a very handsome young man, leaping suddenly forward from Kanzakura, the sacred *cherry tree* in which he lives. He will offer her a bough of cherry blossom, promising love in the future.

Mwaro　A communal shrine. See *New Caledonia.*

Myo-Jo　('Bright Love') The planet Venus in Japanese astrology.

N

Nakatsu Hime (Shinto goddess, Japan)

Na Atibu   The first man and demi-god in the myths of *Kiribati*. He died so that the earth would be prepared to receive humankind. His right eye is the rising *sun*, his left eye is the full *moon* in the western *sky*. His brains, full of sparks, have become the *stars*. His limbs, scattered on the ocean, became the *islands*, while his bones became the tree trunks. He is compared to *Tangaroa*. See also *Kai-n-Tiku-Aba; Nareau; Ta'aroa*.

Na Kika   In the myths of *Kiribati*, the Octopus-God, whose many arms served him well when he shoved up the earth from the bottom of the sea to form the *islands*, the beaches and the rocks. See also *Creation; Nareau*.

Nabangatai   The village of *souls* in the Fijian Land of the Dead. See *Hades*(4).

Nabhipura   See *Phra In*.

Nabi Isa   Jesus. See *Epic*.

Nabi Khadir   See *Kilir*.

Nabi Khidir   See *Kilir*.

Nabiata   See *Creation*(15).

Nadaka The disloyal servant of Shiva (see *Siwa*). See *Narayana*.

Naga

1. In the myths of the Malay mariners, one of a species of many-headed *dragons* of enormous size.
2. In *Java* and *Thailand*, a mythical *serpent* or dragon, a *serpent-god*, a ruler of the *Nether World* who possesses immense wealth. In Java, also called *Sesa*. In Thailand, a naga is often seen sculpted in temples as a dragon with five heads. It is the emblem of *Narayana*.

Naga Muchilinda In Cambodia, Naga Muchilinda is the *serpent* serving the *Buddha*, drawing its 'hood' over his head to protect the Lord against a rainstorm. This shows that the Buddha is identified with Vishnu-Narayana (see *Narayana; Wisnu*).

Nahk In *Thailand*, a boy of 10–13 years who is dedicated by his parents to become a monk. In a colourful ceremonial procession taking place once a year, such boys are introduced to the local temple.

Nakatsu-Hime ('The Lady of the Middle World') In Japanese cosmology, the Goddess of the Eight Island Country directly below *heaven*. See also 'Gods of Japan' under *Gods*.

Nakula One of the sons of King *Pandu*. See *Pandawa*.

Namora See *Creation*(1).

Namu-Amida-Butsu 'Save us, Merciful Buddha', a Japanese invocation frequently used by the followers of the popular movements.

Nana-Ula A pioneer seafarer who led his people from *Tahiti* (*Kahiki*) to *Hawaii*, perhaps more than 1,000 years ago. During the voyage of over 4,000km (Columbus sailed about 5,000km), Nana-Ula encouraged his men and their wives to be patient, brave and steadfast, while his famous bard and astrologer, Kama-Hua-Lele, recited the *epic* poems celebrating the history of the ancestor heroes and their odysseys.

After his people had settled on the *islands*, Nana-Ula became the first king of the island of Hawaii. From him descend the kings of Hawaii. Initially each of the seven major islands of the archipelago had its own sovereign, but the King of Hawaii was the first among them. See also *Hawaii*.

Nangananga A Fijian goddess. See *Hades*(4).

Naniumlap In Carolinean myths, the God of Festivities. People would pray to him in the hope that he would make women have babies, make the crops grow fast and the animals grow fat. He was associated with the *turtle*, which only chiefs were allowed to eat.

Napoleon See *Indonesia*.

Nara In *Japan*, near Nara, there is a famous *Buddha* temple with a huge statue of the Buddha, erected by the Emperor Shomu in 752. See also *Maitreya*.

Nara-Simha See *Lion*.

Narada In Javanese mythology, a sage who warns people of impending disasters. He is a messenger of the *gods* and in that capacity knows the future.

Narai See *Wisnu*.

Naraka See *Jigoku*.

Narasinga See *Narayana; Wisnu*.

Narayana In Thai mythology, Narayana is the god Vishnu (*Wisnu*). His emblems are the conch, discus, mace and *naga*. In the Thai *epic* work called the *Narayana Sippang*, the god Narayana lives in an ocean of milk and appears on earth in 10 *incarnations*:

1. Wild *boar*, Varaha;
2. *Tortoise*, Kurma;
3. *Fish*, Matsya;
4. *Buffalo* (in which incarnation Narayana had to slay another buffalo);
5. Ascetic, Sanyasi (in order to obtain Shiva's lingam from Tripuram);
6. *Lion*, Narasinga (in which appearance Narayana had to slay the demon Hiranyapakasura);
7. Hunchback dwarf, Vamana (in which form Narayana defeated the demon Tavan);
8. Krishna (see *Kresna*);
9. Celestial nymph, (in order to kill Shiva's disloyal servant Nadaka);
10. Rama, the hero of the epics of *Ramayana* and *Ramakirti* (see *Ramakien*).

See also *Dasarata; Garuda; Wisnu*.

Nareau In the myths of *Kiribati*, he was the Spider-God and *Creator*. In the beginning he walked alone in the oppressive darkness (see *Te-Po-ma-Te-Maki*). He took water and earth, out of which he fashioned *Na Atibu* and Nei Teuke, the first human beings, man and woman. They procreated the *gods*: Te Ikawai, 'The First', Nei Marena, 'The Goddess', Te Nao, the God of Waves, *Na Kika*, the octopus, and Ruki, the *sea-serpent*.

Narsuen A sixteenth-century Thai leader. See *Thailand*.

Navel of the Earth, the (Hawaiian, Ka Piko o ka Honua) The Hawaiian goddess *Pele* was born in Honua-Mea, part of *Kahiki* (*Tahiti*). She was of such eruptive temper that her father Kane Milohai (see *Kane Hoalani*) exiled her from their home island. She was given a canoe and travelled north in search of an auspicious land in which to make her home. She went ashore on many islands, including Kaula, Lehua, Niihau, Kaua'i and Oahu, Molokai, Lanai and Maui. In many places she started digging, thinking to make the foundations of her new house, but every place appeared unsatisfactory for some reason or other. The pits she dug can still be seen, as immense craters, relics of extinct volcanoes now filled with water. Finally she alighted on *Hawaii*, where she created Mount Kilauea, her own home at last. She became very happy there because it was the Navel of the Earth. There, the *gods* began *Creation*.

This search for a divine home is commemorated in a famous *hula* song accompanied by a solemn dance which was still performed at the turn of the century. The image of the navel as centre of the earth is well known in *Java*.

Navigators The Polynesian navigators were great scholars and national leaders. They were elders with a long experience of ocean sailing. It is often supposed that the Polynesian migrants set out on luck-or-loss voyages in arbitrary directions, that they were dreamers trusting their *gods*. Close study of the Polynesian culture and customs has shown that this was never the case. There may have been pioneer voyages of a few dare-devil mariners, out for profit and fame to discover new land or perish, but they did little dreaming during their voyages. They had to stay awake to observe attentively every detail of the seascapes they passed through: the presence and identity of seabirds, the shape, colour and distribution of the clouds, the colour, smell, taste and 'thickness' of the *sea*, the shape and frequency of the waves. The ocean is different in different places so that an experienced navigator can tell where he is by studying the sea. The result was that such skilled sailors could find their way back home without map, compass, sextant or heliometer. Thus the pioneers returned to their home island to tell the elders what they had found, and if they could report an important discovery, only then would an expedition be launched to explore the new-found island and assess its suitability for settlement. Thereafter one or more proper migrations would be prepared with women, children, food and baggage stored aboard a fleet of up to 100 ships.

The navigator functions as master of the ship, standing in the bow and giving directions to the helmsman. He watches the ocean very closely, not only with his eyes. His ears will perceive sounds which tell him about the way the waves and the foam move and hit the ship, his nose tells him of any changes in the smell of the sea, while his feet tell him how the ocean 'swells', i.e. where its currents roll to.

When a storm rises, the sails are rigged, and women and children are securely tied to the ship. The crew ride out the storm, hoping they will survive. The Polynesian craft are not likely to capsize, but they could be broken up by the storm. When the storm subsides, the oldest navigator's great knowledge of the ocean will help him to determine the ship's position, which may be hundreds of miles off course. From there, he can conclude where the nearest landfall must be. That knowledge saves the people.

See also *Aremata-Rorua and Aremata-Popoa; Expansion; Kaho; Nana-Ula; Oripo; Polynesians; Ru(2); Storm; Tangi'ia.*

Nawang Wulan See *Dewi Nawang Wulan*.

Ndauthina In the Fijian myths, the God of Fishermen and Seafarers. His name means the 'torch bearer', a vital function for fishing at night. They say he wanders around at night seducing women. See also 'Gods of the Pacific' under *Gods*.

Ndengei The *Creator* in Fijian mythology. Ndengei is represented as a *serpent* coiling and curling in a cave deep inside the mountain, so causing the people to feel the earth quaking.

Ne-Te-Reere See *Taburimai*.

Needles It is written in the *Malay Annals* that in the reign of Sultan Mansur Shah (1458–77), ruler of the Malay Peninsula, the Emperor of China sent an entire ship full of needles, explaining in a letter that every Chinese citizen had contributed one needle. The sultan smiled and sent the ship back full of threshed *rice*, *beras*, explaining that each of his subjects had contributed one grain. The emperor decided that he had found his match in political sagacity, so he sent the sultan a ship with 500 beautiful women on board.

Negrites See *The Philippines*.

Nei Marena ('The Goddess') See *Nareau*.

Nei Teuke The first woman. See *Nareau*.

Neititua Abine In the myths of the people of *Kiribati*, the Goddess of Vegetation. She had a red skin and eyes which flashed like lightning. King Auriaria fell in love with her. He was a red-skinned giant. Soon after their marriage Neititua Abine died and was buried. Out of her head sprouted the *coconut* palm, out of her navel the almond tree and out of her feet the pandanus.

Nembutsu (*nem* = 'feeling, caring') Nembutsu is caring *Buddhism*, in Japanese religious philosophy. This practice of 'personal Buddhahood' is based on the faith that *Buddha* will bring salvation.

Nether World The Nether World, the Land of the Dead, is always down below the earth. Among the Bagobo of Mindanao, one of the Philippine islands, it is said that the Nether World is surrounded by the Dark River. There, the *souls* of the *dead* will meet a giantess with many breasts who will suckle the souls before they enter the real Land of the Dead, Gimokodan. The land has two sides: the Red Region is reserved for heroes killed in battle; the White Region is for ordinary people's souls who will rest in daytime, limp like dewdrops on petals. At night they will wander about.

The entrance to the Nether World in the coast of Waipio has long since silted up. It is said that the spirit of the great Hawaiian King Kamehameha I (see *Hawaii*) could be seen there from time to time, marching with his procession of great warriors.

See also *Avaiki*; *Hades*; *Hiku*; *Hiyoyoa*; *Merau*; *Milu*; *Miru*; *Naga*; *Other World*; *Pare*; *Patal*; *Paradise*; *Ratu-Mai-Mbula*; *Reinga*; *Rohe*; *Underworld*.

Nets See *Fairies*(1).

Nevi Yanan An Indonesian sea-god. See *Kay Islands*.

New Britain The largest island of the Bismarck Archipelago, which was named after the great German statesman in 1884 after it was occupied for the Kaiser. New Britain has an area of 36,500 sq km, larger than Belgium or the Netherlands. It lies just off the north-east coast of *New Guinea*. It has active volcanoes, the highest reaching 2,438m (8,000ft). Cocoa and palm oil are produced in plantations, *coconuts* and timber are its 'natural' products. Rabaul is the largest town. New Britain has a population of 250,000 and belongs to *Papua* New Guinea. The people speak several Melanesian languages.
　　See also *Adam and Eve*(6); *Monsters*(1); *Spirits*(5); *Sumua; Wallaby*(2).

New Caledonia The original people of this island are often erroneously referred to as *canaques* (the origin of this word is the Hawaiian *kanaka*). They distinguish between a god, *tamate*, and a human spirit, *ko*. When someone has died, his corpse is laid in the bush and attempts are then made to capture his *ko*. The priest and some elders keep a vigil near the body until they hear something, a rat or a *lizard*. This is the *ko* of the deceased. The priest quickly catches the animal in a cloth. With it, he runs to the river and plunges into the water. He re-emerges with a stone, affirming that the *ko* has petrified in the stone. These round ancestral stones, *bao*, are kept in a special communal shrine, *mwaro*. The *bao* which contains the *ko* of a redoubtable warrior and brave hero, is called *panyao* and receives special attention, since its spirit is powerful enough to cause thunder. The souls of the dead float down the rivers toward the ocean where they will live on the sea-bed and where they are ruled by the Shark-God.
　　See also *Black; Gecko; Moaro; Race*(2); *Tomb; Totem*(2).

New Guinea The island of New Guinea, although larger than France and Italy together, was discovered by accident, by a Portuguese captain, Dom Jorge de Menezes, in 1526, while sailing from Malacca. He missed the *Moluccas* and landed on the big island which looked to him like the coast of West Africa, so he called it New Guinea. The Spaniard Alvaro de Saavedra sailed along the north coast in 1527–8, convinced that he had discovered *Terra Australis*, the Great Southland. It was only in 1605 that Luis Vaez de Torres sailed between New Guinea and what is now called Cape York, which he thought was an island. He gave his name to the strait between New Guinea and Australia, but his report was kept secret by the authorities.
　　The first expedition from Holland, led by Captain Willem Janszoon in 1605, was unlucky. Part of the crew, searching for water and food at Duyfken Point, south of Cape York, were killed by the aborigines. Captain Janszoon was the first European to set foot in Australia, and he mapped the south-west coast of New Guinea.
　　In 1642, Abel Tasman discovered the eastern point of New Guinea after sailing round Australia, Tasmania and *New Zealand*. The south-east

coast of New Guinea was first mapped by James Cook in 1769. In 1874 a British High Commissioner was appointed by Parliament, who would administer 'the western Pacific' with his headquarters at *Fiji*, just occupied for the purpose. His new empire included New Guinea east of the 143rd meridian (at present the 141st meridian is the western border of *Papua* New Guinea). New Guinea was little explored and not administered at all, enabling Bismarck to claim the north-eastern quarter of the island in 1884, even though in 1871 he had declared that he wanted no overseas colonies. With characteristic energies the Germans began to explore and map their new colonies, which included the Bismarck archipelago; they called their part of New Guinea Kaiser Wilhelmsland, and it was German scholars who published the first descriptions of some of the *languages* of New Guinea, proving them to be totally unrelated to those of the surrounding islands of Melanesia.

In that same year, 1884, Lord Derby declared to want 'neither Zululand nor New Guinea'. So as early as 1887, south-eastern New Guinea (in 1905 called Papua) was attached to the Queensland administration because the Australians were fearful of the French acquiring islands in the western Pacific. In 1914, Australian troops occupied German New Guinea, which was placed under civil administration only in 1921, after the League of Nations declared Australia the mandatory power. Parts of the island were occupied by the Japanese in 1942–5. Papua and Australian New Guinea were united in 1949 and achieved formal self-government in 1973. Full independence was inaugurated on 16 September 1975.

See also *Austronesia; Bird of Paradise; Black; Butterfly*(3); *Cargo; Cassowary; Creation*(1); *Devil; Fire*(3)(5); *Germans; Gherkins; Goddess*(1); *Head-He-Go-Round-Man; Ihova*(1); *Iko; Indonesia; Ivo; Kangaroo; Korwar; Kyaka; Language; Maori*(2); *Mask; Medicine Man; Mirage; Moon*(2); *Morning Star; Mu; New Britain; Pacific Peoples; Pigs*(1)(2); *Python*(1); *Race*(3); *Rain-Making; Sex; Sky*(1); *Snake*(1)(2); *Spirit Woman; Sun*(1); *Tambaran; Totem*(1); *Woman*(2); *Yam*(1)(3).

The New Hebrides See *Vanuatu*.

New Ireland A mountainous island in the Bismarck Archipelago which belongs to *Papua New Guinea*; it is long and thin: 320 by 11km (200 by 7 miles). The population of less than 100,000 speaks several Melanesian languages. It lies just north of *New Britain*.

See also *Ginger; Malanggan; Solanang; Spirit-Canoe*.

New Year

1. In *Japan* this was originally a feast to welcome back the ancestral *spirits*, for whom branches of pine and bamboo were placed in the house to 'perch on'. Today it is a family get-together for which everybody makes 'a clean slate', settling old grievances and paying debts.

2. In *Thailand*, Songkran was the New Year festival when the ancestors
    were worshipped with scented water. Later it became a water orgy.

New Zealand New Zealand was so named by Captain Abel Tasman
after his native Zeeland, a province in the Netherlands, when he first
sailed along its eastern coast in 1642. (The Tasman Glacier on South
Island was named after him some 200 years later.) With an area of
268,046 sq km (103,493 sq miles), it is rather larger than the United
Kingdom, but its population is still less than 4 million (UK 57 million).
Of these, some 300,000 people are *Maoris*, a considerable increase on
50 years ago, when these people, the largest surviving Polynesian nation,
seemed to be threatened with extinction.

See also *Avaiki Tautau; Black; Dawn Maiden;* 'Gods of the Pacific'
under *Gods; Hahau-Whenua; Hina-Keha; Iho-o-Kataka; Indonesia; Kiwi;*
Kupe; Lizard(1); *Maui; Maori*(1); *Pitaka; Polynesia; Polynesians; Poukai*(2);
Samoa; Storm; Tane; Taniwha; Tonga; Waitiri; Waka.

Nga-Atua The Polynesian sixth *heaven*. See *Tawhaki*(3).

Ngabal *God*, in Oewat (Uwat) on the *Kay Islands*, the protective spirit
who lives in a *fig tree*, to whom a billy-goat is sacrificed in times of need.
The priest will pray: 'God, Sun, Moon, Ngabal, we fear you and bring
you this meat, that we may receive all we need. Protect us, we pray,
against fever, smallpox, blindness, sickness, death, witchcraft and
destruction, that we may be healthy and happy with our families.'

Nganga The *Maori* God of Sleet. See *Fire*(4).

Nganaoa A *Maori* hero who slays three sea-monsters and accompanies
Rata on his odysseys. In the stomach of one of the aforementioned
monsters, he found his long-lost father Tairi, and his mother as well.
They were still alive and could walk out of the beast.

Ngani-Vatu (also called Ngutu-Lei) The man-eating bird of *Fiji* myths.
A hero called Okova was happily married until one day, as he and his
wife were fishing at sea, the bird Ngani-Vatu swooped down low over
their canoe and picked up Okova's wife. Okova turned his canoe and
sailed after the bird but lost sight of it, as it was too fast. After many
days he landed on Sawailau, the island of the killer-bird. In a cave he
found a finger which he recognized as his wife's. It was the only thing
that remained of her.

Later, Okova and his wife's brother Rokoua waited near the entrance
of the cave, which was filled with skeletons, till the bird arrived. It
obscured the setting sun, its shadow plunging the cave into total
darkness and its wings causing a storm. It did not notice the two men,
who were hidden behind the rocks, but started tearing up the big body
it had brought with it. Quietly the two men positioned themselves, then
rushed forward and stuck their spears into the bird's belly. Although
they were long spears, they went in all the way. The bird fell down onto
the edge of the rocky ledge, starting an avalanche. The men decided to
take a tail feather to replace one of their old sails but it was too big for

their ship, so they pulled out a smaller feather from one of the huge wings. Finally they pushed the bird into the sea where it caused a tidal wave as it sank.

Ngarara (also called Karara-Hu-Ara, Ngarara Huarau) In *Maori* myth Ngarara was an *atua*, a divinity or, according to others, a *pitua*, a demon, who was an attractive woman except that she had a long tail. Some writers think of her as a mermaid because she looks superficially like an attractive woman, and can live in the sea. However, Ngarara can walk too because she has feet, so she may have been a water-lizard woman or even a sea-serpent woman. She lived on an island with two servants, Kiore Ti and Kiore Ta.

One day a young man called Ruru landed on the island in search of fresh water and fire. His two brothers sent him ashore to ask for fire at the place where they saw smoke rising. Ruru called at the *marae* (front yard) and was kindly received by the two servants who gave him some fire. He was just on the point of departing when Ngarara arrived, in the shape of a beautiful woman. She took a liking to him, put her hands on his shoulders and wound her tail round his neck. 'You must stay and share our meal,' she said.

Ruru knew he could not escape, but he managed not to eat from the food that was put before him, for he knew it was prepared with Ngarara's scales. Had he eaten from it, he would have developed scales too. As soon as he saw a chance, he ran for freedom. The servants helped him in this way: Kiore Ti disappeared into a stone so Ngarara stumbled over it; picking it up, she scratched it. Kiore Ta then quickly became a *tekoteko*, a magic statue above the entrance gate, so Ngarara had to stop and admire it. She cried after Ruru: 'I will catch you in the mist.'

Quickly the brothers built a reed hut on the beach with a statue in it that looked exactly like Ruru. The next day there was a mist and Ngarara arrived while the brothers hid. Seeing the statue she wound her tail round its neck. The brothers then hastened to set fire to the hut and Ngarara could only escape by leaving her tail behind. The fire purified her so she had no more malice after that.

Ngarara Huarau   See *Ngarara*.

Ngaro   The food of the *dead* in Polynesian mythology. See *Reinga*.

Ngaru ('Waves, Surf') Ngaru was a great hero in Polynesian mythology who dared the King of the Sharks, Tumuitearetoka, to catch him, but was never caught because he invented the surfboard. He married fair Tongatea but she was shocked and fled when she discovered that he was black and entirely hairless. He blanched himself in a limepit, and at the request of his grandfather, *Moko*, King of the Lizards, the god *Tangaroa* gave him nice wavy locks. He was no doubt originally a fish-god, whom the *Creator* reshaped into a handsome man. When Tongatea saw him again she fell in love with him.

He also climbed up into the *sky* (see *Spirits*(2)). See also *Hades*(2); *Lizard*; *Shark*.

Ngelmu The Javanese word for the science of *magic*. Books have been filled with magic formulae in Javanese script, to be recited under special circumstances by medicine men who have studied for years to master the art. If memorized, these secret formulae give the magician the power to change himself or others into an animal. The magic formula itself is called *rapal*. *Ngelmu gadungan* is the power to change oneself into a tiger and back again. See also *Firefly*(3); *Guna-Guna; Macan Gadungan; Magic; Medicine Man*.

Ngirungiru The white-breasted blue tit, the *Maori* lovebird. See *Fairies*(3).

Ngurai A Fijian god. See *Rat*.

Ngutu-Lei See *Ngani-Vatu*.

Ni-Hon-Go ('The Rising Sun Country') See *Japan*.

Nichiren ('Sun-Lotus') A Japanese scholar and founder of a famous school of *Buddhism*, also called Nichiren. Before his birth in 1222, his mother dreamed that she saw the sun (her son) resting on a lotus, a symbol of the world.

Nichiren saw that the people of his time had become corrupt. He decided that Buddhism should again concentrate on the doctrine of Shaka Muni (*Buddha*) himself. His fervent sermons caused a confrontation with *Japan*'s government, which ordered his decapitation, but the sword broke the moment it touched his neck. At the same time lightning struck the Regent Tokimune's palace at Kamakura, while Nichiren's head was surrounded by a bright aureole. These omens moved the authorities to pardon the saint.

Later, Nichiren was exiled from the capital and decided to settle on Mount Minobu where he meditated. While he was meditating, a lovely woman appeared, but the saint told her: 'Resume your natural shape.' Suddenly she became a long, golden-coloured *snake* with teeth of iron.

After his death in 1282, Nichiren was buried at the temple of Kuonji in Yamanashi province. His teaching had revived moral *law* in times of corruption. His followers call him an *incarnation* of Bosatsu Jogyo, one of the early Bodhisattvas.

Night One day Lejo, a young Dayak chief, made a sacrifice on the occasion of the sowing of his rice-fields. At nightfall, when the priestesses had already left, he came back to the altar to look for his knife, an heirloom from his father. To his surprise he found goddesses there, busy consuming the sacrificial meal. As soon as he appeared, they vanished, but one of the goddesses could not leave, for she had very long hair which became entangled in the trees. When Lejo came closer, he saw that she was very beautiful. He said to her, 'Daughter of Heaven, do not fear, I wish you to become my wife and live on earth with me.'

The goddess, whose name was Mang, consented, but she wanted to return to *heaven* first, to collect her clothes. She came back to earth with a plaited bag, which she took to her newly prepared bedroom. She was tired from the journey and soon fell fast asleep. While she lay there, a child came in and, seeing the bag, was curious to know its contents. He made a little hole between the reeds and darkness crept out. The goddess Mang, not wanting to be seen while she was being embraced by an earthling, had collected some darkness from the night *sky* and brought it down in a milk-basket. For in those days, there was no darkness on earth yet; the sun shone day and night. When Mang woke up, she quickly picked up the child and put him outside the door. But she was not careful enough for, at the same time, 'darkness' escaped from the bedroom and out into the world. This was the first time this phenomenon was observed on earth. Terrified, the earthlings ran in all directions hunting 'darkness', trying to sweep it up with brooms and catch it in baskets and sheets – in vain, for 'darkness' had come to stay on earth! It spread like fire, like water, like dust carried by the *wind* which gets into all the corners. The earthlings called it 'night'. They prayed and made sacrifices until suddenly the cocks began to crow. Slowly, darkness became thinner until it lifted altogether. But after 12 hours it came back and this is how it has been ever since.

Chief Lejo and goddess Mang had a daughter. When she had grown up, Mang felt her longing for heaven grow stronger and one day, after her daughter was married, she went back forever to Apu Lagang, the World of the *Spirits*.

See also *Maui*.

Nikko-Bosatsu In *Japan*, the Bodhisattva of smiling sunshine and good health. See also 'Gods of Japan' under *Gods*.

Nikobo An Japanese exorcist. See *Fire-Face*.

Nila Utama The first ruler of *Singapore*. See *Malay Annals*.

Nilawati ('Indigo-Flower') In Javanese mythology, she was a nymph who was born from a *serpent*. The serpent was a *gandarwa*, a spirit who had sinned and was condemned by the god *Siwa* to live as a serpent until its body was killed by a prince, who would find his reward in it. Prince Bambang Kalingga Sakutren, son of Manumayasa, killed the serpent, then married Nilawati and they had a son, Sakri.

Nini Muni In Indonesian mythology, a horrible old *witch* who lives in the Forest of Spirits (see *Kaseteran*). She will threaten the visitor unless he brings dishes of *rice*, roast chicken and sweet cakes, 77 of each. While eating she becomes ever younger and prettier until she is a buxom girl demanding that the man make love to her. After that she will give him what he has come for: Obat Hidup, the medicine that revives the *dead* and heals all wounds.

Ninigi Prince-Ear-of-Rice and Plenty, a young rice-god in Japanese mythology, grandson of the Sun-Goddess *Ama Terasu*. His grandmother gave him precious stones and the *sword* of her brother *Susanowo*, before sending him down to rule the earth. Accompanied by his sister, the vivacious *Uzume*, he broke through the clouds and landed on earth at the point where eight paths lead in all directions of the compass. There he met the terrifying Deity who guards the Floating Bridge to Heaven, who frightened him, but not Uzume. Therefore the God of the Paths guided Ninigi to all the regions of his terrestrial kingdom. Pleased with this service, Ninigi gave Uzume in marriage to him. He himself married *Ko-no-Hana*. His sons were *Hoderi and Hoori*. See also *Bridge of Heaven; Iha-Naga; Sengen*.

Nioo   The patron saint of Japanese wrestlers. See also 'Gods of Japan' under *Gods*.

Niu   The *coconut*, which in *Polynesia* is believed to have grown from the head of *Tuna*, the God of the Sea-Snakes or Ocean-Eels.

Niwareka   The daughter of Uetonga, King of the Fairies. See *Turehu;* also *Fairies*.

Niwaru   The name of the first *canoe*. See *Rata*.

Noa   See *Language*.

Nobapuri   See *Phra In*.

Notu   A magical white *tortoise*. See *Tortoise*(2).

Nuku-mai-Tore   ('People of the Other World') See *Atua*.

Nu'u   In Hawaiian myth, Nu'u was the equivalent of the Patriarch Noah. He was the first man to build a large vessel with a cabin on its deck. On it he loaded *pigs, dogs, kava*, roots and *coconuts*, and escaped to safety from the *flood* which was caused by a tidal wave. Then *Kane* sent a rainbow.

Nyai Belorong   See *Ocean-Goddess*.

Nyai Gedé Segoro Kidul   See *Ocean-Goddess; Storm*.

Nyai Lara Kidul   See *Ocean-Goddess*.

Nyawa   See *Firefly*(2); *Soul*.

Nyi Pohatji Sri   The *Rice-Goddess* of the Sunda people of West *Java*. See *Dewi Nawang Wulan; Rice Mother*(2).

Nyilitimo   See *Creation*(7).

Nyorai   The Japanese word for *Buddha*, often after a name, as in Dai-Nichi-Nyorai, 'The Great Sun Buddha', i.e. *Vairocana*. See also 'Gods of Japan' under *Gods*.

O

Oni demon disguised as a monk (Japan)

O Ai San See *Fudo*(2).

Oa Iriarapo See *Fire*(5).

Oa Rove In the mythology of the Roro people of *Papua*, Oa Rove is the God of Changes. Like Proteus, he could change his appearance at will. From an inaccessible rock he threw down a bow and arrows, a spear and a club which since then men have used in warfare.

Oanamochi The God of the Crater of Mount Fuji. See *Fujiyama*.

Obat Hidup A medicine to revive the *dead*. See *Nini Muni*.

Ocean-God See *Tangaroa*.

Ocean-Goddess The people along the southern coast of Central *Java* worship the Goddess of the Southern Ocean, the personification of the Pacific, called Nyai Lara (Loro) Kidul or Nyai Belorong or Ratu Loro or Nyai Gedé Segoro Kidul, 'Great Queen of the Southern Ocean'. She is also known as Ratu Lara Kidul, 'Virgin Queen of the Southern Ocean'. In Javanese mythology she is identified with *Kali*, wife of *Siwa*. She lives in a splendid palace on the sea-bed and employs many *spirits*, who live in the caves along Java's southern coast. A Javanese will not risk himself in those stormy places before undertaking elaborate sacrifices, prayers and fasting, performed while dressed in a special costume of sackcloth, with uncovered head and specially made straw sandals.

Certain places are particularly devoted to the goddess, such as the cave Karang Tretes, east of the river Upak. Only kings and princes have, during Java's long history, found the courage to enter that cave, where the goddess grants revelations to her favourites. A period of retreat and meditation there was needed for a prince before being acclaimed as sovereign of Java (see *Senapati*). It is said that the goddess even granted her favours to the chosen monarch, appearing to him in 'real' physical form.

Ratu Kidul is also the Goddess of Rains and Storms and as such causes the *rice* to grow as soon as she sends the monsoon rains. In the town of Rongkob, on the coast due south of Surakarta, there is a temple for her, reverently greeted by all passers by, where only the priest may enter. It is his task to keep the Goddess' house clean and ready for her arrival. From time to time it pleases her to rise up from the ocean floor and take up residence in her 'house'. During such a time, a great sacrificial meal is held, by and for the pickers of swallow nests (which are sold to the Chinese as a delicacy), who have to risk life and limb climbing down sheer rocks to the caves where the swallows nest, right above the seething ocean. Many fall into the sea.

The Ocean-Goddess also receives worship from the fishermen who have to risk their lives in their small proas. Those who collect shellfish, squids, barnacles, oysters and other seafood for the marketplace are likewise dependent on her whims.

See also 'Gods of the Pacific' under *Gods; Jin Laut; Pere; Sea-Goddess; Storm*.

Octopus See *Kupe*.

Oda Nobunaga A sixteenth-century Japanese nobleman. See *Japan*.

Oedipus In *Thailand*, a myth relates that King Kong of Si Wi Chai had a very lovely queen. One day she gave birth to a healthy son, but the wise men predicted that he would one day murder his father. King Kong ordered his most trusted officer to kill the child in the forest. The officer took the baby to the jungle and left him there, convinced that the child would perish without him having to shed innocent blood. In the jungle, at that time, lived an old woman called Phrom. She heard the baby crying, found him and took him home. Her childless younger sister, Hom, adopted the baby and called him Phan.

When he was a strong youth, Phan went to see the capital city of Ratpuri (Rajapura). It so happened that at that time the royal *elephant* had broken loose and was running wild in the city. When it saw Phan it went for him, but he seized it by the tusks and forced it on to its knees, showing he had divine power. Soon the whole city was talking about nothing else and eventually the king heard of it too. He ordered Phan to be brought before him and decided to adopt him.

The city of Ratpuri owed annual tribute to King Kong, but when Phan was charged with the mission of offering this tribute in gold and silver, he went to the countryside instead where he recruited an army. When King Kong arrived, seated on his elephant, with his army, to demand the tribute, Phan mounted the royal elephant and slew King Kong with his long lance. Thus he killed his own father. King Kong's army fled back to Si Wi Chai. Phan pursued them and made himself king of that city. He entered the palace where, he was told, King Kong's beautiful widow lived. He entered her apartment at night, intending to make love to her. However, at dawn she recognized him by a birthmark as her own son. He prayed for a sign from *heaven*: 'If this woman is my mother, may milk flow forth from her breasts at this moment!'

At once, the lovely queens's breasts overflowed with milk. So there was no doubt that she was his mother! However, in due course, she gave birth to Phan's son who later succeeded him. King Phan atoned for his sins by building a pagoda 'as high as the birds fly'.

See also *Incest; Sinta.*

Ogre See *Spirit Woman.*

Oho-Kuninushi ('The Landowner') In Japanese mythology, a deity of Kitzuki who rides at night on a *bronze horse.*

Oho-Yama The Japanese Great Mountain God. See 'Gods of Japan' under *Gods; Iha-Naga; Ko-no-Hana.*

Oi-E See *Trinity.*

Oil of a Thousand Charms In Malay mythology, Prince Lela Muda owns a bottle full of this magic aromatic oil which makes any woman fall in love with him if she is sprinkled with it.

See also *Love-Magic.*

Ojin A Japanese emperor. See *Hachiman; Tide Jewels.*

Okova See *Ngani-Vatu.*

Okuni-Nushi A god in the Japanese pantheon who married *Susanowo*'s daughter through trickery, tying up his father-in-law. See 'Gods of Japan' under *Gods.*

Old Daddy Grasshopper See *Malay Tales.*

Olena See *Turmeric.*

Olo Dusun A branch of the *Dayaks* of *Borneo.* See also *Heaven.*

Olo-i-Nano See *Owl*(1).

Olo Keu See *Owl*(1).

Olofat The son of *Lugeilan* in the mythology of the *Caroline Islands.* He is the god who travels between heaven and earth and so is comparable to Hermes. Olofat also brought *fire* from heaven to earth.

Olopana The King of Oahu. See *Laa.*

Omang   *Gnomes* whose feet point backwards. See *Demons*(3); *Gnomes*.

Omikami   ('Illustrious Goddess') See *Ama Terasu*.

Omitsunu   The King of Izumo on *Japan*'s west coast, grandson of the Storm-God *Susanowo*. He enlarged his kingdom by pulling up *islands* from the sea with a rope, like the Polynesian God-King *Maui*. See also *Izumo*.

Omokage-no-Ido   ('Image-well') A sacred well near Idoji in *Japan*, created by *Kobo* with his staff. If the pilgrim can see Kobo's face in the water before drinking it, good luck will follow; if not, disaster will strike.

Omonga   See *Moon*(4).

Ompu Tuhan Mula Jadi   ('The Lord the Root of Becoming') See *Creation*(9).

Onang Kiu   The wife of Raja Suran. See *Malay Annals*.

Oni   In Japanese mythology, *demons*, evil *spirits* who cause disasters like famine and disease. They look human when manifesting except that they have three eyes, big mouths, horns and sharp nails. They fly around and seize the *souls* of dying sinners. Annually the *oni-yarahi* ceremony is deemed necessary to expel these *devils*.

The sage *Nichiren* saw the *oni* at work in the scourges of this time: enemy invasions, earthquakes and eclipses. He attributed the evil to the sinfulness of his Japanese contemporaries, so he founded a special school of *Buddhism* to reform the people.

See also *Jizo*; *Kobo*.

Ono   In the Marquesas Islands, the God of Song. See also 'Gods of the Pacific' under *Gods*; *Lono*.

Opo-Geba-Sulat   ('The Lord who Forms People') See *Creation*(15).

Opossum   In the Kagua Valley in the highlands of *Papua New Guinea*, people relate that in the beginning there was only one man on earth. He had many banana trees, but opossums kept coming and eating the fruit. The man used to shoot them but they always ran away with his arrows in their backs. One day he tied a long string to an arrow before he shot it. He hit an opossum and again it ran away with the arrow, but this time he could follow the string. After a long time he came to a deep cave. Inside there were many women, weeping over the opossums he had killed. They told him that those opossums were their husbands. The man told them, 'Opossums are not for marrying, they are for eating. I will be your husband.'

He cooked all the opossums, and all the women ate some, after which they all married him, and they all had many children, filling the land with people.

Oracles

1. In *Hawaii* the king was, at certain times, confined in a structure of wickerwork where he could not be seen by profane eyes. At such times the spirit of a god would enter the king's body so that it shook. The god would then answer questions through the king's mouth.

   In the southern Pacific the deity would frequently enter the appointed medium, whose will-power would be taken over by the god, so that he or she spoke entirely under supernatural influence. The medium would become violently agitated, his limbs convulsed, his body swollen and his eyes wild and strained. He even would sometimes roll on the ground, his face distorted, foaming at the mouth, shrilly crying divine words which would be interpreted by the expert priests in attendance.

2. In *Indonesia* the descent of a spirit into a medium is demonstrated by shaking and trembling. After this the medium becomes quiet and may answer questions. Often the medium will begin to dance, performing a *menari*, which has been described as a typical shaman's dance (see also *Shamanism*). Some dancers hold a *sword*, swinging it against the enemy: the evil *spirits* of the village.

See also *Ganindo; Heiau; Korwar.*

Orchid   In *Thailand* there is a tradition that two lovers, a prince and a princess who grew up together in the forest where their royal parents lived in exile, swore to love each other forever in purity or to die. One night an evil bushman broke into the princess' hut and raped her. The princess drowned herself in the river, hoping her *soul* could be purified although her body was defiled. The prince followed her into death. Their souls became two orchids: she became an *Ua*, he a white *Khulu* orchid. See also *Love.*

Oripo   In Tahitian, a bard, a sage who can recite the genealogies of the captains and *navigators* who first settled the *islands*, and their descendants.

   The recital used to begin: 'The earth rose from the sea, and the people rose from the earth.' The earth, i.e. the islands, 'rise up' from the horizon for the first explorers. This is also, however, the myth of *Creation*, in which the islands rise to the ocean surface like giant *whales*, after which the people 'rise' like the trees and plants from the belly of the land.

Oro

1. In Tahitian mythology, the God of War and Peace, son of the *Creator Tangaroa*. In peacetime his name was Oro-i-Te-Tea-Moe, 'Oro with the Spear Down', but in wartime he was known as the killer of men, for he took pleasure in human sacrifices and he was present in battles. He was also the patron of the Areoi, the Argonauts of the Pacific. He was the son of Hina-Tu-a-Uta, the Earth-Goddess Hina. Oro had three daughters: Toi-Mata, 'Axe-Eye', Ai-Tupuai, 'Head-Eater', and Mahu-Fatu-Rau, 'Escape from a Hundred Stones'; and one son, Hoa-Tapu, 'Faithful Friend'.

2. In Rarotongan mythology in the *Cook Islands*, the son of Tangaroa and ancestor of the Rarotongan people.

Oro-Tetefa See *Areoi*.

Other World The Other World houses all the *gods* and *spirits* (not just the evil ones, as the *Underworld* does). It can be anywhere, not necessarily beneath the earth, as the *Nether World* is.
    See *Atua; Hades; Nether World; Reincarnation*(1); *Ru*(1); *Semangat; Shaman*(1); *Shamanism*(1)(2)(3); *Spirits*(3); *Tuma; Underworld*.

Otohime The daughter of the *Sea-King*. See 'Gods of Japan' under *Gods; Toyo-Tama*.

Otoku-San A girl-doll. See *Tokutaro-San*.

Otter In *Japan*, an otter can play the same tricks on a man as a *fox* or a *badger*, so the people say.
    One day a fencing teacher called Rokugo met a beautiful girl on the road whom he suspected to be a spirit's illusory shape. He drew his *sword* and struck just to the right of the apparition, since he knew that the girl he saw was only an illusion, but that the fox or other animal causing it was on its right, real but invisible. Sure enough the sword struck home and there lay a dead otter.

Ovo Akore The red *coconut* palm. See *Sex*.

Owl

1. In a Samoan myth two brothers, Olo Keu and Olo-i-Nano, while endeavouring to cut trees in a sacred grove, came upon an owl fighting for its life as it was being encircled by a *snake*. Suddenly the owl turned to the brothers and said, 'I am the lord of this forest. If you help me now, I will help you build your boat. If I lose my life, your boat will never sail.'
    The brothers quickly seized the snake and slit its throat. Thereupon the liberated owl spoke again: 'Now you can cut down my trees and build your canoe with its outrigger. Call it Va'atele, "Swift Yacht".' This they did.
        See also *Canoe*.
2. In *Malaysia* it is related that the owl once fell in love with the Princess of the Moon. When he proposed to her, she spat out her *sirih* (quid of *betel*) all the way down to earth, telling this foolish lover to go to earth and find it. Alas, on earth, the quid became a honey-bird (or bee-eater) and flew away. The owl never found it. It can still be seen looking lovingly and hopefully to the moon.

Oya-Shima-Guni ('Parent-Island-Country') The original eight *islands* of Japanese cosmology, the first parts of the solid world created out of the primeval ocean. *Izanagi* and *Izanami* dropped brine from a spear point and, in this way, caused the inhabitable world to take shape. See also *Creation*.

P

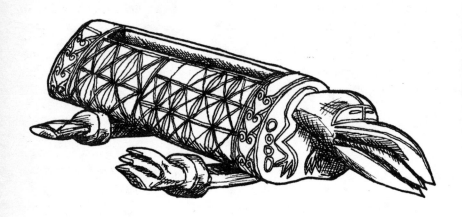

Papua drum: men's house drum depicting magic bird
(mid-Sepík, Papua New Guinea)

Pa Bilalang ('Old Daddy Grasshopper') See *Malay Tales.*

Pa Pandir ('Daddy Stupid') A Malay folklore character who always does the opposite of what is advisable or necessary and so always fails. See also *Malay Tales.*

Pacific Gods See 'Gods of the Pacific' under *Gods.*

Pacific Peoples The Pacific peoples are many and varied. They arrived in waves over a very long period. *New Guinea* was 'discovered' by its first settlers *c.*25,000 years ago during the last Ice Age. At that time the level of the ocean was much lower than today, so many *islands* were then linked that are now isolated. As a result there was no Torres Strait and the first people could just walk over to Australia. As the waters rose, Australia and New Guinea were separated from the other islands and the new settlers had to travel in boats which, of course, they had to invent first. It was the brilliant invention of the outrigger *canoe* that enabled the Malayo–Polynesians to roam freely across two oceans, from the Kenyan coast to Easter Island (*Rapanui*), a distance of 27,750km, more than half-way round the earth along the Equator. The Malayo–Polynesians were a group of peoples all speaking the languages of one family. They include the Malaysians, the Indonesians (but not the peoples of Irian Jaya, *Papua* New Guinea) and the *Polynesians*.

There is a great deal of debate among scholars regarding the date of this *expansion*. *Polynesia*, it is now claimed, was reached by the first Polynesians *c.*3,000 years ago, whereas Madagascar was settled by peoples speaking closely related dialects as late as 1,000 years ago. This confirms that there have obviously been several waves of expansion.

In spite of the exceptional ranges in both time and distance, these Austronesian islanders of the Indian and Pacific oceans display many common characteristics. Obviously, between the Australians of 25,000 or more years ago who migrated on foot into Australia, the Melanesians, Papuans and other black inhabitants of the islands who came after them, and the first Austronesians, many centuries elapsed. It is attractive, therefore, to hypothesize the arrival and/or transition of several other groups of peoples. The languages of Australia and New Guinea are not related to each other nor to the Austronesian languages of the Malayo–Polynesians, so we may posit not only a different history but also a distinct origin. Scattered groups of black peoples, including pygmies, have been found in *Malaya*, the *Philippines* and on the Andaman Islands. Conversely, scattered groups of Polynesians have settled in Melanesia and *Micronesia*.

Padanda A Balinese priest.

Padanda Boda A Buddhist priest.

Pagar Ruyung A Malay ruling dynasty. See *Malay Annals*.

Pagui See *Stingaree*(2).

Pahuanui In Tahitian cosmology, one of the *demons* of the sea.

Pai Hutanga The first wife of *Uenuku*.

Paikea The Polynesian God of Sea-Monsters, son of *Papa*; in Hawaiian, Paiea, the soft-shell crab.

Pajajaran See *Bantam*.

Paka'a In Hawaiian mythology, the God of Wind, comparable to the Greek Aiolos. He was a grandson of *Loa* the *Creator*. Paka'a invented the sail and gave it to the mariners of the *islands* (see also *Navigators*). See also 'Gods of the Pacific' under *Gods*.

Pakasa Uru ('Big Wallaby') See *Wallaby*(2).

Palatehan of Pasai See *Sunan Gunung*.

Paliuli The Hawaiian Garden of Eden where the *breadfruit* grows.

Pampahilep See *Tree-Spirits*(7).

Panakawan The comedian or light entertainer in the *wayang* performances. See also *Semar*.

Panangsang A Javanese prince. See *Jaka Tingkir*.

Pancha-Sila ('The Five Virtues') In *Indonesia*, the basis of the national constitution, based on ancient Hindu lore. They are:

a) The belief in an Almighty God.
b) Humanism, civilization (*adab*), and justice (*adil*).
c) *Persatuan* – unity (of the nation).
d) Democracy led by wisdom, diplomacy and consultation of representatives.
e) Social justice for all the people.

These principles are acceptable to all.
  See also *Adat; Law*.

Pancha-Tathagata (The Fivefold Buddha) The myth of the five sacred kings of Central *Java* during the Middle Ages. These kings were believed to be *incarnations* of the five Dhyani Buddhas. Their names are Kartanagara, Jayanagara, Rajasanagara, Jayawardhana and Rajasawardhana. They were kings of Singasari and Majapahit, perhaps in the eleventh and twelfth centuries, but their historicity has been disputed. Needless to say that they possessed infinite wisdom and knowledge, courage and self-control. During their reign *Buddhism* flourished on Java, and great works of art and literature were created. See also *Colours and Compass*; 'Gods of Bali' under *Gods*.

Panchatantra See *Panja Tanderan*.

Pandawa (or Pandowo) In Javanese mythology one of the five sons of King *Pandu*. They are *Yudistira, Bima, Arjuna*, Nakula and Sadewa, the heroes of the *Mahabharata*. See also *Bratayuda*.

Pandowo See *Pandawa*.

Pandu In Javanese myths King Pandu is the father of the five *Pandawa*s including Puntadewa, *Arjuna* and *Bima*. He is the blind son of *Kresna*, the god of the 'good' side in the *wayang* and *epic poetry* of old *Java*.

Pangeran Bonang See *Sunan Bonang*.

Panja Tanderan The Indian *Pancha Tantra* in Malay and Javanese. This ancient book of fables is well known in many Indonesian languages. Its original purpose was to teach princes and chiefs' sons the art of how to make friends, how not to lose them and how to manage people. The main characters are two jackals, called Karataka and Damanaka in Sanskrit, Kalila and Damina (Dimna) in the eleventh-century Arabic version. Both fable books have found their way to *Indonesia*, adding to the vast treasure of Indonesian animal fables already in existence. The two jackals are parasites, spongeing on the *lion*'s catches. They tell each other fables on the art of useful behaviour and politics. In the end they even manage the affairs of the lion, the King of the Animals. Here the fables teach princes how to control their courtiers and recognize self-interested liars. See also *Kanchil*.

Panji (also Chekel Waneng Pati and many other aliases) A prince in Javanese mythology whose story is performed in the *wayang gedog*. He meets the Princess *Chandra Kirana* ('Golden Moon'), but only after numerous adventures in which he slays *serpents*, *demons* and *giants* of all sorts is he allowed to marry her.

There are many variations on this theme, which has grown into a literary genre known as the *Panji Romances* in Malay and Javanese. The opening chapter usually introduces *Wisnu* and his beloved wife *Dewi Sri* in *heaven*, deciding to incarnate in a prince and a princess in the respective kingdoms of Kahuripan (Koripan) and Daha, so that they can combat evil and in the end, marry. However, these tales are no longer as popular as they used to be.

Panyao A stone containing the *ko*, 'spirit', of a brave hero. See *New Caledonia*.

Panyasa-Jataka See *Jataka*.

Paoro The *Maori* Goddess of Echoes. See *Woman*(1).

Papa (or Enua, Hotu-Papa, Whenua) The earth, a goddess, and the first woman in Polynesian mythology. Her husband is variously called Wakea, Vatea or *Rangi*. Some traditions relate that this first couple came to *Hawaii* from the Society Islands in a *canoe* with two pigs, two dogs and two fowls. Others relate that their original homeland was Ilolo (Jilolo) or Ololoi in the *Moluccas*, now part of *Indonesia*. This name, Muluka or Moloka ('Molucca'), was the origin of the name Molokai, one of the Hawaiian *islands*.

See also *Adam and Eve*(2); *Goddess*(4); 'Gods of the Pacific' under *Gods; Heaven*(2); *Rangi; Rehua*(1); *Sky*(2); *Tane*.

Papare The *moon* in Orokolo mythology. See *Yam*(2).

Papua Papua New Guinea is the eastern half of the island of *New Guinea* and adjacent islands. At 461,691 sq km, it is somewhat larger than Sweden. It has 4 million inhabitants, speaking over 400 languages between them. It is rich in food products: coffee, tea, cocoa.

See also *Coconut*(1); *Creation*(2); *Demons*(2); *Dogs*(3); *Dudugera; Epalirai; Evara; Fire*(2)(5); *Germans; Ghosts*(4); *Goddess; Goga; Head-He-Go-Round-Man; Hiyoyoa; Ihova*(2); *Kyaka; Life After Death; Maori*(2); *Mask; Matabiri; Matagaigai; Moon*(2); *Mu; New Britain; New Guinea; Oa Rove; Opossum; Pigs*(1)(4); *Python*(1); *Semangko; Sorcery*(2); *Tambaran; Taro; Vailala; Vaimuru; Wallaby; Woman*(2); *Yama Enda*.

Paradise (or Pulotu, Purotu, 'Beauty') In central Polynesian mythology, Pulotu is the abode of the *gods*. In that valley there is a lake called Vai-Ola, '*Water of Life*', in which old people can bathe – if they can find it. They will come out young. There is also a tree, *Pukatala*, which can supply all one's needs. Its fruits are better than any on earth.

One arrives in Pulotu by floating down a narrow river. All the *spirits* of the *dead* pass through that gorge into the *Nether World*, old and young,

rich and poor. After bathing, and so regaining their youthful beauty,
they live in perfect happiness. At night they may float upwards into the
sky like *will o' the wisps*, and visit earth. They may also appear to their
relatives in *dreams*, but they must be back in Pulotu before sunrise.

See also *Bulotu; Jodo; Hades; Heaven*(1); *Khuna; Reinga; Ten; Tokoyo-no-Kuni; Tuma.*

Pare In *Maori* legend, Pare was a *puhi*, a noble virgin of such high class
that no man may touch her until she finds a suitor of equal rank. She
lived alone with her maids-in-attendance in a house surrounded by three
circles of palisades. One day a young chief named Hutu came to the
playing field in front of her villa to throw darts and javelins. Pare could
watch the games because her house was built on a hill. From afar love
stole into her heart as she watched Hutu's strength and agility. As she
watched, one of his darts was blown off course by a gust of wind and
landed at her feet. Hutu came up to the gate and requested whoever was
inside to throw it back. Great was his surprise when he heard a girl
answer: 'Come and get it! I want to speak to you!'

Hutu knew that behind the enclosure lived a *puhi*, so that the place
was *tapu* (taboo) for him. Cautiously, he declined to enter. When Pare
opened the gate and took him by the hand, he suddenly turned and ran
back to his own home. Overcome by grief, Pare dismissed her servants
and took her own life. Hutu was arrested and accused of being
responsible for her *death*. He agreed and consented to be executed, but
requested three days respite to arrange his affairs.

'But do not bury the body,' he added. 'Just leave it in her house.'

This was agreed and Hutu left. He travelled to the *Underworld* where,
at the gate, *Hine-Nui-Te-Po*, the Goddess of the Night, barred his way
until he gave her a *mere* or greenstone, probably cassiterite. She then
showed him the 'Path of the Dead Men', leading down into Te Reinga
(*Hades*). After a long search he found Pare and by his ingenuity was able
to persuade her to go back to the Upperworld with him. He told her
to embrace him tightly, whereupon he climbed a tree. In the
Underworld, trees grow from the roof downwards, just as in a cave the
roots stick out downwards from the ceiling. Thus Hutu clambered up
the tree until he reached the roots. He then dug his way upward until
he emerged on the other side, which is our earth. When they saw Pare,
the people rejoiced, and they agreed that a man with so much *mana*
(magic power) was a worthy husband even for a lady of high birth who
had just risen from the dead. (It is not told how the spirit was reunited
with the body. For that, see *Eleio*.)

Pari Penganten See *Rice-Bride and Bridegroom*.

Parrot The Malay collection of fables, *Hikayat Bayan Budiman*, 'Parrot
Tales', is still very popular in *Indonesia*. In a certain tree lived a flock of
parrots. They chased away the *cemperling* (starling) who also lived in that
tree, because he was different. It was a lucky escape, though, for a
birdcatcher came and cast his net around that very tree. The leader of

the parrots, however, instructed all the birds to simulate death, so the birdcatcher threw them away. He caught the leader last, by which time all the other parrots had flown away, so the man no longer believed the leader-parrot when he feigned death. The chief-parrot then spoke, saying in good Malay, 'There you see, I kept my word to those birds but they are not loyal to me. Leadership is an ungrateful task. Take me to the market and sell me for a high price because I can speak your human language.'

The birdcatcher sold the leader-parrot to Hoja Maimoon, a rich merchant. One day Hoja had to go on a long business trip and left his faithful parrot in charge of the house. Hoja's wife was very beautiful. One day the local prince saw her and made her fall in love with him by means of magic incantations. At nightfall, she wanted to go out and join her lover, but the wise parrot said: 'Wait! Do not fall into the same trap as Princess Hasana!'

'How does that story go?' asked Hoja's wife.

The wise parrot then began the first of the 70 tales of the loyal parrot who is trying to prevent his mistress from being unfaithful to his master. Each tale lasts until morning, when it is too late for women to join their lovers. There are 70 tales because the merchant stayed away for 10 weeks, during which the wise parrot succeeded in keeping his mistress indoors simply by keeping her enthralled by his story-telling.

The origin of this cycle is the *Sukha-Saptati*, the Sanskrit book of the 'Parrot's Seventy'. The Persian version, *Tuti-Nameh*, 'Parrot Book', (1329) is equally popular and probably the source of the Malay *Parrot Tales*. Not all the collections of these tales are complete.

See also *Sijobang*.

Parvati See *Prawati*.

Patal (or Patali; Sanskrit, Patala) In Thai, Javanese and Balinese cosmology, the *Nether World*, where *demons* live. See *Hades*(3); *Hanuman*.

Patinaya Nei ('Queen-Mother') See *Mother-Goddess*.

Pau-Makua A famous chief of Oahu. See *Laa*.

Paulet An Englishman who annexed *Hawaii*. See *Hawaii*.

Peach In Japanese, *momo*, a highly valued fruit. Myth relates that an old woman once found a big shining peach floating on the river. She took it home and inside it found a baby. See also *Momotaro; Mollusk*.

Peacock See *Manyura*.

Pear In *Japan* it is said that beside a lake there stands a tree laden with mountain pears. One pear will cure the sick and even revive the *dead*. But in the lake lives a monster who will devour all but the quickest climber. See also *Mango*.

Pelandok See *Kanchil*.

Pelanduk See *Kanchil*.

Pele The Goddess of Fire, and Goddess of the Kilauea Volcano in
Hawaii. Naturally her temperament is impetuous and passionate. She
must never be crossed, of course, but to be loved by her is equally
dangerous.

1. A chief called Kahawali was once challenged by Pele, who appeared
   to him in the form of a shapely woman, to a sledding match down
   the mountain slope, on a *holua* (the forerunner of the modern
   toboggans). The chief accepted, unaware of the power of his
   opponent, yet Pele lost the match, since Kahawali had more
   experience. Incensed, she came after him, sliding on the rolling
   stones which soon became lava, as the goddess' wrath set the
   mountain on fire. Kahawali had to run for his life. Just in time he
   reached the seashore. There lay a boat. Kahawali jumped into it and
   pushed off, while Pele rained stones on him, without hitting him.
   Behind him she had resumed her fiery form.

2. One fine day Pele fell in love with Lohiau, the handsome Prince of
   Kaua'i, who was a master of drumming and graceful dancing. She
   appeared to him as a ravishing beauty, even lovelier than the girls
   of Kaua'i. They talked for a while in elegant phrases. Of course the
   prince fell in love with Pele and so they agreed to be married, even
   though he knew neither her parents nor her homeland. After many
   happy weeks Pele suddenly decided she had to go back to her
   volcano. She promised her husband that she would come back, then
   flew away, invisible. After a month or two, Lohiau, refusing food,
   died of grief. Many people had ignorant opinions about his death,
   but one man, an old seer or prophet, *Kaula*, advised the people not
   to enquire any further, since he said Lohiau's wife must have been
   a goddess who had returned to the world of the immortals and had
   invited the spirit of Lohiau to join her there.

   Meanwhile, Pele sent her faithful sister *Hiiaka* to fetch Lohiau's
   body. Hiiaka travelled to Kaua'i disguised as a mortal, only to find
   out that Lohiau had died and that his soul was imprisoned by the
   lizard women Kilioa and Kalamainu on a lonely cliff by the shore.
   Fortunately, being a goddess, Hiiaka could penetrate the spirit-
   prison and gather up Lohiau's life-soul. Then, abandoning her
   human form, she flew through the air to the death chamber with
   Lohiau's soul in her arms. There, in the funeral hall in the middle
   of the night, she reunited Lohiau's soul with his body. He woke up
   confused and was taken to the beach where, in the fresh breeze, he
   soon recovered. From there, Hiiaka and Lohiau travelled to *Hawaii*
   and fell in love. When Pele perceived this, furious, she decided to
   destroy the husband she had taken so much trouble to 'have and
   to hold'. She poured molten lava over him so that he became a pillar
   of stone and died.

   Hiiaka then descended into the earth to the kingdom of *Milu*, the
   God of Death, to await the arrival of Lohiau's soul. However, his soul
   was hovering over the ocean and the *islands* in search of her. There

it was discovered by the god Kane Milohai (see *Kane Hoalani*), father of the *gods*, who came sailing past in his miraculous ship. He caught Lohiau's soul like a bird in the air and returned it to the stone pillar on the mountain slope where, he knew, the prince's body was hidden. He removed the stone covering that concealed Lohiau's body and allowed the soul to enter its abode once more. As Lohiau regained consciousness he found himself standing on the slope of Mount Pele. Suddenly he saw the goddess standing before him. Even though he recognized her as his wife, he was ready to beg her for mercy, knowing that she had killed him once already. But Pele was an unpredictable goddess. She had not only forgiven her husband but was ready to give him away now that he was reborn. She said: 'Do not fear me. I was your wife in your previous life. Now I cannot expect you to love me any more. I have been hasty and unjust. My sister Hiiaka loves you.'

She vanished, and in her place stood Kane Milohai, who said, 'Here is a magic seashell which, if you put it in the sea near the shore, will become a ship. Board it and it will take you wherever you want to go. When you arrive, do not forget to pick it up. It will become a seashell again so you can carry it in the palm of your hand. You will find the one you love.'

The god vanished and Lohiau placed the shell on the waves where it grew at once into an elegant yacht. He sailed to Kaua'i but landed on Oahu along the way. This was the will of destiny because Hiiaka, too, was there. The King of Oahu was holding a *kilu*, a song competition. When it was Hiiaka's turn to sing, she sang a song of her own composition, praising Lohiau. When she had ended, Lohiau, who had been watching among the hundreds of spectators, quickly began to sing a hymn in praise of the goddess Hiiaka. Reunited, they set sail for Kaua'i in the miraculous ship.

(This myth is strongly reminiscent of the Greek myth of Aphrodite who loved Adonis. Young Adonis died every year and was revived each new spring with the anemones. Diana–Artemis was the goddess who killed her own lover, Aktaion.)

See also *Kamapua'a; Navel of the Earth*.

Pelesit In *Malaysia*, a *spirit* in the shape of a *cricket*, used by *sorcerers* to accompany a *polong* (see also *Bajang*) or bottle-imp, which sucks the blood of the sorcerer's enemies. To conjure up the spirit, the sorcerer will dig up the body of a first-born child, freshly buried, take it to an anthill, bite off its tongue and bury that in a certain place, dipped in fresh coconut oil. It will then turn into a *pelesit*. This is one method; there is another (see *Polong*). They have different results.

Penan (or Punan) See *Borneo*.

Penanggalan In *Malaysia*, it is said a woman may become the devil's apprentice. She will learn to fly, but only her head with the entrails attached to it will actually fly, while the rest of her body stays behind.

She will suck the blood of her enemies at night. See also *Witch*(4).

Penates   See *Atua*.

Penis   See *Inuvaylau; Sex; Squirrel*.

Penyakit   The Sickmaker. See *Spirits*(4).

Peony

1. In *Japan*, it is said that the peony shrub (*botan*) has a spirit like a young man. Once this flower-spirit fell in love with a princess, Aya, but she had already been betrothed to a young lord, Ako. One day she was walking in the garden when she stumbled in the flower bushes, but a young man prevented her from falling. His *kimono* had peonies embroidered on it. Princess Aya fell in love with him and became ill. Her father asked her maid why, and she told her master the secret of the Peony Youth. The king sent a guard to seize the youth, but all he found in his hands was a large peony. Aya kept the flower, but when she married Lord Ako, it died.
2. Yone was a young woman in Japanese mythology. She died, but in the moonlit night of the *Bommatsuri* celebration, she came back from the *dead* carrying a paper lantern decorated with peonies. She had taken the lantern from her own grave.

Perahu   A boat or small sailing vessel. See also *Indonesia*.

Pere   The Polynesian Goddess of the Waters of the Ocean which surrounds the *islands*. Her mother was Tahinariki or Haoumea, or *Papa*. She married Wahiaroa. One morning Pere wanted to travel, so her mother gave her the ocean in a jar to take with her and later to carry her in her royal yacht. In the beginning there was no sea at all, so Pere poured it out wherever she wanted to go. At first she carried the ocean in a jar on her head, and later, when she had poured it all out, the ocean carried her in her lovely divine ship. Thus a mother will give birth to a son who will one day 'support' her.

Peri Dewa   A prince of *Sumatra*. See *Cow; Maniaka*.

Perry, Commodore Matthew   See *Japan*.

Persatuan   ('Unity' (of the nation)) One of the Indonesian Five Virtues. See *Pancha-Sila*.

Petara   See *Creator; Siwa*.

Petruk   One of the sons of *Semar*.

Phan

1. A Thai king, the son of King Kong. See *Oedipus*.
2. The King of Nakhon Pathom who used the *elephant-tiger* to breed a new race of war elephants. See *Elephant-Tiger*.

Pheasant In Japanese, *kiji*, a bird which may be the *soul* of a woman who has died.

The Philippines The Philippine peoples (total population approaching 60 million) are divided into 'tribes', better described as ethnic groups, with their own religions, many of which remain to be studied and described, and 33 *languages*, all related to each other, to Indonesian and to the Polynesian languages, and yet quite distinct, not mere dialects. In addition, English is understood by many, Spanish by some. Filipino, the national language, is a 'Creolized' form of *Tagalog*, the language of the Manila area.

Of these 'tribes', six are described as 'Negrites' which in practice means that they do not care for Western 'civilization' or Christianity, but prefer to live in their traditional ways, following their ancient religions and speaking their own beautiful languages. Their names are *Ita, Ayta, Dumagat* and *Agra* on Luzon, *Ati*, which is scattered on all of Panay and much of Negros (though the 'great' language of Panay is *Iloilo*) and *Ata* on Southern Negros. Those peoples will remain for as long as the forests that support their lives are left in place. The 'tribes' are again divided into sub-tribes, some composed of only a few hundred members, each with its own dialect. They feel no loyalty towards any central government. Similarly the four Muslim groups, Maranaw and Samal on Mindanao, and Yakana and Tausug on the *Sulu Islands*, see themselves as culturally completely separate from the ruling circles in Manila.

People speaking Indonesian languages settled in the Philippines well before the birth of Christ, and found the islands already occupied by a *race* of small dark-skinned people of whom only pockets now remain. They are the 'real' Negritoes.

The famous Portuguese navigator, Fernao de Magalhaes (Magellan), in the employ of the Holy Roman Emperor, Charles V, was the first European to set foot on the Philippines, on the island of Samar (1519) which he called St Lazarus. He managed to persuade the chief of a neighbouring island to accept baptism, but was killed in a skirmish with some 'rebels'.

The Philippines were then visited by Captain Lopez de Legaspi, the first Spaniard to land there. He named the islands after his king, Philip II (1558–98). The Spaniards invaded Manila in 1570 and discovered a foundry where bronze canons were made, as well as copper and tin, Chinese porcelain, iron and steel. Indian textiles were also readily available all the way from Cambay.

While the Portuguese built their fortresses in Tidore (now in north-east Indonesia) (1578) and Macao (1557), the Spaniards built theirs in Manila. When Philip became King of Portugal as well, in 1580, he came to rule a vast commercial empire, reaching from Sumatera to Firando on Kyu-Shu on the Japanese coast. Later, the Spanish government instituted a regular shipping service from Mexico to Manila. Until 1821, the Philippines were administered from Mexico as part of the Spanish king's dominions.

Gradually a middle class developed of a Spanish-speaking educated bourgeoisie. Young men went to study in Spain and France and came back with new ideas. The best known of the political thinkers in the Philippines was José Rizal, author of *El Filibusterismo*. Thanks to his promotion of equality and independence, he was exiled in 1893 and executed in 1896.

In 1898 the Spanish–American war broke out over Cuba, which gave the Americans a chance to open a window toward China, where they had extensive interests. Admiral Dewey steamed into Manila Bay and destroyed the Spanish fleet. The Philippines were then 'bought' from the Spanish crown by President Th. Roosevelt for US$ 20 million. The peace of Paris ratified this. Some Filipinos continued their guerrilla actions, now against the Americans, until President F. D. Roosevelt gave them independence in 1937.

In 1941, war broke out and on 2 January 1942 the Japanese occupied Manila and heavily defeated the Americans at Bataan and Corregidor. When Douglas McArthur landed in the Philippines, a further series of brutal and famous battles were needed to wrest the islands from the Japanese, one after another, culminating in the last great battleship to battleship confrontation of history, the triple battle of Leyte in October 1944. The Japanese even offered 'independence' to the Filipinos but it was too late. Independence returned on the 4 July 1946, when most of the war damage was repaired and the Americans were ready to leave the islands.

Between 1946 and 1965 there were five presidents. From 1965 to 1986, the Philippines were ruled by Ferdinand Marcos. Initially he reduced the crime rate, but communist agitation was supported from abroad. Gradually its suppression made the regime more tyrannical until Corazon Aquino, the widow of Marcos' enemy, won countrywide elections and became President.

See also *Adarna; Ape; Bats; Boroka; Heaven*(1); *Indonesia; Lioness; Mary*(1)(2); *Monsters*(1)(2)(3)(4); *Nether World; Pacific Peoples; Pregnancy; Sangiang; Stingaree; The Sulu Islands; Tinoso; Tortoise*(2); *Witch*(6).

Phosphorescence of the Sea   The Malaysian fishermen attribute this wondrous phenomenon to Hantu Air, the Sea-God.

Phra In   (or In, Inthra) In Thai mythology, Phra In is the God of Wealth, the Lord of Heaven, King of all the Gods, who decides all things. He possesses a third eye, like Shiva (see *Siwa*), with which he can see all things that are hidden from mortal eyes. It was thus that he once saw that the people of Lawa, one of the numerous clans of the Thai nation, were distressed because they were plagued by evil *spirits*. Phra In sent a dream to an ascetic telling him that the people on earth must always speak the truth and think the truth. The ascetic prophesied that the people would be freed from the evil spirits as soon as they had made their minds absolutely pure of all lies and insincerity. They obeyed by beginning to lead pure lives. Soon Phra In, being pleased with the people's virtue, caused three miraculous wells to open in the earth, one made of *crystal*, one of silver and one of gold. Every citizen who prayed devoutly and regularly near one of the wells would find in it whatever he wanted. Thus the people lived in complete happiness.

Alas, the world is wicked. Numerous jealous and dishonest men descended on the town, which was called Nobapuri or Nabhipura, 'Navel City', and started stealing from the wells. When the citizens prayed fervently to Phra In, he sent two giants from heaven, carrying a huge metal pillar between them. This they erected near the golden well in the city. The pillar radiated virtue. Its effect was incredible. All the thieves arriving from foreign lands became honest traders overnight. This happy condition prevailed for many years so that Nabhipura became a great centre of commerce and wealth. Alas, nothing will last. In the end the people forgot their prayers, just took what they wanted and soiled the sacred pillar. One day the two giants returned, lifted the pillar up and carried it back to heaven. All too soon the country was poor again.

Phra Sao In Thai mythology, the Planet-God Saturn, 'the God of Fickle Fortune'. When Saturn visits a person, he is invisible, only a shadow, yet a *mirror* image will betray his approach. Like the classical Saturn–Kronos, he is the father of the gods, whose wrath will cause terrible misfortune. Prayers are due to him when he approaches one's Zodiacal sign, and it is advisable to perform sacrifices. The god does not strike his victims physically with hail or lightning, but his displeasure is announced by the five signs of ill-boding: profuse perspiration, paleness, shivering, darkness before the eyes, and a feeling of gloom in the heart. That melancholy forebodes bad luck. One's best friend dies, one's horse breaks a leg, one's son falls ill. Saturn can humble the proud. Only he can cause the fall of tyrants. Worst of all, Saturn causes illusions, so that evil men pursue their own death.

See also *Sword*(2).

Phrom

1. The Thai form of the name *Brahma* the *Creator*. See also *Bromo*.
2. The old woman who found the baby Phan, the son of King Kong, in the forest. See *Oedipus*.

Phrom-Kuman ('Boy-God') See *Elephant*.

Phrot Thai form of *Bharata*, one of the heroes of the *Mahabharata*. See *Bratayuda*.

Pia In *Maori* traditions, a frozen land where rocks float in the white sea, colossal *fish* play in the ocean and it is dark most of the time: Antarctica.

Pigeon

1. In *Malaysia*, the *tekukur*, *Geopelia striata*, is the subject of a tale in which she was a girl whom her parents kept confined to their home.

So one day, dressed only in her necklace, she flew away, having changed herself into a pigeon. Today the pigeon still has a speckled collar.

2. There is a Malay myth of a speaking pigeon which tells the king it has three rubies in its stomach. The credulous king pursues it through the forest but never catches it. The pigeon mocks him and so do his subjects, who somehow learn of the event. The king is deposed and exiled.

Pigobara   See *Spirits*(5).

Pigs

1. In the East Sepík district of *Papua New Guinea*, the people relate that there was a time when they did not yet have pigs. So what else could they eat except other people? Then a pregnant goddess, whose little son had been designated as the meat for the next big meal, told the boy: 'Your father intends to swap you with the neighbours' child, for slaughter. I do not want to give birth to a human child. I will make a pig.'
    She gave birth to a little daughter with many teats like a sow. The mother herself turned into a big sow with two rows of teats. The people called this new animal a pig. They tied up the mother pig and carved her into many pieces for the participants of the big meal. The little girl pig grew up and gave birth to many piglets.

2. In the New Hebrides (see *Vanuatu*) and some other areas of Melanesia and New Guinea, the pig is the supreme object of sacrifice, to the extent that the pig takes the place of, or is identified with, the sacrificer. The pig represents wealth, power and fertility. It lives for sacrifice.

3. In the New Hebrides it is related that a man once climbed a tree. The bark rubbed against his testicles, which began to swell. He returned home and told his friends to cut stakes and put them securely in the ground. Meanwhile his testicles went on growing until they were enormous. Finally they burst and five pigs ran out of each testicle. Some were caught by the men and tied to the stakes. Their offspring became the domestic pigs. The others ran into the forest where their offspring became the wild pigs. This is the origin of pigs of different colours.

4. Pigs were first created by a god called Yabuling, according to the myths of the Rai coast peoples of northern Papua. His sanctuary is still near Gabumi in that area.

5. The Dairi people of west *Sumatra* believe that the *souls* of the *dead* transmigrate into wild pigs. In Minangkabau, people are said to come back as bush pigs, or as *snakes*.

6. In the Javanese book of *magic* (*Kitap Ngelmu*, see *Ngelmu*) there is a special formula for changing one's enemy into a pig.

Pili   The Gecko-God. See *Gecko;* also 'Gods of the Pacific' under *Gods*.

Piliwale A King of Oahu. See *Kelea*.

Pillow In Japanese mythology, a *magic* pillow will transport the sleeper who has laid his head down on it to a distant country. A man called Rosei was once on a long journey. Tired, one night he arrived at the inn of Kantan and fell asleep almost immediately, unaware that his head was lying on a magic pillow. At once, he saw an ambassador who addressed him thus: 'I am sent by the Emperor of Ibara to inform you that His Majesty wishes to relinquish the throne. He invites you to take his place.'

Rosei was led out of the inn, where a palanquin was waiting. Liveried lackeys carried him through the clouds to a country of indescribable beauty. Rosei was enthroned as its emperor and reigned for 50 years during which he enjoyed every pleasure, both spiritual and sensual. Finally he decided he had had enough and returned home to end his days in meditation.

Pinang See *Betel*.

Pine Tree (Japanese, *matsu*) In *Japan* the pine tree is the symbol of good fortune and long life. It is often represented in art as the very image of Japan, and its evergreen presence is found in every garden. It is said that it is auspicious to grow a male and a female pine tree in the family garden, no matter how small, to ensure a long, peaceful marriage. Houses are built from pine timber so that the tree can shelter all the family. Its resin is used to prepare fragrant and medicinal unguents.

In mythology, pine trees are said to have *spirits*. Two of these are called Jo and *Uba*, 'Mr and Mrs', symbolizing marital love and fidelity. Pine tree branches are used for decoration during a feast, *matsuri*, in Japan, especially *Sanganichi*, Japanese *New Year*. See also *Matsu; Raicho; Uba*.

Pintara See *Creator*.

Pipi Korovu See *Butterfly*(3).

Pipiri The star Castor. See *Gemini;* 'Gods of the Pacific' under *Gods*.

Pitaka A *Maori* hero who, with 170 brave men, marched up into the mountains where an enormous man-eating dragon-like monster lived in a cave. It was as large as a hill, shaped like a huge *lizard*, and was called a *taniwha*. The hunting party laid nooses of thick ropes on the ground and trapped the monster by quickly pulling on them when it came forth to attack them. They started hitting it with their stone battleaxes and their long spears, while the monster lashed out at them with its long tail, on which sharp spines grew, and tried to catch them between its numerous teeth. It did manage to catch some of them, but finally succumbed to the many wounds inflicted upon it. When the men cut open the monster's stomach they found inside piles of human bodies.

Pitaka's fame travelled through *New Zealand*, so the chiefs of Waikato district sent a message to Pitaka asking him to come and slay another *taniwha*, which lived in a lake in the mountains near Te Awa Hou. Pitaka soon arrived with his intrepid men. Taking one end of a long rope, he told his men to hold on to the other end and to start hauling it in as soon as they felt a pull on it. Then he dived down to the bottom of the lake, holding his end of the rope firmly in his hand. With his *karakia*, his magic formula, which he repeated continually, he so confused the *taniwha* that he managed to approach it from behind and quickly tied the strong rope around its tail. As soon as the men on the shore felt the rope pulling, they hauled it in, singing their *karakia*, which put a spell on the monster so it could not escape. The stomach of this fish-lizard was likewise full of dead people.

A third monster lived in a cave near Rotorua. It had large green eyes with which it stared at its victims, thereby paralysing them.

Pitua A demon in *Maori* myth. See *Ngarara*.

Plum Tree In *Japan*, plum trees are revered as givers of beautiful blossom and delicious fruit, *sumono*.

An old gardener, Hambei, had an ancient plum tree in the garden handed down to him from his grandfather. Alas, a nobleman coveted it and sent a messenger to negotiate the purchase of the tree. Hambei refused flatly to sell his grandfather's tree, even though he knew that the nobleman had friends at court. But the nobleman simply sent a bag of gold and announced that the next day his gardeners would arrive to transplant the plum tree. That night Hambei heard sobbing in his garden. He went out and saw a beautiful woman weeping near his tree. She was Sumono, the spirit of the plum tree. He asked her why she cried so sadly and she replied: 'For so many years have I lived in this garden that I remember your grandfather when he was a boy. Now I have to be uprooted, cut off from my earth, and placed in a foreign land.'

The next morning when the nobleman arrived, Hambei told him the story, returned the bag of gold and pleaded with him to leave the tree where it was. Unaccustomed to being contradicted by a peasant, the impatient nobleman drew his sword and would have killed the gentle Hambei if the spirit of the tree had not intervened. His sword slashed through something that was not the peasant's neck. Nor was it the tree-ghost, for she appeared in front of him, and then disappeared just as suddenly. A branch from the tree then fell on the nobleman;s head. His sword must have gone through it, though he did not understand how it could have happened. Contrite, he withdrew, but the delicate tree died. So did the nobleman's father, the same day.

See also *Cherry Tree; Tree-Spirit; Willow Tree*.

Po ('Night', Polynesian) See *Creation*(5); *Milky Way; Trinity*.

Poe Mpalaburu See *Crocodiles*(1).

Pokeka A Polynesian ceremonial *robe* of honour.

Pokop See *Masalai*.

Polecat In *Malaysia* it is said that the polecat, *musang*, is a spirit, *hantu*. Charms are worn against it. See also *Bajang*.

Polong In *Malaysia* it is said that a *polong* is a 'bottle-imp' as small as a child's little finger. It can be made by a *sorcerer* taking the blood of a murdered man, putting it in a wide, round, narrow-necked bottle and muttering secret incantations over it. After 7 to 14 days a *pelesit*, a cricket-shaped spirit always associated with the *polong*, will begin to stir and chirp.

The *polong* has to be fed on blood, so the sorcerer will send it to his or her enemy at night. The cricket will enter the victim's body tail first, and the *polong* will follow, to suck his blood. The victim will fall ill, so the *medicine man* will have to be fetched. He will ask the *polong* inside the patient: 'Who is your master?' The *pelesit* will then answer through the patient's mouth, giving the sorcerer's name in a high pitched cricket's chirping.

Polynesia Polynesia is comprised of the innumerable *islands* lying within the 'Polynesian Triangle' defined by Easter Island (*Rapanui*) in the east, *Hawaii* in the north, *Fiji* in the west and *New Zealand* in the south, the last three island groups lying almost in a straight line.

The history of Polynesia can be pieced together on the basis of the oral traditions which are still present in the minds of some men and women. The backbone of their history is the genealogy of both the male and the female lineages of the ancestors. These are remembered in some cases as far back as the twentieth generation. The names of these ancestors used to be recited in a traditional cantilating fashion at special festive occasions, when the *spirits* of the ancestors were commemorated and venerated. Specially memorable events and exploits were also mentioned, such as great voyages of exploration and discovery, with the names of the islands concerned, where they passed and sojourned and where they finally settled, who the navigators were and how they sailed.

On this basis, Alain Gerbault, himself a sailor, concludes that the *Polynesians*, whom he calls *Maoris*, arrived in Porapora and Raiatea, where he collected data, in about the middle of the ninth century, not later, using very large *canoes* (longboats) or proas. It is said that these ancestors were *gods*, but the reason for this is that they were deified in the course of subsequent history. This fact should not exclude our treating these recitals as the skeleton of Polynesian history, with an admixture of mythical material.

The ancient Polynesian noblemen married their sisters because there were no other women, nor could better husbands be found for them. They were not only expert *navigators* but also astronomers and geographers, since it appears they knew where they were going. It is said that they were travelling east, so we may conclude that they came from the west originally. However, the majority of Polynesian traditions begin at a much later stage, when the people were settled in central Polynesia (Opoa) and from there voyaged north to Hawaii, south to New Zealand, east to Tuamotu, the Marquesas and *Rapanui*, and west to Fiji. Only Fiji and the islands further west were inhabited before the Polynesian expansion; from those islands we hear of wars which, however, ended in a merging of the two populations into a new *race*.

See also *Atlantis; Austronesia; Hawaii; India; Indonesia; Islands; Java; Malaya; The Moluccas; New Zealand; The Philippines; Samoa; Tonga.*

Polynesians These are a well-known and distinct *race* of people, uniquely adapted to sail the high seas in small open craft. For this trying life they need courage, knowledge and grim perseverance; also the ability to survive heat and cold, and the constant spray of salt water, which, when it dries, leaves the skin cold, oversensitive and covered in crystals. The Polynesians can survive for days and nights without food, fresh water or sleep and yet remain cheerful and optimistic. They are the Greeks of the Pacific, intrepid sailors, and scholars with a firm grasp of geography, ocean lore and astronomy. They are also poets with a fine gift for music and song, including *epic* songs. In their poetry is embedded one of the richest mythological traditions on earth, remarkably coherent, over the largest area ever covered by an ethnic group before the Portuguese expansion. They are incredibly inventive and great artists when weaving, painting boats and decorating houses with wooden sculptures.

The Polynesian languages are very closely related, including Hawaiian, Samoan, *Maori* and even *Rapanui*, the language of Easter Island. They form a genus of the Malayo–Polynesian family of the Austronesian language phylum.

Apart perhaps from Fiji, the Polynesians were the first and only settlers of the Polynesian islands until *c.*1800 when British, American, French and Chilean ships brought new settlers. They migrated because they had to: the islands were very small and supported only a limited population. When that limit was passed, new islands had to be discovered, or the people would starve.

See also *Adam and Eve*(2)(3); *Amai-Te-Rangi; Ao; Aremata-Rorua; Areoi; Atua; Atutuahi; Auraka; Avaiki; Brain Coral; Breadfruit; Canoe; Creator*(4); *Dance; Dawn; Death*(1); *Deluge; Earthquake; Eel*(2); *Eva; Expansion; Fish; Gemini; Giants*(1) 'Gods of the Pacific' under *Gods; Hades*(2); *Haronga; Hawaiki; Heaven*(2); *Heiau; Hina-Ika; Hina-Keha; Hina-Uri; Hiro; Io; Ika-Tere; Infanticide; Ira; Ira-Waru; Iva; Kaikomako; Kanaka; Kane Hoalani; Kapuku; Kava; King; Kohara; Kumara*(2); *Law; Lizard*(5); *Lona; Lua-o-Milu; Mahiki; Makutu; Mana; Manawa; Maohi; Maori; Mapere; Marae; Marama; Mareikura; Maro; Maru; Matariki; Maui; Mauri; Milky Way; Milu; Miru; Navigators; Ngaru; Niu; Papa; Paradise; Pere; Pomare; Rain-God; Rangi; Reinga; Rongo-Mai; Ro'o; Sky*(2); *Songbirds; Spirits*(3); *Sport; Storm; Sweet Potato; Taboo; Tai-Moana; Tane; Tangaroa; Tapairu; Tevake; Tiko-Kura; Tini Rau; Tui; Turehu; Uekera; Uru; Utu; Waiora; Waka; War; Wind; Yam.*

Pomare The name of a series of queens of *Tonga*. Pomare IV lifted the ban on marriages with non-Polynesians. As a result, diseases spread among the members of the once pure *race*.

Ponaturi Sea-fairies, the *spirits* of the Pacific, the ogres of the ocean. These strange beings have often been at war against the heroes of the *Maori* traditions.

Rua-Pupuke had a son who went swimming with the other boys of the village. When his friends came back home, Rua-Pupuke asked them where his son was. They answered simply: 'He sank.'

The father asked the boys to take him to the exact spot where his son was last seen. There, in the surf, he changed himself into a large *fish* and dived down to the sea-bed. He found the palace of the Sea-God, built entirely of beautifully carved human bones. Rua-Pupuke recognized his son, whom the Sea-God had placed above the lintel over the front gate, as a *tekoteko*, a gable ornament. The boy cried out to his father, as he recognized him even in the shape of a fish. Rua-Pupuke, who was a very big fish (perhaps a *whale*), took the boy in his huge mouth and carried him back to the beach where he spewed him out. His mother, who was waiting there anxiously, received him with open arms.

Rua-Pupuke resumed his human form and started giving orders. An old house was repaired in such a way that not a ray of light penetrated it. Meanwhile the boy, who was still recovering from his ordeal under water, was carried to a secret place in the woods. That night at dusk some people arrived whom Rua-Pupuke, with his great knowledge of the unseen, perceived to be the *Sea-King* and his suite in human disguise. He met them at the entrance gate of his compound with great courtesy and led them to the newly repaired house, which he put entirely at their disposal, ordering his cooks to prepare a sumptuous meal for his guests. Rua-Pupuke knew they were searching for his son, for once the Sea-God has a human *soul* he will never let it go, but nothing was said of this of course. The guests retired for the night in the house, because as they were pretending to be human beings they would naturally have to seem to be in need of sleep. As the house had been hermetically sealed, the next morning the sea-spirits could see no light. When the sun was high, Rua-Pupuke ordered his men to set fire to the house so that all the bodies in it were burnt to ashes. The spirits themselves escaped, of course, but without bodies, so they had to fly straight back to the sea.

See also *Dwarfs; Fairies; Gnomes; Hema; Menehune; Tawhaki*(2); *Tipua*.

Poros See *Malay Annals*.

Porpoise It is related in *Malaysia* that some poor unlucky fishermen once met a mysterious wise man who told them to pick loads of mangrove leaves and scatter them on the sea. Then he changed into a porpoise and jumped overboard. The leaves changed into *fish* so the next day the fishermen hauled in their nets heavy with fish.

Possession (Japanese, *kitsune-tsuki*, 'fox-lunacy') This occurs, we are told, mostly in women. The fox spirit enters through the fingernails or the breast. See also *Tadanobu*.

Pou Matangatanga The daughter of the *Maori* chief Tawheta. See *Uenuku*.

Pou-Tere-Rangi   The Gate of Heaven. See *Turehu*.

Pouakai   See *Poukai*(2).

Poukai

1. A man-eating bird in *Maori* myths. When a man went to a certain
    river to fetch water, this bird would emerge from its hiding place in
    a cave, swoop down, pick him up with its enormous bill, and take
    him to its cave, where it would kill him by smashing his head against
    the rocks. The hero Pungarehu went down to the river with his
    companion, told his friend to go and stand in the river pretending
    to fill a water pot, and just wait. The bird soon came. It wheeled over
    them but just at the moment it would have seized his friend,
    Pungarehu hit it with his stone axe so hard that its left wing broke.
    A second blow broke the other wing. The bird fell down and
    Pungarehu beat it to death. The companions climbed up to the bird's
    cave where they found piles of human bones and skulls. When they
    came home they found their wives sleeping with new husbands
    because they had been away for so long. When the two women woke
    up, they were overjoyed at seeing the 'lovers of their youth', and sent
    their second husbands away. As the proverb says: 'The old key fits
    the lock best.'
2. On South Island, *New Zealand*, there once lived an even larger bird
    called *pouakai*, which could fly so fast that it could seize a running
    man in its claws. No one could escape it. It took men, women and
    children, all of whom it carried up to its nest on the rocks for its
    young to devour. Its cry was a blood-curdling scream, which it
    emitted just before it swooped.

    One day the hero Hau-o-Tawera came to offer his help to the
    terrified people. He instructed them to plait a strong net 60ft across,
    from tough saplings. Acting as a decoy, he waited for the bird to dive
    down on him, and just managed to escape under the net where 50
    men armed with spears were hiding. In its effort to grasp Hau-o-
    Tawera, the bird became entangled in the net and could not escape,
    so the men were able to stab it to death.

See also 'Gods of the Pacific' under *Gods*.

Prabu Makukuwan   A Javanese king. See *Python*(3).

Prambanan   In Central *Java*, between Jogyakarta and Surakarta, in the
valley of Kali Dengkeng, stands a magnificent temple complex, almost
1,000 years old. The main temple was dedicated to *Siwa* and his spouse
Dewi *Kali*, whose statues are still there. It is flanked by temples for
Brahma, *Wisnu*, Rama and Durga Sakti (see *Lara Jonggrang*). In the
vicinity are several *Buddha* temples all dating from the twelfth century.

It was here that Prince *Senapati* stood on a hill praying to the Goddess
of the Southern Ocean (see *Ocean-Goddess*) (Kali is also the Goddess of
the South and of Death), while his enemy, *Jaka Tingkir*, the Sultan of
Pajang, was encamped in the valley, ready to attack. The goddess sent

thick black clouds unchaining a terrible rainstorm, while to the north the great volcano Merapi erupted, vomiting flames and rocks. These signs of the gods were watched by the Sultan of Pajang. His generals urged him to order the attack, but he called the battle off, adding, 'I, Jaka Tingkir, Sultan of Pajang, ruler of Java, will soon die. He, young Prince Senapati, will rule Java after me.'

Rocks rained down on the camp and his soldiers fled. The next day, the Sultan of Pajang fell from his elephant and died.

Pramuni See *Durga*.

Pratiwi, Dewi Pratiwi In Javanese mythology, the Goddess of the Earth, identified with *Dewi Sri*, spouse of *Wisnu*. See *Wijaya-Kusuma*.

Prawati The Balinese form of the Sanskrit Parvati, the Mountain-Goddess of Meditation and Virtue, wife of *Siwa*. See *Kali*.

Predestination (Indonesian, *nasib*; Japanese, *ummei*)

1. In Indonesian and Japanese cosmology, predestination is taken for granted. Very common is the tale of the man who, dissatisfied with his lot, goes to the Lord of Heaven to complain. The Lord agrees to let him choose again and – disaster – he again chooses the fate he already suffers from. In both Buddhist and Islamic philosophy the life of a person is determined by his birth.
2. The Tontemboan people of north *Sulawesi* relate that when a child is born, the God of Fate, Kumokomba, son of the *Rice-Goddess* Lichambene, lights a fuse in *heaven*. If it burns quietly to its end, that child will have a long life. If a man dies young, they will say, '*Suwang-na kolek* [His fuse was short].'
3. The Sea *Dayaks* of *Borneo* believe that whenever a child is born, a flower will grow up in Soul Land. If that person suffers illness, they say that his flower is wilting. A *shaman* is called who will go to Soul Land and purify the soil surrounding that person's flower.
4. The *Batak* people of *Sumatra* relate that the *soul*, on its way from heaven to earth, is led past a gigantic tree. Each of its leaves carries in it an aspect of human destiny: wealth, poverty, power, honour, happiness, misery, sickness and early death. The soul is told to pick a leaf, and thus pick his or her own future life.
5. On Nias, they say, the soul before birth is given a parcel. Baliu, the God of Life, will ask the soul if he or she wants a light or a heavy parcel. If he or she answers, 'A light parcel', he or she has a short life on earth. Thus the soul should ask for a heavy parcel.

Pregnancy In Philippine myths a pregnant woman often has odd wishes, while in *Indonesia* there is even a special word for such whimsical desires: *idamidam*. The husband must at any price fulfil these caprices, for ill-luck will befall the child in his wife's womb if he does not. The mythical origin of this necessity is the belief that if the infant is a son, it may be the husband himself who is being reborn in a new body, or perhaps his father or uncle. This belief is widespread.

See also *Puntianak; Reincarnation.*

Pua Ariki ('Royal Flower') See *Ru*(2).

Pua-Ne A *magic* arrow. See *Hiku.*

Pua Tu Tahi ('Coral Rock Standing Alone') In Tahitian cosmology, this was a dangerous demon living under the sea.

Pue di Songi The Supreme God of the Torajas. See *Shamanism*(2).

Pugot See *Monsters*(1).

Pugut See *Monsters*(1).

Puhi In *Maori* legend, a *puhi* is a noble virgin of such high class that she is *tapu*, kept apart, sacred, so that no man may touch her until she finds a suitor of equal rank. See *Pare.*

Pukapuka See *Danger Island.*

Pukatala In Polynesian mythology, the miracle tree in *Paradise* which produces honey or nectar on which the *spirits* live.

Pulotu See *Paradise.*

Puna

1. Child of the *moon*. See *Mahina.*
2. A Polynesian king. See *Moikeha.*

Punan (or Penan) See *Borneo.*

Pungarehu A *Maori* hero. See *Poukai*(1); *Spirits*(3).

Puntianak In *Indonesia*, a universally feared terrible female ghost, who haunts the living and causes miscarriages or stillbirths when women see her. In the hope of preventing such a tragedy, women will sacrifice a chicken at the riverside, which is where the spirit lives. She is described as a wild naked woman with dishevelled hair, wailing like a woman in labour. She died in childbirth and her open, bloody vulva can be clearly seen, a sure sign of witchcraft. She hates men, so she will appear to them as a ravishing beauty but when one tries to make love to her, she will tear off his genitals. When a woman has died in childbirth, some Indonesian people will nail her hair to the coffin so that she cannot rise to cause misfortune.

Some Malays say that the proper name for the child of such a female ghost is *langsuyar* or *langsuir*, 'stillborn child', and that *punti anak* is the same as *matianak*, 'death of a child'. These dead children, or their souls, were said to live on an island off the west coast of *Kalimantan*, hence the name of the city which now stands there. It is related that the founder of the city, Sultan Abdu Rahman, ordered his fleet to open fire on the uninhabited island to frighten away all the *ghosts*. After the bombardment he jumped on the shore armed with an axe and started chopping down trees to prove to his superstitious followers that those who trust in Allah have nothing to fear from evil *spirits*.

Elsewhere the *puntianak* is described as a night-owl, hooting its horrible predictions; or as a black crow which magically penetrates the body of a pregnant woman, causing an abortion (*Achin*). See also *Vampire*(2).

Purarata A *Maori sorcerer*. See *Hakawau*.

Purba Rarang See *Lutung Kasarung*.

Purba Sari See *Ambu Dewi; Guru Minda; Lutung Kasarung*.

Pure Land, the See *Amida*.

Purnavarman A Javanese king. See *Indonesia*.

Purotu See *Paradise*.

Puru See *Malay Annals*.

Pusat Tasik ('The Navel of the Ocean') In Malay cosmology, the deepest part of the sea. *Raja Naga*, the King of the Sea-Serpents, has his palace here. See also *Sea-Serpent*.

Puteri Bualu Julah Karangan ('Golden Princess from the Rock') See *Creation*(6).

Puteri Sembaran Gunung The Giantess of the Mountains in Malay mythology. She spins on top of a mountain, like fate-goddesses. She has breasts as large as mountains which can keep a whole tribe in good health.

Puteri Tunjung Buih ('Daughter of the Foam') See *Malay Annals*.

Putuperereko See *Spirits*(5).

Pyramids These structures of stone were built in Tuamotu, the Friendly Islands, the Marquesas and the Society Islands. They were called *marae* or *morai*, suggesting that there was a temple, a 'house of God' in the centre of each pyramid. The one in *Tahiti* was 267ft long, 87ft wide and 50ft high. It was built in a dozen terraces from blocks of coral a metre long, which had been brought in by canoe from other *islands*. The missionaries had these structures razed, no doubt because they observed the religious ceremonies which were still performed there in those days (*c*.1820), and because of the awe and reverence the people showed with regard to those structures. Yet their religious function is not well understood. Some pyramids had stone altars standing in front of them some 10ft high and it was said that human sacrifices were performed there, although that may well be what some missionaries wanted to believe, so as to show the superiority of Christianity. It is probable that the ancient *kings* were buried there and their *spirits* were no doubt worshipped, like the spirits of the Pharaohs in 'pagan' Egypt.

Python

1. In the East Sepík district of *Papua New Guinea*, people relate that

a man once found a python's egg and gave it to his wife. She cooked it and ate it, but the young python inside did not die. It grew until the woman's belly was swollen, making it look as though she were pregnant. One day when she was chopping dead wood, the python stuck its head out of her vagina and started eating the grubs and maggots that fell out of the rotting wood. When her husband saw this, he quickly cut off the young python's head. The head fell down, then flew away and was never seen again. However, the body of the python withdrew back inside the woman's belly and for a few days blood leaked from her vagina. That is how women came to have periods. From then on the woman had babies, which grew out of the python's body, one by one.

(In Islamic countries there is a widespread belief that women – with some exceptions – have an evil spirit inside them in the shape of a vicious serpent.)

2. In *Polynesia*, half-man, half-serpent *Tuna*, slain by the Sun-God *Maui*.

3. In Javanese mythology, King Prabu Makukuwan (who was *Wisnu*) married a *snake* (*Python pittacus*) he met in the *rice* fields. It was the goddess Lakshmi (*Dewi Sri*), who entered his queen, the Princess of Mandang Kamolan.

See also *Serpent; Snake.*

R

Rua woodcarving (New Zealand)

Ra See *Tama Nui-Te-Ra*.

Ra Torua ('The Day of the Two Sunsets') See *Uenuku*.

Raa The *Maori* Sun-God. See *Woman*(2).

Race

1. On the island of Bilibili, north of *New Guinea*, people relate that in the beginning Anut (*God*) created the black people. Later, some of them took off their black skins. Underneath they had white skins, so they became white people. God told them to go and live far away.
2. In *New Caledonia* the first white men who landed were James Cook and his crew. They were regarded by the New Caledonians as their own ancestors, the *spirits* of the *dead*, coming back for the first time in visible form to the land they once owned.
3. In New Guinea, white men were believed to have returned from the Island of the Dead, hence their colour, white, like bones. This whiteness was the result of their sins having been cleansed.

See also *Austronesia; Kanaka; Polynesians; Tangata; Wallaby*(1).

Raden Rahmat (also known as Malik Ibrahim) First preacher of Islam on *Java*, to whom numerous miracles are attributed. He married one of the princesses of East Java.

Radin A legendary hero among the Iban people of *Borneo*, one of the Dayak-speaking tribes (see *Dayaks*), Radin won the battle of Betong, taking many *heads*, so he gave a big feast (*selamatan*) in honour of Sengalang Burong, the God of the Head-Hunters, that is, the War-God. This god appeared in the form of the great *hornbill*, and his wooden image stood in the longhouse where the men celebrated. After the feast, the image was to be removed and the village abandoned, as the magic power of the god would be too strongly present. So Radin took the wooden statue to the forest, but he was so attached to the longhouse that he stayed there. Some days later the village was struck with smallpox. Every night a bird was heard singing in the longhouse, which was filled with the sick and dying. One night Radin, himself ill with the disease, rose, took his *keris* and swung it at the shadow of the singer. He heard a body falling but nothing was visible. The next day the statue of the bird was found in two halves. This time the people did abandon the village.

Raeit Ngabal An Indonesian forest-god. See *The Kay Islands*.

Raffles, Sir Thomas Stamford See *Indonesia; Singapore*.

Rahi A Tahitian chief. See *Tai-Moana*.

Raho See *Rotuma*.

Rahoua See *Rua*.

Raicho The Japanese Thunder-Bird. It looks like a rook, but can make a terrifying noise. It lives in a *pine tree*.

Raiden (literally *rai*, 'thunder, *den*, 'lightning') The Japanese God of Thunder, depicted with claws, red skin and a demon's head. It was Raiden who prevented the Mongols from invading *Japan* in 1274. He is shown in art sitting on a cloud sending forth a shower of lightning-arrows upon the invading fleet. Only three men escaped. See also 'Gods of Japan' under *Gods; Japan; Kamikaze*.

Raiju ('Thunder Animal') A Japanese demon of lightning, sometimes painted in the shape of a *badger*, a *cat* or a weasel. During thunderstorms it becomes extremely agitated and leaps from tree to tree. If a tree shows the scars of lightning, they say Raiju's claws have scratched it open. Raiju likes hiding in human navels so, if afraid, a person should sleep on his belly during a thunderstorm, to be on the safe side.

Raiko

1. A Japanese hero. See *Demons*(1); *Spider-Boy; Spider-Woman*.
2. A Japanese miser. See *Spider*.

Rain-God Many parts of the Pacific receive, curiously, insufficient rain, and prolonged periods of drought are very well known in *Polynesia*.

When drought continued too long, the Tikopia would circumcise one of the young scions of the old chiefly family of Tafua, because Tafua was also the name of the Rain-God. Prayers were recited and vows were made before the ceremony. This may be a relic of a very ancient custom of sacrificing a first-born to the Rain-God, a custom which is also reported elsewhere. See also *Rain-Maker*.

Rain-Making   Among the Kayakaya in western *New Guinea*, the rain-maker is a magician who endeavours to force the elements to his will. After a prolonged period without rain he will put heavy stones in a canoe, then shake the boat so that the stones roll about in it, making a thunderous noise. Since in his country thunder is always followed by rain, it is believed that the noise he makes will soon have the desired effect. See also *Rain-God; Thunder Baby*.

Rainbow   See *Ina; Kahukura*.

Raitaro   ('Thunder Child') See *Thunder Baby*.

Raivuki   See *Serpent-God*(2).

Raja Angin   ('King of the Wind') The Malaysian Wind-God. See also 'Gods of the Pacific' under *Gods*.

Raja Hantuen   The King of the Ghosts in the mythology of the *Dayaks* of *Borneo*. See *Illness*.

Raja Naga   In Malay mythology, the King of all the Sea-Serpents, the largest of all the *dragons* in the ocean, who lives in the *Pusat Tasik* palace. See also *Sea-Serpents*.

Raja Jinn Peri   The King of the Fairies. See *Malay Annals*; also *Fairies*.

Raja Sulana   A ruler of *India* and *Malaya*. See *Malay Annals*.

Raja Suran   A ruler of *India* and *Malaya*. See *Malay Annals*.

Rajasanagara   One of the Dhyani Buddhas. See *Pancha-Tathagata*.

Rajasawardhana   One of the Dhyani Buddhas. See *Pancha-Tathagata*.

Raka   The Polynesian God of the Winds. See also 'Gods of the Pacific' under *Gods*.

Raka Maomao   The *Maori* God of the Winds. See also 'Gods of the Pacific' under *Gods*.

Rakan   See 'Gods of Japan' under *Gods*.

Raksasa   (Javanese *reksoso; reksasi*, female) In *Indonesia* a demon or demoness of the wilderness, usually a man-eating giant.

Rama

1.   A line of Thai kings. See *Thailand*.
2.   An *incarnation* of *Wisnu*. See *Dasamuka; Ramakien; Ramayana*.

Rama Khamheng   ('Rama the Brave') A thirteenth and fourteenth-century Thai king. See *Thailand*.

Ramadhipati (or Ramatibodi) A fourteenth-century Thai king. See *Thailand*.

Ramakien (or *Ramakirti*) The Thai version of the Sanskrit *epic* myth of the *Ramayana*, the contents of which may have come to the Siamese people via medieval *Java* and Cambodia. Its earliest records date from the thirteenth century, though at that time it seems to have found expression only in the form of shadow-play and dances (Sanskrit, *Chayanataka*). Later figures representing the characters were cut from leather and colourfully painted. This is called *hnang* in Thai and *wayang kulit* in Javanese. It was only *c.*1780, in the reign of Rama I, that the first narrative poems recounting Rama's exploits were composed in Thai, some by the king himself. His son Rama II (1809–24) composed a dramatized version which was performed by masked players in the form of stylized, delicate *dances*.

The 45 episodes describe the exploits of *Hanuman*, *Rama* and Laba defeating numerous demons, in order to rescue Sita (see *Sinta*), Rama's queen.

See also *Ramayana*.

Ramakirti See *Ramakien*.

Ramatibodi A fourteenth-century Thai king. See *Thailand*.

Ramayana A long *epic* in the old Javanese language, written *c.*900AD. Its central theme is the abduction of Sita (see *Sinta*), Rama's wife and an *incarnation* of the goddess *Dewi Sri* (Lakshmi) by the demon Rawana *Dasamuka* ('with 10 faces'), who keeps her prisoner in Langkapuri (Sri *Lanka*). Prince Rama (an incarnation of *Wisnu*) organizes an army of *monkeys* under their general, *Hanuman*, to liberate Sita. There are numerous sub-plots and sub-stories; the romance of Rama and Sita has proliferated, especially on *Java*, into numerous myths and sagas, love stories, wise tales and fables. Many have been rewritten as *lakons*, the scripts for the *wayang* plays. The Thai version is *Ramakien*.

Rangi ('The Sky', or Hanui-o-Rangi, 'Father of the Winds', or Lagi, Langi, Langit) The Sky-God in Polynesian mythology, comparable to Ouranos in ancient Greece, Rangi was originally united with his wife *Papa* (the earth, Gaia) in an eternal embrace. Their children decided to separate them because their was no room on earth for any creatures to grow, to walk or to fly. So, the young *gods*, all the earth's children, endeavoured to separate earth and sky. They all failed until *Tane*, the Forest-God, firmly planted in the earth and unable to stop growing, lifted up the sky so that it remained suspended above the trees. The sky complained because the separation from his beloved wife was painful, but Tane replied that their descendants needed light in order to live and grow. Light then became visible upon earth and at the same time numerous creatures appeared that had been hidden between their parents' bodies: reptiles, mammals and even the first human beings rose up and stood blinking in the light. There was also Rongo ma-Tane, the

God of Vegetation, vegetables and all cultivated food.

See also 'Gods of the Pacific' under *Gods; Haronga; Heaven*(1); *Rehua*(1); *Sky*(2); *Tane.*

Rangi-Haupapa   A cloak given to *Mataora* in *heaven*. See *Turehu.*

Rangi Tuarea   See *Rehua*(1).

Rangima   ('Bright-Sky') See *Creation*(5).

Rangiuri   ('Night-Sky') See *Creation*(5).

Rangkong   A Sumatran princess. See *Hornbill*(2).

Rangsang   According to myth, Rangsang was King of Java, grandson of *Senapati*. He was so devout that he flew to Mecca every Friday to attend the noon prayers there, flying back the same afternoon on his prayer rug. He was also known as Sultan Agung.

As Javanese myths have been woven around known historical figures, Rangsang was probably the original Javanese name of the Sultan Agung Abdur Rahman (1613–45) before, as a Muslim ruler, he adopted the name Sultan Abdur Rahman. See also *Java.*

Ranguma   See *Devil.*

Raos   See *Rasa.*

Rapal   A magic formula. See *Ngelmu.*

Rapanui   Easter Island, the easternmost island of *Polynesia*. Rapanui is also the name of the island's *language*, which is closely related to the dialects of French Polynesia. Rapanui has its own script but it cannot be read since all the local scholars have died. The island is now a Chilean colony, so Spanish has all but replaced Rapanui. The island is full of magnificent medieval sculptures whose significance and symbolism remain a mystery.

See also *Ahu; Hiro; Indonesia; Lizard*(6); *Pacific Peoples; Polynesia; Polynesians; Tangi'ia.*

Rarohenga   Land of the *Turehu*, Rarotonga, one of the *Cook Islands.*

Rasa   (Indonesian; *raos* or *roso*, Javanese) Feeling, refined taste, mystic gift for the discernment of the esoteric significance of cosmic phenomena, acquired by prolonged deep meditation.

Rat   An animal associated with wealth by many nations, the rat is the familiar of the Japanese god *Daikoku* and is the vehicle of the Hindu–Javanese god *Ganesa*; both *gods* are very popular and are often invoked for success. The Fijian god Qurai (Ngurai) turned himself into a rat to be present at the gods' council unseen. See also *Goddess of the Sky; Takara-Bune.*

Rata   A *Maori* hero, son of Wahie Roa, son of *Tawhaki*. Wahie Roa was killed by the ogre Matuku, so when Rata was full grown he had to go and take revenge for his father's death. He took his ancestors' axe and went to the forest, where, after many adventures, he succeeded in obtaining the first *canoe*, built by the wood elves. He named it Niwaru. After more adventures Rata reached the mountain cave where the man-eating giant Matuku dwelt. He told his men to place nooses on the ground in such a way that the monster would step on them as soon as it emerged from its bone-filled cave. That was what happened. Matuku, smelling people, came out to hunt them down, but the men pulled at the nooses and he fell. They cut off his head but his spirit escaped and became the bird Matuku, the bittern.

One day Rata wanted a tree to make a canoe. He felled the tree he had chosen, then went home, for in those days chopping a tree down took a whole day if not two. When he came back the next morning the tree was standing as before. This happened again the next day, but on the third evening, Rata, having felled the tree yet again, hid in the bushes nearby. He suddenly heard a rustling without seeing feet and a singing without seeing people or birds. The singing charmed the tree into re-erecting itself. Rata sang his *karakia*, forcing the singing *spirits* to become visible, or his eyes to see them. He jumped out of his hiding place and, grasping hold of one of the spirits, demanded to know what the reason was for this interference in his work. The spirit answered that Rata should have performed the ceremonies due to *Tane*, the Lord of the Forests.

'Go home, perform the rites and leave the rest to us, your ancestors,' he said.

Rata went home and brought offerings to Tane, with his mother's help. When he came back to the tree the next morning he found a finished canoe in its place. See also *Heron*(1); *Lata*; *Nganaoa*; *Tane*.

Rati   The Balinese Goddess of Love, Desire, Fertility and Motherhood. She is portrayed in Balinese sculpture as heavily pregnant, with voluminous breasts, while her womb is full of life like a river full of fish. See also 'Gods of Bali' under *Gods*.

Ratna Dumilah   ('Shining Jewel') On Central *Java*, one of the names of the *Rice-Goddess*. Ratna Dumilah is born from a jar as the daughter of *Batara Guru*, the Supreme God, and becomes 'the Food that Never Ends': *rice*. The god falls in love with her and embraces her, but she dies. She is buried in Mandang Kamolan and after 14 days, its king, Prabu, sees a light shining from the grave. Out of Ratna's navel grew the rice stalk, out of her feet the nutmeg tree.

See also *Tresnawati*.

Ratna Jumilah   A princess of Madiun (East *Java*), who was left behind by her fleeing father to kill *Senapati* when he entered the palace. She fired pistols at him, thrust a spear into his chest, stabbed him with a *keris* and slashed his face with a razor, but his skin showed not a scratch. No man can die as long as the gods protect him. At last, she fell in love with the great conqueror and submitted to his advances.

Ratu Baka A legendary Javanese king. See *Lara Jonggrang*, who is said to be his daughter.

Ratu Lara Kidul See *Ocean-Goddess*.

Ratu Loro See *Ocean-Goddess; Storm*.

Ratu Mai Bulu See *Serpent-God(2)*.

Ratu-Mai-Mbula In Fijian myth, a *serpent-god* who ruled the *Nether World* where the *dead* live. He made the plants and trees grow. See also *Naga(2)*.

Rawana See *Dasamuka; Ramayana*.

Red Bird The guardian of the southern quarter of the Japanese Zodiac.

Rehua

1. The Polynesian Star-God, son of *Rangi* and *Papa*, ancestor of *Maui* and his four brothers. Rehua lives in the topmost heavens at a place called Te-Putahi-Nui-o-Rehua, 'The Great Crossroads of Rehua', in the tenth heaven called Rangi Tuarea. No mortal being has ever been there. Rehua's son Kaitangata fell down one day and his blood coloured the sky. We call it sunset.
2. Rehua is also the Polynesian name for Pollux. See *Gemini*; 'Gods of the Pacific' under *Gods*.

Reincarnation

1. In Melanesia it is said that the *spirits* of the *dead* who are tired of their life in the *Other World*, *Tuma* (*Hades*), will travel back to earth, to their native island, and find a woman who belongs to the same clan as they did. They will first bathe in a clear well, *sopiwina*, 'cleansing water', then they will enter the womb of a chosen mother and be born as babies, after the normal gestation time.

   Others say that the spirits have to bathe in the ocean and will float on its foam. Fishermen will sometimes hear the baby-souls crying. When a woman conceives, the child descends from her head to her stomach, that is why she suffers from headaches and sickness. The spirit, who may once have been the woman's father or mother, is carried to her by a 'god-spirit', another dead relative, who offers the spirit-baby to her as a present. This relative, usually in the female line, will appear to the mother in a dream and announce that she is going to present to her a new child. The woman will tell her dream to her husband and other relatives. All will accept it as a fact.
2. In *Japan* there are several myths concerning the reincarnation of a soul into another body. The soul of the Samurai Takadai who died, broken-hearted, by throwing himself off a boat clasping a big stone, was later seen as a seagull crying and winging over the spot where he had died in the sea. A monkey who had spent many years daily bringing fruits and nuts for the sustenance of a Buddhist monk who was copying the scriptures was reborn as a wise nobleman. A devout

monk was drowned in Lake Biwa near the sanctuary of the goddess *Kannon*. After his death he became a priest living on the bottom of the lake, where he rescued people trying to kill themselves by drowning, whose time on earth had not yet passed. He would console them and lead them back to the shore, having cured all their ailments, telling them not to attempt suicide again.

See also *Migration of Souls; Monkeys*(6)*; Predestination; Pregnancy; Snake*(3)*; Tiger*(3).

Reinga   (or Te Reinga, with the definite article *te* ('the'), Polynesian) *Hades*, the *Nether World*, in Polynesian mythology. According to some, it is beneath the earth, and can be reached by entering a pit in the ground, an abyss in the mountains or a cave on the coast. The *spirits* 'live' deep down in the cavernous spaces in semi-darkness. They eat *ngaro*, a special diet for the *dead* which visitors from earth must not touch or else they will never be allowed to return to the world of the living.

Polynesian myths express no great fear of the dead or even of dying, and the spirits seem to be reluctant to come back to their bodies and live again; they have to be persuaded. The god and guardian of the dead is Limu (Rimu) who lives in a vast palace. According to other myths, the dead *souls* travel up to *heaven*, or down to the bottom of the ocean, where they live in beautiful palaces, having received *fish* bodies.

Some sailors say that the dead become mermaids who will lure unwary seafarers away from their straight course in search of the lovable shades who sing so beautifully. This myth is an exact parallel to the Greek tale of the *Sirens*, who were also the souls of the dead, singing for the sailors on the lonely seas.

Other Polynesian myths describe the land of the dead as the distant region where the sky descends to meet the ocean. The winged souls will hover forever over the waves and shores whispering into our ears. Other spirits dwell near their graves, in the earth or in the trees.

The saga of the Island of the Lovers is also known in *Polynesia*, the Islands of the Blessed, or the Islands of Eternal Souls, the Lotophagoi. Whoever lands there will forget the time and his home. There is no day or night there, the sun is forever on the horizon and the Blessed live there, forever singing happily. See also *Avaiki; Hades; Hiku; Lua-o-Milu; Milu; Miru; Paradise; Pare; Reincarnation*.

Rejuvenation   It was related on the *Trobriand Islands* that long ago people whose skins had wrinkled with old age could slough them like crabs, *lizards*, *snakes* and other creatures who live on the earth. But since those happy days of eternal youth, humanity has lost the secret of rejuvenation. See also *Waiora*(1).

Replacement

1. In the *Moluccas*, a doll is made from leaves which is intended to replace a seriously ill person. The doll is dressed up in nice clothes and, with prayers and ceremony, is offered to the evil spirit who has made the patient ill.

2. The Torajas call this replacement ceremony *tolokende*, 'swapping for a child'. The doll gets real hair from the patient.
3. In the Minahassa in *Sulawesi*, special wooden dolls are made for the purpose which are kept with the *fosso* statuettes, i.e. the ancestral images. These dolls are called *tetele*, which means in the Toumbulu language, 'that for which one buys', in other words, a ransom for a sick relative. The dolls are revered with the ancestors for they are of great value: the price of a life.
4. The *Dayaks* of *Borneo* use a *sadiri*. When an ancestral spirit has made someone ill because he wants to have him or her close by in Spirit Land, then a *sadiri* doll, made of flour, on which the patient has to spit, is offered, in order that its *gana* ('spiritual essence') will become the property of the ancestral spirits. If they are satisfied with this replacement, they will then release the soul of the patient.

Rice Rice is the staple food of the vast majority of the *Pacific peoples*.

1. In *Japan* it is said that rice has the power to drive away the evil *spirits*. Women throw rice in the air and scatter it on the ground before the ceremony of divining can take place. It is believed that rice fields were created by *Ama Terasu*, the Sun-Goddess. This is how the bounty of rice was given to humanity. Ever since, the emperors of Japan, the descendants of the Sun-Goddess, have cultivated rice ceremonially as part of the ritual of their enthronement. Blessed is the nation whose ruler is a farmer. There is no healthier labour. This explains why rice cultivation is a sacred work to the Japanese; rice production cannot be left to foreigners, it is too important, it is the life of the nation. In autumn, the paddy fields have to be 'washed', when the mountain streams are in flood. *Susanowo*, the Storm-God, is blamed for breaking the dikes, whereas it is simply a necessity of the season.
2. In *Indonesia* the rice is personified as a goddess, whose special animal is the *cat*, since cats hunt the arch-enemies of the rice: rats and mice. The rice must be treated with reverence. Once, it says in a Buginese myth, the women entered the rice shed without the necessary solemnity and improperly dressed, so the *Rice-Goddess*, Sangiang Sari, went to live elsewhere, leaving famine behind.

See also *Dewi Nawang Wulan; Dewi Sri; Rice-Bag; Rice Bride and Bridegroom; Rice-Goddess; Rice Mother; Rice Soul; River Spirit; Tresnawati*.

Rice-Bag A bag of *rice* which could not be emptied. It was given to the hero *Hidesato* by the Dragon-King of Lake Biwa, as a reward for killing the *Centipede*. The rice-bag fed his family for centuries.

Rice-Bride and Bridegroom In *Indonesia*, especially in East *Java*, the sacred day of the divine wedding couple is celebrated annually on the day before the rice harvest, named Pari Penganten, 'The Bridal Couple of the Rice'. The two biggest ears of rice are picked, wrapped in fine cloth, rubbed with cosmetic oil and solemnly carried to the rice-shed,

where they are placed together on a sleeping mat. See also *Rice-Goddess;*
Rice-Mother(2); *Tresnawati.*

Rice-Goddess

1. In Indonesian mythology she is identified with Dewi Seri or *Dewi*
    Sri, equal to the Indian goddess Lakshmi, who arises from the
    ploughed field as Sita in the *Ramayana*. In West *Java* she is called
    Tisnawati, from the Sanskrit Trishnavati, 'thirsty', because the *rice*
    plant requires an abundance of water. Also, Lakshmi is the Goddess
    of Holy Matrimony, 'thirsty for love'.
2. In a ceremony, an old Javanese custom, the people expressed the
    basic wisdom that a good wife is as difficult to obtain and to keep
    safely as is good rice. Both are essential for Man's survival. When
    Batara Guru, the Supreme God of ancient Java, desires to marry
    Tisnawati before the proper conditions have been fulfilled, she dies.
    She is buried on Earth, in a forest. Out of her head grows the *coconut*
    palm, maize grows up from her teeth, bananas from her hands and
    rice from her genitals. Thus Tisnawati is the goddess who gives life
    after she has died and been buried.

See also *Dewi Nawang Wulan; Inari; Ratna Dumilah; Toyouke-Omikami;*
Tresnawati; Uma.

Rice Mother The Rice Mother is one of the most ancient goddesses
of South-East Asia. She was later identified with Lakshmi, the Indian
Goddess of Agriculture.

1. Annually at the beginning of the harvest in *Indonesia*, the biggest
    ear of *rice* in the field is picked first. It is believed that the spirit of
    the rice (*semangat beras*) is especially concentrated in the 'super-ear',
    the mother of all the ears of rice. It is carefully placed in the *lumbung*
    (rice-shed) and all the harvested rice is added later, after it has been
    threshed. It is believed that the Mother of Rice will keep the shed
    well filled until the next year's harvest. She is the *Rice-Goddess*.
2. On *Java*, the growth of rice stalks in the paddy fields is regarded as
    the *pregnancy* of the Rice Mother. She is worshipped with offerings
    in a *maisonette* built specially to house her. Music has to be played
    to keep away evil *spirits*; the Rice Mother is fed, and given acidic
    fruits, which pregnant women like. Special precautions are needed
    to prevent the strength (see *Mana*) or the *soul* (see *Semangat*) of the
    Rice Mother from escaping when the rice has to be cut. This is done
    with the same knife that is used for the circumcision of women.
    Finally the 'wedding' is celebrated of the 'Bridal Rice Couple', the
    two tallest rice stalks in the field. In the Hindu period these two were
    identified with *Wisnu* and *Dewi Sri* (in Sunda *Nyi Pohatji Sri*) who
    are united cosmically. See also *Rice Bride and Bridegroom.*

Rice Soul In Indonesian *languages* the word for *rice* soul is the same
as the word for human soul. If there is a blight causing the rice plants
to wilt, a *dukun sawah*, a 'rice field healer' will be invited. By a special

ceremony he will 'call back' the soul of the rice, using almost the same rites as he would perform for a sick person. In *Sulawesi* and Halmahera, the rice soul is pictured as a bird. The *Batak*s believe she is a *snake*.

Rimu The Polynesian God of the Dead. See *Reinga;* also *the Dead.*

Rinjin The Japanese *Sea-King.* See 'Gods of Japan' under *Gods; Ryujin; Sea-King; Sea-King's Palace.*

Rinzai A form of Japanese Zen *Buddhism,* introduced by the priest Eisai (d.1215) in which the student is confronted by a series of enigmatic, puzzling, contradictory questions, until a sudden flash of enlightenment occurs in his mind. See also *Koan; Mondo; Soto.*

River Spirit In *Malaysia* it is said that every river has its spirit or *spirits.* If a *canoe* or proa is threatened in the rapids, the oldest of the fishermen will scatter *rice* on the troubled waters, praying to the spirits to release the boat. See also *Toniwha.*

Robe Prince Yamato received a silk robe (*kimono*) from his aunt, the Priestess of Ise, the temple of the Sun-Goddess, when he set out to fight the bandits of Kiushiu. When he put his robe on, it changed his appearance into that of a woman. In this disguise he entered the robbers' tent, served them wine and then slew them.
  See also *Pokeka.*

Roh See *Soul.*

Rohe In *Maori* myth, the wife of *Maui.* She became dissatisfied with her husband so she went to the fifth stratum of the *Nether World*, Uranga-o-Te-Ra, where she became the ruler.

Rokoua See *Ngani-Vatu.*

Rokugo See *Otter.*

Rona See *Ina.*

Rongo (Polynesian; Rongo ma-Tane, *Maori;* Lono in Hawaii; Lo'o in *Samoa*)

1. The Polynesian God of Agriculture, Fruits and Cultivated Plants, especially *kumara,* the indispensable *sweet potato*es. Son of Vatea (Wakea), born in Auau. Ceremonial hymns are sung to him during harvest festivals.
2. In Easter Island mythology, the *Creator,* with *Tangaroa.*

See also 'Gods of the Pacific' under *Gods.*

Rongo-Mai ('Water-Food') In Polynesian mythology, the God of the Whales who himself appears as a huge *whale,* and is also the God of Comets. See also 'Gods of the Pacific' under *Gods.*

Rongo ma-Tane See *Rongo.*

Ro'o On *Tahiti*, Ro'o was the great Healer-God, the Polynesian Asclepios. He was called Ro'o-i-Te-Hiripoi, 'Ro'o in Distress', because his name was invoked by sick people whom he cured by driving out the spirit of *illness*. Ro'o was the son of the Sky-God *Atea*, and taught curative chants to the healers on earth.

Roro Nawang Sih ('Lady Large-Eye Love') See *Dewi Nawang Wulan*.

Rosei A Japanese traveller who became emperor of a miraculous country. See *Magic Pillow*.

Roso See *Rasa*.

Rotuma The lonely island of Rotuma lies 500km north of *Fiji* and more than a 1,000km west of Savai'i in the *Samoa* group. Yet it was peopled from Samoa, according to the following myth. There was once a man named Raho who loved his granddaughter Maiva, and she loved him, but the other people in Samoa did not love them. So one day Raho had a new boat built. One night in secret he brought food on board and a basket of earth, and with Maiva he sailed to where the *sun* had set. At a given moment, Raho emptied the basket of earth outside his boat. The earth did not sink but floated on the ocean. The heap grew and grew until it had become an island. The descendants of Raho and Maiva still live on the island, speaking a language that is close to Samoan. They called their island Rotuma.

Roua See *Rua*.

Ru

1. In the mythology of Mangaia, he is the ancient God of the Other World. One day his cheeky son Maui (not the Maori hero) challenged him. Ru threw him up into the air, but Maui quickly changed himself into a bird and alighted safely on the earth. There he grew to gigantic size, picked up Ru and threw him, in turn, up into the sky so far that he remained up there, since he had become entangled in the silvery webs that hold the stars together. So, Ru is now known as the Sky-God. See also *Other World; Sky*.
2. A legendary navigator from Raiatea who selected a star and persuaded his friends and relations to sail with him away from his island of Ra'iatea in the Society Islands because: 'At home the hills are thick with people.' At the time there was famine on the island due to its overpopulation. So, many people sailed with Ru to Aitutaki west of the *Cook Islands*, a distance of 550 miles. On the way, Ru prayed to the God of the Sea, *Tangaroa*, to keep the star visible. It was probably Venus. The name of the ship was Pua Ariki, 'Royal Flower'. The voyage is still celebrated.

Ru-Wu See *Chaking*.

Rua (also Roua, Rahoua, Tubua) The *Creator* of the Tuamotu Islands. The 'Creation Hymn' to Rua begins:

Rua! Great is his descent.
He slept with his wife the dark Earth.
She gave birth to the sun, our great King.
With him was born the day. He cast shadows.
Rua! He embraced his wife.
She gave birth to the moon, our Queen.
She gave birth to the Star, the god of the morning,
    a guide to the seafarers.

Rua-Pupuke A man whose son was stolen by the sea-fairies. See *Ponaturi*.

Rua-Tapu ('Forbidden Path') The murdered father of the Polynesian Wind-God Hau. See 'Gods of the Pacific' under *Gods*.

Ruarangi See *Fairies*(3).

Ruau-Moko The youngest child of *Papa*, the Earth-Goddess. See *Earthquake*.

Rujung See *Dolphin*.

Ruki A *sea-serpent* in *Kiribati* mythology. See *Nareau*.

Rukmini See *Dewi Sri*.

Rukutia (Hawaiian Lu'ukia) The wife of chief *Tamanui* whom she deserts for *Koropanga*. See *Tamanui*; *Tattoo*.

Rupe See *Hina-Keha; Ina*.

Ruru See *Ngarara*.

Ruwakruwak See *Heron*(2).

Ryobu See *Fujin*.

Ryugu See *Sea-King's Palace*.

Ryujin In Japanese myth, the Dragon-King of the Sea, the *Sea-King*, who controls the tidal flow with his magic jewels. He is depicted with a large mouth. His daughter married Prince *Hoori*, or 'Fire Fade', and they became the ancestors of the imperial dynasty.

Ryukyu See *Sea-King's Palace*.

S

Singa lion (Besekih temple, Bali)

Saavedra, Alvaro de   A Spanish explorer. See *New Guinea*.

Sabah   A state on the north coast of *Borneo*. See *Borneo; Malaysia*.

Sadana   See *Sadono*.

Sadewa   One of the sons of King *Pandu*. See *Pandawa*.

Sadono   (or Sadana) In Javanese mythology, Vishnu (see *Wisnu*) as God of the Growth of Crops.

Saicho   A Chinese priest. See *Jobutsu; Tendai*.

Said of Kalijaga   A *wali* (saint) of *Java*, one of the first missionaries of Islam in South-East Asia, performer of many miracles.

Sakana   See *Fish*.

Sakata Kintoki   See *Kintaro*.

Sake   See *Shojo; Susanowo*.

Sakri   The son of *Nilawati*.

Saksit   In Thai mythology, the dangerous, unknown and unpredictable world of the capricious *spirits*, where human laws do not work. Offerings and gifts are necessary to keep those evil forces at bay. Saksit powers are not always evil, but one can never know in advance.

Sakti (or Sekti, Shakti) In old Javanese and Balinese mythology, a name for the goddess *Kali*, *Durga*, *Uma* or Batari, wife of *Siwa*, in her aspect of divine power, the driving force of *creation* and procreation. See also *Dewi*; *Kali*; *Lara Jonggrang*; *Soul*.

Sakyamuni See *Fuku-Nyorai*; *Shaka*.

Sam Muk This is the name of a small rocky island in the Gulf of *Thailand*, where, the fishermen say, there is a deep cave. Inside, if anyone can penetrate below the sea level, there is an immense treasure of golden plates, silver ornaments and the finest porcelain bowls. This treasure was the property of a female spirit whose name was Sam Muk. She was once a lovely girl, deeply in love with a handsome young man. However, his parents were high-born and rich, so they told her that she was not good enough for their fine son and must never see him again. In despair she went to the lonely rocky island, which at that time was still linked to the mainland by a neck of land. She climbed the highest rock and threw herself from its summit.

Her spirit lived on on the island, and whenever a farmers's wife needed plates and bowls for a wedding feast she could come and borrow them from the spirit, after praying and burning incense. Long ago people were honest and returned all borrowed property. One day however, a miserly farmer kept a golden plate and returned a brass plate in its stead. No one has been able to find any crockery at all in that cave since that time.

Even today the fishermen bring offerings to the rock and pray to Sam Muk for fine weather, bringing *rice* for a favourable wind and *coconuts* for a calm, smooth sea. If the sacrifices are forgotten, Sam Muk will send a sudden storm, shaking their frail boats.

Samantabhadra See *Jizo*.

Samebito In Japanese mythology, a black monster with green glowing eyes and a spiky beard like a *dragon*. It was confronted by the hero Totaro on the Long Bridge. But, instead of attacking him as one might expect from a monster that is half-shark (*same* = shark) and half-man, it entreated him to give it food and shelter, for the *Sea-King* had expelled it from the ocean. Totaro took Samebito to the lake near his own castle where he fed it. Some time later Totaro fell in love with a girl, Tamana, whose father had set the bride price at 10,000 precious stones. Totaro went home and lay ill until he was dying. Meanwhile Samebito was shedding tears for his benefactor, until it was discovered that these tears had turned into rubies, pearls and emeralds. With these precious stones Totaro could pay the bride price and so marry the lovely Tamana.

Samoa Eastern or American Samoa is a group of five islands, forming a state with its own legislative body and a governor, heavily subsidized by the US. The total land area is 197 sq km, the population 40,000.

Western Samoa has an area of 2,831 sq km and a population of 170,000. Its capital, Apia, is on the island of Upolu. Western Samoa is now a democratic republic under a king. It belonged to Germany from

1889 to 1919 and to *New Zealand* from 1919 to 1962. Most people are now Christians. The main islands are Savai'i and Upolu. Almost every family still has its own *fale*, a thatched cabin. R. L. Stevenson lived here.

See also *Adam and Eve*(4); *Atonga; Atu; Bua-Taranga; Creation*(5); *Fale-Aitu; Fe'e; Fiji; Fue;* 'Gods of the Pacific' under *Gods; Islands; Kai-n-Tiku-Aba; Lata; Losi; Matagi; Nana-Ula; Owl*(1); *Polynesians; Rongo; Rotuma; Sava; Sina; Sisimatailaa; Taburimai; Talaipo; Vaitupu.*

Samulayo   The Fijian God of War and Death in Battle. See *Hades*(4).

Sang Gala Raja Jin   In *Malaysia*, the black King of the Jins, or *demons*, to whom prayers for protection are addressed. Sang Gala is a corruption of old Indonesian Sangkara, *Siwa*. See also *Jin.*

Sang Hyang Tunggal   In Javanese, the Supreme God. See *God.*

Sang Pertala Dewa   See *Cow.*

Sang Utama   See *Singapore.*

Sanganichi   Japanese *New Year*, when people pray to the *Shichi Fukujin*, the seven Gods of Good Luck, after cleaning their houses thoroughly. See also *Pine Tree.*

Sangen   See *Creation*(6).

Sangiang   The *Dayaks* of *Kalimantan* tell of the existence of a group of beings called *Sangiang*, usually translated as *demi-gods*, or mediating gods. The same word, *Sangiang*, is also found in *Java, Sumatra* and *Sulawesi* and is the equivalent of *Sanian* in the *Philippines*.

According to the Dayaks, the *Sangiang* used to live on earth until men invented iron and became dangerous. They then left and went to live in the celestial sphere above the clouds.

Tempon Telon is the only *Sangiang* to whom regular prayers are addressed. He conducts the souls of the dead to Soul Land. His brother Lilang is invoked by the fishermen when they are in a dangerous storm, hoping that he may 'part the waves and make a path'. When the danger has been averted, tobacco is thrown into the sea. Lilang's companion, Asai, is the God of the Pioneers. On land he cuts down trees with his knife-edged shinbones. At sea he stands on the bow, his fiery body like a beacon in the night. See also *Creation*(6); *Illness.*

Sangiang Dewata   *Mahatara*, the Supreme God of the *Dayaks.*

Sangiang Sari   See *Rice*(2).

Sangkuruwira   See *Creation*(7).

Sanguma   In Melanesian mythology, the method of killing a person by *sorcery*. A lone traveller may suddenly be attacked and tormented by evil *spirits* in the guise of living persons, after which he will die or go mad.

See also *Magic; Makutu; Medicine Man; Sorcerer; Tohunga; Witch.*

Sanian   See *Sangiang.*

Sanjo A Japanese princess. See *Hammer*.

Santang Goddesses See *Mahatara*.

Sanyasi An ascetic. See *Narayana*.

Sanzu no Kawa The River Styx. See *Bommatsuri*.

Sapurba A King of Sumatra. See *Malay Annals; Sumatra*.

Saraswati On *Bali*, the Goddess of Streams and Freshwater Sources and so also of the 'fountains of knowledge'. Her domain is *bayu*, action and learning, and more than one institute of learning on the island is named after her. Scribes and scholars honour her as their patroness, but it is the farmers who especially worship her as the goddess who supplies the vital water to their fields and orchards, their animals and households. The goddess is celebrated annually with hymns such as the following:

> O sacred goddess whom I praise
> Saraswati, receive my song
> I bring thee flowers fragrant fresh
> My strong devotion to express
> Thou art the sacred aim of those
> Who walk the path to scholarship
> The knowledge of all that exists
> All things that thou hast made to grow
> Pray thee for love, favour and sympathy
> Thou art the goddess of all precious things
> Of beauty, virtue and the highest truth.

In Balinese art, Saraswati is represented as an elegant young woman of unique beauty, with *melati* (jasmine) flowers in her hair, accompanied by her swan and peacock (*manyura*). See also *Benten*.

Sarawak A state of northern *Borneo*. See *Borneo; Hawk*(2); *Honey Tree Song; Malaysia; Snake*.

Sarong On *Java*, we are told, certain magicians possess pieces of sarong (skirt) just long enough to wrap round their big toes. But such a *magic* sarong can be stretched until it covers the whole body. Its colour is yellow with black stripes. By putting it on the owner changes himself, or a friend, into a *tiger*, in order to go out killing.

Satori (or *Sattori*, 'Awakening') In Japanese Zen teaching, the moment of revelation when the novice experiences the enlightenment of real knowledge which cannot be expressed in words or otherwise defined. It is an intuitive, sudden insight into the real nature of things and how the world is structured.

Satria The noble knight in the masked *wayang* plays. See *Topeng*.

Satrud In Thai mythology, the Indian Shatrughna, 'Enemy Slayer', one of Rama's brothers. See *Ramayana*.

Saturn See *Phra Sao*.

Sava A boy who settled the Samoan island of Savai'i together with his sister I'i. Their numerous offspring became a nation.

Savali The messenger of the Samoan Ocean-God and *Creator* Tagaloa. See *Islands*.

Sawah A submergeable *rice* field surrounded by a dam. See *Indonesia*.

Sawailau The island of the man-eating bird *Ngani-Vatu*.

Sawara A Japanese painter. See *Kakemono*.

Scorpio One of the signs of the Zodiac. Its tail was used by *Maui* the *Maori* Sun-God as a fishhook to fish up *New Zealand*.

Sea-Fairies See *Ponaturi*.

Sea-Goddess (Polynesian) Some *navigators* have seen her, standing up in one of those huge waves that look like moving walls. She has long waving hair and is so beautiful that the men just stare at her, transfixed. See also *Creation*(16); *Tara*(1); and the Javanese *Ocean-Goddess*.

Sea-King A name for the God of the Ocean in most Pacific religions. He is called *Kala* in *Java*, *Waruna* in *Bali*, *Rinjin* or *Ryujin* in *Japan*.
   See also 'Gods of Japan' under *Gods*; *Kala*; *Kyai Blorong*; *Malay Annals*; *Monkey*(5); *Otohime*; *Ponaturi*; *Samebito*; *Sea-King's Palace*; *Tangaroa*; *Tide Jewels*; *Toyo-Tama*; *Turtle*; *Waruna*.

Sea-King's Palace ('The Evergreen Land'; Japanese, Ryugu or Ryu Kyu, literally 'Dragon's Court') The *Sea-King*, who is one of the *dragon gods* in Japanese mythology, owns a many-storeyed palace under the sea which is well guarded by colourful dragons. It is said to stand on the bottom of the ocean near the Ryu Kyu Islands. The palace is built from red and white coral. Human fishes serve the king as courtiers. On the eastern side of the palace there is the Hall of Spring where butterflies visit cherry blossom while the nightingale sings. On the southern side is the Summer Hall where the cricket chirps in the warm evening. On the western side is the Autumn Hall where the maple trees glow in bright colours. On the northern side is Winter Hall, were snow falls all the time. Once inside this palace, a visitor should never think of home on earth and never wish to go back, for all his kinsmen will have died: a day in the Sea-King's palace is like 100 years on earth.
   Urashima, a young fisherman from Tango, once caught a *tortoise* but he let it free again. It was the Sea-King's daughter in disguise. She invited him to come and live in her father's palace under the sea, where she appeared to him in the shape of a beautiful girl, and married him. After three days he wanted to see his parents, but when he came back to earth he found that 300 years had passed. He himself then died. He is still venerated.

Sea-Serpent Near one of the Oki Islands, in the ocean off the coast of *Japan*, it was said there once lived a sea-serpent, almost 30ft long, in a cave, guarding priceless pearls and the statue of an evil god. It had four legs with sharp claws, a long tail, sharp teeth and it was entirely white, shining brightly like mother-of-pearl. Once a year a 14-year-old girl had to be sacrificed to it. One day a girl of 18 years old, who had learned swimming from the pearl divers, dived down to the cave where the *serpent* lived. She hit it with a dagger in one of its eyes, then, while its vision was blurred by its own blood, she hit it in the heart, so that it died, and with it the evil spirit, which had been born from a curse.

See also *Heron*(1); *Nareau*; *Snake*; *Serpent*; *Serpent-God*; *Pusat Tasik*; *Raja Naga*; *Ruki*; *Sesa*; *Yofune-Nushi*.

Seido See *Bronze*.

Sejarah Banten See *Bantam*.

Sejarah Melayu See *Malay Annals*.

Sekti See *Sakti*.

Selindung Dalima See *Epic*(1).

Semadi (Sanskrit, *Samadhi*) In *Indonesia*, spiritual concentration by meditation, aimed at achieving a higher degree of mystic perception. In this way the hermit hopes to obtain knowledge of his people's destiny.

Semangat (*Batak, tondi*; Toraja, *tanoana*) In *Indonesia*, the individual *soul* of a living person. The classical Malay spelling is *sumangat*, also translated as 'consciousness': what one loses when fainting. It can also mean a protective spirit, the deity of a town: *sumangat negari*.

This living spirit is distinct from the dead *soul*. The *sumangat* lives independently from 'its' person and can be seen as the body's shadow, on which no one may step. Old people who have not long to live have a very thin shadow. A person in anger is said to have lost his *sumangat*. So children must not be beaten because they would gradually become so angry that they would die, i.e. their *sumangat* would not come back. A person raving in fever is said to be talking to his ancestors' *spirits* who are calling him or her to the *Other World*. One must not disturb the person by, for instance, administering medicine, because the *sumangat* might not return.

Dreaming is the travelling of the *sumangat* away from the body to other countries, including the Land of the Dead. Do not step over a sleeping person, for his *sumangat* might not come back. The *sumangat* can also be stolen by *magic*. However, a priest may then succeed in luring it back into the body before the owner has died definitively.

Semangko The *ghosts* of the *dead* of the Kyaka people of western *Papua*. They are divided into six categories. See *Ghosts*(4).

Semar In Javanese mythology, the elder brother of the Supreme God *Batara Guru*. Semar lives on earth to protect the children of the *gods*, i.e. the *Pandawas*, during their numerous adventures. He is, like *Kresna*, disguised as their servant and senior counsellor. He has two sons, Petruk and Gareng. This trio has a special entertaining function in the *wayang* performances. See also ·'Gods of Bali' under *Gods; Panakawan; Wijaya-Kusuma*.

Sembadra   The 'Black Lady' of Javanese mythology. See also *Subadra*.

Semi   Japanese for the tree *cricket*.

Semmai-Doshi   (literally, 'clear words') In *Japan*, a tablet or a page with the *Buddha*'s secret names on it, which pilgrims buy at shrines for a cure.

Senapati   (Commander of the Army, Sanskrit) This title became a personal name during the Middle Ages in *Java*. The Senapati of Javanese myths was the ideal embodiment of all the virtues which the Javanese expect in their kings: modesty, courtesy, diplomacy, moderation, composure and prudence, but also fortitude, physical strength, virility and attractiveness to women, even to goddesses.

The *historical* Senapati was King of Central Java; he died in 1601. His real name was Sutawijaya Sahidin Panatagam. He is the ancestor of the princes of Mataram and was the last of the Hindu rulers of Java. He lies buried in Kuta Gedê. Whether the historical king gave rise to the mythical ruler of all Java is a matter for literary historians to decide. Numerous sagas are told about his exploits and wondrous adventures which all signified that he was, by the will of the *gods*, destined to be King of Java.

One day Senapati went swimming in the southern ocean. A fish carried him to a palace in the sea, the most beautiful palace he had ever seen. There he was welcomed by a graceful young lady at the pearly gate. She led him past silver halls over ruby floors to her divan of golden silk. They were served by *fairies* and sea-nymphs. She taught the prince to command the *spirits*, the jins and fairies. Finally she encouraged him so they united in love for three days and nights. No man except the future King of Java by divine grace, can ever be loved as a husband by the Goddess of the Southern Ocean, Ratu Lara Kidul. This myth signifies that he was identified with *Wisnu* (Vishnu or Rama), the God of the Ocean. Finally, Senapati walked home over the sea, as if its waves were only hills. That night a *star* fell down near his head and said, 'You will be King of Java and your son and grandson will rule after you.'

In those days Mataram was a vassal state of the sultanate of Pajang. Senapati's greatest asset was his wise uncle Juru, who served as his prime minister. When Senapati wished to rebel against the sultan, his suzerain, Juru, told him: 'The son must never rebel against the father. Sultan Pajang rules by divine protection. You can never destroy him. Do you not know that steel cannot cut him? Do you not know that water will not drown him? Even the night cannot make his head dark. It stays light!'

Senapati accepted his counsellor's advice, realizing that *Jaka Tingkir*, Sultan Pajang, ruled by the will of *God*.

One night an assassin named Bochor sneaked up to Senapati from behind and stabbed his back. But the dagger would not pierce the skin: Senapati too, was protected by divine will. Bochor fell on his face at Senapati's feet, abjectly begging forgiveness of the man he had intended to kill. Senapati forgave him. What could he lose?

See also *Prambanan; Ratna Jumilah.*

Sengalang Burong The Iban people's War-God. See *Radin.*

Sengen (also known as Asama, 'Dawn of Good Luck', or Ko-no-Hana-Saku-ya-Hime, 'The Princess who Makes the Tree-Blossom Bloom') Daughter of the Mountain-God, she is the Goddess of Mount Fuji, the Blossom-Goddess of *Japan.* She guards the secret well of eternal youth, giving only a few people some of its *water of life* (see also *Elixir*). She is depicted as a young girl scattering pink camellias, *tsubaki.* See also *Fujiyama;* 'Gods of Japan' under *Gods; Yosoji.*

Sengen is also known as *Ko-no-Hana,* the wife of *Ninigi,* mother of the Fire-Gods *Hoderi and Hoori.*

Senju In Japanese iconography, the image of *Kannon* with 1,000 arms.

Sennin ('Master') The immortal spirit of a Japanese saint living on in the mountains, a hermit who has acquired so much merit by his asceticism (*Yosho,* for example, ate only one grain of millet a day) that he can perform miracles, such as speaking after death, flying on the back of a tortoise, or on a cloud, or causing a gourd to give birth to a horse. Sennins may speak to mortals in *dreams* or appear in the shape of ordinary men, accompanied by their *familiars:* a *toad* (see *Gama-Sennin*), a horse or a tortoise.

Sensu See *Fan.*

Sentaro See *Immortality*(2).

Seri Bunian A Malay princess. See *Epic*(1).

Seri Turi Buwana The name taken by Prince Nila Utama on becoming first ruler of *Singapore.* See *Malay Annals; Singapore.*

Serpent In the ancient city of Chieng Saen in *Thailand* there is a huge gate tower in the south-western wall, now partly in ruins, which is still called 'The Gate which the Burmese could not enter'. It is related that when the pit was dug for the foundation of the tower, a convicted criminal was brought from prison, bathed, shaved, dressed in a white garment and placed in the bottom of the pit. He was told to assume the position of meditation, and sit with folded hands, motionless. Then the huge foundation stone was slowly lowered into the pit, fitting precisely. It squashed the sitting convict, as planned. A priest was officiating, praying to the dying man's spirit to protect the city in the future. He did. Many years later a Burmese army arrived to attack the city. Suddenly, out of the gate tower, a huge white serpent emerged, two feet thick and ten fathoms long, threatening the attackers. Swords and spears, arrows and javelins had no effect on it, nor did fire or stones. It threatened to devour whoever came too close. It seemed to have an enormous appetite and was too quick for those who thought they could run past it. The Burmese soldiers were soon convinced that it was the powerful spirit of an ancient king or the protective deity of the city.

See also *Ahoeitu; Basuki; Creation(3); Malay Annals; Naga(2); Naga Muchilinda; Ndengei; Nilawati; Python; Ratu-Mai-Mbula; Snake; Sea-Serpent; Serpent-God; Toad; Tuna; Uwabami; Yamato Take; Yegara-no-Heida.*

Serpent-God

1. In Fijian mythology the first Serpent-God was *Degei* (see also *Creation(3); Flood; Sky-King*).
2. It is also related that a serpent-god was venerated on the Yasawa Islands just west of *Fiji*. His name was Ratu Mai Bulu, God of Growth and Fertility. His spouse was Raivuki, Goddess of the Seasons. Ratu Mai Bulu created the island of Viwa from a mere atol ring, by raising the ocean bottom above the sea level. Then he created *coconuts* to supply fresh water. If someone offended the god, *snakes* would be found all over his house and food.

Sesa (= Basuki; Sanskrit, Shesha or Vasuki) The hooded *sea-serpent* on which *Wisnu* reclines, in Balinese cosmology. See also *Naga(2)*.

Sex The people of Orokolo district in south *New Guinea* relate that the first people, Kerema Apo and Ivi Apo, had no genitals, so they were sexless. They lived happily on the beach, being fed by their brothers the red *coconut* palm and the black coconut palm. One day, Ovo Akore, the red coconut palm, called Ivi Apo and Kerema Apo to the seashore and said: 'Stand here with your feet in the waves and take one of the seashells you see passing.'

At first the two timid human beings were afraid to touch the *mollusks*, but when Ovo Akore urged them again to obey, Kerema Apo finally caught a cone snail (a snail-shell shaped like a long cone) with his foot. It crept up his leg and attached itself to his groin where it grew into a penis. Ivi Apo also caught a shell with her foot. It was a large cowrie and it became her vagina.

Shah Jehan A ruler of *Malaya*. See *Malay Annals*.

Shair (or *Syair*) A Malay saga or legend in *epic* form.

Shaka (Sanskrit, Shakyamuni, Shaka Muni or Sakyamuni) In Buddhist–Japanese religion, Shaka is the Silent Sage, the embodiment of perfect virtue, the first appearance of the *Buddha* on earth in bodily form. Shrines dedicated to his worship are to be found in every monastery. The great festival of Shaka is celebrated in *Japan* on 8 April, called Hana-Matsuri, 'Flower Festival'. Amoghasiddhi is his Bodhisattva aspect.

See also 'Gods of Japan' under *Gods*.

Shaka Muni See *Shaka*.

Shakti See *Sakti; Soul*.

Shakyamuni See *Shaka*.

Shaman

1. A shaman is a seer who in the spirit (but not in a dream) travels to the *Other World* where he meets the *spirits*, after which he comes back to the world of the living to instruct them about what he saw and heard. On the *Trobriand Islands*, certain men have narrated to the living what they have seen in *Tuma* or *Paradise*.
2. In Korean, the word for shaman-woman, *mudang*, is glossed in the dictionary as 'witch, sorceress, exorcist', and is now considered derogatory, although 'exorcist' is a better English rendering, considering the functions of the person who is usually referred to as 'shaman' when Koreans speak in English. Those shamans refer to themselves as *mansin*, which literally means '10,000 gods'. The *mansin*'s chief function is to perform the big *kut* ceremony at a family dwelling, exorcising all the 'foul' spirits. She also 'fumigates' wood-imps from the house and will even lead the souls of the dead to Paradise, like a real shaman. A woman becomes a shaman through a traumatic experience, usually a severe illness or bereavement. She will have visions and/or become possessed, after which a period of apprenticeship with a 'spirit-mother' will lead up to initiation into the profession.
3. Among the *Batak* people of *Sumatra*, the shaman was called *sibaso*, usually a woman, who after dancing accompanied by drumming, would converse with the spirit asking about the well-being of distant relatives or the future of sick people.

See also *Kut; Shamanism; Sudo; Tree-Spirits*(8).

Shamanism

1. Among the *Dayaks* of south-east *Kalimantan* the celebration feast, *tiwah*, for the deceased is very elaborate. The bones are placed in a coffin which is beautifully decorated. The priest calls Tempun Telon (see *Tempon Telon*), the Ferryman of the Dead, to come and take the deceased across the water to the Land of the Souls. The priest will accompany the deceased and relate his adventures to the villagers when he returns. He is even believed to drink palm wine with the *souls* of the *dead* at their home in the *Other World*.
2. The Toraja priests of *Sulawesi* have a special language for the recitation of litanies, which are conversations with the *gods*. They intone them with closed eyes, because they are mentally 'in' the Other World.
    A Toraja myth relates that a sick woman had disappeared from her hut. After a few days she came back cured and told her fellow villagers how the souls of sick people can be fetched back from Spirit

Land. The Toraja priestess, *tadu*, will sit at the patient's side with a piece of bark cloth over her head. She prays to the spirits, *wurake*, who come and take her in their boat, which is the rainbow, to *heaven*. On the way they meet many evil spirits and other dangers which have to be neutralized. This is done by chewing certain herbs and spitting at these spirits 'to clear the sky', for by that time they are flying in the clouds. The Wind-God is then called to help the good spirits. He will carry the boat to heaven.

There, the Supreme God, Pue di Songi, receives the priestess. She prays for God to release the soul of her patient. God tells her not to worry: he will send the soul back, for he is satisfied with the sacrifice which the relatives have made. Often the priestess has to accompany the good spirits and join them in their war against the evil spirits, who are holding the soul of her patient to ransom. If she has a dream in which it is revealed to her that some dead relative has taken her patient's soul, she has to travel to the *Nether World* to fetch it back. If it is not allowed to return, the patient will die.

3. The priestess, *walian*, of the Tontemboan people of northern Sulawesi begins to sing her song with closed eyes seated on a bench accompanied by her assistants. A spirit will descend from heaven, down a wooden ladder and alight on her neck, between her shoulder blades. From there it will enter her, then it will conduct her soul on a tour of the heavens, past the mountains of Lokon, Lolombulan (the Mountains of the Moon) and Sinosaya. Many gods and spirits live on these ramparts in Spirit Land. The priestess and her guide visit them and receive their blessings. The spirit speaks through the mouth of the *walian*, describing their adventures. The conversations with each of the spirits in the Other World are heard as she sings in different voices. Finally, the blessings are given over to the host of a big feast, which can begin as soon as the *walian* has returned safely from the Mountains of the Gods.

See also *Hakawau; Oracles*(2); *Sorcery*.

Shark

1. In a Melanesian myth, a girl is raped by her father. She is so ashamed that she goes to the beach and asks a shark to come and devour her.
2. In Fijian mythology the Shark-God is the scourge of the fishermen, eating their *fish* as well as the men who fall overboard. His name is Dakuwanga. However, one day he meets his master, the giant octopus, guardian of the reef. The octopus wins the battle and the Shark-God has to promise never to attack the men of Kandavu.

See also *Flores; Mango-Roa-i-Ata; Monkeys*(5); *New Caledonia; Ngaru; Samebito; Taburimai; Tini Rau; Tumuitearetoka*.

Sheikh Ali In Malay mythology, a terrible king who commands three regiments: one of flying horses, one of flying lions and one of flying elephants.

Shesha See *Sesa*.

Shi-Ryo In Japanese myth, a ghost, a dead man visiting the living at night. See also *Ghosts*.

Shi Tenno Four guardian *spirits*, one on each corner, who protect *Japan* against attacks by evil spirits. In the east rules Jikoku; in the south, Komoku; in the west, *Zocho*; in the north, Tamon or Bishamon Tenno. They are depicted as fierce-looking, fully armed and armoured, loyal soldiers. See also 'Gods of Japan' under *Gods*.

Shichi Fukujin ('Seven Happiness Beings') The seven Japanese deities of good fortune, viz. *Benten, Bishamon, Daikoku, Ebisu, Fukurokuju, Hotei* and *Jurojin*. They are invoked when one starts a new venture. See also 'Gods of Japan' under *Gods*.

Shikaiya Wasobioye The Japanese Gulliver. See *Immortality*(1).

Shindai ('Fortune') See *Daikoku;* also *Shichi Fukujin*.

Shinden In *Japan*, a temple, the palace of the deity.

Shinge A Japanese princess. See *Violets*.

Shinju In Japanese, to commit double suicide, to die together for *love*, usually by jumping down together off a rock into the ocean or a river. First, the lovers will pray to the goddess *Kannon*. They hope that their desperate love will be more fortunate in their next lives, when they meet again. See also *Love*.

Shinto The collective name for all forms of Japanese national religion, as opposed to 'imported' religions like *Buddhism*. The word *Shinto* is rendered in the dictionaries as 'The believers, the faithful', as a community. It is composed of *shin*, 'faith, belief and trust', and *to*, 'a group'. This ancient national religion of Japan was purposely divided into two aspects: the Jinja-Shinto, simple veneration of the heroes of the past and the Shukyo-Shinto, the real religion, which includes the worship of the emperor. In every school there was an empty chair behind a curtain. Every morning all teachers and pupils bowed to it, before the omnipresent spirit of the emperor.

See also *Kokutai-Shinto; Shinto Shrines*.

Shinto Shrines A prominent Japanese priest, Toyonosuke Takemoto, wrote of the *Shinto* shrines before the war (1939):

> The ceremonies in the Shinto shrines form an essential part of the Empire. In these shrines is found the nation's religion. If these shrines should cease to exist that would mean the end of the Empire, because they are the Empire itself. The gods of the shrines are connected with the foundation of the nation. Worshipping them is identifying oneself with the Empire.

Another Japanese scholar wrote in 1933:

The way of the gods, that is Shinto, nature-worship and ancestor worship, the chief deity being the Sun-Goddess Ama Terasu, and the Great Ancestors of the Japanese Imperial House.

Shippeitaro   See *Dog*(1).

Shiratake   A Japanese mountain. See *Fudo*(2).

Shishi-o   ('Master of Lions') A famous Japanese *sword*. See *Yorimasa*.

Shito Dama   In Japanese mythology, an astral spirit. Its shape is described as oval or spherical, like a *fireball*. Its colour is bright red. It is the wandering spirit of a dead person. See also *Spirits*.

Shiva   See *Siwa*.

Sho Ten   See *Ganesa*.

Shoden   See *Ganesa*.

Shodo Shonin   A famous Japanese saint and founder of the temple at Nikko. One day while walking a mountain path, Shodo's way was blocked by a river. He prayed for a bridge and then suddenly saw a giant, dressed in dark blue robes, with a garland of skulls around his neck, evidently *Siwa*.

'Here is your bridge,' roared the god, and threw two *snakes* – one blue, one green – across the river.

Unafraid, the saint walked along the living snakes' backs, across the raging torrent in its deep gorge. When he stood safely on the other side, the snakes and the god vanished.

Shoguns   See *Japan*.

Shojo   A kindly creature with red hair, living on the bottom of the Sea of *Japan*. The word *shojo* can mean a maiden or a man, especially an *orang utan* or wild man. The *shojos* are naked but for a skirt of green seaweed; their skin is pink or red. They brew a medicinal white wine *shiroi sake* (*eau-de-vie*), and other medicines. If a good person drinks the *sake*, it will taste sweet and delicious. If a wicked character sips it, it will taste like poison and kill him, unless he repents at once.

Shokujo   See *Tanabata*.

Shoryobuni   Japanese soul-ships. See *the Dead*.

Shotoku   A Japanese prince who was deified as the *reincarnation* of Siddhartha, and, it is believed, will come back as *Miro*, the future *Buddha*. He could speak as soon as he was born, and he predicted the future. See also 'Gods of Japan' under *Gods*.

Shri-Vijaya   See *Indonesia*.

Shugendo   In *Japan*, a syncretistic form of Buddhist esotericism which incorporates elements of asceticism as well as *magic*.

Si Boru Deak   See *Creation*(9).

Si Jari See *Tom Thumb*.

Si Junaha In Indonesian tales, the clever character who invented the 'Knife which Grinds Meat'. He sold it to his creditor, who waived his debt. Next, he invented the 'Weed-Killing Guitar', which saves its owner employing weeders when it is played in the fields. He sells this to his next creditor, etc. See also *Malay Tales*.

Si Luncai See *Si Lunchai*.

Si Lunchai (or Si Luncai) A clever character in Malay–Indonesian tales. Si Lunchai is a poor peasant who marries the princess by outwitting the king. The king had sentenced him to death by drowning, but he escaped and came back dressed as a Hajji, claiming he had been in *heaven* but that God had sent him back. He described heaven in such heavenly terms that the king wanted to see it too, and had a glass coffin made for himself. Then the coffin was dumped in the sea at the king's express command.
See also *Malay Tales*.

Siambuka A Papuan *Creator*. See *Woman*(2).

Sibaso See *Shaman*(3).

Sibauk A Sarawak hero. See *Honey Tree Song*.

Sidin The groom to a Sumatran prince. See *Hornbill*(2).

Sijobang The name of the eponymous hero in the Minangkabau *epic* poem of west *Sumatra*, a type of odyssey in 26 episodes, with a total of 40,000 lines. The hero's full name is Anggun Nan Tungga. He sails along the *islands* of the west Sumatran coast, then up to *heaven* to be taught magical lore. The ship descends back to the ocean and the hero arrives on an island where he marries his uncle's daughter, Dandomi, who gives him a son in three days. Nan Tungga gives his son a magic mat on which he can travel anywhere. He continues his voyage accompanied by Dandomi's naughty *parrot* who possesses the art of speech and intelligence. The parrot flies round Nan Tungga's women, telling them about his love affairs. His first betrothed, Gondoriah, retreats to the mountains, and finally disappears. Her jacket becomes a white monkey.
Nan Tungga later becomes involved in a tournament and, after magically calling his faithful helper, Abang Salamat, who arrives flying on a magic horse, he wins the contest. Finally, however, he goes to the seashore, saddened by the loss of his betrothed, plunges into the ocean and becomes a *dolphin*.

Sihai The Wind-God of Nias. See *Creation*(10).

Siloo The sister of Dapie, the Seran Moon-Goddess. See *Sun*(9).

Sina Sina was a moon-goddess in Samoan mythology. She kept an *eel* in a jar but when it grew as long as a man she let it swim in a pond. One day while she was bathing, the eel assaulted her so she cried for help. The people of Upolu sentenced the eel-man to death. He was the god *Tuna*. Before dying he told Sina to bury his head in the sand on the seashore. This she did and out came the first *coconut* palm, a gift from the gods.

See also *Danger Island; Eel; Snake-King; Tuna*.

Singa In Balinese myth and art, the Winged *Lion*, an image of the Hindu Fire-God Agni, associated with *Siwa* as God of the Funeral Pyre, and with *Wisnu* as Narasinga.

Singapore It is said that Singapore island is especially blessed by the *gods*. Furthermore, that it was founded in antiquity as a sanctuary dedicated to the god Vishnu (*Wisnu*) in his *avatara* as a lion-man: Narasinga.

It is further related in the Malay traditions that on Mount *Mahameru*, source of the Malayu river in *Sumatra*, there was born a divine prince, Sang Utama, later called Seri Turi Buwana, son of Surana, descendant of Alexander the Great. Sang Utama set out on a voyage and landed on the green island of Bambam. He liked it so much that he decided to build his capital there, which he called Singapura, 'Lion City'. His descendants ruled the city for many generations. One day, however, Singapura was betrayed to the Javanese invaders by its own *manteri* (prime minister).

During the sixteenth century, Singapore was in Portuguese hands, but was overshadowed by Malaka. It became part of the Dutch East India Company's territories in 1619, and in 1819 Stamford Raffles raised the British flag on the island which, he foresaw, would have a great future. It became the centre of the extensive British trade in South-East Asia, and later the base for the Royal Navy.

In 1942, on 15 February, General Parcival surrendered Singapore to General Yamashita, unconditionally. The Japanese took 80,000 prisoners, of whom 20,000 were killed in concentration camps. It was not until 4 September 1945 that British Indian forces returned to Singapore.

Singapore was later made a very unhappy member of the Federation of *Malaysia*, but broke free on 9 August 1965 under the leadership of its able premier Lee Kuan Yew, who made it the world's second biggest port, after Rotterdam.

See also *Malay Annals*.

Singapura See *Malay Annals; Singapore*.

Sinta (or Dewi Sinta; Javanese form of the Indian Sita) In Javanese mythology, an incarnation of *Dewi Sri*, spouse of *Wisnu*, who in the same cycle of myths (which have been assembled in the old Javanese epic *Ramayana*) incarnates as Rama. Sinta is abducted by the evil demon Rawana, who is an incarnation of *Dasamuka*. An army of *monkeys* under the command of *Hanuman* liberates her. Unwittingly, she marries her own son, Watu Gunung, but when she discovered that her husband was her son, she decided never to see him again, so that further *incest* was avoided.

Sireh   (or *Sirib*) See *Betel*.

Sirens   On the island of Siau, north of *Sulawesi*, it is said that beautiful maidens lure the fishermen ever further out to the open sea. See also *Reinga*.

Sisianlik   See *Goddess*(1).

Sisimatailaa   In Tongan mythology, a certain woman used to go fishing in the ocean, standing naked in the sea on the western side of her island, as the sun was setting. By her the Sun-God begot a son called Sisimatailaa. When he had become full grown, he boarded a boat and sailed northwards to *Samoa*. There he met a girl with whom he fell in love. He proposed and she agreed to marry him, but he had to ask his parents' consent. So he sailed back to *Tonga*, where his mother told him to climb a hill near the beach and ask permission of the rising sun, his father. Sisimatailaa prayed to the sun and at noon two parcels fell from the sky. One said: 'Open Now', the other 'Open Never'. Out of the first parcel came gold and silver, so Sisimatailaa was a rich man. He sailed back to Samoa to marry. One bad day, as they were sailing together, his wife found the second parcel, hidden by her husband in the bilge. She could not read, so she opened it while he was asleep. Out came rain and hail, storm, lightning and thunder and whipping winds. The boat was driven off course and was never seen again.

Sisinjori   See *Kangaroo*.

Sison   In Thai mythology, Sison was a king who loved Princess Thewi Suthat. She was a princess who by her generosity and kindness to beggars expunged the king's sins and so restored his royal dignity, an incarnation of the *Goddess of Mercy* (see *Kannon*). Theirs is a long story, first of life as two flowers living in the shallow stream, then of life as a young peasant and a poor girl. Each time their marriage was prevented by disaster: the flowers were washed away by the floods; the girl was killed by robbers. Finally as king and princess, they married and remembered their previous lives. See also *Ananta Nakhon*; *Love*; *Shinju*; *Sword*(2); *Tipaka*.

Sita   In Thai and Javanese mythology, daughter of King *Janaka* and queen of Rama. She was an *incarnation* of the goddess Lakshmi (see *Dewi Sri*). See also *Ramayana*; *Sinta*.

Siva   See *Siwa*.

Siwa   The Indian god Shiva is well known in *Indonesia* under different names, viz., Macassar: Batara; Sea-Dayak: Petara; *Philippines*: Bathala, Mahacabatara; Dayak: *Mahatara*; also *Guru*, *Kala*, Siwa. He is the Balinese Mountain-God of the East, husband of *Prawati* or *Uma* or *Sakti*.
   On *Bali* they relate that a certain farmer, Diarsa by name, was addicted to cockfighting. In spite of his optimism he always lost his wagers, and he had to sell all his possessions until finally he had only one cock left. Even his house was in ruins, except the shrine for the god Siwa, which

was properly kept, with new offerings being placed on it every day.

One night Diarsa met an old sick beggar and invited him into his home. He killed his last cock for him and his wife cooked their last bowl of rice. The next morning the beggar took Diarsa's only son, Wirachita, with him as his apprentice. When they had reached the summit of the mountain, the beggar sat down on a golden throne. He was no longer a beggar but a strong, handsome young man with four arms, each holding an object: his mace *katwanga* with a skull at the top, a rosary which was a necklace of skulls, the *fan* to fan the sacrificial fires and *pinaka*, the trident of lightning. Siwa! Wirachita sank down on his knees to perform *sembah* (worship) to the god with a *snake* round his neck and the crescent in his hair. Siwa gave the boy a lotus flower to eat so that he could fly with him up to *heaven*. There, they were surrounded by serving *demi-gods*. Wirachita was allowed to bathe in Siwa's lake so he grew stronger than other men. When his time in heaven was up, Siwa sent him down to earth as a king. Meanwhile, Siwa sent to Diarsa a cock which defeated all the other cocks of Bali, so Diarsa became very rich. Finally the people made him king.

See also *Ambu Dewi*; 'Gods of Bali' under *Gods*; *Kala*; *Kaseteran*; *Krailasa*; *Mahayogi*; *Sang Gala Raja Jin*.

Siwa Mahayogi   The Sundanese name for the Javanese *Batara Guru*. See also *Lutung Kasarung*.

Skeleton   In *Japan* there is a mountain called Hakkotsu-San, 'Skeleton Mountain'. It was said that a priest once lived there, called Ajari Joan, who once loved a girl, which is a sin for Buddhist priests. He became a *devil*, *okuma*, destroying his own temple. As an old man he recovered his wits and sat down to pray. He went on muttering prayers after he had died, becoming a praying skeleton.

Skulls   The Japanese artist Hiroshige painted a scene of a garden under snow. The attentive observer will realize to his horror that the snowflakes, when touching the ground, gradually turn into human skulls. No doubt he hoped to express the glaciality of *death* and the fatality of snow.

Sky

1. The people of Matu in central *New Guinea* relate that in the beginning the sky was much closer than it is today, indeed it was only six men high, so people were able to climb up to it with a rope ladder. Up there they found plenty of good food: sugar cane, bananas, melons and pumpkins. At that time an old man lived in the sky, a god, whom people called Heduru, 'The Helper'. When the people had to go out fishing and hunting, Heduru would descend from *heaven* and look after the children. The children loved him for he brought them fruits. However, each time he went back to heaven he took a child with him. One day two men decided to hide, before Heduru arrived, and spy on him. When they saw him depart with

a child, they ran after him but he was too quick. In their anger, they cut the rope ladder with the result that the sky rose up and flew away out of reach.

2. In *Polynesia* the Sky-God *Rangi* and the Earth-Goddess *Papa*, who lived in perpetual embrace during *Creation*, engendered the following gods:

   a) *Tangaroa*, the Ocean-God,
   b) Rongo ma-Tane, the God of Food and Plants, especially *kumara*, the *sweet potato* (see *Rongo*(1)),
   c) Haumia Tiketike, the God of Wild Roots and Ferns,
   d) Tane Mahuta (see *Tane*), the God of Forests, Birds and Insects,
   e) *Tawhiri-Matea*, the God of Winds and Storms
   f) *Tu-Matauenga*, the God of War, the first man, and
   g) *Ruau-Moko*, who was never born. He moves from time to time inside his mother Papa; he is the God of Earthquakes.

For each god there is a special *karakia*, hymn or prayer.

See also *Earthquakes*; 'Gods of the Pacific' under *Gods*; *Heaven*(1)(2); *Sky-King*; *Storm*; *Tane*; *Ten*; *Wind*.

Sky-King In the mythology of *Fiji* it is related that long ago the Sky-King married a woman on earth and had a son by her. The boy grew up bigger and stronger than the other boys, but he never played with them because they teased him: 'Where is your father?'

When he answered: 'In the sky,' they just laughed.

One day he planted his stick in the ground and went to sleep near it. The next morning it had grown up high into the air. So the boy climbed it and reached the sky country where he found people, plants, trees and running streams. Eventually, the Sky-King was pointed out to him.

'Who are you?' asked the Sky-King.

'I am the Boy-Challenging-Men.'

Hearing the boy boast thus, one of the Sky-King's courtiers laughed. The boy went up to him and struck him with his fist, then took the man's own club and crushed his skull with it. The Sky-King was amused: 'I can see that you are my son. You are a man.'

The boy fought and defeated all the king's enemies in Skyland. Having made his father unopposed ruler, he sat beside him on the throne. But soon he grew tired of the quiet life and went back to earth in search of a wife. On earth he conquered all the *islands* until he came to Kauvadra where the great serpent Dengei (see *Degei*) lived. Dengei addressed him thus: 'Welcome, Slayer Son of the Sky-King! Why should we fight? Come and marry my daughter, Princess Sweet-Eyes, and let us live in peace.'

Thus was done, and peace reigned.

Skyland See *Sky-King*.

Snake

1. On the Admiralty Islands, north of *New Guinea*, people relate that

a certain woman met a long snake who proposed to her. After some hesitation, the woman agreed. They were married and she gave birth to a boy and a girl. The snake taught the children to catch fish. He also taught them to make fire, and cook their food so it tasted better.

2. The people of the island of Siar, just off the north coast of New Guinea, relate that long ago when their ancestors still lived on the mainland, the men caught a snake in a tree (probably a *python*). They decided they would eat it the next day. That night all the women had a dream in which they saw the snake, which told them: 'If you eat me, the whole village will be drowned.'

No one took the dream seriously except one woman, Bubuli, who took a canoe and paddled to Sial, a neighbouring island, with her two children, a boy and a girl. The villagers ate the snake, but in the middle of their feast water surrounded the village, which suddenly capsized, like a boat going bottom-up in the sea. All the people drowned and there was no trace left of the village, only a pool. Bubuli stayed on Sial and her children married each other because she said: 'You are the only ones left of your clan.' They had many children who now populate Riwo and Siar. See also *Dreams*.

3. In *Indonesia*, if a man sees a snake on his path he will immediately return home and stay there, convinced that it is an unlucky day. The snake may be the *incarnation* of an evil character or an enemy-spirit, announcing misfortune and early *death*. The Torajas tell their children not to play on the cemetery, otherwise the ancestral *spirits* will emerge as snakes from holes in their graves. In Sarawak some Dayak chiefs have prohibited the killing of snakes because they are their ancestors reincarnated. The same conviction is found around Macassar, on Tanimbar and Timor Laut.

Many peoples in Indonesia believe that the snake entering the house announces death to the person who sees it first, but a sacrifice may avert the impending fate. Some people will even move house, hoping to evade their doom.

In some parts of Java a snake is called *siluman*, 'spirit', and addressed as *kyahi*, 'grandfather', because it is a jin.

See also *Cobra; Demons*(3); *Dugong; Gama-Sennin; Goga; Kahausibware; Nichiren; Owl*(1); *Python; Rice Soul; Serpent; Serpent-God; Shondo Shonin; Snake-King; Violets; Yatim Nustapa.*

Snake-King In Thai mythology, Thonamun is the King of Snakes and Eels. One day he was offended by Sura Uthaka, King of the Khmer. The Snake-King called on all his creeping subjects to go and undermine Nong Han, King Sura's capital. The *snakes* dug tunnels under the city, so that it sank into the earth. Thonamun then wound his long body around King Sura and drowned him in the Khong River.

Snow-Spirits Snow-women are *spirits* of people who have died in the snow. They have no feet, for they float in the air like a freezing vapour. They are greatly feared, for they can kill people with their icy breath.

A snow-woman can blow open the door of an isolated hut and lie with a lonely traveller sleeping there. In her embrace he will freeze to death. Beware of their cold beauty!

Much snow falls in the province of Niigata, yet the peasants are so poor that they can afford only flimsy houses. One night during a snowstorm a man heard someone knocking on his door. He refused to open it, even though a girl's voice from outside pleaded for help. She came in all the same, since *ghosts* require no opening of doors to enter. If a man is alone in the house with a snow spirit he will soon die of cold.

See also *Skulls; Yuki-Onna*.

Sodzu Baba See *Bommatsuri*.

Solanang The Supreme Deity of *New Ireland* who arrives annually seated on a fish-boat in two forms: a god and a goddess. See also *God*.

The Solomon Islands The Spanish explorer Alvaro de Mendana, who first visited these *islands* in 1568, on his way from Peru to the *Philippines*, named them after the Biblical king, reputedly because he hoped to find gold there, i.e. Solomon's mines. No one ever did. The archipelago consists of six large islands (Choiseul, Santa Isabel, New Georgia, Guadalcanal, Malaita, San Cristobal) and a few dozen smaller ones, as well as a few hundred coral rocks. It stretches for some 1,000 miles (1,600km) north-east of the Queensland coast, with an area of 29,785 sq km. The capital is Honiara on Guadalcanal. The republic has been an independent member of the British Commonwealth since 1978. The 300,000 inhabitants live on fishing and coconuts. Some of their lush forests have been cleared to make room for palm oil plantations. They are Melanesians and speak 87 distinct languages between them. The Solomons were the scene of fierce fighting in 1942–3 between the Japanese and American fleets and armies, especially Guadalcanal.

See also *Adaro, Ganindo; Kahausibware*.

Songbirds These were first brought to earth from the Eternal Land, according to Polynesian tradition. See also *Hine-Nui-Te-Po*.

Songkran See *New Year*(2).

Sopiwina ('Cleansing water') A clear well. See *Reincarnation*(1).

Sorcerer In Melanesia, the sorcerer can be recognized by those who are brave enough to follow him at night. They will see that he emits flames in the dark, that he is good friends with the owls, and that he can disappear at will.

See also *Kahoali; Medicine Man; Pelesit; Sanguma; Sorcery; Witch*.

Sorcery On Halmahera, when someone has been freshly interred, a person who possesses the second sight is told to keep a vigil on the graveyard. First, at seven when it is almost dark, he will see a dog and then a *cat*. These are the 'devil's spies'. Suddenly, a fire will be visible, and only after that will the 'devil' appear, looking like an ordinary man. He wants to have a few morsels from the dead body, but one thrust with a spear will kill him. Such a devil is called *kitoka*. Some people want his help so they bring him offerings. He will then teach them the *magic* to make people sick or insane (by 'eating' their *liver* so that they die) or to make the crops fail. Gradually the pupil will destroy even his own family. This ability for sorcery can also be inherited, as is the ability to change oneself into a carnivorous animal, in order to kill someone. Some sorcerers belong to known 'killer clans'.

See also *Hakawau; Karakia; Love-Magic; Makutu; Medicine Man; Sanguma; Sorcerer; Tiger; Tohunga; Were-Dog; Witch.*

Soripada ('The Earth') See *Creation*(9).

Soryo A Japanese priest or *bonze*. Some priests can recite prayers which will expel evil *spirits*. See also *Gaki; Kitsune.*

Soto In *Japan*, a school of Zen which has restored the original contemplation to *Buddhism*. It also stresses that all our preconceived ideas have to be replaced by new thinking. See also *Koan; Mondo; Rinzai.*

Sotoba Japanese form of the Sanskrit *stupa*, a Buddhist sanctuary.

Soul In Indonesian *languages* there are many words for soul: *roh*, the spirit; *nyawa*, 'breath', that which flows away at the end of one's life and *semangat*, 'living essence'.

Badi is the soul who can wander when a dreamer is 'travelling'. The *badi* of a *tiger* can enter a man and make him bloodthirsty. It is therefore best to let sleeping people lie. A man who, one night, woke his wife, was suddenly confronted by a fierce tigress.

The *bayang*, 'wind-life', permeates a person's whole body and survives him like the 'shade', looking like the person.

Tondi (*Batak*) is the essence of life, the soul-power that keeps a person alive. After death the *tondi* becomes a *begu*, 'ghost'.

In Javanese, *kesakten* is the cosmic soul, the vital principle of the universe, the animating power which the Indians call *shakti*, equated with the goddess *Uma-Kali*.

In *Thailand*, *windjan* is the soul which leaves the body at *death*, a person's consciousness. *Khwan* is the soul that may wander about when a person is dreaming.

See also *Arugo; Banoi; Birds*(1)*; Black; Bluebottle; Bommatsuri; Bubwayaita; Butterfly*(1)(2)*; Cat*(1)*; Corpse-Eater; Crow; the Dead; Death; Degei; Demi-Gods; Dragonfly; Fairies*(3)*; Firefly*(1)(2)*; Flores; Fly; Fox; Futon; Gods; Hades; Harai; Hina-Matsuri; Hiyoyoa; Honey Tree Song; Hototogisu; Illness; Iva; Jizo; Kabu; Life After Death; Love; Manawa*(2)*; Mareikura; Mauri; Migration of Souls; Milu; Miru; Monkey*(6)(7)(8)*; Nabangatai; Nether World; Pheasant; Pigs*(5)*; Predestination; Reincarnation; Replacement; Rice Soul; Semangat; Shaman; Shamanism; Spirits; Topileta; Tree-Spirit*(5)*; Tuma; Waterlily; Yamato.*

Sparrow In Japanese mythology the Sparrow-God possessed great wealth so people tried to find him. One washer-woman, greedy for wealth, went to visit the Sparrow-God, who offered her a small box and a big one. Although her neighbour had warned her to choose the smaller box, the jealous woman distrusted him and chose the bigger box. She took it home and opened it, but oh disaster! It contained evil *demons* who soon devoured her.

Spectre Huntsman   This Malayan myth is the Malay equivalent of the Flying Dutchman. A hunter was told by his pregnant wife to go and find her the meat of a mousedeer doe who was pregnant of a male young. He swore that he would not come back unless he was successful. He never was, so he never returned home. Meanwhile his wife gave birth to twins, a boy and a girl, who knew nothing of their father. When the boy grew up a playmate teased him once: 'Your father is an evil spirit!'

The boy asked his mother, who confessed that it was all her fault. She told him on his insistence what his father's 'home name' was, and he went in search of him. He found his father at last, still wandering in the forest, looking like a ghost, or a corpse with moss all over him. The Spectre Huntsman told his son that he must become a doctor and cure the people whom he, the Huntsman, had made ill by his *magic*. So the boy went home and became a famous physician.

This ending resembles the Flemish tale of Godfather Death. Another variant relates how the woman joined her husband in the forest and had more children with him.

The Spice Islands   See *The Moluccas*.

Spider   (*kumo*) In Japanese mythology, the deity *Inari* may assume the shape of a spider in order to teach wicked men a lesson.

Once a huge spider sucked the blood of a miser, *Raiko*, every night until he repented, while other Japanese myths tell of gigantic spiders, bigger than a man, with eyes as big as saucers, sharp teeth and legs as long as men's. They will hide in old castles, looking like innocent heaps of clothes. Unsuspecting travellers, seeking shelter and lying down to sleep, will wake up finding themselves imprisoned by huge sticky spider webs, too tough to be undone except by *magic*.

See also *Marawa*(1); *Spider-Boy*; *Spider-Woman*..

Spider-Boy   The Japanese hero *Raiko* was ill one day and a little boy entered his room every night to bring him his medicine. However it did not cure him, indeed it made him sicker. The medicine was poison. His suspicion aroused, Raiko struck the boy one night when he came in. The boy threw something at him which quickly grew and became a sticky net, enveloping the hero entirely, so that he could not move. The boy fled, but was stopped by Tsuna, the chief retainer, at sword's point. The boy threw his web over the retainer too, then fled again. He was later found in a cave and killed. The boy was a spider-spirit, a little demon with a *magic* weapon.

Spider-Woman   Once the Japanese hero *Raiko* saw a skull flying before him, then disappearing into a ruined building. In the building Raiko found an old hag, entirely white with hanging breasts. A moment later he saw an old nun with a large face. Finally he saw a beautiful woman.

As he stared at her, she enveloped him quickly in a sticky net. He struck
her with his sword but its point broke off. Tsuna, Raiko's chief retainer
arrived and liberated Raiko from the huge web. The woman had
vanished, but after a thorough search they found a huge *spider* with the
tip of Raiko's sword sticking out of its stomach. As they pulled it out,
the white spider died. Inside the body they found numerous human
skulls, those of the spider's victims; in addition many 'baby' spiders, as
large as children, came creeping out. The heroes slew them all, thus
liberating the country of the age-old plague of mountain spiders, a race
of evil demons.

See also *Spider-Boy*.

Spinach See *Spirit Woman*.

Spirit-Canoe In Melanesia, this is a long boat in the shape of a *fish*,
carved in wood and manned by the images of the ancestors all dressed
in their totemic *masks*, ready to attend a feast in their honour in *New
Ireland*.

See also *Canoe*.

Spirits

1. The *Maori* tradition mentions Tau-Titi, son of *Miru*, Queen of the
    Spirit World. A *dance* is named after him, which is held during the
    night by moonlight. The four beautiful daughters of the Spirit Queen
    would sometimes arrive at the dance after sunset, unrecognized. As
    soon as the *morning star* appeared, they would vanish and return to
    their gloomy home in *Avaiki*, in the deeps.

2. The Rarotongan tradition is very similar. The spirits, they say, live
    in crevices in the earth, or beyond the waters. If a chief desires to
    see beautiful spirit-women, he will order fresh banana leaves to be
    cut and spread out at one end of the dancing ground lest the spirits'
    feet should be soiled by the earth or hurt by rock.

    The *sky* too, is inhabited by spirits, of a different kind, more
    cheerful. They even practise ball games with great skill, which
    Ngaru, 'Waves', the Polynesian explorer who one day climbed up
    into the sky, learned from them. *Ina*, the *moon's* wife, is able to keep
    seven balls in the air at the same time, probably an allusion to the
    Pleiades. These sky spirits were fair-skinned, says the tradition, and
    it has been suggested that they were an ancient *race* whom the
    Polynesians encountered during their wanderings, and whom they
    count among their ancestors.

3. The Polynesians believe the spirits of the *Other World* eat their food
    raw, as do the primitive peoples of the jungle. One day a man called
    Pungarehu went fishing with a friend. A storm drove their boat far
    away to an unknown coast. They wanted to make a fire to cook their
    meal but found no dry wood. So they took some wood from their
    boat and put it under their armpits to dry. Meanwhile they went and
    explored the country. They came upon two men who said: 'We will
    take you to our village for a meal, but you must never laugh or you
    will be killed.'

They arrived in the village of the 'Gloomy Ghosts' and were given raw whale-meat to eat. The next morning they showed the villagers how to make a fire and cook their meat. The spirits have no fire; they are condemned to suffer cold.

In *Polynesia*, the spirits are numerous in all the *elements* too: in the *air*, the water, the *earth* and the fire of the volcanoes. They are occasionally vaguely seen but sometimes they look like human beings or like fishes, *birds* or *lizards*. They may be only weak voices or powerful, strong *giants*. Some are worshipped, some are propitiated, all are taken seriously.

The spirits of the *dead* have to travel to the World of the Dead (see *Hades*), where they will join their relatives and old friends. In a Maori prayer to a deceased father, the children pray: 'My father, farewell. Go to the spirit world, go to Hawaiki, to your ancestors, to your elders. Farewell, our protector, our breastwork, our shelter from the fierce winds, our shady tree . . .'

The spirits of the deceased travel in the direction of the setting sun to *Hawaiki* Nui in the land of Irihia. Some spirits, it is believed, travel downward to Tahekeroa in the heart of the earth. Others travel upward to Aratiatia, to the kingdom of Io in the skies. Soon all their memories of earth will have faded in the sunny skies among the bright clouds, the true home of spirits.

4. In *Malaysia*, the people believe in many dangerous spirits, e.g. Hantu Kuang, the Ghost with a Hundred Eyes; Datu Jinn Hitam, the King of the Black Jins; Hantu Uri, the Placenta Spirit who may cause trouble after birth; Penyakit, the Sickmaker; Bujang Sembelih, the Throat-Cutting Demon; and Mambang Kuning, the Spirit of Sunset. The *jin* or *jan* are *internal* spirits, i.e., spirits who may possess people by entering their heads or bodies and controlling their speech or movements. *Jins* can be manipulated by black magicians (*sorcerers*) to make their enemies sick, mad or childless. The *bomoh* is the specialist who can deal with some of these *demons*. Spirits can be controlled by praying to the *Buddha* while facing a Buddha image, or by reciting the holy Koran, or other holy scriptures. A 'Black Shadow' is a spirit which visits people every night, causing pain in the neck. It is often sent by a greedy, jealous rival.

5. Included among the spirits and ghosts among the Lakalai of central *New Britain* are the following:

A *balepa* is a corpse wrapped in its funeral mat, flying over the village.

A *halulu* is the shade or *soul*, the life of a person which leaves him when he dies.

A *hituhitu* is the spirit of a dead man when it appears to humans.

A *kalulu* is the individual spirit, which consciously experiences adventures.

A *pigobara* is a 'bleeding woman', a mother who died in childbirth, becoming a dangerous and horrifying bleeding spectre. See *Puntianak*.

The *putuperereko* is a spirit with huge testicles who devours people.

A *tarogolo* is a spirit who seduces people of the opposite sex, killing them by cutting up their genitals.

A *tatabu* is a *fetish*: a spirit confined to an object to serve its owner. The *taua* are a large group of spirits disguised as animals or even plants. Many are *monsters* combining parts of different animals. Some *taua* spirits belong to certain clans, but most spirits are dangerous because they steal souls, or cause violent *storms* and *earthquakes*. A woman once ate a fish which was a *taua*. It spoke to her from her own stomach, then killed her by tearing it from within. However, these spirits sometimes help their clan-mates. Four fishermen of the cassowari (see *Cassowary*) clan of south Irian were caught in a storm. Their boat sank, but four cassowaries appeared and carried the men to safety. A tree once prevented another tree from falling on its clan-mate. The helpful tree was a strong protective clan spirit, a father or grandfather during its human life.

A *vis* is a vampire. It flies at night shining brightly and it scratches out people's eyes with its long nails.

See also *Atua; Child-Spirit; the Dead; Hotoke; Iki-Ryo; Illness; Kami; Masalai; Matabiri; Miru; Shi Tenno; Shito Dama; Snow-Spirits; Soul; Spirit-Canoe; Spirit-Twin; Spirit Woman; Tambaran.*

Spirit-Twin On the *Trobriand Islands*, it is related that every human or animal being has a spirit which can travel independently from the body. Objects also have their spirit-twins, so that when the living give the *shaman* gifts for their dead relatives in *Tuma* before he travels there, he will carry only the spirit-twins of those objects to the spirit world.

Spirit Woman In the lower Sepík area of northern *New Guinea*, there is told the following horror tale.

A 'good' woman was travelling along the path with a spirit woman. The spirit woman said to her companion, 'Let me carry your child.'

The good woman agreed, for she had a net full of *sweet potatoes* as well as a bundle of firewood to carry. They walked on, the spirit woman now carrying the child. The spirit woman then pulled one of the child's arms off and ate it up. The good woman asked, 'Why does the child cry?'

The spirit woman replied, 'He cries in his sleep.'

She then pulled off the other arm and proceeded to eat it. The good woman asked the same question again, and the spirit woman again replied, 'He is crying in his sleep. He is all right.'

As they walked on the spirit woman devoured the rest of the child. When the good woman said she wanted to have her child back, the spirit woman put a piece of wood in her carry-net. Finally the good woman realized who her fellow traveller was. She fled and escaped to her hut. The spirit woman hungrily pursued her and scratched at the bamboo walls with her huge nails. Then she changed into a flying dog and flew up to the trees to eat bananas. (All spirits have an endless hunger for human flesh, hoping to become human again. The bananas were only a part-replacement for the whole woman.)

Later, the husband of the good woman lured the spirit woman into his house where he was roasting big nuts (like chestnuts) in a fire which was blazing high. As she came in to pick up the nuts from the fire, he attacked her from behind with a forked stick he had placed nearby for the purpose. He then held her down in the fire until she was totally consumed. In her place they found *gherkins* and *aibika*, a *spinach*-like vegetable which is highly prized. The evil spirit had been transformed into these good things by the purifying fire and the good husband's strong willpower.

Sport Polynesian games included regattas, archery, javelins and wrestling and were often linked to the choosing of spouses. See *Polynesians*.

Squirrel (*Tupai*) In *Malaysia* it is said that the squirrel was originally born from a certain large caterpillar. The dried penis of the squirrel is believed to be a powerful aphrodisiac. It is called *chula tupai* (*chula* is the Sanskrit word for the horn of a *dragon*).

Sri In Javanese mythology, Lakshmi, the kind Goddess of Rice and Birth. See also *Dewi Sri; Rice-Goddess*.

Sri Lanka See *Lanka*.

Sriwijaya A kingdom in eastern *Sumatra*. See *Indonesia*.

Star Repeatedly we read in the Javanese chronicles that a star was seen after the *death* of a *king*. It would happen at night when one of the princes, sleeping peacefully, would suddenly be brightly lit by a falling star or a ray of moonlight. The star sometimes spoke, saying, 'This one will be King of Java.'

The most senior *guru* (sage) or *mantri* (minister) had to see the star so that he could hail the new king as ruler of *Java*. The *mantri* would then hail that prince as *God*'s chosen king.

See also *Atutuahi;* 'Gods of the Pacific' under *Gods; Matariki; Milky Way; Morning Star; Ru*(2); *Senapati; Star Spirit*.

Star Spirit In ancient *Thailand* there once reigned a divine king called Thung of Ruang, whose religious convictions included prohibiting the killing of animals. When animals emerged from the woods to eat the people's rice, the farmers complained to the king. So the king ordered fences to be built around all the cultivated fields, but it was not effective. So then he ordered all the farmers to place stars, made from bamboo, on stakes in all their fields, gardens and orchards. The spirit of the star protects the crops because the animals respect it. Farmers in Thailand still place bamboo stars in the corners of their rice fields and vegetable gardens.

See also *Atutuahi;* 'Gods of the Pacific' under *Gods; Matariki; Milky Way; Morning Star; Ru*(2); *Star*.

Stingaree (Stingray, *Vari*) A large Pacific fish of the family of *Dasyatidae*. It has a long tail with a poisonous sting at the end.

1. In Melanesia there is a myth in which a stingaree emerges from the sea to sting a mother of five sons. All the sons flee except for the youngest. He prepares five spears made of the wood of different trees in order to be prepared for the next (fifth) attack of the stingaree. After a fierce battle he kills the monster. The flesh is given away because it is *taboo*. A curious detail of the myth is that the stingaree emerges singing a song in which it threatens to cut up the five clitorises of the mother of five sons.
2. In the *Philippines* this skate-fish is called *pagui*. Its tail is very efficacious against *witches* and other evil *spirits*. It will even convince a giant that its owner is too strong to attack.

Stingray See *Stingaree*.

Stones

1. Stones are sometimes venerated in *Japan*, especially those which have been touched or blessed by *Kobo*. These stones are kept in the temple and can be borrowed by the people to cure skin diseases. In several places the *Buddha* and other saints (including Kobo) left their footprints in the rocks. This belief signifies that the weight of the Buddha's spirit and knowledge is such that his body sinks in rock as if it were soft mud. See also *Footprint of the Buddha*.
2. In western Papua *sorcery* is practised by means of small prehistoric figurines upon which pig's blood is smeared. If such a stone is waved at a man he will soon die.
3. On Timor, if a man finds a stone of a certain shape – round, oval, cylindrical or of animal appearance – he will take it home. If, that night, he dreams that the stone is his friend, then he knows he is in luck: inside the stone lives a spirit who is concluding a covenant of friendship with the finder. However, the stone may ask for a sacrifice of an animal or even a human being. If the finder cannot satisfy the stone's desire he may become ill, or his children may die, so he needs a magical expert who can make the covenant ineffective. For this, the stone is placed on a mound which will become sacred: no one may cut wood there forever after.
4. On Halmahera, before its conversion to Christianity, many stones were venerated. For instance, in the village of Baratako a stone *tortoise* was the protective deity of the area. It was said that it turned its head whenever the wind changed. People sacrificed to it.
5. The Torajas worship seven tall stones representing the clan ancestors.
6. In Minangkabau there was a cat-shaped stone which, it was claimed, could make rain.
7. In south *Sulawesi* the god *Karaeng Lowe*, 'Great Lord', is worshipped by burning incense before a big stone in a cave on the coast.

See also *Amulet*(3); *Bezoar Stone; Creation*(8); *Death-Stone; Fetish; Kongo; Moonstone; New Caledonia; Rain-Making; Tide Jewels; Vajra.*

Storm   In Polynesian mythology there are many storm-gods, including *Tawhiri-Matea* of *New Zealand;* Apu-Hau, 'Fierce Squall', of *Hawaii;* the *Maori* Apu Matangi, 'Howling Rainfall', and Awha; and the Samoan Afa.

There are also many measures to placate them. On the south coast of *Java* the fishermen sacrifice to Ratu Loro or Nyai Gedé Segoro Kidul, the 'Great Queen of the Southern Ocean', hoping to persuade her not to cause storms while they are out fishing. On the Aru Islands the fishermen drop a gong in the sea for the Sea-God Taidue, before sailing out. The Malay fishermen of Selangor pray to the Sea-God in the shape of a black *turtle* when they see a storm brewing.

In East Javanese myth, the Sea-God *Kyai Blorong* has a palace of living people who have drowned in storms.

See also *Navigators.*

Suac   A Philippine hero. See *Monsters*(2).

Subadra   In Javanese mythology, the younger sister of *Baladewa* and *Kresna;* she marries the hero *Arjuna.* There is a special *wayang* drama, *Subadra Abducted.* See also *Durga; Sembadra.*

Suchada   See *Diamond Buddha.*

Sudo   (Korean, 'asceticism, spiritual discipline') Even today, men and women may retire – not necessarily after their active life in society has ended; some are still young – to the wooded hills or to a *sudo-won*, a monastery, to meditate. This may not necessarily be after their active life in society has ended; some are still young. Such a person is by no means always a Buddhist *sudo-sung*, monk, but he or she may be a beginner *shaman* whom the *spirits* call.

Sudo-Sung   In *Korea,* a Buddhist monk. See *Buddhism; Sudo.*

Sudo-Won   A Korean Buddhist monastery. See *Buddhism; Sudo.*

Suharto   The ruler of *Indonesia.* See *Indonesia, Modern History.*

Suijin   The *kami* (deity, god, goddess) of the *water* in Japanese cosmology, or a water-nymph. The *suijin-matsuri* (feast) is celebrated on 1 December.

Suisho   See *Crystal.*

Sujata   See *Diamond Buddha.*

Sukarno   The first ruler of independent *Indonesia.* See *Indonesia, Modern History.*

Sukha-Saptati   See *Parrot.*

Sukhavati   The Land of Happiness. See *Amida.*

Sukuna-Biko   A dwarf-god of Japanese religion. King of Izumo, he was skilled in the arts of healing and agriculture. See also *Dwarfs; Izumo.*

Sulawesi One of the big islands of *Indonesia* (the third largest), with an area of 179,370 sq km, more than twice the size of Scotland, lying between *Borneo* (*Kalimantan*) and the *Moluccas*, north of Flores, south of Mindanao. Its population is over 10 million, also twice that of Scotland.

Sulawesi houses many cultures, from the Christian Menadonese in the north to the Muslims of the south in the towns of Macassar, Goa, Bone and Bugi. There are more than a dozen ethnic groups speaking as many quite distinct languages. The best known are the To-Raja, 'Royal People', usually referred to as Torajas. They live in central Sulawesi and are in turn divided into a number of sub-tribes, each with its own ancestors and other gods.

In the Minahassa (the 'neck' of northern Sulawesi), there live the Bolaang-Mongondow peoples with their own language and myths.

See also *Amulet*(2); *Creation*(7)(8)(11); *Crocodiles*(1); *Eel*(3); *Goddess*(2); *Gnomes*; *Indonesia*; *Moon*(3); *Mouse*; *Predestination*(2); *Replacement*(3); *Rice Soul*; *Sangiang*; *Shamanism*(2)(3); *Stones*(7); *Sky*(4); *Sun*(6); *Tadu*; *Tree-Spirit*(5); *Walian*; *Witch*(3).

Sultan Pajang See *Jaka Tingkir*.

The Sulu Islands An archipelago of over 400 *islands* covering 982 sq km, the Sulu Islands lie between Mindanao and *Borneo* in the Sulu Sea. Their Islamic culture and preference for the Malay language makes the inhabitants (400,000 in number) incline towards *Malaysia* or *Indonesia*, but they became part of the *Philippines* in 1940. They had their own sultans on Jolo until *c*.1890.

Sumangat See *Semangat*.

Sumangat Negari See *Semangat*.

Sumatra (Sumatera is the official Indonesian spelling) See *Abdu'l Ra'uf of Singkel*; *Bukit Seguntang*; *Creator*; *Demons*; *Eggs*; *Hornbill*(2); *Indonesia*; *Iskandar*; *Keris*; *Korinchi*; *Mahameru*(2); *Malay Annals*; *Malaya*; *Maniaka*; *Pigs*; *Predestination*(4); *Sangiang*; *Shaman*(3); *Sijobang*; *Sunan Gunung*; *Tiger*(3)(5).

Sumono See *Plum Tree*.

Sumua On *New Britain*, the Lakalai people have a myth about Sumua, a forest spirit, portrayed as a handsome, tall youth, who was born from a *cassowary* and a human mother who gave birth to him after she had died. According to some he was a stillborn baby who was left in the bush. He became a powerful god who gave to his people the *taro*, the *sweet potato*, the pig, the chicken, *fire* and sago. He travels with the *winds* and can cause *floods* or volcanic eruptions at will. Sumua has 10 human wives. He receives the *souls* of the *dead*.

Sun Worship of the sun is prevalent throughout the Pacific.

1. In Binadere, northern *New Guinea*, people relate that long ago the sun was owned by a young man who kept it in a dish. He had

inherited it from his father who was a magician (i.e. a god). The young man lived with his sister who made food for him. But when she was married, her husband brought him *stones* instead of the food she had cooked. So, the young man decided to live elsewhere. He took his sun one evening and travelled away in his *canoe*.

In his village he left darkness behind. He sailed until he arrived in the east. There he landed on a beach and went to sleep. The next morning he saw many young women arriving with food and gifts. They said they were his wives and welcomed him as king to their island. The young man was now rich, because he brought sunshine, and the only man on the island. Meanwhile in his home village the people found they could grow no food in the darkness so they starved. The young man's sister then went in search of her brother, the owner of the sun. At last she saw a streak of light in the east, and finally landed on the island where her brother was king. She persuaded him to come back home with her. He put the sun, which had the shape of a shining round seashell, in his boat, and together they travelled westward. The starving people soon felt better when they saw the sun rise at last. They could cultivate food again and so, they lived. But the owner of the sun did not stay, He sailed away again to his island where he was king. However, he promised to return every morning and he has kept his promise to this day.

2. On the *Moluccas* it is related that Upu Lero, the 'Lord Sun', is worshipped during special ceremonies during which the people hang an elaborate lamp, *palita*, in a *fig tree* above their heads. Once a year the Sun-God descends onto the holy fig tree to fertilize the entire earth.

3. On the Watubela Islands in *Indonesia* the people invoke the 'Lord Sun' whenever they want to undertake a journey, when a woman has a difficult confinement, in case of illness or when war threatens. On the island of Buru in Indonesia, a white chicken was dedicated to the Sun-God.

4. The Torajas of central *Sulawesi* relate that the Sun-God, Ilai, who lived in heaven, married the Earth-Goddess, Indara, 'The Maiden'. See also *Creation*(8).

5. In Irian Jaya too, the worship of the sun is documented as early as 1705.

6. In the Minahassa in Sulawesi, the Sun-God, Muntu-Untu, is the law-giver and judge.

7. On Nias it is said that Lature who lives in the sun, owns all the people on earth, just as men own pigs. Some people proffer sacrifices to Lature hoping that he will continue their lives by giving them shadows on earth forever. A priest has to perform a daily ritual to keep people's shadows on earth.

8. In central *Malaya* the people relate that there are two Sun-Gods: the White Deity is the God of the Noon, the Yellow Deity is the God of the Sunset. This latter deity is a daily danger for children as he could take their *souls*.

9. On the island of Seran (Ceram) just west of New Guinea in
Indonesia, it is related that the name of the *Creator* is Tuniai who
made the earth, while the God of Heaven is Lahatala. The oldest
god, however, is Tuwale the Sun-God. One day Tuwale was travelling
on earth, disguised as a sick old beggar. He met two sisters, Siloo
and Dapie the Moon-Goddess. He went to Dapie's parents to ask
for her hand in marriage, offering gold and silver as bride price, but
they refused because he had pimples on his face. They dressed up
a sow to look like Dapie. She disappeared in the river when her
husband had found out the deceit, but she promised she would
come out in three days. Pigs love to cover themselves with mud. The
Moon-Goddess is identified with a sow.

See also *Dudugera; Gods; Sisimatailaa; Tama Nui-Te-Ra.*

Sunan Ambu See *Ambu Dewi.*

Sunan Bonang Ibrahim ibn Rahmatallah Nyakrawati is better known
as Sunan Bonang, though it is uncertain whether he was ever *sunan,*
'sovereign'. He seems to have referred to himself as Pangeran Bonang,
'Prince' of Bonang.

Bonang is on *Java*'s north coast, near Semarang, downstream from
Demak, where Sunan Bonang was *imam* for a time and where he built
the mosque, which is still there. Legend relates that he was one of the
nine saints of Java responsible for the Islamization of that large island,
and that he died in Bonang, which was his father's town. The date of
his birth is not known, but he was active in Tuban between *c.*1475–1500,
and died *c.*1525. He studied in Malacca which was then, before the
Portuguese destroyed it in 1511, a great centre of Islamic scholarship.

After his *death*, his body was shipped to 'Ampel' (perhaps this is
Karang Ampel near Cheribon) to be buried near his father's, but a storm
pushed the ship ashore near Tuban, where he now lies, 'because God
so willed it'. Many miracles are told of him. See also *Wali.*

Sunan Gunung ('Mountain King') This was the title of a Javanese
saint who lies buried on Gunung Jati, 'Teak Mountain'. His real name
was Palatehan of Pasai, *Sumatra*, from where he migrated to Bantam in
1520. From there he conquered Sunda Kalapa, 'Sunda United', a city
better known as Jayakarta, 'Creator of Victory', the present Jakarta. He
died in 1570 and is still venerated as the first Muslim prince in *Java.* See
also *Wali.*

Sunyata (Sanskrit, 'emptiness') See *Borobudur.*

Suprabha See *Arjuna-Wiwaha.*

Sura Uthaka The King of the Khmer. See *Snake-King.*

Suria The Javanese Sun-God. See *Karna; Wilotama.*

Suryananta The Sun Prince. See *Kalimantan.*

Suryavarman See *Angkor-Wat.*

Susa-no-o See *Susanowo*.

Susanowo (or Susa-no-o; in full: Takehaya Susanowo) Susanowo is the Japanese Storm-God. Just as storm clouds obscure the *sun*, so Susanowo harassed his sister *Ama Terasu*, the Sun-Goddess. This aroused the hostility of the *gods* of the land and the bright skies, who restored Ama Terasu to her proper place, after she had hidden her shining visage from the tempest, and punished Susanowo with exile and confiscation of his goods.

While wandering in exile, Susanowo met and fought the great *dragon* of *Izumo* with eight heads. Having killed it, he found a *magic sword* in its tail. Its name: Kusanagi-no-Tsurugi, 'Grass Cutting Sword'. This name implies that people are like grass before the sword's cutting edge. He sent this sword to Ama Terasu as a symbol of submission to her superior power. She in turn gave it to her descendant, the first Emperor of *Japan*, and that sword is an emblem of imperial power to this day. Susanowo also planted the mountains with his own hairs, which became *pine trees*.

According to another variant of the same story, once, while walking upon earth, Susanowo heard weeping and found a beautiful girl with her parents. The girl, Kushinada, was the youngest of eight sisters; seven had been devoured by the Eight-Clawed Monster. Soon it would come for her. Susanowo offered to rescue Kushinada, if he was allowed to marry her. The parents agreed. Susanowo changed Kushinada into a comb (*kushi* = comb) and stuck her in his hair. Soon the Eight-Clawed Dragon appeared. It had red eyes, eight tails and was as large as eight hills. Susanowo gave it *sake*, which he had asked the girl's parents to prepare, and when it was drunk, he slew it.

Like Poseidon and *Tangaroa*, Susanowo is the God of the Ocean as well as of the storms that rage over it. He is the God of the Autumn Storms, riding his dark clouds like wild horses, while the sun withdraws for the winter. When she reappears, he is banished to the Land of *Yomi* (*Hades*) leaving the green hills of earth brown.

Often, like Shiva in *India*, so in Japan, Susanowo is also the God of Destruction, as when he ruined his sister's *rice* fields by breaking the dividing embankments, or when he disturbed her weaving. In this we see an expression of early human philosophy, as reflected in ancient religions, proving wiser than some modern philosophy. We cannot build all the time. Often we have to destroy our own works before we can build the new things we need.

See also *Ama Terasu*; 'Gods of Japan' under *Gods*; *Izanami*; *Kompera*; *Ninigi*; *Omitsunu*; *Rice*(1); *Tengu*.

Sutawijaya Sahidin Panatagam See *Senapati*.

Suyudana See *Duryudana*.

Swan There once was a rich man in *Thailand* who lived happily with his wife. However, nothing is eternal, so one day the man died and went to *heaven*. There he was reborn as a golden swan, and lived happily on the Heavenly Lake. Soon, however, he remembered his wife and when he looked down to earth he saw that she lived in poverty. Overcome with love and compassion, the golden swan flew down to earth and alighted at his widow's feet. He said, 'I cannot bear to see you living in distress. Pull out one of my golden feathers and sell it in the city.' This she did and he then flew away.

The woman sold the unique golden feather for much money and bought all the things she needed. Every day the golden swan came down and gave her another feather, so that she lived comfortably. However, she wanted more than that, so one day when the swan-husband offered her a feather, she seized him and quickly plucked out all his feathers. Alas! All the feathers suddenly became white. The swan flew away and never came back.

Sweet Potato (*Ipomoea Batatas*, a tuber of the *Convolvulaceae* family; Javanese, *uwi*; Malay, *ubi*; Maori, *kumara*) This plant keeps voyagers alive and is the staple food of most of the *Pacific peoples*, *Polynesians* and Indonesians. It was brought by the Polynesians from *Hawaiki*, which is usually interpreted as *Indonesia*, where it grows wild. The Maori god Rongo ma-Tane (see *Rongo*) is the protector of this very special plant. It is so powerful that if it is buried in the path of approaching enemies they will go mad and run away.

See also *Fue*; *Taro*; *Yam*.

Sword

1. In Japanese mythology it is related that the sword is the symbol of the unity of the nation.

    A sword was once found by a pearl diver off the coast of Amakusa. It was standing on a rock shining brightly. It was brought ashore and placed in a special temple. Since that day there were no more *earthquakes*, and there was always plenty of *fish*, since the spirit of the sword was duly worshipped.

    It is said, in *Japan*, that a special old sword, made for a great prince, may have a spirit of its own. Such a spirit was seen at night near Cape Fudo where a sword lay on the bottom of the ocean. It was the sword of *Susanowo* and Prince *Yamato*. See also *Susanowo*; *Yorimasa*.

2. In Thai mythology it is related that King *Sison* of *Ananta Nakhon* possessed a sword which he could wield only with the consent of the god *Phra Sao*, the God of Destiny and Luck in Warfare. If the sword was raised, all the enemies who saw it flashing in the sunshine on the morning of the battle would perish. If however, no proper sacrifices had been offered to Phra Sao, the king's own soldiers would suddenly die.

Syair See *Shair*.

Syarul Baria The wife of Alexander the Great. See *Malay Annals*.

T

Tangaroa (Rurutu, Austral Islands, Tubuai)

Ta'aroa

1. In Tahitian religion, Ta'aroa was worshipped as the *Creator, Tangaroa*. There is a hymn to Ta'aroa, preserved in the oral tradition:

> Ta'aroa is his name
> He has always been
> When there was no earth, no sky
> There was no sea, there was no man.
> Then, Ta'aroa called
> and He became the universe
> He is the origin of rocks, of sand
> He is the germ, He is the light
> He is within, He is the form
> He made the sea, He made the sky
> He made the sacred land Hawaii.

2. On the Tuamotu Islands, he was the first god, who was born from the union of heaven and earth. The sky was so close to the surface of the earth that it was like an egg's shell, and Ta'aroa was in it. He cracked the shell from the inside, crept out and crowed, but no one answered. He made rocks out of his eggshell, clouds out of his skin, a mountain range out of his spine, the rich earth out of his flesh,

the trees and shrubs out of his feathers, the *fish* from his nails, the lobsters, shrimps and eels from his guts. He used his blood to dye the sky red. The *sun* then rose: the first day.

See also *Creation*; 'Gods of the Pacific' under *Gods*; *Na Atibu*; *Tangaroa*.

Taboo (Polynesian; from *Fiji*, *tabu*; Hawaiian, *kapu*; in the other Polynesian languages *tapu*; also, not identical but related, *topu*) A state of being set apart. A murderer or adulterer was *tapu*, untouchable. This 'guilt' could only be removed from a person by means of elaborate ceremonies, or by exiling him. All the statues of the *gods* were *tapu*, sacred, so they must not be offended; a temple was *tapu* so that no fighting was allowed in it, and enemies must behave there like brothers. *Tapu* can also be a noun.

See also *Bomala*; *God*; *Hawaii*; *Io*; *Kava*; *King*; *Pare*; *Stingaree*.

Tabu See *Taboo*.

Taburimai In the myths of the people of *Kiribati*, Taburimai was the ancestor of the people, son of the demi-god Bakoa. He had a brother Teanoi, the hammer-headed *shark*. One day the people of his island plotted to kill Taburimai but Bakoa got wind of the evil plans. He asked Teanoi to carry his brother to safety. This he did by swimming away across the sea. Then, having left his brother safely on the beach at *Samoa*, Teanoi flew up into the sky where he can still be seen (probably as the constellation Pisces).

Taburimai married and had a son, Te-Ariki-n-Tarawa, who took to wife Ne-Te-Reere, Goddess of Trees. They had a son called Kirata-n-Te-Rerei who was 'so beautiful that he had children without a wife'. Evidently he was an androgynous *Creator* deity.

Tadanobu A retainer of the Japanese hero *Yoshitsune*. A *fox*, an evil spirit, wanted to take revenge on Yoshitsune, so he entered the body of Tadanobu and possessed him. See also *Possession*.

Tadu In the *language* of the Torajas of *Sulawesi*, the word for a *shaman*, usually a woman. It is her speciality to travel to *heaven* and pray for the return of a patient's *soul* from Pue di Songi, *God*. See *Shamanism*(2).

Tafua The name of an ancestor-king and his descendants, an old ruling family of the Tikopia of *Polynesia*, and also the name of their *Rain-God*. See *Rain-God*.

Tagaloa The Samoan Ocean-God. See *Creation*(5); *Tangaroa*.

Tagalog The national language of the *Philippines*, spoken originally only in Manila district. It is related to the Indonesian languages. It is not an easy language, so that a type of Creole developed from it, mixed with English, called Filipino.

Tagaro In the religion of the people of the New Hebrides (see *Vanuatu*), he is the *Creator*, the Benevolent Great Spirit who made the first people after he had descended from *heaven*. He sometimes appears as a man but normally he is only visible to the *dead*. In the beginning he lived on earth like a man and taught human beings to walk upright on two legs, not like pigs on four. One fine day he caused winged women to come down from heaven. These girls alighted on the beach, shed their wings and plunged into the ocean for a bath and a swim. The men hid their white wings and married these girls. However, one girl managed to find her wings and flew back to heaven. See also *Cassowary*.

Tahekeroa The Spirit Land in the heart of the earth. See *Spirits*(3); also *Nether World*.

Tahinariki See *Pere*.

Tahiti The largest island of French *Polynesia*, 402 sq miles (1,042 sq km) in area, and the main island of the Society group which, together with the Tuabua group, forms Tua-Motu, 'The Islands of the Other Side', the easternmost archipelago of Polynesia. Tahiti is the Polynesian Paradise; its beauty is matched by that of its language and the songs sung in it. It was painted by Paul Gauguin, who arrived there in 1891. Many of the oral traditions remain to be recorded. Numerous writers (Loti, Melville, Gerbault) have exulted about it. However, both the luxuriant forests and the golden coral reefs are in danger of dying.

See also 'Gods of the Pacific' under *Gods*; *Kahiki*; *Nana-Ula*; *Oripo*; *Oro*(1); *Pahuanui*; *Pua Tu Tahi*; *Pyramids*; *Ro'o*; *Tai-Moana*; *Ta'aroa*(1); *Waka*.

Taho One of the five Bodhisattvas. See *Amida*; 'Gods of Japan' under *Gods*.

Tahu See *Atea*.

Tahua A *Maori* hero and symbol of the faithful messenger. Chief *Manawa* visited the town of Chief Tuwhakapau to confirm the betrothal of his son to the latter's daughter. He hoped that in this way the two families would be reconciled, since his men had killed one of Tuwhakapau's sons. That murder was not forgotten, however, and the unsuspecting visitors were ambushed. Manawa was killed with a stone axe, and only one man escaped, Tahua, by jumping down a 30ft cliff and running away along the beach. He warned the party waiting in their boats that they must re-embark and row home at once.

Tai-Moana (Tahitian, 'Threnody of the Ocean') A type of long *drum* which accompanies the *Polynesians* on their long voyages. There is a legend of a Tahitian chief, Rahi, who discovered such a drum, as long as a *canoe*. Inside it he heard a sweet voice singing softly. Rahi opened the drum and found inside it a beautiful princess whom he married: her name was Hotu-Hiva. They became the ancestors of the kings of Hauahine.

Taidue The Sea-God of the Aru Islands. See *Storm*.

Tairi See *Nganaoa*.

Taishaku The Japanese name for *Indera*.

Taiwan An island 500m east of *Hong Kong*, 300m north of the northern tip of Luzon. The history of Taiwan is full of myths. Firstly, the island was not 'discovered' by the Chinese until the fifteenth century. Before that it was inhabited by a people who are still there, speaking Malayo–Polynesian dialects closely related to the Philippine languages. Secondly, though the Portuguese 'discovered' the island in 1540 and called it 'Ilha Formosa', 'Beautiful Island', quite rightly, they did not settle it, but in 1622 a Dutch admiral arrived to ask the Chinese inhabitants if he could buy some land to build an office. There was never a Dutch 'invasion', as one can read in some of the books on Taiwan and its history. Thirdly, the 'hero' Coxinga, who arrived in 1662 and 'took' the island or 'liberated' it, was a common pirate. Fourthly, the original inhabitants of the islands are not 'head hunters' or 'cannibals' as the Japanese (prior to 1944) and the Chinese (after 1949) reports want us to believe. Nor are they 'hill tribes hidden in a few mountain recesses'. In 1932 they still occupied more than half of the island, but the Chinese invasion of 1949 has driven them away to the farthest southern corners of the island. They are called 'aborigines' and number some 400,000, much more than the number of original Hawaiians, Fijians and *Maoris* at present alive. But against a vast influx of 19 million Chinese from the mainland they had no chance to maintain themselves. They are now rapidly and forcefully being 'assimilated' and a few are 'kept' in 'ethnic' villages to be visited by tourists who may buy their handicraft work and watch their 'quaint' dances. That is the fate of minorities in their own country.

Taka-Rita The second wife of *Uenuku*.

Takadai A Japanese Samurai. See *Reincarnation*(2).

Takami-Musubi In Japanese mythology the *Creator*, or rather the great generative Spirit of Divine Love from whom all beings spring.

Takara-Bune In Japanese myth, the treasure-ship, with the Seven Gods of Good Luck on board (see *Shichi Fukujin*). The treasures are the Inexhaustible Purse, the Invisible-Making Hat, the Lucky Coat, the Wealth Mallet, the Ghost-Chasing Rat, the Full Bag of Rice, and the Magic Key. Pictures of the ship are laid under children's pillows, so that they have lucky dreams.

Takehaya Susanowo See *Susanowo*.

Taksin An eighteenth-century Thai king. See *Thailand*.

Talaipo In Samoan myth, a miraculously swift *canoe*, built in one night by the bird-spirits from their own trees. It was inherited by generation after generation of sea-chiefs, but it survived them all. Each chief gave it a new name when he received it. It is said that it sailed west to Fiti (*Fiji*) and east to Tongareva.

Tama The handmaid of a Japanese nobleman. See *Fly*.

Tama Nui-Te-Ra ('The Great Son of the Sun'; or Ra, for short) The Polynesian Sun-God. See *Auahi-Turoa and the Fire Children; Creation*(4); *Dawn Maiden;* 'Gods of the Pacific' under *Gods; Maui.*

Tama-Rangi An ancestor of *Maui.* See *Maui.*

Tamana A Japanese girl loved by Totaro. See *Samebito.*

Tamanui ('Great Son') A *Maori* hero whose history sounds almost like that of Agamemnon, except that when his wife had eloped with a foreign prince, he did not take his revenge on the prince and his city, as did Agamemnon, but punished his wife by forcing her to be reborn, like an Indian goddess. The story is as follows.

Tamanui was a chief who lived happily with his wife *Rukutia* and four children until another chief named *Koropanga* arrived, whose masculine beauty, ornamental garments and agile performance at the dance so outshone Tamanui's limited abilities that the latter went and sat moping in the temple, saddened in his heart by the brilliant red feathers the guests wore at their dance. Meanwhile, Koropanga stole into Rukutia's bedroom, seduced her and then sailed away with her. Of course Tamanui had to take action and revenge this mortal insult. Firstly he travelled to *heaven* to consult his ancestors; they taught him the art of *magic* and tattooed his body, so that he became irresistibly handsome (see *Tattoo*). Thus he brought the art of tattooing to the earthlings.

When he decided to return home, his ancestors gave him several goodbye presents, including a *pokeka*, a ceremonial robe of honour. He then travelled down to his home, greeted his children and went out in search of his wife Rukutia. Though Koropanga had placed obstacles in his way, such as tangled brambles and other impenetrable bushes, Tamanui could sing the obstructions away with his secret magical *karakia*. He disguised himself as a servant and fell in with a group of servants carrying firewood for the fires that would illuminate the dance feast at which Rukutia, now the wife of Koropanga, would dance that night. Tamanui kept to the shadows when the feast began. Then, when Rukutia started her dance, he muttered a *karakia* to make tears stream down her face so she had to stop to wipe them away. This happened several times, so that Koropanga, disappointed by his wife's poor public performance, hit her in the face. Later, when the people were all asleep, Tamanui opened a phial of secret *rotu*, heavenly perfume, which his celestial ancestors had given him. The powerful fragrance aroused Rukutia. Its magic reminded her strongly of her first husband. When he set sail in the morning, she swam to his ship. But when he pulled her out of the sea, Tamanui cut off her head and sailed home with it, leaving her body to be washed ashore at her lover's feet.

In his own palace, Tamanui took the head and placed it in a magic box (this may have been a large calabash), which he buried under the floor. After waiting patiently until the fruits of the new season were ripe, he uncovered the box and heard a humming in it, as of bees singing. He opened the box and there was Rukutia, whole and healthy.

Tamapo   The Tongan God of the Heavens. See *Laufakanaa*.

Tamasik   See *Tumasik*.

Tamate   See *New Caledonia*.

Tambaran   In *Papua New Guinea* the spirit of an ancestor. A *tambaran-house* (now spelled *haus* in Tok-Pisin, the national language of Papua New Guinea) is a temple, a 'cult-place', a building where the elders congregate to perform rituals on behalf of the ancestors. It is said that there are no *gods* in New Guinea, but why can ancestors not be gods? The Romans worshipped Mars and Venus as their ancestors.

Tamon   See *Shi Tenno*.

Tanabata   (or Shokujo) Tanabata was the daughter of the Japanese God of the Firmament. She was the first *weaver*, weaving garments for her father to wear. One day she saw a cowherd called Hikoboshi. The two fell so deeply in love that they neglected their work of weaving and herding the cattle. So *God* the Father created the heavenly river, the *Milky Way* to separate them. Only once a year, on 7 July, are the lovers able to meet, when a big flock of magpies arrive to form a bridge across the river. Over their fluttering wings Hikoboshi hurries to his sweetheart in the morning, returning that same night. Tanabata is celebrated in Japan on 7 July with decorations and poetry.

This myth is reflected in the *sky*, where Tanabata is also the name of the constellation of Vega, in which the early astronomers saw a loom, *hata*. In *Korea*, the three bright stars in Aquila, the constellation of the Eagle, are the image of a prince (the Korean version of the cowherd), who loves the Weaver or Spinning Damsel in the constellation Lyra.

See also 'Gods of Japan' under *Gods*.

Tanaoa   See *Tangaroa*.

Tane   (*Kane* in *Hawaii*) The Polynesian God of Artistic Beauty, the primeval ancestor of all the Polynesian nations, who know themselves to be related. He was also the God of Light, often invoked by swimmers because for a diving swimmer the light is where life is, the side of survival. Tane is also the God of the Forest (as *Tane-Mahuta*) in *New Zealand*, where the trees grow towards the light, and the Lord of the Fairies (*Tapairu* the Peerless Ones) as was Oberon in Shakespeare's woods.

Tane was the son of *Rangi*, 'heaven', or 'sky' and Papa-Tu-a-Nuku, the Mother of the Gods, Rangi representing the light in the sky, *Papa* the dark of the earth. These two deities clung together in a perpetual embrace until Tane persuaded them that 'Rangi must stand above us, and Papa must lie under our feet.'

In that way, by suspending the sky far above the earth, light could inhabit the space between the two and illuminate the land. Tane covered the naked body of his father Rangi with Kohu, the God of Mist, Ika-Roa, the *Milky Way*, and their shining children, the *star*s. Rangi's black cloak has a red lining at dawn. Tane's mother, Papa, also lay naked, so he covered her with forests, ferns and other plants. It seems that in the beginning the trees grew out of the sky pointing downwards. Tane pointed them the right way up and planted them firmly in the earth.

See also *Adam and Eve*(2); *Atea*; *Dawn Maiden*; 'Gods of the Pacific' under *Gods*.

Tane-Mahuta The God of the Forests. See 'Gods of the Pacific' under *Gods*; *Papa*; *Sky*(2); *Tane*.

Tangaloa The Tongan Ocean-God. See *Tangaroa*.

Tangaroa (*Maori*; *Kanaloa*, Hawaiian; *Tangaloa*, Tongan; *Tagaloa*, Samoan, *Ta'aroa*, Tahitian) The Polynesian God of the Ocean, the Polynesian Poseidon, son of the Earth-Goddess *Papa*, who had so much water in her body that it swelled up one day and burst forth, becoming the ocean. Tangaroa breathes only twice in 24 hours, so huge is he. We call that the tidal movement. His brother is *Rongo*, who was, according to some myths, the same as *Maui*, the Fisher of Islands, the inventor of sail-ships.

Tangaroa is shown in some famous sculptures as the *Creator*, out of whose body the creatures emerge, including human beings. The Indian god *Brahma* created nature in a similar fashion. The myth of the Ocean-God as the Creator is explained by the myth of *Ika-Tere*, the Fish-God, some of whose children were partly human, like mermaids and mermen, although often the right side was fish while the left side was human. Gradually they became all-human.

In Tahuata (the Marquesas), Tangaroa is known as Tanaoa, the God of the Primeval Darkness (like Chaos, one of the oldest gods, according to Hesiod). At a given morning a new god, Atea, 'Space', emerged, freeing himself so that there was room for Atanua, 'Dawn', to arise. She married Atea, since light can only exist in, or together with, space. Their child was Tu-Mea, the first man. Tanaoa was confined to the depths of the ocean where darkness and silence still reign.

See also 'Gods of the Pacific' under *Gods*; *Losi*; *Sea-King*; *Tanaloa*; *Toyo-Tama*; *Veeteni*.

Tangata The original *Polynesians' name for themselves. See Giants*(1); also *Kanaka*; *Race*.

Tangi Elegies sung for the *dead*. See *Death*.

Tangi'ia A famous navigator who led a fleet from *Avaiki* (*Indonesia?*) to Rarotonga, and another from *Fiji* to *Rapanui* (Easter Island). He voyaged throughout his life. See also *Navigators*.

Tangi-Kuku The brother of the Moon-Goddess in the mythology of the *Cook Islands*. See *Ina*.

Tangotango She was a fairy of the heavenly race in *Maori* myth. When she heard of the handsome young god *Tawhaki*, she looked for him and found him one night, while he was sleeping in the woods during a journey. She lay with him night after night until she became pregnant. She later had a daughter Arahuta.

Taniwha A huge monster like a *dragon* or an enormous *lizard* which once lived in numbers in the caves and lakes in the mountains of *New Zealand*. Two of them were slain by the hero *Pitaka*.

Tanuki Japanese for a roguish fox spirit. See also *Fox; Kitsune-Tsuki; Inari; Possession*.

Tapa

1. Bark cloth. On the Polynesian Hervey Islands Autu and Manui, it was related that *Marama* was the name of the Moon-God who was in love with *Ina*, daughter of Kui, an old blind earth-god. Ina is the Goddess of Light, like the Roman goddess Lux. She married the Moon-God and lives in the sky in daytime, when her husband is rarely visible. She makes *tapa* from the trees that grow on earth. As soon as a piece of bark cloth is well beaten she hangs it out on the blue sky where it sits like a cloud, white and grey. She fixes the pieces of cloth with large *stones* and when she removes a piece the stones roll away causing what we call thunder.
2. In *Indonesia*, a hermit who lives in the woods on the mountains, meditating and living abstemiously, thus accumulating *tapas* ('merit').

Tapairu ('Without Equal') Name of a race of Polynesian nymphs who may ascend from limpid pools on moonlit nights to join dancers, disappearing again at *dawn*. They also inhabit the pool that leads to the *Underworld* and are sent out by their mother *Miru*, Goddess of the Dead, to seduce men away from the earth. See also *Hades*(2).

Tapas (literally, 'heat') In *Indonesia* the mystic merit which accrues for a man or woman by the assiduous performance of severe asceticism. See also *Tapa*(2).

Tapu See *Taboo*.

Tara

1. The Polynesian Sea-Goddess. See also *Maui*.
2. The Buddhist Goddess of Love. See also *Kannon*.

Taraipo ('Built in a Night') In *Maori* tradition, the name of the first *canoe*, which the bird-spirits of the forest of Kupolu in Aitutaki built in one night for the hero *Rata*, while the woods rang with their song. See also *Rata*.

Taranga (Polynesian; *Bua-Taranga*, Samoan) The mother of *Maui*. See *Maui*.

Taro The *Maori* word for the plant *Colocasia esculenta* of the *Araceae* family, also called *dasheen*, in Japanese *imo*. The tubers (better: corms) are edible provided they are well cooked. They are the native staple crop in the western Pacific. There are two types: the white and the (superior) red taro. Its protective god is *Losi*.

1. In the language of the Orokolo on *New Guinea*'s south coast, this tuber is called *ipomavea*, no doubt the origin of the word *Ipomoea*, the botanical name of the *sweet potato*. They relate that in the beginning of time a *fish* called Maivia Kivavia lived in the river Pulari. One day he lay on a sandbank in the sunshine and decided he would rather live on land. He grew arms and legs instead of his tail and fins, and stood up like a man. He planted sago and taro on the hills Mari and Hola where he settled. Without a wife he had two daughters, Moro and Mavu, and two sons, who became the clan's ancestors.

2. The peoples of the Finisterre hills and the Rai coast of *Papua* have several myths concerning the origin of the taro root. In one myth the red taro was created in *heaven* and brought to earth. A goddess called Meanderi created the red taro root and the sugar cane 'from under her skin' while she was in Asang, somewhere west of the country of her worshippers, indicating that those plants were probably introduced from the west, perhaps *Indonesia*.

See also *Sweet Potato; Yam*.

Tarogolo   See *Spirits*(5).

Tasman, Abel, Captain   The European discoverer of *New Zealand*. See also *Maui; New Guinea*.

Tatabu   See *Spirits*(5).

Tatsu   See *Dragon*.

Tattoo   *Maori* legend relates that a nobleman named *Tamanui*, 'Great Son', was deserted by his wife *Rukutia* for a chief named *Koropanga*. When Tamanui asked his children why their mother had forsaken them, they answered: 'Because of your unattractiveness.'

Tamanui took the shape of a beautiful silvery white *heron* and flew up to *heaven* to consult his ancestors. He marvelled at their beauty and asked them how they had acquired their colourful appearance. They told him that they would paint him as they themselves were. Once Tamanui was back in his own shape, they did so, but when he went bathing in the sea, it was all washed off, so he went back to his ancestors (who are known by name in this myth) and demanded to know the secret of real body decorations such as they had on their own backs, arms and shins. They told him: 'If you really want to be tattooed, you must realize that you may die of the pain.'

Unafraid, Tamanui submitted to their tattooing operations, which consisted of cutting long gashes in his body, then filling the wounds with secret substances that would cause definitive colourations. He fainted several times during the operation, which took all day. After that, it took three days before the pain subsided and Tamanui could walk again.

Soon afterwards, he decided to go back to earth, and after several adventures was reunited with Rukutia, who was amazed by his tattooed beauty. See also *Tamanui*.

Tau-Titi   The son of *Miru*, ruler of the *Nether World*. See also *Spirits*(1).

Taua   See *Spirits*(5).

Tautohito   A *Maori* sorcerer. See *Hakawau*.

Tauva'u   A type of *incubi*. See *Witch*(5).

Tavan   A demon. See *Narayana*.

Tawhaki   The *Maori* God of Thunder and Lightning and also of Good Health, the son of *Hema*. He became an expert at building fine houses and plaiting decorated floor mats. His son was *Matuku*.

1. One day Tawhaki met Hine Piripiri and they soon fell in love with each other. However, her cousin, to whom she had been betrothed since childhood, decided to kill Tawhaki. He and his fellow murderers left him for dead near a pond where he had been bathing, but Hine Piripiri went in search of him, found him and nursed him back to health. When he had recovered, they went and built a fortified dwelling on a hill top and there they had a son named Wahie Roa. One day Hine Piripiri's cousin climbed the hill intending to kill Tawhaki, but Tawhaki raised his arms. Lightning flashed from his armpits which drove the intruder away. Tawhaki then prayed to his ancestors for revenge. In reply the ancestors sent torrential rains which destroyed his enemies.

2. Then Tawhaki and his elder brother Karihi set out to take revenge for their father Hema who had been killed by the *Ponaturi*. These semi-spirits lived under the sea by day but at night they came ashore, to spend the night in Hema's house. They had hung his skeleton under the eaves of his own home. They had spared Urutonga, Hema's wife, but she had to stay outside the house. She hid her sons until nightfall when they saw the Ponaturi arrive, flying in from the sea, thousands of them. They all piled into the house and went to sleep there. When no more came, Urutonga told her sons to close every opening and crack in the house. When they had finished, dawn was approaching. The Ponaturi chief called from inside: 'Urutonga! Is it dawn yet?'

    'No,' she replied. 'It is still pitch dark.'

    This went on until the sun rose. Then the brothers opened the door and all the Ponaturi died in the bright sun rays, except Kanae, who became a flying fish, and Tonga-Hiti, the headache-demon.

3. One day Tawhaki's grandmother Waitiri gave him a vine which grew up to heaven (like Jack's beanstalk). Tawhaki climbed up it and first met his ancestors, one after another. He knew them all by name. He met Uru Rangi, the God of Winds, and his wife Maikuku. He saw the palace of *Maru* the War-God, who taught him weaponry and the

art of chanting spells to paralyse his enemies. Tawhaki also saw the moon and there on the beach he met *Rongo-Mai* the Whale-God. Finally, Tawhaki reached the sixth heaven, called Nga-Atua, where his former lover *Tangotango* lived with their daughter Arahuta. She embraced him and they lived happily in heaven ever after.

Tawhiri-Matea The Polynesian Storm-God, the smiter of trees, the lasher of waves. Nothing is safe from him, he blows whatever he dislikes away. See also 'Gods of the Pacific' under *Gods*.

Tawheta A *Maori* chief. See *Uenuku*.

Te-Ariki-n-Tarawa See *Taburimai*.

Te Ikawai ('The First') See *Nareau*.

Te-io-Ora See *Motoro*.

Te Kanawa See *Fairies*(2).

Te Nao The *Kiribati* God of Waves. See *Nareau*.

Te-Po-ma-Te-Maki ('The Darkness of the Embrace') In the cosmology of the people of *Kiribati*, this was the primeval matter, the dark earth of our origin. Upon it walked the *Creator*, the Spider-God *Nareau*, who by his walking, started movement and with it, evolution. Nareau still appears on earth, as a spider.

Te-Putahi-Nui-o-Rehua ('The Great Crossroads of Rehua') See *Rehua*(1).

Te Rangi Whakaputa See *Maru*(2).

Te Reinga See *Reinga*.

Te Rongo The Polynesian *Creator*. See also *Rongo* and *Lono*.

Te Toi-o-nga-Rangi The highest *heaven*. See *Io*.

Tea Tea is native to Assam whence it came with *Buddhism* to the Far East, *Indonesia* and *Thailand*. See *Chaking; Daruma; Dengyo*.

Teanoi A hammer-headed *shark*. See *Taburimai*.

Tekoteko A wooden sculpted statue standing above the lintel of the entrance gate to the *pa*, the *Maori* village. These very artistically carved figures have the shape of men, animals or *demons* and possess great *magic* power. See also *Ngarara; Ponaturi*.

Tele The first man on Upolu, according to Samoan myth. See *Islands*.

Temasik See *Tumasik*.

Temmu The Japanese emperor (672–86), who ordered the first law books to be codified and established the shrine of the Sun-Goddess *Ama Terasu* at Ise, and with it, his descent from her. See also *Japan*.

Tempon Telon (or Tempun Telon) The Ferryman of the Dead. See *Sangiang; Shamanism*(1).

Tempun Telon See *Tempon Telon*.

Ten Japanese for the *sky, Paradise, heaven*, Providence, *God*. See also 'Gods of Japan' under *Gods*.

Tencho A Japanese emperor. See *Kobo*.

Tendai A Buddhist religious movement brought to *Japan* from China by the priest Saicho in 805 AD . Its doctrine is based on the famous *Lotus Sutra*, teaching morality, rigorous meditation and attributing to Man the essential nature of the *Buddha*. See also *Jobutsu*.

Tengu In Japanese mythology, a race of *demons*, evil *spirits* known for their ferocity. Some look semi-human but they are 'normally' *giants*, and have wings, large claws, red ugly faces, a long beak or a bill-nose, feathers, long hair and a stormy temperament. They are reborn spirits of proud and aggressive people who possess living beings. Some *tengu* are meteors, fiery spirits emanating from the Storm-God *Susanowo*. We are told that there are also female *tengu*, with the heads of animals, long ears, and noses as long as an arm, upon which a man can sit. A *tengu* may thus carry a man while flying all day. The teeth of these *she-tengus* are so strong that they can pierce armour. It seems that 'originally' they were long-billed bird-spirits. These devils often harass people, playing jokes on them. They live in the wooded mountains, and people who meet them become insane.

Tenjin The Japanese God of Calligraphy, who taught men to write their language. See also 'Gods of Japan' under *Gods*.

Tennin In Japanese Buddhist mythology, an angel or fairy, a heavenly, beautiful person who may appear on a mountain. To meet one, the pilgrim has to climb to the summit. See also *Angels; Fairies;* 'Gods of Japan' under *Gods*.

Tenno Heika ('His Majesty the Son of Heaven') This title is the formula by which the Japanese national anthem refers to the Emperor. He is traditionally considered as the direct descendant of the Sun-Goddess *Ama Terasu*, via her grandson *Ninigi* and his great grandson *Jimmu Tenno*, the first Emperor of *Japan*, the founder of the dynasty, unbroken to this day.

Tenrikyo ('The Doctrine of Heavenly Wisdom', 'The School of the Laws of Nature') This is the largest and most energetic of the *Shinto* sects of modern *Japan*. This Japanese faith-healing sect teaches the belief in the One God. It was founded by Miki Nakayama, a perspicacious woman who organized games and dances, accompanied by orchestras and attended by thousands.

Tevake In western *Polynesia*, a gannet, a seabird that roams freely and has become a symbol of the *spirits*.

Thailand The name *Thai* means 'free men', i.e., the descendants of the men who were never subservient to the Chinese when the latter conquered their southern province of Yun-Nan during the Sung (Song) dynasty. The Thai migrated south from the upper Mekong area and formed an independent state, Pa Yao, around the confluence of the Me Ping and Me Wang rivers in the hills of what is now north-western Thailand. They were probably still indistinguishable from the Shan. The name Siam is probably the Portuguese spelling of Shan (we owe many Oriental names to the Portuguese). This state flourished in the eleventh century. In the next century further Thai ('free') states were created in what is now northern Thailand and also around Luang Prabang, which remained part of Thailand until the end of the nineteenth century.

In the year 1238 two Thai chiefs took the ancient city of Sukhotai and made it the capital of their state. The first kings of that state, Mangrai (Mengrai), Indraditya and especially Rama Khamheng 'Rama the Brave' (1283–1317) were renowned warriors. Rama reduced the Thai *language* to its written form, by modifying a variety of the Khmer script, itself ultimately based on the Sanskrit alphabet. He used the new characters for the first time in his famous inscription of 1292, the oldest document in the Thai language.

The Thai form of *Buddhism*, the Theravada, originated from Sri *Lanka*, and relations between the two countries were maintained by scholars travelling across the mountains, down the Salween river and across the sea. Even today, Buddhist scholarship is the worthiest profession for a Thai man, even a nobleman. The Thai scribes acquired, copied and translated the *Manuscripts of the Law of the Buddha*. Rama's son, Lo Thai Dharmaraja, (1317–47), was a pious Buddhist. His son Lu Thai abdicated in 1361 to enter a monastery. The next king, Ramadhipati (Ramatibodi) I (d.1369), was the founder of the new capital, Ayodhya or Ayuthya on an island in the Menam river. He also promulgated the first Thai code of *Law*.

In the sixteenth century Thailand suffered repeated attacks from the Burmese. Finally the Burmese sacked the beautiful temple city of Ayuthia in 1569, but in 1584 the Thai leader Narsuen overcame the Burmese and declared Thailand independent once more. In 1686 an agreement was finalized with the French ambassador which formed the beginning of French interests in South-East Asia. However, in 1688 all foreigners were expelled, including the French.

The year 1767 was disastrous for Siam, after a golden period under King Boromakot (1733–58). The Burmese sacked Ayuthia once more and it has remained a ruin to this day. Fortunately, the new king, Taksin (1769–82), restored the monarchy and overcame the Burmese. He made Thonburi his capital. In 1782 Rama I ascended the throne and made the small traders' town of Bangkok his residence. A wise choice. From then on a continuous line of nine kings, all calling themselves Rama, ruled Thailand. The present king is Rama IX, though his 'off-duty' personal name is Bhumibol.

A disaster for Thailand was the French conquest of the country which is now called Laos but which is ethnically and linguistically Siamese (1893). The French lost their South-East Asian colonies in 1941, regained them in 1945 and lost them again in 1954, dividing Vietnam and so starting the war in which North Vietnam eventually occupied not only South Vietnam but also Cambodia and Laos.

Meanwhile modern Thailand has flourished and is on its way up among the South Asian nations.

See also *Ajapal*; *Amulet*(1); *Ananta Nakhon*; *Ananta Thewi*; *Angkor-Wat*; *Anomatan*; *Bewitched City*; *Boar*(1); *Chedi*; *Chomphu Thawip*; *Dasarata*; *Deer*(1); *Dewi Sri*; *Diamond Buddha*; *Dwarawati*; *Ear Ornaments*; *Eel*(1); *Elephant*; *Elephant-Tiger*; *Emerald Buddha*; *Hades*(3); *Hanuman*; *Himaphan*; *Hiranyaksa*; *Iswara*; *Jataka*; *Kham Daeng*; *Khrut*; *Khuna*; *Kinnara*; *Krailasa*; *Krengjai*; *Kupera*; *Lion*; *Love*; *Machanu*; *Maenam*; *Makara*; *Mango*; *Mendicant*; *Migration of Souls*; *Milk*; *Mountain Spirit*; *Naga*(2); *Nahk*; *Narayana*; *New Year*(2); *Oedipus*; *Orchid*; *Patal*; *Phra In*; *Phra Sao*; *Phrom*(1); *Phrot*; *Rama*(1); *Ramakien*; *Saksit*; *Sam Muk*; *Satrud*; *Serpent*; *Sita*; *Snake-King*; *Soul*(5); *Star Spirit*; *Swan*; *Sword*(2); *Thewi Suthata*; *Tiger*(2); *Tipaka*; *Tosachat*; *Tree-Spirit*(2); *Umbrella Mountain*; *White Elephant*(1); *White Raven*; *Wisnu*; *Witsanukam*.

Thewi Suthat (or Thewi Suthata) See *Love*; *Sison*.

Thonamun See *Snake-King*.

Thunder Animal See *Raiju*.

Thunder Baby Bimbo, a poor Japanese peasant, during a long drought, prayed to the *Buddha* for rain. Suddenly, rain fell in sheets, accompanied by a loud peal of thunder. In the dazzling light, Bimbo saw a handsome baby lying on the grass. Bimbo and his wife adopted the baby, calling him Raitaro, 'Thunder Child'. He grew up into a healthy dutiful boy, helping his foster-father in the fields. Whenever there was too little rain for the crops, Raitaro would simply call the clouds and order them to rain. As a result, Bimbo became a rich farmer. When he was 18 years old, Raitaro thanked his foster parents for their loving care, turned into a white *dragon* and flew away.

Thunder-Bird See *Haida*; *Raicho*.

Thunder God See *Raiden*.

Thunder Woman See *Kaminari*.

Thung of Ruang A Thai king. See *Star Spirit*.

Ti Tsang See *Ksitigarbha*.

Tiang Maleh Rupa A Malay magical formula to turn men into crocodiles. See *Crocodile*(5).

Tide Jewels In Japanese myth these are two precious stones, the High Tide Jewel and the Low Tide Jewel. Many centuries ago the Empress *Jingo* planned an invasion of *Korea*. She prayed to the *Sea-King* and sent

Isora the Beach-God to the *Sea-King's Palace* where he was given the Tide Jewels for the empress. When the Japanese fleet sailed towards Korea the Korean fleet sailed out to confront it. Quickly the empress threw the Low Tide Jewel into the sea so that the tide receded at once and the Korean fleet was beached. The Koreans all jumped out onto the mudflats but at that moment the empress threw out the High Tide Jewel. At once a tidal wave drowned the men on the mudflats and carried the Japanese fleet on to the coast, into the harbour and to victory. Later the Sea-King personally presented the Tide Jewels, on a beautiful pink seashell, to Prince Ojin, son of Empress Jingo (see also *Hachiman*).

See also 'Gods of Japan' under *God*.

Tiger

1. There are numerous Malay stories about the wicked boy who was whipped by his teacher until he turned into a tiger; the tiger's stripes are the weal marks of the whip. In the City of the Tigers the houses are built from human bones.

2. Long ago there lived in *Thailand*, near a shrine on the road to Chieng Mai, a monk who, by his long studies, had learned the art of changing himself into a tiger. In the daytime he was a learned monk who would receive offerings from travellers to pray for their safe arrival. At night, however, he would prowl the campsites where the cattle drivers slept, nightfall temporarily halting their journey to the city. Nearby, where they tied up their cattle, the tiger would find and devour their fattest calf. At dawn he would suddenly resume his original form. A real Jekyll and Hyde character! One day, however, the cattle herds were accompanied by a merchant who met the monk and was astute enough to suspect him. That evening the merchant fashioned buffaloes from bamboo, then muttered magic mantras which turned the bamboo skeletons into real buffaloes. In the small hours the tiger approached yet again to steal a calf. The merchant, alone, was awake. He muttered his magic words, clapped his hands and suddenly the buffaloes came to life, ran towards the tiger, surrounded him and wounded him with their horns. The tiger escaped, but the next day the monk was found lying in the temple, dead.

   Also in Thailand there are *sorcerers* who control tigers as their *familiars*. These tiger-familiars have a king in Phom.

3. In Minangkabau (central *Sumatra*), if a dying sinner prays to *God* that he may be allowed to come back to do penance in an other life, his body will revive after a week, only the head will be that of a tiger's. Gradually the whole body turns into a tiger's. He then escapes from his grave where people will find only an empty hole.

4. In Malay mythology, 'tiger men' are men who may change into tigers, collectively or individually, for one night, either after they have died or, more commonly, during their lives. Purchasing the powerful magic to become a tiger will consume a man's total savings, but it is considered worth it. As a tiger, a man can take revenge for

a lifetime of injustice. A pride of tigers is said to have devoured a cruel and avaricious landowner along with his likewise mean-minded sons.

5. In *Indonesia*, it is said that there are, deep in the jungle, entire villages inhabited by beings who look like tigers, but when one of these tigers leaves his village to visit a people-village, he will suddenly look like a man. In other villages one may meet ordinary-looking people who, however, when going out, will change into tigers. It is said on Sumatra that if you see a tiger without a tail, be extra careful for he is a man. A man suspected of such evil practices must have his back examined. If it shows a black spot, that is where his tail was burnt off.

See also *Amulet*(4); *Crow; Elephant Tiger; Feathers; Gerjis; Jilted Lover; Korinchi; Leyak; Macan Gadungan; Sarong; White Tiger.*

Tiki

1. The first man, the divine ancestor of the *Polynesians*, who led his people in their fleet to the *islands* of *Polynesia*. See *Adam and Eve*(3); *Woman*(1).
2. The sister of *Veeteni*.

Tikokura ('Storm-Wave') In Polynesian mythology Tikokura is a god of monstrous size and enormous power whose angry temperament easily flares up, unprovoked.

Tindalo An oracle-god. See also *Ganindo*.

Tingiano See *Tinguian*.

Tinguian (or Tingiano) A shy people living in the mountains of central Luzon, believers in Tadaklan the Thunder-God, who lives in the sky together with his dog Kimat, the lightning. When his master orders him to, Kimat will 'bite' a house, so it burns.

The Tinguian have elaborate funerary rituals by which they hope to secure the safe arrival of the *maglawa*, the ancestral soul, in the next life.

Tini Rau Chief Tini Rau was married to the Moon-Goddess *Hina-Keha* in southern Polynesian mythology. She always supplied him and his people with plenty of fish. He was a double-natured god who could appear as a handsome young man or as the terrifying Shark-God. *Hina-Uri*, sister of *Maui*, fell in love with him and pursued him in the deep seas.

See also *Hina-Keha*.

Tinoso (Tinyoso) Don Juan Tinoso is a Philippine hero whose exploits are sung in five Filipino languages. He liberated the giant Mauleon because he felt pity for the giant's plight.

Tinyoso See *Tinoso*.

Tioman Tioman is a beautiful island off the east coast of the Malay Peninsula. It is related by the people that Tioman was once a beautiful princess who fell in love with the handsome son of a neighbouring king.

But the proud prince spurned her devotion, so she turned into a dragon and swam away. Finally she became the island of Tioman with the tail at Salang and the horns becoming the twin peaks at the south of the island, where Bali Hai mountain is. (Bali Hai was the background of the mythical island in the film *South Pacific*.)

Tipaka In the Thai myth of King *Sison* this was the king's miraculous horse which could fly and would carry him wherever he wished to go in the blinking of an eye, even to *heaven*.

Tipua Goblins, wicked *demons*, in *Maori* myth, who can take whatever shape they wish. See also *Gnomes*; *Ponaturi*.

Tisnawati See *Rice-Goddess*; *Tresnawati*.

Tistawa A king in Javanese mythology. See *Dewi Gandari*.

Tiwaiwaka The guardian of the ascent to *heaven*. See *Turehu*.

Tjalon Arang A Balinese *witch*. See *Witch*(2).

To-Kabinana See *Adam and Eve*(6).

Toad In *Japan* it is said that a little girl, whose father had promised her to the rain-serpent if it would cause the rain to fall, managed to make the serpent kill itself. That same day she met an old woman, the Mother of Toads, who expressed her gratitude to the girl for having disposed of the dangerous killer of toads, all of whom were her great grandchildren. She gave the girl her old toad skin, by means of which she could disguise herself in any shape she wished. The girl went to the royal palace disguised as an old woman and was taken on as a cook. Soon she revealed herself in her true shape, that of a lovely girl, to the prince, who fell in love with her and married her.
  See also *Devil*; *Gama-Sennin*; *Ghosts*(1); *Sennin*.

Toar See *Creation*(11).

Tohunga (*Maori*; *Kahuna*, Hawaiian) An expert, especially in spiritual and ritual matters, so, a priest. A *tohunga* is called to perform the necessary rites when a person has to be purified from some *tapu* (state of being untouchable) that adheres to him because of some wrong he has done. The *tohunga* also performs the funeral rites. Furthermore, he is familiar with the *spirits* of the air, the water and the earth, the gods of the forest, the sky and the ocean. He understands their *language*, so he knows the past, present and future. In that respect he is a *shaman*. See also *Fairies*(3).

Tomarind A hero of Luzon (in the *Philippines*). See *Witch*(7).

Toi-Mata The daughter of *Oro*. See *Oro*(1).

Tokoyo A Japanese maiden. See *Yofune-Nushi*.

Tokoyo-no-Kuni ('The Eternal Country') In Japanese cosmology, *Paradise*, the Spirit World, a 'distant land across the ocean'.

Tokugawa Ieyasu A seventeenth-century Japanese ruler. See *Japan*.

Tokutaro-San In Japanese mythology, this is a life-size boy-doll, a child of two years. There is also a girl-doll, Otoku-San. These dolls are alive. They do not talk, but they can cry and run away when the house they live in is on fire. When they are neglected they will be cross and bring misfortune upon the family with whom they live. They may survive the passing of several generations if properly looked after. If kept in good repair and dressed in fresh clothes regularly, they will bring good luck to 'their' family and, it is believed, cause babies to be born in good health. Such luck-bringing dolls will be borrowed by other families in the hope that they too will have some good luck through looking after them for some time. When a doll is old, worn, broken and finally declared 'dead', it is laid to rest under an *enoki* tree. See also *Hina-Matsuri; Kojin; Tree-Spirit*.

Tolharubang Korean ancestor figure. See also *Chedu-Do*.

Tom Thumb (Malay, Si Jari, 'Finger-man') Tom Thumb is still a popular character in *Malay tales* because he outwits the giant, *Raksasa*.

Tomb On *New Caledonia* they relate that a woman once gave birth to a son after she had died and was laid out in a forest grave (see also *Ghost-Mother*). The baby not only survived, but sucked his mother's breasts which still contained milk. When he could walk he escaped from the grave and went to his father's house. His father wanted him to stay but the boy said he must say goodbye to his mother first. He went back to his mother's grave and told her that he would from then on live on earth. His father and grandfather were standing outside, weeping. They could hear the boy talking to his mother and crying, but they could not hear the mother.

Tomwaya See *Beyawa*.

Tomwaya Lakwabulo See *Tuma*.

Tondi See *Soul*.

Tonga ('South') The Tonga group of *islands* is the southern segment of the vast archipelago of central *Polynesia*, with the *Samoa* group in the centre. In *New Zealand*, tradition relates that the *Maoris* sailed from Tonga to New Zealand, following the planet Venus. The Tongan language is a very old form of Polynesian.

Tonga is also the name of the first woman on Tonga, according to Samoan mythology (see *Islands*) and the South-West Wind (see *Matagi*).

See also *Ahoeitu; Ata; Bolotu; Islands; Kava; Laufakanaa; Pomare; Sisimatailaa*.

Tongatea See *Ngaru*.

Toniwha In *New Zealand*, a protective spirit who usually lives in wells, rivers and ponds, keeping the water fresh for the people. A *toniwha* is often regarded as a benign ancestral spirit. See also *River Spirit*.

Topeng The *mask* of the Javanese mask-dance, a form of *wayang*. The mime artists, actors and dancers perform scenes from the Panji myths, while the *dalang* recites the tales and directs the *gamelan* music. Female parts are played by boys. The parts of the *satria* (noble knight) and *kelana* (pirate) are played by professionals. The masked *wayang* dances are at least 1,000 years old. They include pre-Hindu characters such as giants and clowns.

Topileta According to Trobriand myth, the Gatekeeper of Paradise. He is a spirit with the shape of a man with enormous ears, as large as the wings of a flying fox. The dead *souls* will meet him on the path to *Paradise* (see also *Tuma*). Topileta will demand objects of value before letting the soul through. If it is a woman's soul, he will have sex with her.

Torajas The To-Raja, 'Royal People'. See *Sulawesi*, where they live; also *Amulet*(2); *Creation*(8); *Crocodiles*(1); *Goddess*(2); *Mouse*; *Pue di Songi*; *Replacement*(2); *Semangat*; *Shamanism*(2)(3); *Sky*(4); *Stones*(5); *Tadu*; *Tree-Spirit*(4); *Wurake*.

Torii In *Japan*, the main gateway to a Buddhist temple complex. Richly decorated, these ornamental entrance structures serve no defensive purpose. It is said that, in more rustic times, they served as a perch for domestic fowl during the night so that the monks could clearly hear the roosters' crowing in time for the pre-dawn prayers.

Another myth states that the sun will perch on the *torii* in the shape of a *hoho* bird and bring good tidings of love and peace. Other deities too are believed to use the *torii* as a footstool.

Other scholars maintain that the *torii* is the entrance to the world of the gods, or the gate towards the *Buddha*'s straight path.

Torres, Luis Vaez de A Spanish explorer. See *New Guinea*.

Tortoise

1. The Black Warrior, guardian of the northern signs of the Japanese Zodiac.
2. On the *Philippines* they tell the story of Yusup who caught a white tortoise and called him Notu. Notu stayed in the bow of Yusup's boat, when he went fishing, looking steadily in one direction, and when Yusup had sailed for some time in that direction, the tortoise would slowly hide his head in his shell, as if going to sleep. There, Yusup would catch fish in abundance. One day, however, Notu guided Yusup due east for three days and nights. Suddenly a huge sea-monster raised its head and thundered out directions, pushing Yusup to a bay in an island, by blowing into his sails. On the beach stood a palace. It belonged to the monster, who was a bewitched prince. He could be cured if Yusup could fish up a magic ring which

the prince had lost. The white tortoise found the ring for Yusup, who was richly rewarded.

3. In *Annam* it was related that a Golden Tortoise lived in the waterfall of Ma Cho. It owned a *magic flute* of pure gold. The Golden Tortoise was consulted by the king in times of need.

See also *Jurojin; Narayana; Sea-King's Palace.*

Tosachat In *Thailand*, the last 10 legends from the Buddhist cycle of *Jataka Tales.*

Toshogu In *Japan*, a temple complex for the *spirits* of the Shogun rulers.

Totaro A Japanese hero. See *Samebito.*

Totem The mythical ancestor of a clan, usually an animal, sometimes a plant, tree or even a stone.

1. Several patrilinear clans of Orokolo on the south coast of *New Guinea* have a *fish* as their totem, i.e. the fish 'belongs' to their family. They alone may catch it, but they may not eat it, so they give it away to friends and neighbours (see also *Goddess*(1)). There is a tale connected with each totem, relating its origin and its relation with the clan's ancestors.
2. On *New Caledonia*, the totem follows the bride to her new home. There, it is kept in a little shrine. When she dies, it is 'liberated' and resumes its 'natural' shape, appearing as a fish, *lizard*, *snake*, crab or bird.

See also *Gecko.*

Totomono See *Kobo.*

Toucan (Malay, tukang) A hornbill-bird. Its horn is made into buttons with *magic* knowledge: they turn black when touching poison, and when the owner is about to fall ill, they will turn green to warn him. See also *Hornbill.*

Toyo-Tama ('Luminous Jewel' or 'Rich Jewel', or Otohime) The daughter of the Japanese *Sea-King* or Sea-God Umi-no-o. She married Hoori, the son of *Ninigi*, and gave birth to a son, after which she turned into a *dragon*. This was her father's original form.
  See also 'Gods of Japan' under *Gods; Hoderi and Hoori; Sea-King.*

Toyo-Uke-Bime The Japanese Goddess of Earth and Food. See also 'Gods of Japan' under *Gods.*

Toyonosuke Takemoto A prominent Japanese priest of the twentieth century. See *Shinto Shrines.*

Toyouke-Omikami In Japanese religion, the Goddess of Grain, whose shrine, *geku*, is traditionally served by a priestess, *saigu*. See also 'Gods of Japan' under *Gods; Rice-Goddess.*

Tracey Islands See *Vaitupu*.

Treasure-Raining Sutra Verses from this textbook of Buddhist doctrine are used in *Japan* to keep out *ghosts*. The doors and windows of a haunted house are fastened with strips of paper on which the Sutra is written. The evil *spirits* will then be unable to enter.

Treasure-Ship See *Takara-Bune*.

Tree-God In Fijian mythology, Tui Delai Gau, the God of the Mountain, lives in a tree. He is a giant who can take his hands off and tell them to go fishing for him in the sea. The hands can walk on their fingers and they can swim as well. He can also take his head off and send it up into the sky as a look-out. He gave his people (the Gau Islanders) the art of digging with a spade and of cooking food in an oven.

Tree-Spirit

1. In *Japan*, several trees (*cherry trees*, chestnut trees, *pine trees*, *plum trees*, *willow trees*) are known to be inhabited by a spirit which can speak and show itself. In the garden of a certain samurai stood a nettle tree (*Celtis Chinensis*, Japanese *enoki*), which had been there for many generations. The owner wanted to cut it down but his mother had a dream in which a huge monster warned her that 'If the tree dies, every member of the household will die.'

    Her son just laughed and had the tree cut down anyway. The same day he became insane, shouting: 'The tree, the tree is tearing me apart!'

    He died soon after, followed by his wife and all their servants. Only his daughter, a Buddhist nun, remained to pray for their *souls*.
2. King Kuna of Thailand, who lived a long time ago, hunted many *elephants* in the forest. For this offence against Life and Nature he was punished after he died: he was reborn as a tree-spirit, a ghost who had to live in a tree and guard the forest. His soul could find peace only when his son had built a huge pagoda which looked like a gigantic candle-holder, a symbol of the spread of enlightenment. See also *Thailand*.
3. In *Indonesia* very old and big trees are said to be inhabited by one or more tree-spirits, *bela*. The woodcutter will not cut down such a tree before he has brought some food and asked the spirits politely to move house to another tree. A *bela* can cause illness if displeased and it can appear in *dreams*. A priestess may be asked to indicate the *bela* who is responsible for an illness and a priest will pray to the wood-spirits by name, with offerings of rice and a chicken as travel-food, to persuade them to depart.
4. The Torajas fear the spirit of the *fig tree*, *waringin*, which can make people ill.
5. In the Minahassa region of *Sulawesi*, people may ask the tree-spirits to return the soul of a sick person before he has died definitively and gone to live in the forest.

6. On the island of Siau, tree-spirits are *giants* with long arms and legs, who, on moonlit nights, emerge and stand in people's pathways. Anyone touching such a tall leg, which looks like a tree trunk, will die.

7. The tree-spirits of the *Dayaks* of central *Kalimantan* are called Pampahilep. They look like tall handsome men and women, who may take to themselves human partners when the latter are lost in the forest. They can make people ill or insane, but also rich and lucky. The trees in which spirits live must not be touched or else illness will follow.

8. The Indonesian people of Nias relate that the *belas* are *demi-gods* descended from *heaven*, children of a goddess; they will cause visions to someone whom they have selected to become a *shaman*. He will flee to the forest and live with them for a time. He will later be found in a tree, taken back to the village and inaugurated as a priest. He is believed to cure insanity with the help of the tree-spirits.

See also *Plum Tree*.

Tresnawati   In Central Javanese mythology the Goddess of the Dry Rice; the name means 'thirsty' and also 'loving'. She was the daughter of *Batara Guru*, or *Siwa*, the Supreme God of Heaven. One day she saw a young and very handsome farmer ploughing his field on earth and fell in love with him. She grew wings and flew down to earth where she offered herself to him as his bride. Batara Guru punished her for refusing to come back to heaven, by changing her into an ear of *rice*. The farmer joined her as a rice stalk and so they became the *Pari Penganten*, the 'Rice Bride and Bridegroom', whose wedding is annually celebrated just before the rice harvest. See also *Dewi Sri; Ratna Dumilah; Rice-Goddess*.

Trinity   In Hawaiian cosmology, the three prominent *gods*, *Kane* (*Tane*), *Ku* (Ku-Ka-Pau, Tu) and *Lono* (*Rongo*) formed together a unity. They were equal in essence but distinct in attributes. This trinity was called Oi-E or Kane-Oi-E. Together they had existed even before the Night of Primeval Chaos, Po, which they dissipated, or 'broke', by an act of will, thus causing light to enter Chaos. They then created the three heavens for each of them to reside in, and the earth, as their footstool; furthermore the *sun*, the *moon* and the *stars* to serve them. After this they created a host of *spirits* (*angels*) who serve them. Then, together, they created man, in the image of Kane. Lono brought pieces of earth from the far corners of the world. From these, Ku-Ka-Pau, 'Ku the Constructor', shaped the form of man, using his saliva to hold the body together. Finally they breathed over the body and man came to life, rising up when they called him.

See also *Creation*; 'Gods of the Pacific' under *Gods*.

The Trobriand Islands   A group of a dozen *islands* north of *New Guinea*, the only big island being Boyowa (*c*.5–15 km wide, *c*.40 km long); others are Boimapu, Muwa, Vakuta, Kitava, Kaileula. See *Child Spirit; Inuvaylau; Rejuvenation; Shaman*(1); *Spirit-Twin; Tuma*.

Tromelin A French admiral. See *Hawaii*.

Tsubaki *Camellia Japonica* of the *Theaceae* family. The camellia is the plant which belongs to the Goddess of Fujiyama. See *Fujiyama; Sengen*.

Tsuki-Yumi ('Moon-Bow') The Japanese God of the Moon. See *Ama Terasu*; 'Gods of Japan' under *Gods; Izanami; Kaguya; Ladder of Heaven*(1); *Moon*.

Tsuna The chief retainer of *Raiko*, the Japanese hero. See *Spider-Boy; Spider-Woman*.

Tsuyu ('Dew') A girl who fell in love with a young samurai who could not marry her at first and was told later that she had died. She then did die of grief. Her ghost haunted the samurai's house until she finally joined him in his bed. There he was found the next morning, dead, in the tight embrace of a skeleton.

Tu See *Ku; Trinity*.

Tu Matauenga The Polynesian War-God. See *Adam and Eve*(3); *Maru; Sky*(2); *War*.

Tu-Mea See *Tangaroa*.

Tu-Te-Koropanga See *Koropanga*.

Tu-Te-Wehiwehi In *Maori* mythology, the Father of Reptiles. See also *Moko*.

Tua-Uo-Loa The South Wind. See *Matagi*.

Tuakeka See *Maru*(2).

Tubua See *Rua*.

The Tubuai Islands An archipelago, part of French *Polynesia*.

Tueva The father of *Veeteni*.

Tuhuruhuru The son of the *Maori* Moon-Goddess. See *Hina-Keha*.

Tui A bird of the *Prosthemadera* genus, used as food by the *Polynesians*. It was specially created by the god *Tane* as one of the aspects of the *Goddess*, the female essence. In another myth Tane's brother, the Sky-God *Rehua*, shook the bird out of his hair. It looks like a green glossy starling but belongs to the *Meliphagidae* family.

Tui Delai Gau See *Tree-God*.

Tukang See *Toucan*.

Tulagola ('Orphan Dog') See *Wallaby*(2).

Tuli See *Creation*(5).

Tuma In the *Trobriand Islands'* myths, the happy world where the human *spirits* live after *death*. Tuma is the Island of the Blessed where all inhabitants have the status of chiefs, all are handsome, and the men do not have to work there for the women do everything. (This point was conveyed to Dr Malinowski by a man, a seer called Tomwaya Lakwabulo.) Every man will have many wives, all charming. They dance all day, have plenty of food and drink, possess uncounted riches and are decorated with ornaments of many colours. This happy life will last forever, undisturbed.

As soon as a *soul* arrives in Tuma he or she will be met by a group of relatives to keep him or her company, for the dead soul is often lonely and sad at having to leave loved ones behind. A soul of the opposite *sex* will prepare a bouquet of aromatic herbs, over which *magic* words are pronounced. As soon as the newly arrived person smells this fragrant posy, he or she will forget the world of the living and be ready to make love to the souls of the opposite sex in *Paradise*. Thus it has been described by seers who have been there and come back.

See also *Paradise*.

Tumasik   (or Temasik, Tamasik, from *tasik*, 'sea') The island on which *Singapore* now stands. See also *Malay Annals*.

Tumudurere   The Lord of the Dead. See *Hiyoyoa*.

Tumuitearetoka   The Polynesian King of the Sharks. See *Ngaru; Shark*.

Tuna   (or Tunaroa; *tuna*, 'eel'; *tuna roa*, 'long eel', Polynesian; *kuna*, Hawaiian)

1.   The Polynesian Fish-God and Vegetation-God, Tuna lived in a pond near the beach, according to the myths of many Polynesian *islands*. There, one day, the Moon-Goddess *Hina* descended to bathe, like Diana. In the water, Tuna met her and made love to her.

2.   In another version of the myth, related by the inhabitants of Mangaia, an island in the Cook archipelago, one day a girl called Ina Moe-Aitu, 'Ina Love-God', was bathing in a stream when suddenly Tuna appeared and declared his love for her, saying he had been watching her for a long time. After a beautiful time of love, Tuna told Ina that he had to leave her, but he promised her that he would give her something permanent to remember him by.

'Bring an axe tomorrow,' he added mysteriously.

When she came back the next day at dusk, her lover was there, ready to love her. Afterwards he told her to cut his head off. When she hesitated, he explained that great misfortune would befall both of them if she refused. So she cut off his head. Tuna resumed his fish-shape and swam away for good. Ina buried the head out of which grew a *coconut* palm. It produced both food and drink for the people, thatching and matting for their houses and fibre for ropes.

3.   In yet another version, the woman involved was *Maui*'s wife Raukura. Maui was so incensed that he slew Tuna, and hacked him to pieces. Again, out of Tuna's head grew the coconut palm, while out of the pieces of his body grew the various species of fishes – the

middle became the ancestor of the sea-eels and the tail became the freshwater eels – and out of his blood grew the *rimu* or redwood tree. The blood also fell on many trees and *birds*, so they still have red spots to this day, such as the parakeet.

Tunaroa See *Tuna*.

Tunggal Garing Janjahunan Laut ('Lonely Garing, Risen from the Sea') See *Creation*(6).

Tuniai The *Creator* in Seran mythology. See *Sun*(9).

Tunjung Buih ('Lily of the Foaming Water') See *Kalimantan*.

Tupai See *Squirrel*.

Turehu In Polynesian mythology, they are a race of fair-haired *fairies* whose king was Uetonga, grandson of *Ruau-Moko*, the God of Earthquakes. The Turehu live in the land of Rarohenga which is said to be below the earth.

A young prince called *Mataora*, who was a poet and a singer, once fell asleep in a meadow after landing on an unknown island. When he woke up he found himself surrounded by lovely nymphs. Their leader was Niwareka, daughter of the Turehu king. The nymphs shared some delicious fruits with him after which the prince danced the dance of the *taiaha*, a ceremonial weapon. Niwareka joined him in the dance, for she had fallen in love with the handsome prince, who in his turn felt irresistibly attracted to the fair-skinned princess. They were married and lived very happily for several years until, one day, Mataora lost his temper and abused his noble wife. Indignant, she left him and went back to her father's country. Disconsolate and ashamed, Mataora went in search of her. After many days of travelling he arrived at Pou-Tere-Rangi, the Gate of Heaven, which was guarded by Kuwatawata. Mataora asked him if he had seen a fair woman passing. Kuwatawata answered, 'Yes, I saw a lovely white woman coming through this gate, weeping sadly.'

At last Mataora found Niwareka, by singing a love-song which her little sister heard. After many hours, at last he persuaded her to return with him to earth, even though its ways were evil. His father-in-law gave him, as a parting present, a cloak called Rangi-Haupapa, with a belt, the designs of which are still followed by skilled artisans on earth. On their way back to the world they were detained by Tiwaiwaka, the guardian of the ascent, because they had to await the proper season. When they arrived at the gateway leading to earth, Kuwatawata said, 'I will close this gate now. Henceforth no one will return to earth from our world.'

During his stay, Mataora had been tattooed by his father-in-law. Thus the art of *tattooing*, of weaving cloaks and of carving leather were brought from fairyland (see also *Tamanui*).

Turmeric (Hawaiian, *olena*) In *Indonesia* this plant, *kumkuma*, is used as a condiment in rice. It is also used in healing rituals because it is believed to have the power of defying evil.

Turtle   In *Japan*, though some fishermen on the coast eat turtles, many people regard them as too closely related to us to eat. They might be messengers from the *Sea-King* and so, kind spirits. See also *Creation*(2); *Monkey*(4); *Namiumlap*; *Storm*; *Tortoise*; *Toyo-Tama*.

Turukawa   See *Creation*(3); *Flood*.

Tushita   See *Maitreya*.

Tuti-Nameh   See *Parrot*.

Tutu   The first man on the island of Tutuila, according to Samoan mythology. See *Islands*.

Tuumbamuuta   See *Cassowary*.

Tuvalu   Formerly the Ellice Islands, Tuvalu has a total land area of 26 sq km (the island of Manhattan is twice as big). The length of the island chain is 600km.The capital, Funafuti, on the island of the same name, is only 2.8 sq km. in area. The total population is 8,500, with 2,800 being the population of the capital. The Ellice Islands voted in 1974 to break away from the Gilbert Islands (*Kiribati*). Funafuti is just between Kiribati and *Fiji*. Other islands, all atolls, are Nanumea, Nanumanga, Niutao, Nukufeitau, Nuku Laelae and Nui. The people speak Tuvaluan, a Polynesian language.
See also *Infanticide*.

Tuwale   The Sun-God in Seran mythology. See *Sun*(9).

Tuwhakapau   A *Maori* chief. See *Tahua*.

Twins   See *Gemini*; 'Gods of the Pacific' under *Gods*.

U

Uzume surprised in her dance by Ama Terasu (Japan)

Ua The *Maori* God of Rain who had many names: Ua-Roa ('Long Rain'), Uanui ('Heavy Rain'), Uawhatu ('Hail') and Ua Nganga ('Rainstorm'). His son is *Hau Maringi*, the God of Mist or Fog. See also *Fire*(4); 'Gods of the Pacific' under *Gods*.

Ua Nganga See *Ua*.

Ua-Roa ('Long Rain') See *Ua*; *Deluge*.

Uanui See *Ua*.

Uawhatu See *Ua*.

Uba ('Old woman, wet nurse') The spirit of the *pine tree* in *Japan*. She symbolizes fidelity in marriage with her husband Jo ('Love').

Uekera In Polynesian cosmology, the sacred tree that reaches to *heaven*.

Uenuku A great *Maori* chief, descendant of the War-God Tu Matauenga (see *Maru*).
   Uenuku had two wives; by the first, Pai Hutanga, he had five sons. By the second, Taka-Rita, sister of Chief Tawheta, none. Takarita deceived her husband by committing adultery with two men. However, Uenuku discovered this misdemeanour and killed all three of them.

When Chief Tawheta was told that Uenuku had killed his sister for adultery, he said, 'That act was no doubt justifiable. Yet he will pay for it.'

He awaited his chance and soon it came. One day all Uenuku's five children went to the forest to pick certain fruits which were used for pickling food. Tawheta sent his men to the forest to kill them all. Only one son escaped, the youngest, critically wounded. He lived to tell the tale of how his four brothers were slaughtered. Brashly, Tawheta went up to Uenuku's town, pretending to be visiting a friendly kinsman. Sadly and solemnly, Uenuku showed him his sole surviving wounded son. Quickly Tawheta and his men withdrew and fled, fearing they would be killed now that Uenuku knew what had happened. However, Uenuku let the culprits escape, because a guest may not be harmed. Tawheta had, meanwhile, demonstrated his cowardice.

Uenuku assembled his men and went to war, after feeding his dead sons' blood to the *gods*. They surrounded Tawheta's enclosure but he escaped, leaving his men to fight alone against Uenuku's ferocious attack. Every man inside the compound was killed, even Hapopo the priest, who had failed to predict the attack because Uenuku's gods had clouded his mind. The only survivor was Pou Matangatanga, Tawheta's daughter, whom Uenuku took to himself as wife to give him new sons. Still, Uenuku knew that Tawheta must be killed or he would remain a danger forever after.

Finally Uenuku cornered Tawheta, who was hiding in the forest with his men. By *magic*, Uenuku caused a thick fog to descend from the mountains, while his gods clouded the minds of the enemies, so they battled against one another. After a while, Uenuku commanded the fog to lift and his men, still in their boats, were astonished to see so many corpses. Uenuku then released his dogs on the survivors. Drunken with the scent of all that blood, the dogs tore away at the enemies, who could not escape since their hide-out was surrounded by mountains. Finally, Uenuku went ashore with his men. Tawheta had to give battle and was killed by Uenuku himself. The sea was bright red with the blood of the slain as far as the eye could see. Later, when the *sun* set, the sea was again coloured red. Since then, that battle has been known in history as 'The Day of the Two Sunsets', Ra Torua.

Uetonga See *Turehu*.

Uga-no-Mitama The Japanese Goddess of Agriculture. See *Inari*.

Uheita A Japanese peasant. See *Witch*(1).

Uhi See *Yam*.

Uira (also called Kanapu) The Polynesian God of Lightning, ancestor of *Tawhaki*. See also 'Gods of the Pacific' under *Gods*.

Ujigami (from *uji*, 'family lineage') In *Japan*, a tutelary god. Living relatives may ask their house-god for an *oracle* in case of *illness*.

Ukaipu See *Ivo*.

Uke-Mochi See *Inari*.

Ulay A Philippine prince. See *Witch*(6).

Ulupoka The Fijian God of Evil. See *Head*(1).

Uma ('The Golden') The Balinese *Rice-Goddess*, who causes the *rice* to germinate in the ground. Also the benign Goddess of *Tapas*, *Dewi Parwati*, or *Sakti*, wife of *Siwa*. See also *Kali*.

Umbrella Mountain In *Thailand* it is related that one fine day long ago the *Buddha* arrived to preach his doctrine. The king was so pleased with the presence of the Holy One, that he quickly travelled to the place where the Buddha was resting, and offered his royal umbrella, made of pure gold, to shade His Holiness. The Buddha was grateful for the king's devotion and, as a reward to the Thai nation, he left a sacred relic behind on the mountain where he had spent the night and which, he said, should henceforth be called Chatragiri (Ujapapata), 'Umbrella Mountain'. This was done. A temple was built there which has long since fallen into ruin.

  The gift of the relic indicates that what the king saw was not the Buddha but his spiritual appearance. The physical Buddha had already died and entered Nirvana, but his powerful and divine spirit, his Bodhisattva, carried the relic to Thailand. According to some it was the Buddha's skull. Naturally, such a powerful relic will continue to send out spiritual vibrations which will cause people to see apparitions and hear voices. That is the reason why no one ventured to the mountain and, therefore, why the temple fell into ruins. Only one man ever lived near there. He was a criminal and a drunkard who found a cave nearby where he hid from the authorities. One night the Buddha appeared to him and the criminal was so terrified that he converted to *Buddhism* and never again touched alcohol, but lived as a hermit in his cave. He died long ago but his horrifying corpse still walks there.

Underworld The Underworld is home to the evil *spirits*. In Javanese mythology there is a well, Jalatunda, which is so deep that it reaches down to the well in the Underworld, which contains not water but oil, *tala*, which makes the body invulnerable. See also *Bua-Taranga*; *Hades*; *Nether World*; *Other World*; *Reinga*.

Unicorn See *Kirin*.

Upolu The name of the first woman on the island of Upolu, according to Samoan mythology. See *Islands*.

Upu Lero ('Lord Sun') See *Creator*; *Sun*(2).

Uranga-o-Te-Ra The *Nether World*. See *Rohe*.

Urashima A young Japanese fisherman. See *Sea-King's Palace*.

Uriko See *Chopstick*.

Uru (Polynesian; Malay, *hulu*, for 'origin') It has been hypothesized by

Drs Percy Smith and Fornander, William Churchill and A.C. Haddon, that the *Polynesians* originate from Ur (also spelled Uru) in southern Mesopotamia, the capital city of the Sumerians, who had trade relations with the cities in the Indus valley. More recent research has found astonishing similarities between the scripts of the Indus Valley and Easter Island (*Rapanui*).

Uru-Tetefa See *Areoi*.

Utu ('Satisfaction') This is in the sense of seeking satisfaction when honour is impugned or pride wounded. Polynesian chiefs and princes would seek satisfaction when they had been insulted; like the ancient Greeks, they would go to war for an abducted wife. See *Maru*(2); *Uenuku*.

Urutonga The wife of *Hema* and mother of *Tawhaki*. See *Tawhaki*(2).

Uwabami In Japanese mythology, a monstrous giant *serpent* which can fly in the *sky*, swoop down and swallow a man on horseback, whole. It was killed by the hero Yegara-no-Heida.

Uwhi See *Yam*.

Uwi See *Sweet Potato*.

Uzume ('Whirling') In *Japan* the Daughter of Heaven, the Goddess of Good Health, which people obtain by drinking the blessed water from her stream. Uzume is also the Goddess of Happiness and the Dance. Her dance made *Ama Terasu* open the cave-door behind which she was hiding, so that sunshine returned to earth. Uzume is called Heaven's Forthright Female. She was married by her brother *Ninigi* to the Deity who guards the Floating Bridge to Heaven. See *Ama Terasu*; *Bridge of Heaven*; 'Gods of Japan' under *Gods*; *Ninigi*.

V

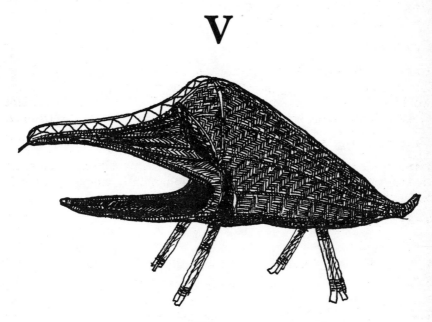

Vaimuru

Va'a See *Waka*.

Va'atele ('Swift Yacht') See *Owl*(1).

Vabusi See *Beyawa*.

Vai-Ola See *Paradise; Waiora*.

Vailala This town in southern *Papua* is famous for the 'madness' that once enslaved the people. A man called Kaehehe committed adultery with a woman in Vailala, so the men there killed him. Kaehehe had an uncle, Kukuhae who was a powerful magician. He cursed the people of Vailala by waving the symbol of the sun at their village from a great distance, pronouncing his *magic* formulae (*karakia*). The next night a woman in Vailala saw a large ship coming down the river. In it were the *spirits* of the *dead* who spoke to her. She went to her people and told them that they must destroy all the *masks* and the men's houses. Then they would see their dead. The people of Vailala went mad. They even stopped cultivating and started living promiscuously. They sang sacred hymns to the *gods* without the cautionary rituals. The 'leaders' of the movement erected posts in the villages with strings attached to them, claiming that the spirits spoke to them through these devices, which looked curiously like telephone wires. It all ended in famine and the dispersal of the survivors.

Vaimuru   A *Papua* tribe who initiate their boys by putting them in a huge fish-shaped basket, from which they are 'reborn' as men.

Vairocana   (also Vairochana, Mahavairocana, Mahavairochana) The first and foremost of the Dhyani *Buddhas*; in Balinese *Buddhism* the Bodhisattva of the knowledge of ideal forms. Venerated all over the Mahayana world, Vairocana is especially revered in *Japan* where he is known as *Dainichi*. He symbolizes the cosmic element of *rupa*, 'form', and he possesses perfect knowledge, which he may impart to his devotees in *dreams*. His season is autumn, his colour is white. His numinous opposite deity is *Yama-Raja*. See also 'Gods of Japan' under *Gods; Kobo*.

Vairochana   See *Vairocana*.

Vaitakere   See *Vaitere*.

Vaitere   (or Vaitakere; 'Full of Water') The father of *Ina*, in Polynesian myth.

Vaitupu   This is one of the Tracey Islands of the Ellice Group north of *Fiji* (see *Tuvalu*). The people of Vaitupu trace their origin to *Samoa*. They relate the following myth of *Creation*: In the beginning there was only sea. Out of the limitless ocean rose, upon one dark night, the coral rocks. The spray of the waves beating the rocks rose up and became a thick vapour spreading out over the entire ocean. When the sun rose it had become the sky. In the centre of the thickest part of this vapour a human being became visible, a man. As the sun rose he walked upon the land. When the sun became hot he began to perspire. The pearls of sweat on his body collected on the earth and there rose up the first *woman*.

Vajra   *Indera*'s lightning-jewel. See also *Kongo* and *Wajera*.

Vamana   A hunchback dwarf. See *Narayana*.

Vampire

1. In *Japan* it is related that Prince Hizen once had a mistress who was in reality a giant *cat*, or who had a feline spirit. Every night she put a spell on his guards and entered the prince's bedroom. Gradually the prince fell ill, his condition deteriorated and soon it became clear that he was dying. At last a soldier by the name of Ito Soda was found prepared to keep watch. He turned a dagger in his flesh so that the pain kept him awake, and so did not fall asleep in spite of the cat-demon's witchcraft. The mere sight of his watchful eyes in the dark made the demoness powerless. She stayed away after a few nights and the prince recovered.

2. In *Malaysia*, a female spirit who can appear in the shape of a beautiful woman and so, gain power over the *sorcerer* who thought he could enslave her by his *magic*. She can even bear him elfin children. She often appears as a bat or a black owl with long claws. She sucks the blood of babies, unless given plenty of fish. See also *Kalong; Puntianak*.

See also *Spirits*(5); *Yasha*.

Vanuatu The new name of the New Hebrides archipelago since 1980, when Vanuatu became independent after nearly a century of Anglo-French condominium. This new parliamentary republic lies 1,750km east of Australia, south-east of the Solomon Islands, north of *New Caledonia* and the Friendship Islands, while the Banks Islands are part of it, though ethnically distinct. *Fiji* is 1,000km further east. Vanuatu comprises 80 *islands*, less than half of them suitable for habitation. The largest of them are Espiritu Santo, Malekula, Maewo, Pentecost, Anbrim, Epi, Mai, Huon, Erromango, Aniwa, Efatē and Tanna.

Though geographically part of Melanesia, Vanuatu speaks 40 distinct languages, some of which are Polynesian in origin. Apart from English and French as official languages, there is a local language called Bislama, described by some as a pidgin, which is widespread, at least in the capital Port Vila on the island of Efatē. This is also where manganese used to be mined. Today the main exports are *coconut* products: copra, coconut oil and coconut-fibre (coir); as well as *fish*, the staple food, and beef.

See also *Banoi*; *Cricket*(1); *Dwarfs*; *Ghosts*(3); *Pigs*(2)(3); *Tagaro*.

Varaha A great boar. See *Hiranyaksa*; *Narayana*.

Varima-Te-Takere ('The Woman of the Very Beginning') See *Goddess*(4).

Varuna See *Waruna*.

Vasudeva In Hindu Javanese and Balinese mythology, a high god (*Wisnu*), the father of Krishna (*Kresna*) and, by extension, Krishna himself.

Vasuki See *Sesa*.

Vatea A *Creator* god. See *Adam and Eve*(5); *Goddess*(4); *Papa*.

Veeteni (pron. 'Ve-e-te-ni') On the island of Mangaia, east of Rarotonga in the *Cook Islands*, the funerary ceremonies for a deceased son or brother are exceptionally elaborate and meaningful, as well as beautiful. The reason for this is, we are told, the memory of the departure of Veeteni, who may be compared to Adonis, the ritually lamented Greek God of the Sunset and the Flowers. Like Adonis, Veeteni was still a young man when he died, and he was the first man ever to die on the island. His parents, Tueva and Manga, and his loving sister Tiki, mourned him through the night by singing dirges, dressed in black *pakoko* cloth. At last, when dawn broke in the east, they saw their beloved son and brother return to them along the red path of the *sun* on the waves. Rejoicing greatly, the family received him back with glad songs, but alas: he was no longer the same, for he now belonged to the spirit world and would have to return to it at sunset. His loving relatives wept bitterly upon hearing this, so Veeteni agreed to pray to *Tangaroa* to ask if he would make the day longer. Tangaroa, in his kindness, agreed to give the day henceforth the same length as the night (see *Maui* for the myth of the lengthening of the day).

So, during the day, the people of the island (who may all have been related) were very happy to have the handsome Veeteni in their midst, but as sunset approached, they grew sadder and when the sun vanished they would cling to Veeteni, wanting to keep him on earth. Alas! It was like embracing the last ray of light at sunset. Mourning songs and dirges are still sung to commemorate him.

Venus See 'Gods of the Pacific' under *Gods; Morning Star; Tonga.*

Vikramavardhana A Javanese king. See *Indonesia.*

Violets (Japanese, *sumire*) In the valley of Shimizutani in *Japan*, there was a well round which violets grew in profusion. The Princess Shinge came there one day to bathe but a snake, who lived in the well, bit her. There she lay, her lovely lips as violet as the flowers around her. Her maids found a young doctor called Yoshisawa, who came at once and cured her. The princess fell in love with him but her father decreed that a mere doctor was not good enough for his daughter. One day, she found her death at the bottom of that same well, and so did young Yoshisawa (see also *Joshi*). Their soft plaintive song can still be heard.

Shinge is no doubt the personification of the violet flower.

Visu The Japanese Rip Van Winkle, who watched two beautiful girls playing for 300 years until they suddenly became *foxes.*

Vitu

1. A name for the island of *Fiji.*
2. In Samoan mythology, the name of the first *woman* on Fiji.

Volcano God In *Indonesia*, the volcanoes were all believed to be *gods*. In the Minahassa (*Sulawesi*), human victims were sacrificed to them.

1. On the island of Siau, north of Sulawesi, Aditinggi is the God of the Volcano Gunung Awu. Every year a child was sacrificed to the god and prayers were recited entreating him not to make the mountain erupt. Later a wooden doll was offered instead, which was chopped to pieces.
2. The Sultan of Halmahera used to sacrifice human heads to the volcano god on that island, imploring him not to ruin his island.
3. In *Java* the God of the Great Volcano *Bromo* (*Brahma*) is still celebrated annually, now, however, with animal sacrifices. For the God of Mount Tengger on Java see *Bromo, the Creator.*

See also *Fujiyama; Pele,* the Goddess of Volcanoes.

W

Wayang shadow puppet (Duryudana, Java)

Wa'a See *Waka*.

Wagon Priest See *Hoteri*.

Wahiaroa See *Pere*.

Wahie Loa ('Long Branch') In Hawaiian myth, the God of Comets.

Wahie Roa The son of *Tawhaki*.

Waiola See *Waiora*(1).

Waiora

1. (Waiola; Vai-Ola in central *Polynesia*) A lake in Polynesian mythology containing the *water of life*, which rejuvenates whoever drinks it or bathes in it. Its location is, however, unknown. See also *Paradise*.
2. The Polynesian Goddess of Health (like the Greek Hygieia). Bathing in her well, a sick person will be completely recovered and be healthy for life.

Waitiri (also Whaitiri) According to the traditions of the Ngai Tahu people of Stewart Island to the south of *New Zealand*, she was a goddess. She descended from *heaven* to marry a human called Kai Tangata whom she taught to fish with barbs. They had a son called *Hema*. One day Kai Tangata offended Waitiri, so she ascended back to heaven from the roof top, coloured white, like a cloud. See also *Tawhaki*(3).

Wajera (Javanese Wajro, from Sanskrit Vajra), the lightning-jewel of the Hindu god *Indera*, well-known in Javanese and old Malay mythology. See also *Kongo*.

Wajro See *Wajera*.

Waka (Polynesian, 'boat, canoe') Captain James Cook reported in 1773 that he saw at *Tahiti* a fleet of over 300 double *canoes*. He also saw two canoes being constructed, each 108 feet long. These boats could have up to 40 men on board and, if skilfully navigated, they could outsail Cook's own ships with ease. They could sail 100 miles in 24 hours. Traditions in several parts of *Polynesia* relate that in the 'real' old days, perhaps 20 generations ago, canoes were built that were very much larger than the ones used at present. Obviously, such big ships could only be constructed on the greater *islands* where an infinite number of tall trees was available, as in *New Zealand*.

Wakea The Hawaiian equivalent of Vatea. See *Adam and Eve*(5); *Papa*.

Wali In *Indonesia* and *Malaysia*, a Muslim saint. The best known medieval saints of *Java* are Sunan Giri, *Sunan Bonang, Sunan Gunung,* Sunan Kudus and Sunan Kalijaga. They are still believed to bless devotees at their graves.

Walian Priestess of the Tontemboan of *Sulawesi*. See *Shamanism*(3).

Wall Oil In *Java*, a certain prince possessed the secret of a magical oil. When, at midnight, he rubbed a wall with it, a section of that wall, just wide enough to let a man through, would sink into the ground. He used this to visit the princesses he loved in the *kraton*.

Wallaby

1. In west *Papua* people relate that in the beginning there were no people, only animals. One day man Wallaby and wife Wallaby had a fight. Wife Wallaby died and man Wallaby went away. There she lay and out of her body crept many maggots. Some of these grew into people, white people. In the beginning they had only sign *language* but soon they developed a proper language. Later, in the night, more maggots crept out and became people, but now they were black people. The white people sailed away. The black people stayed because the climate suited them. They divided into small groups, each with its own language. They never eat wallaby flesh because, they say, the wallaby is their mother. See also *Totem*.
2. In *New Britain*, Pakasa Uru, 'Big Wallaby', is the buffoon and chief character in Lakalai humorous tales. He is usually outwitted by Tulagola, 'Orphan Dog', the inventor of drums.

Wananga Secret knowledge in Polynesian.

War The *Polynesians* are a peaceful race; there are many proverbs in their languages advising against waging war. *Tu Matauenga* (in *Maori* also called *Maru*, in Hawaiian, Ku) was the War-God. He quarrelled with the *gods*, his own brothers, for such was his nature. He devoured their children, like Kronos. He was cast out, exiled to the nether regions of darkness, but once, aided by the shadowy hosts of Anu, he rose up and invaded *heaven*, where the gods could only defeat him after three fierce battles; finally they threw him back. See also *Bratayuda; Maru*(1).

Waringin See *Fig Tree*.

Waruna (or Mahadewa; from the Sanskrit, Varuna) In Balinese mythology the God of Oceans, Rain, Water and the Sea, who rules the west and is married to *Durga*. He is equated with the classical Uranus. See also 'Gods of Bali' under *Gods; Sea-King*.

Water (*Amida-Nyorai*) One of the *elements* in Japanese cosmology.

Water of Life On Timor it is related that a prince found two wells, one shouting, 'Life!' while the other groaned, 'Death!'
    The prince filled a bottle from each well and became a famous doctor. See also *Waiora*.

Water Spirit (Malay, *hantu ayer*) In the South China Sea, St Elmo's *fire* is frequently seen. The Malay fishermen believe it is water spirits, appearing like fire, and tie sugar palm twigs to the top of their masts to prevent the water spirits from perching on them.

Waterlily (*Nymphaea*) This lovely white flower grows out of the dark muddy bottom of a pond, rises up to the light and opens its shining petals to the *sun*. In *Japan* and *Indonesia* it is the symbol of the *soul* in search of serenity.

Watu Gunung A mythical Javanese king who married, unwittingly, his own mother. See *Sinta*; also *Oedipus* for the Thai myth.

Wayang In *Indonesia* and *Malaysia*, the performances of the shadow play. There are two main types, the *wayang wong* (in *Java* and *Bali*), the performance with traditional *dances* by trained actors, and the more widespread *wayang kulit*, played by the expert narrator, *dalang*, who personally handles the dozens of beautifully-painted puppets made of leather, who represent mythological characters. Here are some of the main *wayangs*:

   Wayang Beber: On Java, a recited performance with the scenes painted on large boards.
   Wayang Golek: On Java, a *wayang* performance by means of dressed wooden dolls.
   Wayang Klitik: On Java, the name of a puppet theatre played using small wooden dolls held by long sticks, for the people rather than for the courts.
   Wayang Kulit: On Java, a *wayang* performance by means of over 400 leather puppets.
   Wayang Parwa: On Bali, the *wayang* show of the *Mahabharata* myths.

Wayang Purwa: On Java, the *wayang* show of the myths of the *Mahabharata* (the *Pandawa* cycle) or of the *Ramayana epic* tales.
Wayang Topeng: On Java, a performance by masked dancers.
Wayang Wong: On Java, the epic myths which are performed by trained dancers.

See also *Amir Hamza; Anantaboga; Aneka-Warna; Bima; Bratayuda; Burisrawa; Chandra Kirana; Dalang; Damar Wulan; Dewi Sri; Durga; Gamelan; Gatutkaca; Indera; Janaka*(1); *Kayon; Kelana; Korawa; Kresna; Lakon; Panakawan; Panji; Ramakien; Ramayana; Satria; Semar; Topeng.*

Weddid The oldest surviving Indonesian *race*. See *Indonesia*.

Were-Dog On Timor it is said that a man may change himself, at night, into a dog, while his body remains on his charpoy. He will then steal the *soul* of a sleeping man and change him into a goat or a buffalo with a human head. He will cut that off and offer the animal body to his family. They will partake unsuspectingly and the person whose *sumangat* (soul) was stolen, will die. If discovered, the were-dog will be executed.

Were-Tiger See *Feathers; Macan Gadungan; Tiger.*

Werewolf (Javanese, *anjing ajak*) Werewolves are men whose impure *spirits* change themselves at night into wolves, to devour people.

Werkudara ('Wolf's Belly') In Javanese mythology a nickname for the hungry *Bima.*

Whaitiri See *Waitiri.*

Whakatau See *Matuku.*

Whale

1. In *Taiwan* the whale is honoured at a special festival because it is said that the whale brought millet seeds to the island. The whale is also credited with expelling foreign invaders' ships.
2. In *Japan* a man called Yoda Emon was governor of the Shichito Islands south-east of Japan in the twelfth century. He was once miraculously saved by a whale when his boat was wrecked in a *storm*. He therefore decreed that no whales should be caught off the coast of his province. The emperor approved and confirmed this protection of whales.

See also *Rongo-Mai.*

Whatu The *Maori* God of Hail. See *Fire*(4).

Wheel In *Buddhism*, the symbol of *Buddha*'s doctrine itself. The texts say that just as the wheel crushes all things in its path, so the Doctrine crushes all illusion, error and lust. See also *Kuruma.*

Whenua See *Papa.*

Whiro The *Maori* Lizard-God of the Dead who lives in the dark misty

Underworld and inspires evil thoughts in the minds of people. See also
Lizard; Moko.

White Elephant

1. This is a sacred animal in *Thailand*, a symbol of *Buddha*. In yet older myths, the royal white elephant was a god, protecting the king.
2. In *Malaya* it is related that the white elephant is the King of the Forest. It is credited with divine wisdom.

See also *Elephant.*

White Raven In Thai mythology it is related that long ago the Sun-King Athityarat (Sanskrit, Aditya-Raja), ruler of Lamphun, once received a visit from the King of the White Ravens who told him that near his palace a treasure was buried which had once belonged to the *Buddha.* The white raven indicated the spot, then flew away. King Athityarat built a pagoda on the spot and when he celebrated the ceremony of its dedication, a *crystal* bowl rose out of the ground, laden with fresh fruit, signifying that an age of prosperity had begun.

White Tiger The guardian of the western quarter of the Japanese Zodiac.

Widodari See *Widyadari.*

Widyadari (Javanese; from the Sanskrit, *Vidyadhari*, 'having knowledge') A heavenly nymph who flies to earth to bathe in a lake or river. A young man steals her feather jacket, so she has to stay behind while her friends fly back to *heaven.* She agrees to marry him and they have a child (or two). She gives him the *rice* to feed the child. Finally she finds her wings and flies back home to heaven. Sometimes she is identified with the *Rice-Goddess.* See also *Bidadari; Cassowary; Moon-Bird.*

Wijaya-Kusuma ('Flower of Victory') This flower grows by itself on a small rocky island, Karang Bandung, just off the south coast of *Java.* It grows there only once in a generation, guarded by the King of the Spirits, a servant of the *Ocean-Goddess.* It is poisonous, but *if* a prince should ever manage to pick it and to sail back to Java, he will be the victorious ruler of all Java, *if* the gods favour him. If they do, they will let him pick it.

When Dewi Pratiwi, Goddess of the Earth, was asked to marry *Wisnu,* son of the Supreme God, she wished to receive this flower as a wedding gift. Wisnu went in search of it with the help of *Semar* and his sons and finally found it. Its fragrance revives the slain on the battlefield. Dewi Pratiwi, as Goddess of Nature, possesses the power to recreate all living beings from herself.

Wikramadatta See *Giants*(2).

Will o' the Wisp These are very common in *Japan*, appearing in the form of Buddha-lanterns, badger-blazes, demon-lights, fox-flames, ghost-fires, flash-pillars and flaming-birds. Flames are seen on cemeteries, while fire-wheels come whirling out of the ground. Dragon-torches resemble fiery dragons' eyes.

Willow Tree (Japanese, *higo*)

1. One day a man called Heitaro was told that the beautiful willow tree near his house had to be cut down to be used as timber. Heitaro loved the willow tree, so he wept and offered all the other trees in his garden instead. This was accepted. That night Heitaro met a beautiful woman under the willow tree. She offered to marry him. Her name was Higo.

2. In Japan, a young nobleman, Gobei, saw a lovely lady in his garden the night after his agent had told him that he was bankrupt. The lady was the spirit of the ancient willow tree. She told the Lord Gobei: 'Dear young master! Deep below my roots your great grandfather's great grandfather buried an old treasure chest so that no scion of his line would ever have to sell his house, his land or his garden in times of need.'

   She showed him the exact location of the treasure, then disappeared into the tree. With two faithful retainers, Gobei dug deep into the place indicated by the spirit and found an ancient chest full of golden oblongs, as they struck them many generations ago. Now he could pay all his debts! There was a letter in with the chest, urging the writer's descendant to look after the family property henceforth with good care.

See also *Cherry Tree; Pine Tree; Plum Tree; Tree-Spirit*.

Wilotama In Javanese mythology, a celestial nymph who assumed the shape of a mare in order to carry the Brahmin guru Durna, from *India* (Bharat) to *Java*. During the flight the old sage ejaculated involuntarily, as a result of which Wilotama conceived and gave birth to a son, Aswatama, who grew up in Java. The Brahmin was no doubt the Sun-God Surya.

Wind In *Polynesia*, there are special names for the different winds, as there were in ancient Greece: Hakona Tipu, South Wind, Marangai, East Wind, and Matu, North Wind. See also *Matagi*.

The original Wind-God was Hanui-o-Rangi, 'Father of Winds'. He was the son of the Sky-God *Rangi*. His sons were *Tawhiri-Matea* the Storm-God and all the other wind-gods. See 'Gods of the Pacific' under *Gods*; also *Hau; Storm*.

Windjan See *Soul*.

Wirachita The son of the Balinese farmer Diarsa. See *Siwa*.

Wisnu (In Thai, *Narayana*, Narasinga, Narai or Hari) Indonesian form of the Indian god Vishnu, well known in Javanese and Balinese myths. He is the son of *Batara Guru*, the Supreme God. Vishnu is best known in his *incarnation* as Rama, the god-hero of the *epic Ramayana*. Wisnu and his divine consort *Dewi Sri*, the *Rice-Goddess* (Lakshmi) frequently descend to earth to be born in an *awatara* (*incarnation*), usually as a prince of great valour and a beautiful princess, but in different royal households. It is their destiny to meet and marry in each of their terrestrial existences. Wisnu travels on *Garuda* the Celestial Eagle.

See also 'Gods of Bali' under *Gods; Hiranyaksa; Kresna; Narayana; Sadono.*

Witch

1. In *Japan*, it is said, one may still encounter witches in the forest. A sly old peasant called Uheita met a witch in the forest of Yasunaga. He heard a child crying and knew it was the witch pretending to be an infant. As soon as he came near he knew she would open her huge maw and eat him up. But Uheita was too quick. He picked her up, holding both her hands and her two feet in his strong hands, and carried her home. There he shut the door and the windows and made sure there was not a hole in the room left even for an ant to creep through. He lit the fire and threw the witch in, but when she jumped out and tried to escape, she could find no way out. Then she tried to frighten Uheita by showing her enormous teeth, but he was too wise and kept his cool. Suddenly she vanished. Uheita went in search of her until he discovered there were two statues of the goddess *Kannon* instead of the one he put in the family shrine years ago. Only one could be the goddess, the other must be the witch. But which was which? Uheita took some *rice* and red beans, his traditional offering for the goddess, and held it before the two similar statues. One smiled and held out her hand, so he realized that the other one must be the witch. He picked the statue up, put it in the pot with boiling water which was hanging over the fire, and held the lid down on it. Thunder and lightning were heard, also screaming and hissing. At last nothing was left in the pot but black tar.

2. On *Bali* it is related that the witch Tjalon Arang possessed a *magic* book and was a servant of the goddess *Durga*, who presides over the *spirits* of the cemetery. Her apprentices, Hoghead, Buffalohead, *et al.*, danced there until the goddess appeared and permitted the witch to kill numerous people. The witch made her followers (all female) dance at the crossroads. Soon people began to die of the Cold Fever, and the king commanded his soldiers to kill the witch. They surrounded her house at night but flames darted from her eyes, burning many soldiers, so the rest fled. The next night the witch and her women danced again, like tigresses, naked and with glowing red eyes. They killed a zombie and washed their hair in his blood, draping the intestines round their bodies. Durga appeared again and through the following days so many people died of fever that there was no one left to bury them. Dogs and ravens fed on the bodies. Many people tried to flee to other countries but they fell down dying on the road with their children as soon as the invisible Disease Demons had touched them.

The king ordered sacrifices burnt until *Siwa*, the four-armed, appeared from the fire and named Bharada the ascetic as the one who could cure the epidemic by removing evil. The saint asked his disciple to obtain the witch's magic book. The disciple succeeded by a ruse and brought the book to Bharada. Having studied the book, the saint travelled through the almost deserted towns. Wherever he found people still alive, he cured them with his holy water. Finally he met the witch, who sprayed him with fire from her nostrils, but it was ineffectual. He informed her that Siwa and Durga had decided that she should die that day. He told her the path to salvation if she wanted it. Then she died.

3. In the Minahassa in *Sulawesi*, a witch is said to be a type of person who can send her head and intestines flying through the air, with her ears (or, in some cases, her lungs) functioning as wings. Sometimes the head and intestines change into a bird or a mouse so that the witch can enter the house of her intended victim unnoticed.

4. In Malay, such witches are called *penanggalan*, 'the one who pulls out' (the innards from the body). The intention of the witch is to drink her victims' blood, especially that of women after childbirth. Witches may learn their art from an evil spirit but usually it is inherited. They operate at night and if head and guts are not back with the body by dawn, the witch will die. To cause this to happen the body, if found, can be hidden. The Malays hang thorny branches at the entrance of their houses so that the guts may get entangled, thereby trapping the witch.

5. In Melanesia the witches, or female *sorcerers*, are especially dreaded. They can fly at night, emitting light from their eyes, like fireflies or falling *stars*. They are also associated with flying *foxes*, or *birds*. They feed on the bodies of dead people. They cause instantaneous death at will by inflicting their victims with incurable diseases, which destroy the intestines completely and quickly. In vain will the victim search for a remedy. Some witches are young and attractive so they can put a spell on a man, even a chief, thus acquiring political power. They do not apply their black art for real profit. These witches may have sexual relations with non-human invisible male beings, a type of *incubi* called *tauva'u*, who cause epidemics, venereal diseases and even toothaches. See also *Familiar*.

6. There are many witches in the *Philippines*. They love boys and girls: to eat (see also *Boroka*). They also keep children as little slaves, employing them as cooks, while keeping them in reserve, to eat later. Some witches are young and beautiful, like the one with whom Prince Ulay fell in love. When he married another girl, obeying his father the king, the angry witch changed him into a monkey, his father's capital city into a forest and all its citizens into animals. The witch decreed that the monkey prince would live in the forest for 500 years, until a beautiful girl would come to love him, and live with him in that forest. Thus it happened! Five hundred years later the

love of a poor young girl broke the witch's spell and she found herself loving a prince, no longer an *ape*.

Philippine witches can also change ugly women into beauties and vice versa. The witch of Tipuca was friendly (or perhaps in love) with the hero of Luzon, Tomarind. She commanded her many strong servant-spirits to dig a tunnel for Tomarind to the World of the Dead Souls, and also gave him a stick that made *monsters* friendly.

See also *Cat*(1); *Durga; Fairies; Guna-Guna; Illness; Magic; Makutu; Maori*(2); *Medicine Man; Menehune; Nini Muni; Puntianak; Shaman; Shamanism; Tipua*.

Witsanukam   In Thai mythology, the Architect of the *Gods*; the name is a combination of Vishnu (see *Wisnu*) and *Kama*.

Woman

1. The *Maori* myth of the *creation* of woman is as follows: Arohirohi, the Goddess of Mirages, i.e. mysterious visions on the horizon, was the wife of Raa the Sun-God (see *Mirage*). She took the vibrating heat of the noon sunshine, when mirages are visible, and shaped Woman out of it. She asked Paoro, the Goddess of Echoes, to give Woman a voice, which she did. This first woman, was given a name, Marikoriko (Hawaiian, *mali'o* means 'the first rays of light, aurora'), and a husband, *Tiki*, the first man and co-creator of the earth. They had a daughter, the first child ever born on earth. They called her Hine-Kau-Ataata ('Lonely Gentle Woman' or 'Lady of the Early Gentle Floating Shadows'). Clouds appeared when she was born, announcing the first rain of the season, a very auspicious sign. The rivers flowed, but without overflowing. Then the light of morning broke.

2. The Kamanuku people of *Papua New Guinea* relate that in the beginning there was Woman, although she was not yet a woman because she had no vagina, until one day from high above came Siambuka, a demi-god. He spoke to the woman and she liked him. Then, taking a splinter of bamboo, he made an incision between her legs. Next, he pushed his penis into the incision. When he had finished, he flew away. Later the woman gave birth to all living beings, people and animals.

See also *Adam and Eve; Cassowary; Creation; Creator; Mother-Goddess*.

Wulan   See *Moon*.

Wulleb   A god and the first man according to the myths of some of the Marshall Islands peoples. He was born in an oyster shell from between Loa's legs. When he lifted the top half of the shell, it became the *sky*, while the bottom became the earth. This myth aptly explains the Pacific's colours. See also *Creation; Loa*.

Wurake   The *spirits* in Toraja mythology. See *Shamanism*(2).

Y

In and Yo

Yabuling A god of *Papua*. See *Pigs*(4).

Yaegiri A very beautiful Japanese princess at court who fell in love with Kurando, a handsome officer of the guards. When he was dismissed, she managed to escape from court and, after a long search, found her lover and gave herself to him. Alas! He was depressed by his disgrace and took his life. Later, in the mountains, Princess Yaegiri gave birth to a lovely son, whom she called *Kintaro*, 'Golden Boy'.

Yakirai See *Demons*(2); *Ghosts*(4).

Yakushi-Nyorai ('Master of Medicines'; Sanskrit, Bhaishajya) One of the six *Buddhas* of Meditation in Japan who is much revered as the giver of cures.

Yalafath On the island of Yap in *Micronesia*, the *Creator*, associated with the albatross. He is benevolent and kind.

Yam (*Maori*, *uwhi*; Hawaiian and Polynesian, *uhi*) The 60 species of the genus *Dioscorea* of the *Dioscoreaceae* family are native in South-East Asia, where they have been cultivated since ancient times. The yam was one of the tuber foods that kept the *Polynesians* alive during their long voyages.

1. In southern *New Guinea* the yam is a sacred plant. It may not be
   planted before a special priest has come to the field first to drive away
   the evil *spirits*.
2. Here is the Orokolo myth of the yam:

   There was once a man called Aru Aru who married a girl, but at
   night he discovered that she had her period. He was angry and
   accused her of sleeping with another man. She said, 'You are
   ignorant! All women have this every month. It is caused by Papare
   the Moon.'

   Aru Aru decided to go and kill Papare the Moon for lying with his
   wife. He paddled past many islands until he came to the beach of
   the sky. There he met a little boy who was so strong that he could
   lift Aru Aru's canoe out of the water and on to the beach. This boy
   was really Papare the Moon. He knew that Aru Aru had come to kill
   him, but the Moon is wiser than men. The Moon and his brother
   the Sun, who lived in the same house, entertained Aru Aru
   generously even though they knew of his murderous plans. The
   Moon said to him: 'My brother the Sun gives life to all things; to
   fruits and flowers, even to your eyes. And I marry every woman on
   earth. So, it is you who have taken my wife, not I that have taken
   your wife from you. I had her already before you married her, but
   you may keep your wife now. I know everything. Now I will give you
   a present before you go back to earth.'

   Then the Moon gave Aru Aru the yam plant and taught him how
   to cultivate it. It is a gift worthy of the Moon-God, who travels across
   the earth at night, hearing what people whisper. Aru Aru swallowed
   his pride (because he could not tell his people that he had intended
   but failed to kill the moon) and paddled home in his canoe. He told
   his people how to plant the yams with stakes, so the stalks could
   climb up them. He also told the men they must not approach their
   wives during their periods, because at that time the Moon was
   married to them. Aru Aru then cut all the weeds and prepared the
   fields.

   It is along the 'strings' of vine, Convolvulus and other creepers that
   the *spirits* travel, who come down to destroy the crops. Since Aru
   Aru brought back the yam the wise people of Orokolo have their own
   priest, Hi Haela, 'String Man', who cuts the 'spirit strings'
   ceremonially every year before the yams are planted.
3. In the lower Sepík district of New Guinea it is related that before
   the people had yams, the *dogs* were fat and healthy with shining fur
   while the people were lean and starving. One day a man followed
   his dog to a pond. There at the bottom of the pond lay heaps of
   tubers clearly visible in the water. The dog started eating them, so
   the man called his friends and they all collected the yams from the
   pond and began growing them.

See also *Sweet Potato; Taro*.

Yama Enda A female demon in the forests of the Kyaka people of western Papua. See *Demons*(2); *Ghosts*(4).

Yama-Raja In Balinese mythology, the God of Judgement, the terrifying ruler of the Realm of Death. In Buddhist cosmology, he is the opposite of the benign *Vairocana*. In art Yama-Raja is depicted with bulging eyes, long canine teeth, long nails on his toes and pointed wings. See also *Emma-o*; 'Gods of Bali' under *Gods*.

Yama-Uba A mountain *uba* or protective spirit in Japanese myth.

Yamato The *soul* of *Japan*, the Japanese spirit, the very core and essence of the Japanese nation before its real history began. Also the name of a prince (see *Robe*; *Sword*(1)).

Yamato Take A prince and famous Japanese hero, the son of King Keiko, Yamato Take slew many brigands and rebels, as well as the *serpent* of Omi.

Yasakani The Japanese crown jewels. See *Go-Shin Tai*.

Yasha In Japanese mythology, a vampire-bat, said to be the spirit of a woman whose anger lowered her status in rebirth. See *Migration of Souls; Vampire*.

Yata The star-mirror of the Japanese Sun-Goddess. See *Go-Shin Tai*.

Yatim Mustafa See *Yatim Nustapa*.

Yatim Nustapa (or Mustafa; 'Mustafa the Orphan') The famous hero of a Malay *epic*. The young man's real name was Asmara Dewa, 'Love-God'. Born a prince, he was exiled with his little sister by his older half-brother the king, who jailed their mother, his step-mother. She was wrongfully accused of poisoning her husband, the old king. The two children, banned in the jungle, met the Cobra-King who took pity on them and gave them the 'Emerald which Heals All Wounds' (*Siwa*'s Third Eye). He guided them out of the forest, through to the other side, where they found themselves in the kingdom of Inderanegara. There, the king's daughter had been bitten by a snake and was dying. The king promised her hand to whoever could cure her. Asmara Dewa took the name of Yatim Nustapa and announced that he would cure the princess. Admitted to her presence, he placed the divine emerald on her skin, where the snake's teeth marks were still visible. She rose, cured, and married her healer, becoming his queen when the old king retired. Now, Yatim Nustapa could raise an army and march to his native Inderachita to liberate his mother. When they arrived, the mere sight of the army persuaded his elder brother to free her.

Yawata See *Hachiman*.

Yegara-no-Heida See *Uwabami*.

Yellow Springs The home of the Japanese God of Death, *Emma-o*.

Yenoki A Japanese priest. See *Fudo*.

Yeta In *Japan*, a beggar. Sometimes such a beggar is *Inari* in disguise. A woman who wants a child should give generously to such a beggar, so she may have a son. A priest or a Buddhist sage can see who is human and who only resembles humans.

Yin and Yang See *In and Yo*.

Yo The male element in the Japanese cosmology of *Creation*, the equivalent of the Chinese yang. See *In and Yo*.

Yofune-Nushi In Japanese mythology, a *sea-serpent* which lived in a cave under the rocks of the Oki Islands' coast. Every year on the night of 13 June, the monster had to be given a fair maiden, or else it would cause storms and so destroy the fishing fleet. It was finally killed by Tokoyo, a girl who volunteered to go as its sacrifice. With a dagger, she blinded the monster, then slew it.

Yogi See *Tapa*(2).

Yogodayu A Japanese general. See *Bees*.

Yomi (or Yomi-Land; 'Night-Heart') The Japanese *Hades*.

Yone A young Japanese woman. See *Peony*(2).

Yorimasa A famous Japanese hero who slew a monster on top of the emperor's palace, for which he was rewarded with the Lady Ayame's hand, as well as with the famous *sword* called *shishi-o*, 'master of lions'.

Yoromitsu A hero in Japanese myth who, together with his four retainers, slew *giants*. See also *Kintaro*.

Yoshisawa A young Japanese doctor. See *Violets*.

Yoshitsune A famous warrior in Japanese sagas, the son of Yoshitomo, who was murdered by someone of the Taira clan. Intent on avenging his father, he went to the woods, where he was instructed in all the martial arts by the King of the *Tengu* Demons. Finally, Yoshitsune annihilated the Taira clan.

Yosho A Japanese saint (d. 801) whose spirit lives on to help people. See also *Sennin*.

Yosoji A Japanese youth who went in search of the *water of life* on Mount Fuji for his sick mother. It was finally given to him by the Goddess of the Mountain Streams. See *Elixir; Fujiyama; Sengen*.

Yudistira In Javanese mythology, the eldest of the *Pandawas*, son of *Kunti*, daughter of King Kuntiboja, and *Darma*, the God of Justice. Yudistira is the ideal of the righteous brother, the fair fighter, the conscientious, just ruler. His wife is *Drupadi*. (Yudistira is also the reincarnation of Darma, in that if a god has a son, part of the god's spirit incarnates in the child.)

Yuki-Onna In Japanese mythology, the Lady of the Snow, the Snow Queen or Winter Ghost, who sometimes appears as an earthly woman, marries and has children. Sometimes she will disappear in a white mist. See also *Snow-Spirits*.

Yusup

1. An Islamic prophet. See *Epic*.
2. A man who caught a magical white *tortoise*. See *Tortoise*(2).

Z

Zen in Japanese characters

Za-Zen In Japanese *Buddhism*, 'seated meditation'. The monk *Dogen* introduced this form of Zen meditation.

Zocho See *Shi Tenno*.

Zushi In *Japan*, a miniature shrine for personal use.

Bibliography

Note: This bibliography lists only books in English. The author consulted numerous books and articles in other languages also, which are not listed here.

Alip, Eufonio M., *The Philippines of Yesteryears: The Dawn of History in the Philippines.* Manila, 1964.

Allen, M.R., *Male Cults and Secret Initiations in Melanesia.* Melbourne University Press, 1967.

Alpers, Antony, *Maori Myths and Tribal Legends.* John Murray, London, 1964.

Andersen, Johannes C., *Myths and Legends of the Polynesians.* Harrap, London, 1928.

Aston, Dr William George, 'Nihongi: Chronicles of Japan' in *Transactions of the Japan Society,* London, 1896.

——, *Shinto, the Ancient Religion of Japan.* London 1907.

Baal, J. van, *Dema, Description and Analysis of Marind-anim Culture.* The Hague, 1966.

Bacon, Alice Mabel, *In the Land of the Gods: Some Stories of Japan.* Boston, 1905.

Ballantyne, A. and Jennes, D., *Language, Mythology and Songs of Bwaidoga, Goodenough Island.* New Plymouth, NZ, 1928.

Beckwith, Martha W., *Hawaiian Mythology.* Yale University Press, New Haven, 1940; Honolulu, 1970.

——, *The Kumulipo, A Hawaiian Creation Chant.* Chicago University Press, 1951.

Beier, Ulli, and Prithvindra, Chakravarti, eds., *Sun and Moon in Papua New Guinea Folklore.* Institute of Papua New Guinea Studies, Port Moresby, 1974.

Benneville, James de, *Tales of the Samurai.* London, 1915, 1986.

Bernet-Kempers, A.J., *Ancient Indonesian Art.* Cambridge, Mass., 1959.

——, *Ageless Borobudur.* Pomona, California, 1976.

Best, Elsdon, *Maori Religion and Mythology,* Part 1. Wellington, 1924.

——, *The Maori,* 2 volumes. Wellington, 1924.

Biggs, Bruce Grandiston, *Na Ciri Kalia: The Oral Traditions of Cikopia-i-ira, Northernmost Islands of the Fijian Group.* The University Press, Auckland, 1975.

Binyon, Laurence, *The Flight of the Dragon.* London, 1919.

Bosch, F.D.K., *The Golden Germ.* The Hague, 1960.

Brash. E. See Morea Pekoro.

Brown, G., *Melanesians and Polynesians.* Macmillan, London, 1910.

Brown, Herbert A., *Clan Myths of the Elema, Gulf of Papua.* Institute of Papua New Guinea Studies, Port Moresby, 1975.

Brown, John, *Maori and Polynesia: Their Origin, History and Culture.* Macmillan, London, 1907.

Buck, Sir Peter H., *Regional Diversity in the Elaboration of Sorcery in Polynesia.* Yale University Publications, New Haven, 1936.

—— (Te Rangi Hiroa), *The Coming of the Maori.* Wellington, 1949.

Chamberlain, Basil Hall, 'A Translation of the "Kojiki" or "Records of Ancient Matters" ' in *Transactions of the Asiatic Society of Japan,* Volume X. Yokohama, 1882.

Chaya, Prem, *Magic Lotus.* Bangkok, 1949.

Christian, F.W., *Eastern Pacific Lands: Tahiti and the Marquesas Islands.* London, 1910.

Churchill, William, 'The Polynesian Wanderings' in *Carnegie Institute Publication 134,* Washington DC, 1911.

Clark, Kate McCosh, *Maori Tales and Legends.* London, 1896.

Codrington, R.H., *The Melanesians: Studies in their Anthropology and Folklore.* Clarendon Press, Oxford, 1891.

Cole, Mabel Cook, *Philippine Folk Tales.* Chicago, 1916.

Colum, Padraig, *Legends of Hawaii.* Yale University Press, New Haven, 1937.

Cook, James, *A Voyage in the Pacific.* London, 1784; Cambridge University Press, 1967.

Cowan, James, *Fairy Folk Tales of the Maori.* London, 1925.

——, *Legends of the Maori.* Wellington, 1977 (reprint in two volumes).

Davis, Frederick Hadland, *Japan, from the Age of the Gods to the Fall of Tsingtau.* London, 1916.

——, *Myths and Legends of Japan.* London, 1913; Graham Brash, Singapore, 1989.

Dorson, Richard M., *Folk Legends of Japan.* Charles E. Tuttle, Rutland, Vt, 1962.

Elliot, Griffes William, *Fairy Tales of Old Japan.* London, 1908.

Ellis, William, *Polynesian Researches,* 4 volumes. J.&J. Harper, New York, 1833.

Emerson, Nathaniel B., *Unwritten Literature of Hawaii.* Smithsonian Institute, Washington DC, 1909.

Evans, I.H.N., *The Religion of the Tempasuk Dusuns of North Borneo.* Cambridge University Press, 1953.

Fansler, Dean S., 'Filipino Popular Tales' in *Publications of the American Folklore Society,* Volume XII, New York, 1921.

Firth, Raymond, *The Work of the Gods in Tikopia,* 2 volumes. London School of Economics, London, 1940.

——, *History and Traditions of Tikopia.* New Plymouth, Wellington, 1961.

Fison, Lorimer, *Tales from Old Fiji.* London, 1904.

Fornander, Abraham, *An Account of the Polynesian Race,* 3 volumes. Truebner & Co., London, 1878–85.

——, *Collection of Antiquity and Folklore,* 3 volumes. BP Bishop Museum, Honolulu, 1916–20.

Fortune, Reo F., *Sorcerers of Dobu.* London, 1932.

——, *Manus Religion . . . Admiralty Islands.* Philadelphia, 1935.

Furness, William Henry, *The Island of Stone Money: Uap of the Carolines.* London and Philadelphia, 1910.

Gifford, W., 'Tongan Myths and Tales' in *BP Bishop Museum Bulletin 8.* Honolulu, 1924.

Gill, William W., *Myths and Songs from the South Pacific.* London, 1876.

Grace, A., *Folk-Tales of the Maori.* Wellington, 1907.

Grey, Sir George, *Polynesian Mythology and Ancient Traditional History of the Maoris.* John Murray, London, 1855; Auckland, 1885.

Grimble, Sir Arthur, *A Pattern of Islands.* John Murray, London, 1952.

——, *Migrations, Myths and Magic from the Gilbert Islands.* London, 1972.

Gutmanis, June, *Kahuna La'au Lapa'au* (Secrets and Practice of Hawaiian Herbal Medicine). Island Heritage, Kahai Street, Honolulu, 1987.

Hall, D.G.E., *A History of South-East Asia.* Macmillan, London, 1970.

Hames, Inez, *Legends of Fiji and Rotuma.* Wellington, 1960.

Handy, E.S. Craighill, *Polynesian Religion.* BP Bishop Museum, Honolulu, 1927.

Hearn, Lafcadio, *Japanese Fairy Tales.* New York, 1919, 1948.

——, *Karma and Other Stories.* London, 1921.

——, *Some Chinese Ghosts.* New York, 1927.

——, *Buddhist Writings.* Wildwood House, London, 1981.

Henry, T., 'Ancient Tahiti' in *BP Bishop Museum Bulletin 48.* Honolulu, 1928.

Heyerdahl, Thor, *Aku-Aku, the Secret of Easter Island.* Penguin, Harmondsworth, 1958.

Hooykaas, C., *Religion in Bali.* E.J. Brill, Leiden, 1973.

Hori, I., *Folk Religion in Japan, Continuity and Change.* Chicago, Ill., 1968.

-- *et al.,* eds., *Japanese Religion.* Tokyo and Palo Alto, 1972.

Hurihuri, Te Ao, *The World Moves On: Aspects of Maoritanga*, ed. M. King. Hicks Smith, Wellington, 1975.

I'i, John Papa, *Fragments of Hawaiian History*. BP Bishop Museum Press, Honolulu, 1959.

Il Yon, *Samguk Yusa, Legends and History of Ancient Korea*, 2 volumes. Seoul, 1972.

Im Bang, *Korean Folk Tales*, trans. James S. Gale. London, 1913.

In-Sob, Zong, *Folk Tales from Korea*. Hollym, Seoul, 1987.

Jennings, Jesse D., ed., *The Prehistory of Polynesia*. Harvard University Press, Cambridge, Mass., 1979.

Jensen, E., *The Iban and their Religion*. Clarendon Press, Oxford, 1974.

Johansen, J. Prytz, *The Maori and his Religion in its Non-ritualistic Aspects*. Copenhagen, 1954.

——, *Studies in Maori Rites and Myths*. Copenhagen, 1958.

Kalakua, *The Legends and Myths of Hawaii*. New York, 1888.

Kamma, Freerk C., *Religious Texts of the Oral Tradition from Western New Guinea*, 2 volumes. E.J. Brill, Leiden, 1975.

Ker, Annie, *Papuan Fairy Tales*. London, 1910.

King, M. See Hurihuri.

Knappert, Jan, *A Structural Sketch of the Hawaiian Language*. Leiden, 1954.

——, *Myths and Legends of Indonesia*. Heinemann, Singapore, 1977.

——, *Malay Myths and Legends: Kuala Lumpur – Singapore*. Heinemann, 1980.

——, 'The Myth of the Rice Goddess in Java' in *The World and I*. Volume 1, No.10, pp.160–9, Washington DC, 1986.

Korean Folklore. The Korean National Commission for Unesco, Seoul, 1983.

Lawrence, P. and Meggitt, M.J., *Gods, Ghosts and Men in Melanesia*. OUP, Melbourne, 1965.

Layard, John, *Stone Men of Malekula*. London, 1942.

Leib, Amos P., *Hawaiian Legends in English. An Annotated Bibliography*. University of Hawaii Press, Honolulu, 1949.

Lewis, David, 'Wind, Wave, Star and Bird' in *National Geographic*. Volume 146, No.6, pp.747–55, 771–81, Washington DC, December 1974.

Luomala, Katharine, *Maui of a Thousand Tricks, His Oceanic and European Biographers*. Honolulu, 1948.

Malinowski, Bronislaw, *Argonauts of the Western Pacific*. Routledge, London, 1922.

——, *Coral Gardens and their Magic* I–II. Allen and Unwin, London, 1935.

Malo, David, *Hawaiian Antiquities*. BP Bishop Museum, Honolulu, 1951.

Marett, Robert Ranulph, *The Threshold of Religion* (first mention of the term *mana*). London, 1909; New York, 1914.

May, Reginald Le, *Thai Tales Old and New*. Shanghai, 1945.

McElhanon, K.A., *Legends from Papua New Guinea*. Summer Institute of Linguistics, Ukarumpa, 1974.

Metraux, Alfred, *Easter Island*. André Deutsch, London, 1957.

Mitford, A.B. (Lord Redesdale), *Tales of Old Japan*. London, 1893.

Moerenhout, J.A., *Voyages aux Iles du Grand Ocean*, 2 volumes. Paris, 1837.

Moss, Rosalind, *The Life after Death in Oceania and the Malay Archipelago*. London, 1925.

Mulder, N., *Mysticism and Everyday Life in Contemporary Java*. Singapore University Press, 1978.

Nozaki, Kiyoshi, *Kitsune: Japan's Fox of Mystery, Romance and Humour*. The Hokuseido Press, Tokyo, 1961.

Ozaki, Yei Theodora, *Japanese Fairy Book*. Westminster, 1903.

Pekoro, Morea, *Orokolo Genesis. An Account of the Origin of the World and of the People of Niugini*. trans. Elton Brash, Port Moresby, 1973.

Poignant, Roslyn, *Oceanic Mythology*. Hamlyn, Feltham, London, 1968.

Pukui, Mary Kawena, *Hawaiian Beliefs and Customs During Birth, Infancy and Childhood*. BP Bishop Museum, Honolulu, 1942.

Redesdale, Lord Algernon Bertram. See A.B. Mitford.

Reed, A. W., *Legends of Rotorua and the Hot Lakes*. A. Reed, Wellington, 1958.
——, *Maori Fables*. A. Reed, Wellington, 1965.
——, *Favorite Maori Legends*. A. Reed, Wellington, 1965.
——, *Wonder Tales of Maoriland*. A. Reed, Wellington, 1967.
——, *Treasury of Maori Folklore*. A. Reed, Wellington, 1967.
Rice, W.H., *Hawaiian Legends*. BP Bishop Museum, Honolulu, 1923.
Rivers, W.H.R., *The History of Melanesian Society*, 2 volumes. Cambridge, 1914.
Roth, H. Ling, *The Natives of Sarawak and British North Borneo*, 2 volumes. London, 1896.
Rubinstein, Carol, *The Honey Tree Song. Poems and Chants of the Sarawak Dayaks*. Ohio University Press, Athens, Ohio, 1985.
Satyananda, Puri and Sarakhiran, Charoen, *The Ramakirti or the Thai Version of the Ramayana*. Dharmashrama, Bangkok, 1940.
Schnitger, R.M., *Forgotten Kingdoms of Sumatra*. Leiden, 1939.
Seligmann, C.G., *The Melanesians of British New Guinea*. Cambridge, 1910.
Skeat, Walter William, *Fables and Folk Tales from an Eastern Forest*. Cambridge University Press, Cambridge, 1901.
——, *Malay Magic*. Frank Cass, London, 1965.
Smith, Richard Gordon, *Ancient Tales and Folklore of Japan*. London, 1908.
Smith, R.J., *Ancestor Worship in Contemporary Japan*. Stanford, California, 1974.
Smith, S. Percy, *Hawaiki: The Original Home of the Maori*. Wellington, 1921.
Sorrenson, M.P.K., *Maori Origins and Migrations*. Auckland University Press, 1979.
Stair, J.B., *Old Samoa*. London, 1897.
Steubel, C. and Herman, B., *Tala o le Vavao. The Myths, Legends and Customs of Old Samoa*. Auckland Polynesian Press, 1987.
Stimson, John Francis, *Tuamotuan Religion*. Honolulu, 1933.
——, *The Legends of Maui and Tahaki*. Honolulu 1934.
——, *Tuamotuan Legends*. Honolulu, 1937.
Stutterheim, W.F., *Indian Influences on Balinese Art*. London, 1935.
Swellengrebel, J.L., *et alii. Bali: Studies in Life, Thought and Ritual*. Van Hoeve, The Hague, 1960.
Takakasu, J., *A Record of the Buddhist Religion as Practised in India and in the Malay Archipelago*. Oxford, 1896.
Taylor, Richard, *Te Ika A Maui or New Zealand and its Inhabitants*. London, 1855.
Thompson, Vivian L., *Hawaiian Myths of Earth, Sea and Sky*. University of Honolulu Press, 1966.
Thomson, Basil, *The Fijians*. London 1908.
Thrum, Thomas G., *Hawaiian Folktales*. A.C. McClug & Co., Chicago, 1907, 1917.
Trompf, Gary, ed., *Prophets of Melanesia*. Port Moresby, 1977.
Tyler, Royall, *Japanese Tales*. Pantheon, New York, 1987.
Valentine, C.A., *Masks and Men in Melanesian Society*. Lawrence, Kansas, 1961.
Watson, R.M., *History of Samoa*. Wellington, 1918.
Wavell, Stewart, *The Naga King's Daughter*. Allen & Unwin, London, 1964.
Westervelt, William D., *Legends of Ma-ui, a Demigod of Polynesia, and of his Mother Hina*. Honolulu, 1910, Melbourne, 1913.
——, *Hawaiian Historical Legends*. New York, 1923.
White, John, *The Ancient History of the Maoris, Mythology and Traditions*, 6 volumes. Wellington, 1887.
Williams, Thomas and Calvert, James, *Fiji and the Fijians*, 2 volumes. London, 1885.
Williamson, Robert W., *Religious and Cosmic Beliefs of Central Polynesia*, 2 volumes. Cambridge University Press, 1933; New York, 1977.
Wilson, Charles A., *Legends and Mysteries of the Maori*. Harrap, London, 1932.
Winstedt, Sir Richard, *A History of Classical Malay Literature*. OUP, Kuala Lumpur, 1969.
Worsley, P., *The Trumpet Shall Sound. A Study of the Cargo Cults in Melanesia*. London, 1957.